CRITICAL
CREATIVE
PROCESSES

METROPOLITAN COLLEGE
OF NEW YORK LIBRARY
75 Varick Street 12th Fl.
New York, NY 10013

Perspectives on Creativity
Mark A. Runco, series editor

Reclaiming the Wasteland: TV & Gifted Children
Bob Abelman

The Motives for Creative Work
Jock Abra

Creative Intelligence: Toward Theoretic Integration
Donald Ambrose et al. (eds.)

Remarkable Women: Perspectives on Female Talent Development
Karen Arnold, Kathleen Noble, and Rena Subotnik (eds.)

No Rootless Flower: An Ecology of Creativity
Frank Barron

Critical Thinking and Reasoning: Current Research, Theory and Practice
Daniel Fasko, Jr. (ed.)

Investigating Creativity in Youth: A Book of Readings on Research and Methods
Anne S. Fishkin, Bonnie Cramond, and Paula Olszewski-Kubilius

Creativity and Giftedness in Culturally Diverse Students
Giselle B. Esquivel and John Houtz (eds.)

Quantum Creativity: Waking Up to Our Creative Potential
Amit Goswami

The Educational Psychology of Creativity
John Houtz (ed.)

Flexible Thinking: An Explanation for Individual Differences in Ability
Norbert Jausovec

Enhancing Creativity of Gifted Children: A Guide for Parents
Joe Khatena

Style and Psyche
Pavel Machotka

Social Creativity Volumes One and Two
Alfonso Montuori and Ronald Purser (eds.)

Unusual Associates: Essays in Honor of Frank Barron
Alfonso Montuori (ed.)

My Teeming Brain: Understanding Creative Writers
Jane Piirto

Creativity Research Handbook Volume One
Mark A. Runco (ed.)

Critical Creative Processes
Mark A. Runco (ed.)

Creating Conversations: Improvisation in Everyday Discourse
R. Keith Sawyer

The Young Gifted Child: Potential and Promise—An Anthology
Joan Smutny (ed.)

Underserved Gifted Populations: Responding to Their Needs and Abilities
Joan Smutny

CRITICAL CREATIVE PROCESSES

edited by

Mark A. Runco
California State University-Fullerton
University of Hawaii-Hilo

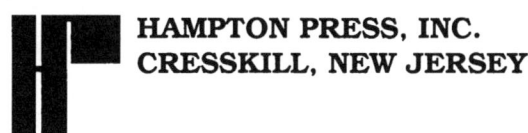

HAMPTON PRESS, INC.
CRESSKILL, NEW JERSEY

Copyright © 2003 by Hampton Press, Inc.

All rights reserved. No part of this publication may be reproduced, stored in a retrieval system, or transmitted in any form or by any means, electronic, mechanical, photocopying, microfilming, recording, or otherwise, without permission of the publisher.

Printed in the United States of America

Library of Congress Cataloging-in-Publication Data

Critical creative processes / edited by Mark A. Runco
     p. cm. -- (Perspectives on creativity research)
  Includes bibliographic references and indexes.
  ISBN 1-57273-134-6 -- ISBN 1-57273-135-4
    1. Creative thinking. 2. Critical thinking. 3. Learning, psychology of. I. Runco, Mark A. II. Series

LB1062.C745 2002
370.15'2--dc21

                                                2001059447

Hampton Press, Inc.
23 Broadway
Cresskill, NJ 07626

This book is dedicated to the three men I most admire. I have devoted much of my career to the study of eminent and creative persons, but the men I most admire are still my father, Ray Runco, and my two older brothers, Christopher and Timothy.

CONTENTS

Preface   ix

PART ONE: INTRAPERSONAL PROCESSES   1

1   Creativity as Variation and Selection: Some
    Critical Constraints
    Dean Simonton   3

2   Picking the Right Material: Cognitive Processing
    Skills and Their Role in Creative Thought
    *Michael D. Mumford, Wayne A. Baughman,
    and Christopher E. Sager*   19

3   Idea Evaluation, Divergent Thinking, and Creativity
    Mark A. Runco   69

4   Creativity, Personality and the Convergent-Divergent
    Continuum
    H. J. Eysenck   95

5   Creative Interaction: A Conceptual Schema for the
    Process of Producing Ideas and Judging the Outcomes
    Edward Necka   115

6   Evaluative Thinking, Creativity, and Task
    Specificity: Separating Wheat From Chaff is Not the
    Same as Finding Needles in Haystacks
    John Baer   129

7	The Role of Intelligence in Creativity *Robert J. Sternberg and Todd E. Lubart*	153
8	Thinking Critically About Creative Thinking *Diane F. Halpern*	189
9	Creative Attributional Self-talk *Thomas E. Heinzen*	209
10	Pragmatic Psycholinguistics as a Framework for the Evaluation of Creativity *Albert N. Katz*	225
11	The Development of Creative Thinking and Critical Reflection: Lessons from Everyday Problem Finding *John F. Wakefield*	253

PART TWO: INTERPERSONAL PROCESSES

12	Teaching Invention as Critical Creative Processes: A Course on Technoscientific Creativity *Michael E. Gorman and Jonathan A. Plucker*	275
13	Evaluative Processes During Group Improvisational Performance *R. Keith Sawyer*	303
14	Motives for Criticism: Some Theoretical Speculations and Introspective Data *Jock Abra*	329
15	Intermediaries in the Creative Process: Serving the Individual and Society *Morris I. Stein*	379
Author Index		395
Subject Index		405

PREFACE

There are at least two interpretations of the title of this book. The first is that there are certain processes that reflect some kind of criticism and influence creative thinking and creative work. The second interpretation is that these processes are critical—in the sense of being crucial—for our understanding of creativity. Perhaps my being explicit about the two alternatives will spoil the double entendre of the book's title. I will take that risk because both interpretations should be kept in mind while reading this volume.

This plurality is also suggested in *Critical Creative Processes*. This is also suggested by the Table of Contents and the distinction therein between intrapersonal and interpersonal critical processes. The chapters in this volume demonstrate that critical processes are varied in the sense of being cognitive, affective, or otherwise extracognitive, linguistic, associational and preverbal. The authors further demonstrate that various kinds of cognition are tied to creative work, as are knowledge, motivation, problem finding, divergent thinking, psycholinguistics, attributions, personality, education, improvisation, and so on. One strength of this volume is that it contains chapters covering a range of critical processes.

The diversity of breadth of perspective is very important for this particular field because there is only moderate consensus about the way to define *creativity*. There is some consensus that creativity is multifaceted, multivariate, and overdetermined. Preferred definitions of creativity call it a *symdrome* or *complex*. This volume does an excellent job of covering the range of processes involved in the creativity complex. Wakefield uses the concept of *complementarity* for taking advantage of both continuity and discontinuity theories. That same concept can be applied generally to the varied perspectives on creativity. Taken together they offer a realistic picture of creativity.

Key Issues

Some books highlight rather than avoid issues and controversies. In *Creativity and Affect* (Shaw & Runco, 1994), I discussed the controversies surrounding intrinsic motivation, drawing from cognitive theory, and suggesting that this popular concept lacks explanatory power. I concluded that we will only understand intrinsic motivation when we look for its underpinnings and I suggested that cognitive appraisals may under intrinsic motivation.

Problem Finding, Problem Solving, and Creativity (Runco, 1994) also dealt with controversy. The debate there concerned the relationships among creativity and problem solving. There are theorists who believe that creativity is a special kind of problem solving, and others who believe the opposite—that problem solving is one kind of creativity. Numerous instances of creativity and self-expression, play, and alternative interpretations were cited and emphasized the latter perspective, that problem solving is one kind of creativity.

With the diverse perspectives contained in *Critical Creative Processes*, and given the complexity of the subject matter, it will be no surprise that the present volume also has a central controversy. It concerns the respective roles of evaluation and judgment in the creative process. Simplifying a bit, many theorists and practitioners believe that evaluation and judgment are detrimental to creativity. Just to name one example, in their book *The Creative Spirit*, Goleman, Kaufman, and Ray (1993) referred to "that dreaded inner voice of self-judgment" (p. 17). Granted that was a mass-market book, but the same position is apparent in what is probably the most popular creativity enhancement technique—brainstorming. As a part of brainstorming judgment is suspended or postponed. Why? Because it ostensibly gets in the way of having a good idea!

At the other extreme we have theories that creativity benefits from, or even relies on, particular kinds of critical, evaluative processes. These theories typically describe a kind of interplay between what have been called *divergent* and *convergent processes*. The theories emphasizing some kind of interplay are well represented in this volume.

Certain evaluative processes are necessary for good creative work. It is a good thing, too, as evaluative processes are natural, spontaneous, and difficult to avoid. As Abra puts it (Chapter 14), "persons with bias do not exist. It is truly said: Everyone is a critic." Abra goes into detail about the various motives for criticism.

Clearly, the inhibitive or facilitative role of evaluative processes in creativity will be largely determined by the specific kind of creativity and the specific evaluative process. When evaluation is defined in a traditional manner, for example, and when it is entirely convergent, it may be the most distinct from divergent creative processes.

Chapter Highlights

Several of the chapters mention both intrapersonal and interpersonal processes. (The placement of these chapters in Part 1 or Part 2 was determined by their emphasis.) Most intriguing is the interaction of intrapersonal and interpersonal processes.

Sternberg and Lubart (Chapter 7) describe several kinds of critical thinking. They start with traditional intelligence and its relationship with creative thinking. They go on to describe three aspects of intelligence. The analytic part involves recognizing and structuring ideas, as well as allocating resources and evaluating the quality of ideas. They synthetic part involves the generation of ideas. The practical part involves the recognition of the need to refine or sell one's own ideas, and perhaps the need to utilize feedback and criticism given by others. Note that Sternberg and Lubart recognize both interpersonal and intrapersonal components of creative thinking. Their chapter talks in some detail about insight, metacognition, and education.

In his chapter reviewing the psycholinguistic view, Katz (Chapter 10) discusses both intrapersonal and interpersonal evaluations. Intrapersonal evaluations, for Katz, may involve tacit knowledge. Of related importance is the pragmatic argument that interpersonal judgments always depend to a certain degree on the communicative context in which they occur. Most important may be Katz's argument about mental models and how these may be internalized and also used as filters for expectations and judgments. According to Katz, whenever an individual is evaluating him or herself or the work of another, he or she is relying on a particular mental model. Research on tacit knowledge and implicit theories tells us a little about what is contained in the mental models of certain groups, although again these are influenced by the particular context. Psycholinguistics informs us about personal interpersonal communications, and these apparently parallel the kinds of interplays that occur between a creator and his or her audience. Any social act of creativity is, in this sense, a dialog. Psycholinguistic research is relevant both because of what it has told us about mental models and the conceptual basis of language, but also because of what it tells us of communication.

Mumford, Baughman, and Sager (Chapter 2) discuss evaluation as a kind of strategy preceding divergent thinking. Evaluation is a "search for key information." Several of the empirical findings reported in this chapter support the idea that some convergent evaluation precedes divergent thinking. It is interesting that one of the strategies identified by Mumford et al. involves voiding a *satificing*. Note also the assumption that all creativity involves problem solving and how some research subjects utilized incongruities.

Runco (Chapter 3) distinguishes between evaluation and more traditional kinds of critical and convergent thinking. Evaluative thinking is involved when the individual judges ideas for their originality rather than correctness. Runco also presents a componential model, showing how evaluation interacts with ideation. He reviews a series of studies which suggest that divergent thinking benefits from particular kinds of evaluation.

Eysenck (Chapter 4) and Baer (Chapter 6) put divergent thinking into a larger context. Eysenck suggests that the divergent-convergent dichotomy is one of "three parallel dichotomies," all related to the notion of creativity; scientific activity can be normal science, in the context of justification, and convergent, or it can be revolutionary, in the context of discovery, and divergent. Baer proposes that evaluation is relevant to divergent thinking (and creativity) at two levels. He suggests a higher level evaluation that is quite general, and lower level evaluations that operate in specific domains.

Several chapters explore practical applications of the key critical creative processes. Mumford et al., for instance, describe intervention opportunities, and Sternberg and Lubart describe programs that have been designed to take advantage of thinking about synthetic and analytical thinking, as well as the selective components of insight and creative thinking. Gorman and Plucker (Chapter 12), Wakefield (Chapter 11), and Stein (Chapter 15) each present highly practical theories of critical creative processes.

Wakefield's (Chapter 11) is a developmental theory. He describes problem finding as understanding. His primary concern is, then, intrapersonal, although most of his chapter applies his theory to education, and in that sense there are interpersonal implications (e.g., for teachers). The critical thinking in the processes outlined by Wakefield are fairly traditional: He discusses logic, for example, the various kinds of inferences predicted by Piagetian theory.

Necka (Chapter 5) takes a structural approach. Creativity, in his view, requires the reduction of the discrepancy between cognitive structures and a particular goal. Necka proposes that there is an interplay between the structures and the goal; hence, there are no stages but an ongoing interaction.

Like Wakefield, Halpern (Chapter 8) is concerned about education. And like Katz (Chapter 10), she appreciates verbal processes. As she put it, "Creative thinking, like critical thinking, also requires the use of verbal reasoning skills because language is so intimately tied to thought that it can direct thought in novel ways."

Heinzen (Chapter 9) and Gorman and Plucker (Chapter 12) discuss applied settings and enhancement. Gorman and Plucker, for example, show how a course designed to enhance the thinking of college students was used with secondary students. They focus on invention. Heinzen also discusses enhancement and "training," but his theory emphasizes "attributional self-talk."

Like Sternberg and Lubart (Chapter 7) and Runco (Chapter 3), Simonton (Chapter 1) discusses both inter- and intrapersonal processes. He applies the idea of selection to problem identification, noting how "the number of potential projects is practically infinite." He also suggests that because interpersonal attributions are external evaluations, failures (which have a constant probability of success) do not necessarily inhibit creative work. This may be good news given how often incentives and rewards are described as detrimental to creative work.

In Chapter 15 Stein extends his theory about the intermediaries in the creative process. The notion of intermediaries rounds out the social perspective (and the interpersonal section of this book). It is simplistic to consider only creators and their audiences: intermediaries are often extremely influential.

Runco (Chapter 3) and Sawyer (Chapter 13) question the realism of separating divergence from convergence and evaluation from other parts of the process. As Runco puts it, evaluation occurs throughout the creative process in a recursive manner. Saywer uses group improvisations to show that creativity may not be accurately delineated into discrete, modular stages.

The beauty of this volume is indeed in the range of processes covered. It is also significant that the contributors practice what they preach: They each take a critical stance, asking pointed questions about creativity and critical evaluation. This volume contains more than just reviews of the subject matter: it presents a creative and critical perspective on the topic.

—Mark A. Runco
La Habra, California

PART I
INTRAPERSONAL PROCESSES

1

CREATIVITY AS VARIATION AND SELECTION: SOME CRITICAL CONSTRAINTS

Dean Simonton
University of California-Davis

Charles Darwin was no doubt a creative genius. His contributions to biology and geology were numerous and varied. Nevertheless, it is clear that his single most important gift to the advancement of science was his theory of evolution by natural selection. This contribution did for the biological sciences what Copernicus' heliocentric theory did for the physical sciences. It removed humanity from the center of the cosmos, and it did so by overthrowing received traditions and established viewpoints. The emergence of the human species was not some privileged act of God, but rather part of a less purposeful universe. Individual organisms simply tried to survive and reproduce; out of the vast variations in their progeny only a select few were sufficiently well adapted to an indifferent environment to be able to survive and reproduce themselves. This chaotic process of variation and selection, preserved through the retention mechanism of genetics, then originated all the diverse species of plants and animals, from the most primitive amoeba to the most complex multicellular creatures. Like most epochal ideas, Darwin's thinking left a mark far beyond the confines of his immediate disciplinary interests. Soon not just nature, but human society was purported to follow evolutionary principles, and thus there emerged the doctrine of

Social Darwinism. Even today, Darwinian inspiration underlies many modern intellectual movements, most notably in sociobiology.

Among these various developments is one that bears directly on the understanding of the creative process. Campbell (1960) advanced the notion that creativity entails a process of "blind variation and selective retention" (p. 380). That is, the mind spontaneously generates ideational combinations in a more or less haphazard fashion; a small proportion of these are then selected for further elaboration, testing, retention, and application. Campbell showed that this Darwinian model was consistent with the introspective reports of creative individuals, such as those of the eminent French mathematician Poincaré (1921). Furthermore, this model was compatible with other Darwinian systems, like evolutionary epistemology and social evolution (Campbell, 1965, 1974).

Others have further elaborated Campbell's (1960) variation-selection model of creativity. In previous work, I developed this model into what I styled the "chance-configuration theory of creativity," with a special focus on scientific genius (Simonton, 1988b, 1988d, 1989, 1993a, 1993b, 1999, in press-b). Kantorovich (1993) added several improvements to my own version, especially by extending it to the output of scientific communities. Eysenck (1993) connected the "Campbell-Simonton" model of creativity with a broad theory of the creative personality (Simonton, 1993a). Finally, Martindale (1990) pushed the Darwinian perspective in a different direction by using it as a foundation for his evolutionary theory of stylistic change in the arts. These and related elaborations promise to help make variation-selection theory one of the most comprehensive and precise frameworks for understanding creative behavior in all its complexity.

Needless to say, not everyone is enthusiastic about these theoretical developments. Many feel that they place too much emphasis on chance, and that they downplay the role of goal-directed behavior. Others may maintain that this Darwinian view understates the role of logical and conscious information processing, the mental processes that are deemed important by those who study creativity using computational models of problem solving. I addressed these and other complaints elsewhere, and have no wish to repeat myself here (e.g., Simonton, 1988c, 1994a, 1999, in press-a). Instead, I develop the model further by discussing some critical constraints on the operation of this variation-selection model (cf. Simonton, 1999). These constraints function to restrain the proliferation of variations, or to seriously curtail those variations that appear too extravagant by some rational or analytical criterion. I start by treating the selection side of the process, and then conclude by examining the variation side.

SELECTION PROCESSES

Any evolutionary theory must begin by specifying the units that are subjected to variation, selection, and retention. For creativity, the units of interest exist at three distinct levels of analysis (Simonton, 1993b, 1999). First, are ideas. These are the units treated by Campbell (1960) and most subsequent workers. Second, are individual creators as the units of selection. This application comes closest to what Darwin envisioned for biological evolution. Third, are groups, and especially cultures, as the fundamental units on which evolution operates. I survey here how the selection processes function at each of these three levels.

Cognitive Selection

According to the theory, creative ideas emerge from a free-associative process, much of which occurs below the threshold of awareness. These vague, ineffable ramblings of the mind often take place when the individual is engaged in some routine behavior or when he or she is relaxed and off guard. Often primed by some random external stimulus, two or more diverse trains of thought may suddenly converge on an integrative idea that apparently synthesizes two or more hitherto separate domains (e.g., Koestler, 1964). Once the creative synthesis thus enters consciousness, it can be subjected to more severe selection. Often, the creator has in mind a set of criteria by which to evaluate any novel idea, and a great many so-called inspirations will not survive this winnowing process. As scientist Faraday expressed:

> The world little knows how many of the thoughts and theories which have passed through the mind of a scientific investigator have been crushed in silence and secrecy by his own severe criticism and adverse examinations, that in the most successful instances not a tenth of the suggestions, the hopes, the wishes, the preliminary conclusions have been realised. (cited in Beveridge, 1957, p. 79)

I cannot overemphasize that this merciless weeding of the ideational garden is absolutely essential to successful creativity. Too much creative potential is wasted because novelties are generated by individuals who lack sufficient self-criticism at this crucial stage in the creative process. The accomplished creator is one who can step back in order to examine an idea from an objective standpoint, from the point of view of a disinterested observer. This is one reason why extreme mental illness is seldom productive of truly creative ideas. Studies of the poetry written by schizophrenics, for example, show that these individuals are unwilling to remove themselves from their work, and cannot accept an alternative perspective on their precious creations. As Rothenberg (1990) said, they just *"won't revise.* Not on your life, not in a million years" (p. 63). The outcome is an autistic variety of creativity that cannot reach beyond the boundaries of a single fragile ego. Contrast this situation with an episode in the creation of one of the landmark works of modern English literature, T. S. Eliot's *The Waste Land.* The first draft was in a terrible state, but Eliot, not being schizophrenic, was willing to expose his aesthetic baby to the merciless criticisms of his wife and his friend Ezra Pound. This vital willingness made it possible for him to convert a rambling and ineffective poem into an epochal masterpiece only half as long.

One crucial criterion for all creative products is the relation between the new ideas and the cultural heritage in which the creativity takes place. To reach a broad audience, to be fully understood and appreciated, an original idea must be interpretable by potential appreciators and admirers. Yet it is built in to the very nature of the human brain that novel experiences are comprehended in terms of past experiences. The creator is thus put in an extremely awkward position of trying to accomplish two diametrically opposed tasks. On the one hand, the creator must maximize ideational originality, for the more original the ideas the higher the odds of attracting attention. On the other hand, he or she must maximize the idea's intelligibility or adaptability in the eyes of potential users. In the specific domain of scientific creativity, Kuhn (1963) styled this contrast an *essential tension,* for "the successful scientist must simultaneously display the characteristics of the traditionalist and of the iconoclast" (p. 343). A similar tension holds for all other forms of creativity as well (see Martindale, 1990). Hence, in a sense, creativity is not just a function of variation alone, but rather of the dynamic interaction of variation and selection. In the absence of either, creativity in any meaningful form vanishes.

One last complication must be inserted into this picture, however. The selection criteria used by a creator can be, and often are, subjected to variation procedures. To appreciate this reality four facts must be recognized:

1. The evaluation of any given creative product requires not one but rather a great many different criteria. For example, to evaluate a musical composition requires the simultaneous assessment of rhyme, rhythm, harmony, counterpoint, formal structure, and a host of other factors, each of which contains a diversity of applicable tests.

2. The creative individual is never completely sure which of the various criteria are most important, or how each criterion fits with all the others. The creator must learn, largely by trial and error, what works and what fails.
3. Because so many different criteria are operative for the production of any given work, the success or failure of that work is only weakly informative about the relative significance and interplay of the judgmental tests. So the relative weights to be assigned to the numerous benchmarks are subject to constant negotiation during the course of a creator's productive career. Each creative product constitutes merely a crude test of a rather complex judgmental hypothesis.
4. The most appropriate mix of criteria does not stay completely stable over time. During the course of any career, aesthetic styles are undergoing changes of fashion, new scientific findings are emerging, novel philosophical questions are being introduced, and the larger sociocultural milieu is experiencing incessant transformation. As a consequence, by the time a creator has finally specified a successful selection strategy, that strategy has probably become obsolete.

Putting this altogether, it is clear that the creative individual must constantly vary not just the ideas produced but also the criteria by which those ideas are appraised. The selection procedures seldom can become routinized, but rather the creator must always experiment and explore new standards and cues. This unstable variability of selection has a couple of interesting implications.

In the first place, the variation of selection helps understand a curious empirical finding about creative careers: the equal-odds rule. If the number of works produced over consecutive time periods is counted, and then these are divided into successful and unsuccessful creations—according to number of citations, frequency of performance, or other appropriate criteria—the outcome is that the success rate stays constant across the career (Simonton, 1988a, 1994b). In other words, the ratio of hits to total attempts neither increases nor decreases with time, nor does it adopt some curvilinear form. This result may seem surprising. It might be expected that with maturity creative individuals might learn how to increase the proportion of successes. Perhaps by the end of their careers, indeed, they might enjoy a long winning streak. Yet this puzzling finding makes more sense when one understands the significance of variation in the creative process. Not only are creators generating new ideas according to a somewhat haphazard process, but additionally they are selecting these ideas according to criteria that are constantly changing by similar trial-and-error procedures. Under these circumstances, the creative person has no immediate control over the outcome of his or her intellectual labors, nor can that individual learn how to improve the chances with experience. The upshot is the equal-odds rule.

Another implication is more narrow but nonetheless provocative. A number of investigators have developed computer programs that purport to make scientific discoveries (e.g., Langley, Simon, Bradshaw, & Zythow, 1987; Shrager & Langley, 1990). These discovery programs operate by utterly logical search procedures: Data input regarding observations on two or more variables are subjected to operations, and then the results tested against some preset criteria. The researchers writing these programs have already claimed many "rediscoveries" of established scientific laws, principles, and concepts. For example, a program called BACON has supposedly rediscovered Kepler's Third Law of Planetary Motion. Even so, if the Darwinian theory of creativity is essentially correct, these discovery programs are terribly misguided. Besides generating hypotheses according to a fixed, logical mechanism, these programs make no provisions for a more dynamic relation between the data, the working hypotheses, and the criteria of adequate fit. This static conception of the creative process in science contrasts greatly with the view that the selection principles themselves are in an unpredictable state of flux. If otherwise, once a scientist acquired the correct criteria for discerning scientific truths, he or she would become an input-output machine, chaotic data going in one end while orderly laws spewed out the other—the two ends being connected by an inexorable logic. This is far from the case, even for the greatest scientific geniuses. Einstein's unified field theory came after his special and general relativity theories, and yet it was no where near as successful.

Interpersonal Selection

Creative ideas are not the only units of selection: Creative individuals can be selected as well. To appreciate this fact, one needs only to examine the phenomenon of multiples in science and technology (Lamb & Easton, 1984; Merton, 1961). This event occurs when two or more persons, working independently, come up with the same discovery or invention. One classic illustration is the theory of evolution by natural selection, which was proposed by both Anthony Wallace and Charles Darwin. Other examples run into the hundreds if not thousands (Simonton, 1987, 1988d). These occasions raise a curious issue: If two or more people actually arrived at the identical idea, who should get the credit? The fair decision would seem to grant the greater kudos to the individual who came up with the idea first. Yet recognition according to temporal priority is not always the deciding factor; other contaminating influences often intervene instead (Campbell & Tauscher, 1966; Simonton, 1979).

Some of these contaminants are apparent in the Wallace-Darwin case. Despite the fact that Darwin saw Wallace's theory as equivalent in all essentials to his own, and notwithstanding the fact that Wallace sought publication of the theory before Darwin, this multiple is credited to Darwin more than to Wallace. Hence, the theory of creativity advocated here is even styled Darwinian. Somehow, Wallace lost out in the competition for recognition. Although the reasons for this are probably complex, one source is that Darwin as a person had assets that elevated his overall standing with the scientific community. Darwin was an older and better established figure, who had already acquired an enviable reputation ever since his voyage on the *Beagle*. Darwin was also far more prolific throughout his career. Additionally, Darwin hailed from a higher socioeconomic stratum than did Wallace. Most significant, perhaps, is Wallace's predilection for Spiritualism, an affection that Darwin definitely did not share. Given all these contrasts, it is fair to speculate that evolutionary theory might not have been as influential had Wallace been its sole advocate. Furthermore, it should not be surprising that Darwin ended up obtaining the lion's share of the credit for their joint theory.

To generalize beyond this example, the fate of individual creative products might often rise or fall according to their creator's own standing with contemporaries or posterity. This standing may depend on a diversity of personal attributes, not all of which may have anything to do with the merits of the person's life work. The most obvious example is when the individual in question is female or hails from an oppressed minority group. Such talents may be ghettoized at best, and at worst cast into a dungeon of permanent oblivion. More subtle are biographical events and character traits whose primary function is to make a person look like the prototypical creative genius (see Kasof, 1998). For example, given individuals with otherwise equivalent accomplishments, those who make it to the top may be those who led traumatic lives and exhibited eccentric or pathological personalities.

Of course, we must acknowledge that individuals can also be favored according to criteria more directly related to creative achievement. Certain childhood experiences and adulthood personality traits may actually promote a long and productive career. No one will ever know how many potential geniuses never made the first cut because they exhibited some weakness or flaw that prevented them from attaining high distinction. For example, when Bolyai learned that Gauss had already anticipated his discovery of non-Euclidean geometry, he gave up on mathematics. A similar episode, in contrast, did not prevent Planck from forging ahead to make a name for himself. Clearly, they differed in persistence, determination, self-confidence, and whatever else it takes to overcome setbacks and obstacles enroute to greatness (see Simonton, 1994b).

Another such criterion for individual selection returns to the question of an individual's judgment. In order for anyone of us to take the time to acquaint him or herself with somebody's creations, the person must trust that this exploration will be worth the effort. He or she must have faith that the creator is not only honest, but also possesses good taste. Creators are expected to do their own editing, and what they finally decide to pass down are only those things that have passed the severest tests. For example, if one seriously doubts an artist's integrity or technique, there is less likelihood of familiarizing oneself with the artist's collective works, although there might be a masterpiece or two among them. Life is short, and so people cannot sacrifice precious time doing the winnowing for sloppy artists.

Or, to return to the realm of science, this attributional process is seen occurring in the difference between Darwin and Wallace. If the latter subscribes to spiritualistic beliefs, how much confidence can one possibly have in his treatment of any scientific question? How much weight can be assigned to Wallace's claim, not shared by Darwin, that natural selection could not explain the evolutionary emergence of the human brain? Thus, creators are partly chosen because they show critical restraints in the exercise of their own creativity.

Sociocultural Selection

It has just been shown that individuals undergo a selection process analogous to what happens within the mind of a single person. Some personalities have what it takes to earn recognition as creative geniuses, whereas others, even if of equal intrinsic talent, slip into the status of also-rans or nonentities. This raises the possibility of yet another selection procedure operating at a higher level of analysis. Societies can vary greatly in the criteria that they apply in evaluating prospective creators and their creative products. For example, in certain times and places, religious fervor reigns supreme, dictating that artists, writers, thinkers, and other creators devote themselves to conveying the appropriate theological and moral messages (see Sorokin, 1937-1941). In many cases, the Zeitgeist dictates the style and content of the creativity produced without spoiling the quality. Thus, great creativity can be seen in the Buddhist, Hindu,

Christian, and Islamic traditions, creativity that compares with what emerges from purely secular civilizations. Other times, however, the prevailing ideological or intellectual commitments may interfere with effective creativity in certain domains. Creators are favored who exhibit only a parochial form of creativity, a type that lacks universality or broad appeal. In these situations, when the society that encouraged the creativity dies, so does the audience for the individuals and their products. Such is the fate of most of the "Aryan art" promoted in Nazi Germany as well as the "socialist realism" that produced so much deliberately pedestrian work in Communist Europe.

In these examples, the sociocultural system selected against creativity, and so when the system dissolved, the practical function of the creative persons and products disappeared. The surviving works and their creators could not stand on their own merits. Justice won in the end. The creativity was so intimately linked with an idiosyncratic ideology that its vigor was stifled. But the story can become more arbitrary. Sometimes the sociocultural system indeed supports the production of first-rate creativity, yet that system looses out in political or economic competition with rival systems. The best illustrations may come from the realm of literature. All major languages spoken by literate peoples have produced imaginative writers of the highest caliber. Each linguistic nation has its William Shakespeare, although the actual name and genre vary with the tongue. Even so, the world's languages differ immensely in international importance, differences that reflect political and economic history rather than the inherent quality of its literary tradition.

For instance, during the late Middle Ages, the Iberian peninsula was the home of several first-rate literary languages—most notably Castilian, Portuguese, Catalan, and Galician. Somehow, through the complex peculiarities of the re-conquest of Spain from the Muslims, the coming and going of various dynastic alliances and marriages, and the repercussions of the discovery and colonization of the New World, only two of these languages achieved international distribution. And of these two, Castilian and Portuguese, the first (as Spanish) attained the distinctive position as the most widely spoken Romance language in the world. The consequence for literary creativity is clear. Spanish authors of any period and place can reach a more populous audience. Should it be a surprise, then, that Cervantes is the most illustrious of all writers to emerge from the Iberian peninsula? Or that authors writing in Spanish have received more Nobel Prizes than those authors writing in any other Iberian tongue?

Admittedly, it could be argued that there is some method to this madness. The sociocultural systems that developed under Castilian and Portuguese peoples may have had certain political, economic, diplomatic, and military advantages that made them more adaptive, and accordingly enabled them to emerge victorious in the struggle of the fittest. Even so, this argument does not remove one stark reality: The reception of literary creations can largely depend on extraneous factors that ignore intrinsic aesthetic worth. So, however logical in a larger environmental context, the critical constraints imposed by sociocultural selection remain capricious and cruel. It is like some beautiful and exotic life forms on some remote Pacific atoll suddenly going extinct when this tiny world is unexpectedly washed over by a tidal wave or paved over by an air force runway.

VARIATION PROCESSES

So far, I have shown how several critical constraints operate at different levels to restrict the ideational variations that are offered in the world. Out of the cornucopia of ideas, only a few survive; from the menagerie of creative individuals, only a small proportion attain contemporary success and fewer still are remembered to posterity; and of the inventory of available sociocultural systems, only a subset make a lasting and extensive contribution to human civilization. Moreover, I have by no means exhausted what can be said about the operation of selection in the winnowing out of variations. For instance, I have ignored the role of schools, paradigms, and styles as units of selection that reside midway between the interpersonal and the sociocultural levels (Hull, 1988; Kuhn, 1970). But rather than expound any further on this mode of group selection, I turn from the receiving end of the variation-selection process underlying creative behavior. Instead, I look, however briefly, at the critical constraints that are imposed at the beginning end of the hypothesized process. These essentially fall into two broad classes.

First, creative individuals must implement limitations on problem identification. In any given creative enterprise, the number of potential projects is practically infinite. Just think of all the natural phenomena that can become the subject of investigation or theorizing! Just imagine all the human experiences that can become the germ for literary treatment! Just contemplate all the poems that might be set to music or all the stories that might become operas? And so forth. At the same time, these myriad potential projects vary immensely in their amenability to creative solution. Indeed, for a particular discipline at a particular time, solutions of some problems may be strictly impossible. To offer a classic illustration, the creation of a heavier-than-air flying machine had to await the development of a motor that had the necessary ratio of horsepower to weight. A large number of would-be inventors wasted large chunks of their lives trying to devise airplanes before this prerequisite was met.

Hence, effective creativity requires the right mix of imagination and pragmatics. From the profusion of conceivable projects a creator must select that subset that are at least possible. This demands a rational and mature assessment of the probable requirements of any particular project and the personal and social resources available for its realization. Those creators who lack the capacity to carry out these appraisals, and instead take up projects willy-nilly, too often will forfeit the achievable for the sake of the chimerical. So good judgment in problem identification is essential for a long and productive career.

Second, constraints are normally imposed on solution generation as well. To appreciate the need for such limitations, let us return to the variation processes that drive biological evolution. Most of the variety in forms that populate a particular species emerges from the Mendelian recombination of genetic material. That means that the combinatory process operates on genes that, with only few exceptions, have proven themselves to have adaptive value in the prior evolutionary history of the species. The contrast between dominant and recessive traits also reflects the gifts of this evolutionary wisdom. Additionally, the phenomenon of linkage interjects further restrictions on the freedom of recombination, restrictions that again are the outcome of the evolutionary past. Hence, the variations that fuel natural selection are produced mostly by a mechanism that represents a compromise between utter randomness and total stability. Only in the case of mutations can it be said that the variation mechanism is totally iconoclastic. Yet, haphazard mutations have a low probability of making any positive, adaptive contributions to the gene pool.

In the variation processes that feed creativity, there are analogous intrusions of constraints. Certainly, when creative individuals contemplate specific problems, they do not generate all possible permutations of all concepts and images available in their minds. Rather, no matter how far-reaching and remote the linkages may appear, they are much more narrow in scope than what could be envisioned under a completely chaotic system. In other words, creativity entails the operation of something more akin to Mendelian recombinations than anything comparable to outright mutations. The variational procedures do not mix up every idea with every other possible idea, but rather all ideas going into the hopper are confined to some domain (see Eysenck, 1993).

Take Gutenberg's invention of the printing press as a case in point (cf. Koestler, 1964). This invention arose when Gutenberg linked block printing, coin minting, and seal imprinting with wine presses. Indeed, it is obvious from immediate visual inspection that the Gutenberg printing press represents an innovative adaptation of the wine press. Now, the latter device may seem rather removed from the other concepts milling around in Gutenberg's mind. Squeezing juice from grapes is a far cry from leaving graphic impressions on paper, metal, or wax. But think again. The wine press is certainly not as remote as, say, freely associating to the taste of wine or the shape of the grape vine, the topography of the Rhine valley, the grammatical structure of the German language, the story of Job in the Bible, or his favorite beer. In fact, all the conceptual components feeding the creation of the printing press share key elements in common. All are mechanical systems. All deal with the application of pressure. And all add value to a raw substance—paper, metal, wax, or grapes—and thereby yield a product that is exchanged on the market. So the analogical reasoning that led Gutenberg to the printing press was not as farfetched as it first appears.

This feature of the variation process enables an appreciation of an important aspect of creative genius. Great creators are seldom one-project-at-a-time thinkers. Instead, they will normally have several projects going on simultaneously, each at a different stage toward completion, and all somewhat loosely interconnected with each other (e.g., Root-Bernstein, Bernstein, & Garnier, 1993; Simon, 1974). In short, creators are engaged in a *network of enterprises* (Gruber, 1988). By jumping back and forth between various projects, creators can bring to one problem the insights and perspectives developed on other problems (see also Garvey & Tomita, 1972). Such a situation increases the likelihood that the creator will chance on a startling solution that might otherwise be missed. It enables the creator to take full advantage of serendipitous episodes. Notwithstanding the novelty of the associative linkage, the creative synthesis will usually incorporate ideas that lie within the general sphere of activities that comprise the network of enterprises. Thus, Poincaré (1921) reported how the solution of one mathematical problem could lead him to the surprising solution of another, supposedly unrelated problem:

> Then I turned my attention to the study of some arithmetical questions apparently without much success and without a suspicion of any connection with my preceding researches. . . . One morning, walking on the bluff, the idea came to me . . . that the arithmetic transformations of indeterminate ternary quadratic forms were identical with those of non-Euclidean geometry. (p. 388)

Yet, significantly, Poincaré did not record any examples of productive interplay between ideas that went well beyond the mathematical sciences. The network of enterprises pretty much defines the ideational territory in which the most productive variations take place.

CONCLUSION

Three related themes permeate the foregoing discussion of critical constraints. These themes enable appreciation of some of the central qualities of the creative process and personality.

First, it has been shown that creativity is a delicate, even precarious activity. Initial ideas are like pollen: Although many grains are tossed into the winds, only a few find the flowers in which they can germinate fruit. Likewise, the creative individuals who produce these ideas are in an equally perilous position. For a sundry capricious reasons, they may find themselves selected out of the competition, whether because they lacked some crucial trait of character or because the sociocultural system on which their contributions were founded lost out in the fierce competition among political entities.

Second, creativity is so often at risk because it requires a tricky adjustment of various trade-offs. For example, creative individuals must find the right response to the essential tension between iconoclasm and traditionalism. And they must conceive the just balance between refining old criteria and devising new ones. Not everyone has the mental flexibility and emotional stamina to engage successfully in juggling acts like these.

Third, this necessity of finding an equilibrium between opposites often results in the occurrence of curvilinear relations between antecedent variables and creative behavior. In problem identification, for instance, creators must find questions that are original yet attainable. This implies that the relation between creativity and the boldness of problem finding will be defined by an inverted-U curve. Similarly, although problem solution demands the activation of a free-associative, variation procedure, this process cannot go so far beyond the domain that it brings about autistic rather than useful syntheses of ideas. Hence, a curvilinear, inverted-U function probably describes the connection between the range of the imagination and the quality of the ideas so produced.

I find the role of such curvilinear relations especially provocative. These functions correspond with the inverted-U curves that so often govern the impact of certain variables on the development of creative talent (Simonton, 1994b). For instance, a certain optimal amount of traumatic experiences in childhood and adolescence may enhance the prospects for creative achievement in adulthood. Likewise, the relation between level of formal education attained and eminence as a creator is often described by an inverted-U curve. A similar curve frequently connects creative distinction with the influence of role models and mentors. These findings imply that these developmental experiences may partially determine whether a young talent will develop the right mix of iconoclasm and traditionalism, imagination and judgment, and so forth. These opposed qualities must be finely balanced for an individual to display exceptional adulthood creativity, and that balance emerges from the events and circumstances of childhood and adolescence. These influences ensure that the individual will have neither too much nor too little. Ultimately, the story of creativity, as told by the variation-selection theory, echoes that of Goldilocks and the Three Bears. Everything must be "just right."

REFERENCES

Beveridge, W. I. B. (1957). *The art of scientific investigation* (3rd ed.). New York: Vintage.

Campbell, D. T. (1960). Blind variation and selective retention in creative thought as in other knowledge processes. *Psychological Review, 67,* 380-400.

Campbell, D. T. (1965). Variation and selective retention in socio-cultural evolution. In H. R. Barringer, G. I. Blanksten, & R. W. Mack (Eds.), *Social change in developing areas* (pp. 19-49). Cambridge, MA: Schenkman.

Campbell, D. T. (1974). Evolutionary epistemology. In P. A. Schlipp (Ed.), *The philosophy of Karl Popper* (pp. 413-463). La Salle, IL: Open Court.

Campbell, D. T., & Tauscher, H. (1966). Schopenhauer (?), Séguin, Lubinoff, and Zehender as anticipators of Emmert's Law: With comments on the uses of eponymy. *Journal of the History of the Behavioral Sciences, 2,* 58-63.

Eysenck, H. J. (1993). Creativity and personality: Suggestions for a theory. *Psychological Inquiry, 4,* 147-148.

Garvey, W. D., & Tomita, K. (1972). Continuity of productivity by scientists in the years 1968-1971. *Science Studies, 2,* 379-383.

Gruber, H. E. (1988). The evolving systems approach to creative work. *Creativity Research Journal, 1,* 27-51.

Hull, D. L. (1988). *Science as a process: An evolutionary account of the social and conceptual development of science.* Chicago: University of Chicago Press.

Kantorovich, A. (1993). *Scientific discovery: Logic and tinkering.* Albany: State University of New York Press.

Kasof, J. (1995). Explaining creativity: The attributional perspective. *Creativity Research Journal, 8,* 311-366.

Koestler, A. (1964). *The act of creation.* New York: Macmillan.

Kuhn, T. S. (1963). The essential tension: Tradition and innovation in scientific research. In C. W. Taylor & F. X. Barron (Eds.),

Scientific creativity: Its recognition and development (pp. 341-354). New York: Wiley.

Kuhn, T. S. (1970). *The structure of scientific revolutions* (2nd ed.). Chicago: University of Chicago Press.

Lamb, D., & Easton, S. M. (1984). *Multiple discovery.* England: Avebury.

Langley, P., Simon, H. A., Bradshaw, G. L., & Zythow, J. M. (1987). *Scientific discovery.* Cambridge, MA: MIT Press.

Martindale, C. (1990). *The clockwork muse: The predictability of artistic styles.* New York: Basic Books.

Merton, R. K. (1961). Singletons and multiples in scientific discovery: A chapter in the sociology of science. *Proceedings of the American Philosophical Society, 105,* 470-486.

Poincaré, H. (1921). *The foundations of science: Science and hypothesis, the value of science, science and method* (G. B. Halstead, Trans.). New York: Science Press.

Rothenberg, A. (1990). *Creativity and madness: New findings and old stereotypes.* Baltimore, MD: The Johns Hopkins University Press.

Root-Bernstein, R. S., Bernstein, M., & Garnier, H. (1993). Identification of scientists making long-term, high-impact contributions, with notes on their methods of working. *Creativity Research Journal, 6,* 329-343.

Shrager, J., & Langley, P. (Eds.). (1990). *Computational models of scientific discovery and theory formation.* San Mateo, CA: Kaufmann.

Simon, R. J. (1974). The work habits of eminent scientists. *Sociology of Work and Occupations, 1,* 327-335.

Simonton, D. K. (1979). Multiple discovery and invention: Zeitgeist, genius, or chance? *Journal of Personality and Social Psychology, 37,* 1603-1616.

Simonton, D. K. (1987). Multiples, chance, genius, creativity, and zeitgeist. In D. N. Jackson & J. P. Rushton (Eds.), *Scientific excellence: Origins and assessment* (pp. 98-128). Beverly Hills, CA: Sage.

Simonton, D. K. (1988a). Age and outstanding achievement: What do we know after a century of research? *Psychological Bulletin, 104,* 251-267.

Simonton, D. K. (1988b). Creativity, leadership, and chance. In R. J. Sternberg (Ed.), *The nature of creativity: Contemporary psychological perspectives* (pp. 386-426). New York: Cambridge University Press.

Simonton, D. K. (1988c). Quality and purpose, quantity and chance. *Creativity Research Journal, 1,* 68-74.

Simonton, D. K. (1988d). *Scientific genius: A psychology of science.* Cambridge: Cambridge University Press.

Simonton, D. K. (1989). The chance-configuration theory of scientific creativity. In B. Gholson, W. R. Shadish, Jr., R. A. Neimeyer, & A. C. Houts (Eds.), *The psychology of science: Contributions to metascience* (pp. 170-213). Cambridge: Cambridge University Press.

Simonton, D. K. (1993a). Blind variations, chance configurations, and creative genius. *Psychological Inquiry, 4*, 225-228.

Simonton, D. K. (1993b). Genius and chance: A Darwinian perspective. In J. Brockman (Ed.), *Creativity: The Reality Club IV* (pp. 176-201). New York: Simon & Schuster.

Simonton, D. K. (1994a). Foresight in insight? A Darwinian answer. In R. J. Sternberg & J. E. Davidson (Eds.), *The nature of insight*. Cambridge, MA: MIT Press.

Simonton, D. K. (1994b). *Greatness: Who makes history and why.* New York: Guilford Press.

Simonton, D. K. (1999). *The origins of genius: Darwinian perspectives on creativity.* New York: Oxford University Press.

Simonton, D. K. (in press-a). The continued evolution of creative Darwinism. *Psychological Inquiry.*

Simonton, D. K. (in press-b). Creativity as blind variation and selective retention: Is the creative process Darwinian? *Psychological Inquiry.*

Sorokin, P. A. (1937-1941). *Social and cultural dynamics* (4 vols.). New York: American Book.

2

PICKING THE RIGHT MATERIAL: COGNITIVE PROCESSING SKILLS AND THEIR ROLE IN CREATIVE THOUGHT

Michael D. Mumford
The University of Oklahoma

Wayne A. Baughman
Christopher E. Sager
American Institutes for Research

Many students have attended classes in social philosophy, sometimes under the guise of history, sometimes under the guise of sociology, and, occasionally, as part of the philosophy curriculum. Often, these courses draw a distinction between two modes of thought: the romantic view, with its focus on the mysterious genius of the individual; and the naturalistic view, where the individual is seen as a flawed entity dealing with a complex world. These notions are not antiquated. In fact, they are apparent in the consideration of the relation between critical and creative thought.

The romantic tradition has played an important role in shaping understanding of creativity (Abra, 1994). According to this tradition, the creative person is often portrayed as an open, unconstrained individual whose personal efforts are the ultimate source of any new idea (Gruber, 1988). This portrayal of creative people influences the assumptions made about the nature of creative thought: This view is implicit not only in the psychodynamic tradition, where the unconscious is held to be an important source of new ideas (Arieti, 1976; Suler, 1980), it is also apparent in psychometric work on the assessment of creative potential. For example, the Remote-Associations Test links creativity to the individual's ability to make unusual connections (Mednick & Mednick, 1967).

In contrast to the romantics, naturalists do not stress the intrinsic worth of the individual's ideas. Instead, they argue that ideas must be carefully evaluated to establish their merits and potential flaws. This tradition is alive and well in the critical thinking literature. Investigators in this area stress the need to evaluate ideas and arguments in terms of their strengths and weaknesses and in light of our biases as human beings (Chaffee, 1990). In this sense, critical thinking represents the antithesis of creative thought. In fact, it is commonly assumed that critical thinking may inhibit creative thought, contributing to the production of useful, new ideas only in the later stages of the creative process, where one must evaluate the merits of a new idea (Lindzey, Hall, & Thompson, 1978).

In this chapter, we argue that this arbitrary distinction between critical and creative thinking is misleading and unnecessary. More specifically, we argue that creativity is based on a set of complex information-processing skills, and that effective application of these skills often requires critical thinking. We then review the results obtained in a series of studies that provide evidence showing that the quality of the information used in executing processes underlying problem solving represents an important influence on creativity. Finally, we consider the broader implications of these findings for understanding creativity and the development of creative potential.

CREATIVE THOUGHT

Creativity

The word, *creativity*, calls to mind images of exceptions, which carry some emotional baggage. Thus, it is germane to begin by defining exactly what is meant by the term, *creativity*. Although creativity has been defined in many ways (Mumford & Gustafson, 1988), most investigators agree that creativity is the production of useful new products and ideas (Amabile, 1983; Ghiselin, 1963; Nicholls, 1972). In this sense, creative achievement must be viewed as a complex form of performance. Thus, like any other complex performance, a host of variables influences eventual achievement. These factors include expertise (Martinsen, 1993), special abilities (Walberg & Stariha, 1992), motives and personality characteristics (Domino, 1994; Rubenson & Runco, 1992), and social evaluation of the proposed new idea or product (Kasof, 1995; Rodgers & Adhikarya, 1979).

Although students of creativity have examined the influence of these factors on the production of new ideas, the field has tended to focus on the crucial issue of how new ideas are generated. Our initial answer to this question, one that appeared quite promising at the time, may be found in the notion of divergent thinking (Guilford, 1950). Essentially, divergent thinking refers to the capacity to generate multiple alternative solutions to novel, open-ended problems. It was assumed that the individual's ability to generate multiple alternative solutions represents the basic capacity accounting for creative achievement and individual differences in idea generation across a variety of domains.

Studies carried out since the 1950s, however, have led many to question divergent thinking as a framework capable of accounting for idea generation and subsequent achievement. It has been known for some time that although divergent thinking is related to creative achievement (Runco, 1991; Runco & Albert, 1985), measures of divergent thinking are not highly effective predictors of idea generation and subsequent creative achievement. Furthermore, evidence compiled by Baer (1994) shows that divergent thinking cannot account for creative performance across different fields of endeavor. Finally, the very notion of divergent thinking may miss the point. Creative achievement depends more on the generation of a single high-quality alternative than on the number of alternatives.

Problem Solving

If one accepts the proposition that creative thought involves not merely the generation of alternative solutions but also the identification of viable, new, alternative solutions, then one must also grant the proposition that creative thought represents a form of complex problem solving. More specifically, the creative person must be able to construct and identify a viable alternative, one out of many potential alternatives, which addresses the issue at hand. Thus, the generation and selection of viable alternative actions represent a form of complex problem solving. Accordingly, many investigators have begun to examine how the understanding of human cognition and problem solving might be used to account for creative thought (Bradshaw, Gangley, & Simon, 1983; Finke, Ward, & Smith, 1992; Mumford, Mobley, Uhlman, Reiter-Palmon, & Doares, 1991; Sternberg, 1986a; Sternberg & Lubart, 1991).

One principle commonly accepted by adherents of this approach is that not all problems individuals confront in their lives call for creative thought (Dillon, 1982). Instead, creative thought is likely to be called for when people have identified or are presented with a novel problem, where a solution cannot be generated simply through the rote application of experience (Mumford & Gustafson, 1988). Creative problems, moreover, are commonly held to be ill-defined in the sense that the nature of the problem situation and potential courses of action are not clearly specified (Frederiksen, 1984). Finally, it is often held that these problems tend to be open-ended, lacking a fixed solution but allowing multiple, potentially viable solutions.

These characteristics of creative problems, however, pose still another question: How can we go about generating viable, new, alternative solutions that go beyond existing expertise if expertise, or knowledge, is indeed the foundation for all problem solving (Anderson, 1993; Chi & Glaser, 1988; Kulkarni & Simon, 1988)? One answer to this riddle can be found in the combination and reorganization of extant knowledge structures (Mobley, Doares, & Mumford, 1992; Mumford & Gustafson, 1988; Simonton, 1988). This model of idea generation asserts that people continue to apply available expertise as they try to solve novel, ill-defined problems. Extant knowledge, however, is not applied in a rote, automatic fashion. Instead, people identify multiple categories, or schema, which might be used to account for the available information bearing on the nature of the problem. These knowledge structures are then combined and/or reorganized to create a new knowledge structure that provides a better basis for understanding the problem situation (Mobley et al., 1992). This new knowledge structure, in turn, provides a basis for the generation of new alternative solutions. It may, in fact, lead to the generation of unanticipated solution alternatives as people explore the implications of new features or attributes of the knowledge structure emerging with this combination and reorganization (Finke et al., 1992).

A variety of evidence is available that points to the importance of this combination-and-reorganization process in creative thought. Studies of eminent achievement in the arts and sciences by Koestler (1964), Kuhn (1970), and Rothenberg (1986) suggests that new ideas are often associated with the sudden fusion or explicit linkage of two or more schemata. Along similar lines, Simonton (1988) has shown that the rate of creative contributions can be accounted for based on the number of concepts available for combination. Other work by Carlson and Gorman (1992) and Mumford and Connelly (1993) suggests that many innovations in applied fields can be linked to the reorganization of available knowledge structures. A case in point may be found in Bell's development of the telephone, where auditory principles allowed for a more effective organization of the relevant electromechanical principles.

Evidence pointing to the importance of combination-and-reorganization efforts is not limited to historic studies. In one set of experimental studies, Rothenberg and his colleagues (Rothenberg & Sobel, 1980; Sobel & Rothenberg, 1980) proved that experimental conditions intended to help combination and reorganization via superimposing different images led to the production of more creative literary and artistic products. In another set of investigations, Mumford and his colleagues (Baughman & Mumford, 1995; Mobley et al., 1992) presented categories (e.g., birds, sporting equipment, etc.) and asked people to combine these stimulus categories to generate a new category that would account for the relevant category exemplars (e.g., for birds—robins, sparrows, owls, and ostriches). They found that more original categories and more original stories were obtained when people were asked to combine diverse, as opposed to similar, stimulus categories. In still another set of studies, Finke et al. (1992) presented various mechanical parts and asked people to combine these parts to create a useful, new tool. They found that the exploration of these new combinations led to the production of creative, original, new products. Along similar lines, Owens (1969) asked engineers to combine and reorganize various parts and mechanical principles to create a new machine. Measures of skill in combining and reorganizing these parts and principles were found to yield correlations of about .45 with patent awards and supervisors' assessments of creativity obtained more than 5 years later.

These studies provide compelling evidence that the combination-and-reorganization process is important to creative thought. Accordingly, more recent studies have begun to examine the mechanisms people use as they attempt to combine and reorganize knowledge structures to arrive at a new understanding of various problems. In an initial study along these lines, Baughman and Mumford (in press) tested the hypothesis that overlapping features of categories provide a basis for people's combinations and reorganizations. In this study, subjects were asked to solve a series of category-exemplar-generation problems drawn from Mobley et al. (1992). Here, however, subjects in the experimental conditions were asked to identify the features of each category (e.g., birds have feathers and fly), and then identify the shared and unshared features of the stimulus categories before generating their new category. It was found that this search-and-mapping operation contributed to the production of more original, high-quality, new categories, when people were presented with relatively similar stimulus categories.

A later study by Mumford, Baughman, Maher, Costanza, and Supinski (1994) examined how people combine more diverse stimulus categories. To accomplish this objective, subjects in one condition were asked to combine categories using only a simple feature search-and-mapping procedure (Baughman & Mumford, 1995). Subjects in the experimental condition, however, were asked additionally to think about what these features might represent (e.g., birds have wings and fly, and *flight* represents *freedom*). This metaphor manipulation was found to contribute to the production of more original, higher quality category combinations when people were asked to work with diverse stimulus categories. Thus, it appears feature search and mapping may be used to combine similar stimulus categories, whereas metaphors, or abstract relations, may be used to combine more diverse stimulus categories.

Processing Skills

Taken as a whole, the studies just described lead to one profoundly important conclusion. The combination and reorganization of extant knowledge structures may represent the key cognitive process underlying the generation of new ideas. This general conclusion, however, has another important, even if often overlooked, implication. That is, the nature and success of these combination-and-reorganization efforts will depend on the nature of the problem the individual has identified and the quality of the information and knowledge structures available for use in the individual's combination-and-reorganization efforts. This observation, in turn, implies that the success of the individual's combination-and-reorganization efforts may depend on the effective execution of several other cognitive processes.

In a recent review of the literature examining the cognitive processes that appear to play a role in creative thought, Mumford et al. (1991) identified eight processes that are commonly held to influence creativity. The processes identified in this literature review include the following:

1. Problem construction or problem definition.
2. Information encoding.
3. Category search.
4. Category selection.
5. Category combination and reorganization.
6. idea evaluation.
7. Implementation planning.
8. Monitoring.

Figure 2.1 illustrates how these processing activities operate in an integrated problem-solving effort.

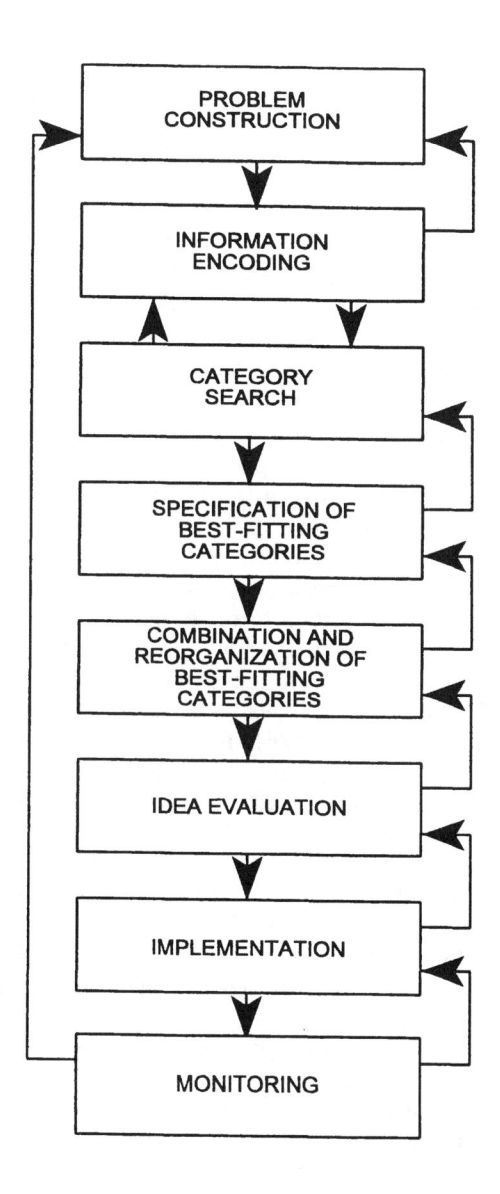

Figure 2.1. Hypothesized relationships among core processes

Within this model, problem solving begins when the individual comes to grips with an unstructured situation by defining or constructing the nature of the problem at hand. Next, the individual uses this initial problem definition to guide a search for relevant information and identify categories or concepts that might be used to account for this information. Subsequently, the best available concepts or categories are identified, and these categories are combined and reorganized to create a new understanding of the problem situation. The new ideas flowing from this combination-and-reorganization effort are then evaluated and a subset is implemented. The success of a particular implementation is evaluated during monitoring.

Regarding this model, three other points are noteworthy: First, people may cycle back through these processes several times during a problem-solving effort. Second, some of these processes may represent particularly important influences on performance on certain kinds of problems. For example, relatively well-defined problems may require less effort in problem construction. Third, the success of an individual's efforts in the later phases of this cycle, particularly combination and reorganization, will depend on the quality of the material provided by prior processing operations. Therefore, the effective execution of all these processes may be required for the generation of successful solutions to novel problems.

In fact, substantial evidence has been obtained in recent years suggesting that these processes can influence the nature and success of creative problem-solving efforts. Getzels and Csikszentmihalyi (1975, 1976), for example, obtained behavioral indicators of problem construction activities (e.g., object handling) before artists started work on a painting. They found that these indices of problem-construction activities yielded correlations between .30 and .50 with judges' ratings of the aesthetic value of artistic products obtained 5 years later. Along similar lines, Okuda, Runco, and Berger (1991) administered a measure of problem-construction activities and found that this scale was a better predictor of "real-world" creative achievement than measures of divergent thinking and intelligence. Other studies by Hoover and Feldhusen (1990); Kay (1991); and Redmond, Mumford, and Teach (1993) also provided evidence for the importance of the problem-construction process, indicating that it can influence creative achievement in such diverse fields as advertising and the physical sciences.

Although recent research has focused on the problem-construction process, there is reason to suspect that the other processes specified in this model also influence creativity and the generation of new ideas. For example, studies by Alissa (1972), Davidson and Sternberg (1984), Kuhn (1970), Kulkarni and Simon (1988), and Perkins (1992) suggest that extended information search and search strategies that result in the identification of key facts and inconsistent information appears to contribute to creative achievement and effective performance as people work through novel problems. In still another investigation, Runco and Chand (1994) found that the kind of standards people apply in evaluating new ideas influences their performance on creative problem-solving tasks. Along similar lines, Mumford, Zaccaro, Harding, and Fleishman (in press) found that people—in the case at hand, organizational leaders—tended to produce more creative solutions to novel organizational problems when they identified the likely consequences of proposed ideas, and then used this evaluative information to revise their initial solutions.

These studies support the proposition that the processes specified in the model proposed by Mumford et al. (1991) represent important determinants of performance on creative problem-solving tasks. Beyond this general conclusion, however, the studies cited here have another noteworthy implication: In one way or another, all these studies examine differences among individuals in the effectiveness with which they applied various processes. Thus, it appears that people differ in how they apply each of these processes in their creative problem-solving efforts.

Some important clues bearing on the nature of these differences have been provided in a recent study by Mumford, Reiter-Palmon, and Redmond (1994). In this study, Mumford and his colleagues were expressly concerned with how people construct and define problems. They argued that people's problem constructions are likely to be based on representations derived from past problem-solving efforts. These representations, reflecting ad-hoc categories are hypothesized to include information about the goals, principles, procedures, and restrictions encountered in earlier problem-solving efforts (Gick & Holyoak, 1983; Holyoak, 1984; Novick, 1990). The idea is that one or more of these representations are activated by the clues present in the problem situation. A subsequent search and screening of the elements included in the activated representations provides the basis for construction of a new representation of the problem situation. This model is illustrated in Figure 2.2. Some crucial support for this model was provided by the finding that conditions calling for active search and screening of representations led to the production of more creative problem solutions.

Mumford, Reiter-Palmon, and Redmond's (1994) model is of interest not only because it provides one plausible description of the problem-construction process. It also suggests two basic ways that individuals might differ regarding the application of a given process. First, they may choose to focus on different kinds of contents in applying a process. For example, with problem construction, one person might focus on goals and another on procedures. These dif-

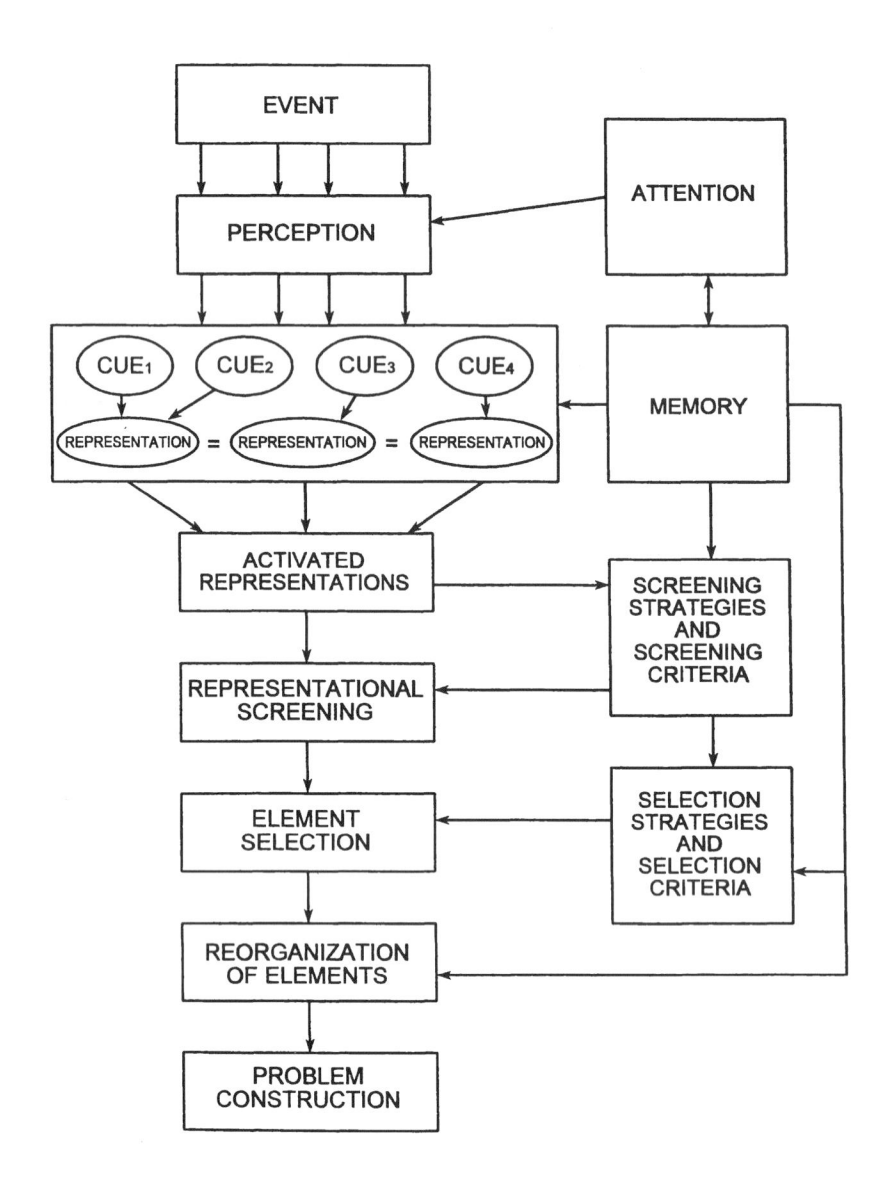

Figure 2.2. Model of problem construction operations

ferences in preferred content may influence the likelihood of producing a useful new idea in subsequent combination-and-reorganization efforts. Second, individuals may choose to apply different strategies in working with material. For example, turning to the case of problem construction, one individual may simply apply the most highly activated representation, while another may retain the two or three most highly activated representations in screening. These strategic differences in the application of processing operations may also influence subsequent creativity with rote retention of the most strongly activated representation, a variation on satisficing, leading to poor performance.

When one considers these observations considering the fact that the effective execution of these processes determines the nature and success of people's combination-and-reorganization efforts, they have several noteworthy implications: To begin, differences among individuals in the content being examined in a given process and the strategies being applied in working with this content will influence their performance on creative problem-solving tasks. Furthermore, one would expect that the tendency to use contents and procedures that result in higher quality, more comprehensive knowledge structures (for use in combination-and-reorganization efforts and subsequent idea generation) would be particularly strongly related to people's ability to produce viable solutions to novel problems. Finally, if these hypotheses are found to hold, they would suggest that critical thought provides a substantive basis for creative thought. This contrasts with the case commonly assumed, where critical thought is imposed only after one has initially generated a new idea. Our intent in the studies described in the following sections of this chapter was to determine what kinds of contents and procedures were related to the production of useful, new ideas with the expectation that the use of contents and procedures that resulted in the availability of viable, high-quality knowledge structures for use in combination, reorganization, and idea generation would be particularly strongly related to performance on creative problem-solving tasks.

CONTENT DIFFERENCES

Study Procedures

To assess the effects of using different kinds of content material during the earlier phases of creative thought, undergraduates were asked to participate in what was purporting to be a 2-hour study of problem-solving skills. Subjects were asked to complete a battery of problem-solving measures. These measures were constructed to assess the very material people used in problem construction, information encoding, category selection, and category combination. The measures intended to assess content preferences in applying each of these skills were administered using a 386 personal computer with a color monitor. To ensure an adequate understanding of the task that was designed to assess content preferences applying to each of these processing skills, subjects were asked to complete a short tutorial. This tutorial described the nature of the task before beginning work on the problem used to assess these content preferences. A series of pilot studies showed that these tutorials and a single practice exercise provided a background needed to perform the tasks.

To determine how these content preferences were related to performance on creative problem-solving tasks, subjects participating in this study were also asked to complete two creative problem-solving exercises. The first set of problems was based on material drawn from the management and public-policy domain, whereas the second set of problems presented material drawn from the advertising domain. Multiple problems drawn from different domains were used to provide some evidence for the cross-domain generality of our conclusions, and these problems were expressly selected to provide a realistic assessment of creative problem solving within an undergraduate sample.

The advertising problems were drawn from earlier work by Redmond et al. (1993), in which subjects were asked to develop an advertising campaign for a new product—the 3-D Holographic Television. Before starting work on their campaigns, subjects read the product description presented in Figure 2.3. Next, they wrote a three- or four-paragraph answer to each of the following instructions:

1. Describe the kinds of questions you would ask in a market survey to obtain information about market characteristics and selling points.
2. Describe a 30-second television commercial that you would use to sell this product.
3. Describe a full-page magazine advertisement that you would use to sell this product.

Solutions to each of these problems were scored by three judges. These (and subsequent) judges were graduate students in industrial and organizational psychology familiar with the problem solving and creativity literatures. The problem solutions were judged for quality and originality using the benchmark rating scales. Scale anchors consisted of illustrations of products reflecting varying levels of qual-

Henderson & Co.
Consumer Electronics Division - New Products Division

NEW PRODUCT INTRODUCTION

New Product: 3-D Holographic TV

Firm: Zenith

Product Description:

One of our clients, Zenith, has developed and patented a three-dimensional holographic television. Using the latest in computer and laser technology, this new home entertainment system takes a standard two-dimensional television or videotape signal and recreates it into a three-dimensional image, a hologram.

The computer technology was developed from research with high-density televisions. Unlike high-density televisions, however, the computer in the 3-D holographic TV generates the normally untelevised third dimension using known objects stored in its extensive memory. All three dimensions are then combined and projected using lasers and mirrors.

As illustrated by the enclosed sketch of the product, the 3-D holographic image is projected to an area *on top of the set*. This 3-D projection allows the created image to be viewed *from all angles* (front, back, and sides). For example, the enclosed illustration of the car scene is viewed from the front of the set. From this angle, the car appears to be traveling towards you. It will appear to be traveling away from you, however, if you were viewing the car scene from the rear of the set.

Other Features:

- Uses standard household current
- High-quality computer chips (Intel 586)
- Extended memory of known objects
- State-of -the-art software
- Computer interface for custom hologram design
- Reasonable image quality
- large image size(24" high, 24" wide, 18" deep.
- Easy to operate controls
- High-fidelity sound (four speakers)
- Wireless remote

Production Schedule:

Zenith currently has a working prototype of the 3-D holographic television build, and will be introducing it into the marketplace in *90 days*.

Retail Price:

The manufacturer's suggested retail price per unit is estimated to be $3,000-$4,000 for the first 10,000 units produced. As more units are produced, however, the average manufacturing cost per unit is projected to curve downward (production experience curve). This projected decline in manufacturing costs will enable Zenith to lower their suggested retail price per unit, as follows:

Retail Pricing Curve

Number of Units Produced	Manufacturer's Suggested Retail Price (per unit)
1 - 10,000	$3,000 - $4,000
10,000 - 100,000	$2,500 - $3,000
100,000 - 1,000,000	$2,000 - $2,500
1,000,000 - 10,000,000	$1,500 - $2,000
10,000,000 and up	$1,000 - $1,500

Competition:

RCA and Sony are also planning to produce 3-D holographic televisions. RCA is projected to introduce their first units in *one year*. However, due to increased development time, it will take Sony *two years* to introduce their first units.

The manufacturer's suggested retail price is expected to be similar for each of the three companies.

Figure 2.3. Description of product to be marketed on the advertising task

ity and originality based on a consensus of the advertising executives (Hennessey & Amabile, 1988; Redmond et al., 1993). These quality and originality ratings yielded interrater agreement coefficients in the .70s. Total quality and originality scores were obtained simply by summing the judges' average ratings across the three problems.

The managerial and policy problems were drawn from case studies presenting novel, ill-defined organization problems (Mumford, Baughman, Supinski, Costanza, & Threlfall, 1994). After subjects had read a description of the case, they were asked to write a brief description of how they would solve the problem posed by the case. Again, a series of benchmark rating scales was developed to assess the quality and originality of the solutions proposed to each problem using anchors defined by a panel of industrial and organizational psychologists. When these rating scales were applied to the solutions obtained from the two management and two public-policy problems, the interrater agreement coefficients obtained from the three judges were in the .80s. Again, total quality and originality scores were obtained by summing judges' average quality and originality scores across the four problems.

Problem Construction

The problem construction measure used to assess the nature of the representational content people applied in structuring ill-defined problems was based on earlier work by Baer (1988) and Redmond et al. (1993). Subjects are presented with six complex, ill-defined situations that might be looked at or structured in several different ways. Next, subjects view 16 restatements of the situation that might be used to define the problem. They were to review the 16 restatements and select the 4 they thought would be most useful in helping them understand the problem situation.

To assess the nature of the content people preferred to use in structuring complex problems, the content of the restatements being presented was varied along four dimensions. More specifically, restatements were presented that reflected a tendency to define problems based on goals, key diagnostic information, procedures, and restrictions. Additionally, within each of these content areas reflecting the basic components of the problem representations (Mumford, Reiter-Palmon, & Redmond, 1994), restatements were developed to reflect two different levels of both quality and originality. Initially, four graduate psychology students were familiarized with the intended design of the measure, and were then instructed to write a set of 16 restatements for each of the six problem scenarios. They were instructed to write the restatements to target each of the 16 possible combinations, given four dimensions with two levels each of quality and originality. This procedure yielded a pool of 64 problem restatements for each of the six problems. The final set of restatements presented on a given problem was selected based on the average ratings of 30 judges concerning the content dimension tapped by the restatement and its quality and originality. In all, each problem presented a set of 16 restatements, representing 2 original and 2 high-quality restatements for each content dimension. Figure 2.4 provides an example of one of these problems and illustrates how the various restatements mapped onto these content dimensions.

For each of the six problems, subjects selected their 4 best restatements from the 16 alternatives. Scores represented how often subjects chose restatements based on original or high-quality goals, diagnostic information, procedures, and restrictions. Table 2.1 summarizes the correlations between these content-dimension scores and scores of quality and originality from the two creative problem-solving tasks. Of the 32 correlations in Table 2.1, 14 were significant or marginally significant. A goodness-of-fit statistic, assuming a base-rate of .10 for marginal significance, provides evidence that the number of significant and marginally significant values appearing in Table 2.1 do not reflect the effects of experiment-wise error [$\chi^2(1)$ = 36.45, $p < .05$]. We report this statistic for the four tables comprising our analysis of content differences.

Across the two creative problem-solving tasks, the tendency to define problems based on high-quality approaches ($r = .19$) and high-quality restrictions ($r = .17$) was positively related to creative performance. The tendency to define problems based on original goals ($r = -.18$) was negatively related to performance. The only other noteworthy finding to emerge in this analysis was related to the use of original restrictions. Use of original restrictions was positively related to performance on the managerial ($r = .17$) but not the advertising ($r = .05$) problems, perhaps because attention to organizational restrictions is particularly important on managerial problems (Mumford et al., in press). Overall, these measures were found to yield average multiple correlations of .34 ($p < .10$) and .38 ($p < .05$) when used to predict performance on the advertising and managerial creative problem-solving tasks respectively. In these analyses, it was found that the use of high-quality procedures in defining the problem ($\beta = .20$), high-quality restrictions ($\beta = .17$), and high-quality information ($\beta = .14$) produced the largest regression weights.

These findings are of interest not only because they suggest that problem-construction skills may influence performance on creative problem-solving tasks. They are also noteworthy because they show that the type of representational content used in problem construction influences the nature and success of people's creative problem-solving efforts. Even more intriguing is the particular nature

SITUATION:

YOU ARE SELECTED TO REPRESENT YOUR COUNTRY IN THE OLYMPIC TRACK AND FIELD. YOU ARE ONE OF THE TOP "HOPEFULS," BUT YOUR DOCTOR HAS ADVISED YOU TO HAVE SURGERY IMMEDIATELY OR RISK A DEBILITATING INJURY. HOWEVER, TO HAVE THE SURGERY WOULD MEAN MISSING THE GAMES.

	QUALITY	ORIGINALITY
GOALS:		
How can I use my fame so as to help others avoid this condition?	HIGH	HIGH
How can I prevent myself from becoming discouraged?	HIGH	LOW
How can I intimidate opponents by convincing the press that I'm not really injured?	LOW	HIGH
How can I attend the games even if I don't participate?	LOW	LOW
PROCEDURES:		
How can I get a bionic replacement part so I can both participate and win?	HIGH	HIGH
How can I find a better solution?	HIGH	LOW
How can I get the games postponed?	LOW	HIGH
How can I convince the coach I should go?	LOW	LOW
KEY INFORMATION:		
How can I find out if other athletes dealt with this same condition successfully?	HIGH	HIGH
How can I find out if I can train to prevent injury?	HIGH	LOW
How can I find out if injured athletes can still make a lot of money?	LOW	HIGH
How can I find out if I can still win the games?	LOW	LOW
RESTRICTIONS:		
How can I make this decision on the basis of what is best for the team?	HIGH	HIGH
How can I participate, but not get hurt?	HIGH	LOW
How can I convince myself that the injury justifies not going to the games?	LOW	HIGH
How can I not let my country down?	LOW	LOW

Figure 2.4. Description of problem-construction task and response options

Table 2.1. Correlations Between Problem Construction and Criterion Measures.

	Advertising Task		Managerial Task	
	Quality	Originality	Quality	Originality
Quality				
Information	-.00	.00	.12	.12
Goals	-.00	.00	-.05	-.01
Approaches	.22**	.17**	.24**	.14*
Restrictions	.17**	.18**	.18**	.14*
Originality				
Information	-.13	-.10	.01	-.00
Goals	-.16*	-.17*	-.20**	-.20**
Approaches	.05	.04	-.04	.00
Restrictions	.05	.05	.20**	.14*

* = $p < .10$
** = $p < .05$

of the representational content that might be related to creative performance. The tendency to focus on high-quality procedures and restrictions yielded the strongest positive relationships. These findings suggest that people who frame an ill-defined problem in terms of viable solution strategies and restrictions on feasible approaches are more likely to perform well on creative tasks. In some senses, this pattern of findings is not surprising, because people who structure problems based on a sound approach that considers likely restrictions have generated a viable and flexible approach to the problem situation.

On the other hand, these results suggest that there is no real need to engage in extensive divergent thought focusing on original elements during problem construction. Use of nearly all of the original representational elements produced negligible or inconsistent relationships with creative performance. The exception here, was the use of original goals. Goal originality, however, produced a consistent negative relationship, perhaps because the tendency to redefine the problem idiosyncratically inhibits performance. Perhaps substantial originality is not needed in problem construction, where sufficient ambiguity has been induced by the nature of the problem itself. Instead, what is needed is a sound set of procedures that allows for likely restrictions. Thus, effective problem construction may require a targeted form of critical thinking, as opposed to a more open, free-flowing approach.

Information Encoding

The information-encoding measure produced a similar pattern of findings, although this measure was constructed using a different set of procedures. Here, subjects were presented with a series of six cards describing either a business or public-policy problem. After reading the material presented on each card in sequence, they were asked to type in a one-paragraph solution to the problem presented in the card set. In working through their solutions, subjects were allowed to page back to a given card as often as they wished. Figure 2.5 describes the nature of this task. In all, subjects were asked to solve two management and two public-policy problems.

To assess the kind of information people tended to focus on in problem solving, the content of the cards was varied, and the time spent viewing each kind of information was recorded automatically as subjects worked on this task. Three of the six cards presented for each problem contained core facts (data) drawn from the relevant source material needed to solve the problem in any fashion. On the remaining three cards, however, other kinds of information were provided. On one business problem and one public-policy problem, one of these three additional cards presented information about principles for organizing information (principles), relevant information that was inconsistent with the facts presented on the three data cards (consistency), and information about how the different facts were related to each other (relatedness). On the other business problem and the other political problem, one of these three additional cards presented information about the goals that needed to be addressed in problem solving (goals), organizational constraints on potential problem solutions (constraints), and additional information about the problem situation that was not specifically tied to the content of the immediate problem (range). These content dimensions were selected based on the available literature concerning the kinds of information that might be related to the production of creative problem solutions (Alissa, 1972; Davidson & Sternberg, 1984; Hogarth, 1986; Kuhn, 1970; Snow & Lohman, 1984; Ward, Byrnes, & Overton, 1990). Kuhn, for example, showed that the tendency to attend to inconsistent observations may be related to good performance on creative problem-solving tasks. Additionally, Snow and Lohman's (1984) findings show that effective problem solving may be related to the use of principles.

Table 2.2 presents the correlations between the time spent encoding these different types of information and performance on the creative problem-solving tasks. Of the 64 correlations, 35 were significant or marginally significant, representing a higher proportion of such significant and marginally significant values than would be expected by chance [$\chi^2(1) = 127.80$, $p < .05$]. Perhaps the most clear-

CARD 1: RESTRICTIONS
Your company, CozyNight Inns, has recently expanded into the national arena by purchasing local hotels and converting them into upscale CozyNight Inns. In order to expedite the change, CozyNight has set up centralized reservations, marketing, finance, interior decoration, methods standardization, and culinary departments at headquarters, but kept the preexisting general managers of each new Cozy Night.

CARD 4: DATA
There are some problems at the local level, too. Hotel managers are often uncooperative with headquarter's policies and are "too busy" to meet with visiting headquarter's staff. Chefs at a number of hotels have complained that nationally prescribed menus violate local tastes, and a Texas head bartender insists that Texas customers want more than 1 ounce of gin in their gin fizzes!!

CARD 2: RANGE
You report directly to the CEO, who has told you, "I know you can handle it, so I'm putting you in charge of the expansion transition. I want my attention free to work on future planning with the board of directors—I don't want to do this day-to-day stuff. You have my authority to do whatever you think is needed to smooth over any transition problems. Just keep me posted once in a while, OK?"

CARD 5: DATA
Although there are problems at the top, you know that CozyNight's problems are restricted to management. The nonmanagerial employees are happy with better wages and benefits, the customers say they are very pleased with the new CozyNight Inns, and the stockholders have seen their shares triple in value. If only the managerial problems could be cleaned up, everyone would be happy with CozyNight.

CARD 3: DATA
Unfortunately, you know that friction is starting among staff departments. Finance is complaining that interior decoration is spending too much on original art work for the new Inns, but decoration insists that the art is essential to the upscale image of CozyNight. Reservations is upset by marketing's many introductory deals, which they say are confusing computers, staff, and customers.

CARD 6: GOALS
So, maybe your task won't be so bad after all. If only you can get the managerial staff to work together, you'll be able to give the CEO a great report. All you need to do is get the managers to agree on corporate priorities, and encourage them to work together to make everyone's life a little smoother. Now, the question is, just what should you do first?

Figure 2.5. Description of information-encoding task

Table 2.2. Correlations Between Information Encoding and Criterion Measures.

	Advertising Task		Managerial Task	
	Quality	Originality	Quality	Originality
Relative Time Spent				
Low-Relevance:Policy	-.21**	-.23**	-.33**	-.24**
Low-Relevance:Business	-.13	-.07	-.06	-.05
Inconsistent:Policy	.16*	.13	.09	.06
Inconsistent:Business	.21**	.15*	.22**	.31**
Principles:Policy	-.01	.06	.11	.09
Principles:Business	-.14*	-.18**	-.36**	-.30**
Restrictions:Policy	.07	.01	-.19**	-.18**
Restrictions:Business	-.05	-.06	-.27**	-.20**
Goals:Policy	-.20**	-.19**	.02	-.01
Goals:Business	-.16	-.12	-.02	-.09
Range:Policy	-.08	-.03	.25**	.23**
Range:Business	-.07	.01	-.16*	-.19**
Facts:Policy1	.18**	.16*	.26**	.20**
Facts:Business1	.08	.14*	.29**	.15*
Facts:Policy2	.13*	.15*	-.04	-.00
Facts:Business2	.18**	.12	.31**	.31**

* = $p < .10$
** = $p < .05$

cut conclusion that can be drawn from these correlations is that people who performed well on the creative problem-solving tasks tended to spend more time encoding key factual information ($r = .16$). This is indicated by the more consistently significant and marginally significant correlations between factual data performance across tasks. Furthermore, in accordance with the earlier observations of Davidson and Sternberg (1984), it was found that people who tended to produce high-quality, original solutions tended to spend less time on irrelevant information ($r = -.17$). In contrast, however, people who produced high-quality, original solutions on the creative problem-solving tasks tended to spend relatively more time examining information. The information they examined was relevant but was not consistent with the other factual data presented on the cards ($r = .17$). This finding is consistent with the earlier observations of Kuhn (1970) and Alissa (1972), suggesting that creative problem solvers focus more on inconsistent or incongruent observations. It also appears that people who performed well on the creative problem-solving tasks tended to spend less time encoding information bearing on relevant principles ($r = -.10$) and pertinent restrictions ($r = -.11$). This pattern of findings suggests that during encoding, creative people tend to focus on a search for relevant information. While engaged in this search, they avoid generalizations, supposed restrictions, and irrelevant information as they look for relevant facts and facts that do not fit the broader pattern of information.

This pattern of findings was confirmed when these measures were used to predict performance on the creative problem-solving tasks. Here, time spent on pertinent factual information ($\beta = .10$) and the tendency to discount irrelevant information ($\beta = -.12$) yielded the largest regression weights. Thus, a critical orientation during information encoding, where people explicitly search for relevant data, appears to contribute to creative problem solving. Moreover, this focused, perhaps critical evaluation of information relevance, was apparently an important predictor of performance on creative problem-solving tasks yielding average multiple correlations with the quality and originality of solutions of .41 ($p < .05$). Thus, the selective search for and evaluation of information may represent a key determinant of creativity (Perkins, 1992).

Category Selection

Of course, once one has identified relevant information, the concepts to be used in organizing and integrating this information must be identified. To assess differences in the kind of categories or concepts people tended to retain for use in problem solving, the work of Mumford et al. (in press) was used to develop a category-selection measure. This measure presented four three- or four-paragraph descriptions of an organizational problem. These problem scenarios, drawn from Shorris (1981), presented a complex, ill-defined situation, where a variety of concepts or schema might be used to understand the problem situation.

To develop a measure of concept or schematic preferences using this material, four doctoral candidates were asked to review each scenario and then identify the concepts or categories that might be used to understand the problem situation. These concepts or categories were then assigned to one of four categories reflecting use of (a) abstract, principle-based concepts (principles); (b) concepts bearing on evaluation of others (evaluation); (c) concepts that focused on long- versus short-term outcomes (long term); and (d) concepts that specified discrete steps for addressing the issues at hand (action plans). The 188 concepts identified in this review were then presented to a panel of five judges who were asked to rate the extent to which each concept reflected these four dimensions. For each content dimension, the two concept statements receiving the highest mean ratings on each of the relevant dimensions, which also had the lowest standard deviations, were identified. Thus, on each problem eight concepts were presented reflecting the four dimensions, and subjects were asked to identify the four concepts they thought would be most useful in illustrating the nature of the problem situation. Figure 2.6 describes the nature of these problems and the eight concepts presented to assess people's preferences for applying concepts reflecting these dimensions.

Responses to these problems were scored simply by finding the number of times concepts drawn from a given dimension were selected for use in problem solving. Table 2.3 presents the correlations between these dimensional preference scores and performance on the two creative problem-solving tasks. Of the 16 correlations, 9 are significant or marginally significant, representing a higher proportion of significant or marginally significant values than would be expected by chance [$\chi^2(1)$ = 34.23, $p < .05$]. The use of concepts reflecting social evaluation and discrete action plans were not related to the quality and originality of the solutions on the two creative problem-solving tasks. The quality ($r = .24$) and originality ($r = .29$) of solutions on the organizational problems, however, was positively related to the selection of concepts reflecting long-term goals ($r = .26$). Along similar lines, the use of concepts based on long-term goals was positively related ($r = .13$) to the tendency to produce original solutions on the advertising problems. Although the use of concepts based on long-term goals was positively related to creative performance, the tendency to select concepts reflecting abstract principles was negatively related to performance on the creative problem-solving tasks ($r = -.23$). One explanation for this pattern of results is that the use of concepts based on general principles may result in the application of concepts that are not sufficiently tailored to the product at hand to result in viable creative products. This is in contrast to the tendency to select concepts based on long-term goals. Thus, again it appears that critical evaluation may be related to creativity, perhaps because concepts based on long-term goals provide a flexible, but appropriate, strategy for organizing information.

Despite the interpretation applied here, however, it appears that this distinctly convergent process contributes to creative performance, although it precedes combination and reorganization and subsequent idea generation. These concept-selection measures yielded average multiple correlations of .25 ($p < .05$) and .33 ($p < .05$) when used to account for the quality and originality of the solutions obtained on the two creative problem-solving tasks. As might be expected, based on our earlier observations, the regression weights suggested that the tendency to use concepts based on long-term goals ($\beta = .17$) contributed to creative performance on the organizational problems, whereas the tendency to use concepts based on general principles ($\beta = -.24$) was negatively related to performance across all problems.

SCENARIO

The amounts charged to the expense account were exorbitant. This was not the occasional three martini lunch or theater tickets—the sales rep was spending more than $150,000 a year—which was more than the whole regional office travel and entertainment budget. The receipts were all there, but the legitimacy of the expenses was questionable. However, the sales rep had been an assistant to the Undersecretary of the Navy during a previous administration and he really knew his way around Washington.

As the regional manager looked over his sales rep's expenses, he wondered why he initialed an expense account that listed $300 dinners night after night. After all, this division sold machinery to manufacturers and parts suppliers and no other sales rep spent a tenth of that amount.

When the rep had moved to the Washington office, he made it clear that the rules for expenses didn't apply to him because he reported directly to the vice chairman of the company. When the issue of meeting sales goals came up, he said it might not be possible to meet them. He told the regional manager if he had a problem with this, he would have to take it up with the vice chair.

Somewhat naively, the regional manager asked the rep why he wasn't working for the vice-chair. The man had responded that the vice chair wanted to keep his lobbying costs down. When the manager asked for a written statement regarding this, the rep merely laughed. The regional manager realized just then that he was going to have to take the blame for the expenses himself, or expose the situation.

RESPONSE OPTIONS:

Abstractness:
- Innocents easily become the victims of political schemes.
- What is ethical and what is practical are not always the same.

Specific Action Plans:
- The regional manager has to decide whether to take the fall or expose the situation.
- The regional manager should consider going to the chairman to try and save his job.

Long-Term Goals:
- Fiscal irresponsibility can set a bad precedent for other reps.
- Politicizing expenses and relationships could be bad for the company.

Social Evaluation:
- The regional manager should take into account ethics, customary Washington lobbying practices, and personal and career considerations in deciding what to do.
- The regional manager could have gone to the vice chair and requested an additional sales rep for his division in order to offset the lack of productivity on the part of the sales rep who only conducted public relations.

Figure 2.6. Description of category-selection task and response

Table 2.3. Correlations Between Category Search and Criterion Measures.

	Advertising Task		Managerial Task	
	Quality	Originality	Quality	Originality
Information Type				
Abstract	-.18**	-.15*	-.28**	-.29**
Social evaluation	-.00	.00	.15*	.06
Long-term goals	.08	.13	.24**	.29**
Specific action plans	-.08	-.16**	-.09	-.16**

* = $p < .10$
** = $p < .05$

Category Combination

The task used to assess the kind of content applied in category combination and reorganization was drawn from the earlier work of Mobley et al. (1992). The six category-exemplar-generation problems presented to subjects presented three categories, or concepts, defined by relevant exemplars. Thus, the category, *sporting equipment*, might be defined using the exemplars, *gloves, skates, bat*, and *ball*. In working through these problems, subjects were asked to review the exemplars defining each of the stimulus categories, and then generate a new category that might account for all presented exemplars. Figure 2.7 presents an illustrative category-exemplar-generation problem.

To assess content as it applies to category combination and reorganization, subjects in the problem-solving skills study were asked to produce three products after they had generated their new categories. They were asked to list the label applying to their new category, the key features or attributes of category members, and five or six exemplars of members of this new category. Here, it was assumed that the category label, the category features, and exemplars of this new category all represented products of the combination-and-reorganization process that might be used in idea generation (Baughman & Mumford, 1995; Finke et al., 1992). Each of these three kinds of products was then presented to a panel of judges comprised of five graduate students in industrial and organizational psychology. These judges were asked to rate each product with respect to its manifest quality and originality. Ratings of the quality and originality of the products derived from the combination-and-reorganization process yielded interrater agreement coefficients in the .80s.

> Your task is to look at these three categories and combine them into one category, imagining that the 12 words are a single list of words, and you had to invent a name for the list.

• seat	• glove	• bicycling
• tire	• baseball	• running
• brakes	• baseball bat	• swimming
• wheel	• football	• lifting weights

Type the NAME of your new category for these words

athletic necessities

Type a CHARACTERISTIC that describes your new category

entertaining
important
physical
enduring

Type a NEW ITEM, or word, that belongs in your new category

aerobics
softball
hockey
ski pole

Figure 2.7. Description of category-combination measure with sample responses

Table 2.4 presents the correlations obtained when these product quality and originality ratings were correlated with the quality and originality ratings reflecting performance on the two creative problem-solving tasks. Of the 24 correlations, 21 were significant (given a base-rate of .05), representing a greater proportion of significant values than would be expected by chance [$\chi^2(1) = 326.70$, $p < .05$]. Perhaps the most clear-cut conclusion to emerge from this analysis was that all three types of product content—category labels ($r = .18$), features ($r = .36$), and exemplars ($r = .28$)—were positively correlated with creative problem solving, as indexed by the quality and originality of the resulting solutions. This finding speaks to the importance of the combination-and-reorganization process in determining performance on creative problem-solving tasks. Of greater interest, however, was the finding that the quality ($r = .30$) and originality ($r = .41$) of the features or attributes used to characterize this new category produced the strongest relationships with performance on the creative problem-solving tasks. This finding is consistent with

Table 2.4. Correlations Between Category Combination and Criterion Measures.

	Advertising Task		Managerial Task	
	Quality	Originality	Quality	Originality
Task Quality				
New category label	.26**	.23**	.12	.28**
Category characteristics	.39**	.40**	.31**	.50**
New exemplar	.24**	.26**	.29**	.41**
Task Originality				
New category label	.18**	.14	.10	.18**
Category characteristics	.32**	.32**	.21**	.44**
New exemplar	.23**	.26**	.26**	.36**

* = $p < .10$
** = $p < .05$

Finke et al.'s (1992) argument that the features emerging from people's combination-and-reorganization efforts are particularly important determinants of creativity. Apparently, both feature quality and feature originality are crucial determinants of the usefulness of new categories in creative problem solving.

Some support for this general conclusion may be obtained by considering the results obtained when our indices of problem-solving performance were regressed on these evaluations of the products derived from new categories. The average multiple correlation of .44 ($p < .05$) obtained in these analyses underscores the importance of combination and reorganization (.41 < Rs < .51). It is clear, moreover, that the quality of the resulting features (β = .66) was the single best predictor of performance on the two creative problem-solving tasks. Apparently, it is more important that people identify viable and appropriate features of their new categories, and then work with these features in problem solving, than it is to identify unusual or original features. Again, this finding suggests that unrestricted, open exploration may be less important to creative performance than a careful evaluation of the merits of the new feature emerging from people's combination and reorganization efforts.

STRATEGIC DIFFERENCES

Study Procedures

Taken as a whole, the results obtained in our first series of investigations indicate not only that the type of content used in applying relevant processes related to performance on creative problem-solving tasks. The results also suggest that use of viable, high-quality content may represent a crucial determinant of creative performance. These studies, however, could not address the second question we raised earlier: How do creative problem solvers differ regarding the strategies used in working with or manipulating this content? To provide at least an initial answer to this question, we initiated a second set of investigations with a second undergraduate sample.

In this set of studies, we assumed that individuals who could effectively apply a given strategy could do two things: First, they could acquire an understanding of this strategy and its implications for performance more rapidly than people who were not used to applying a given strategy. Second, individuals who typically used a viable strategy would apply these strategies more effectively, when they were asked to use them in working through a series of novel, ill-defined problems.

These two principles provided the general framework we used to assess strategy application and its relation to performance on creative problem-solving tasks. Initially, six strategies that might be used in applying each of the four processes—problem construction, encoding, category selection, and category combination—were identified based on a review of the extant literature (Greeno & Simon, 1988; Snow & Swanson, 1992). For problem construction, for example, studies by Redmond et al. (1993) and Rostan (1994) suggested that the tendency to avoid satisficing by extending representational search contributes to effective problem construction. Along similar lines, the work of Davidson and Sternberg (1984) and Perkins (1992) suggests that a search for key diagnostic information may contribute to performance during encoding. Table 2.5 presents a description of the six strategies identified for each of these processing skills.

To assess understanding of application of these strategies, subjects were presented with a general description of the process under consideration. This instructional material was presented in a self-paced, computer-assisted format. The material was intended to provide a background for later efforts to examine strategy acquisition and strategy application. Accordingly, it described the general nature of the skill under consideration, and how this skill influences performance on creative problem-solving tasks. Additionally, material drawn from the general literature was presented describing the nature of the major steps or operations needed to apply this skill in problem solving (i.e., Sternberg, 1986b, 1988).

Table 2.5. Strategies Held to Influence the Application of Problem Construction, Information Encoding, Category Search and Specification, and Category Combination.

Problem Construction	Category Search
Strategy 1: Avoid Satisficing "Don't stop with the first choice that seems to work—keep on looking."	Strategy 1: Category Variety "Look for a variety of categories that help you understand the problem."
Strategy 2: Avoid Goals "Don't think about goals."	Strategy 2: Category Variety "Search for a set of related categories rather than a number of separate ones."
Strategy 3: Reframing "Bring in new information from outside the immediate situation."	Strategy 3: Avoid Goals "Search for categories that provide a general understanding of the situation, not those that related only to goals."
Strategy 4: Key Information "Look for a key piece of information to clue you in to the problem."	Strategy 4: Procedures "Focus on information that shows you procedures about HOW to solve a problem, rather than on simple, concrete information."
Strategy 5: Analogies "Look for analogies to help you create better problem representations."	Strategy 5: Principles "Look for information that produces principles, general rules, or broad understanding."
Strategy 6: Avoid Exhaustive Search "Don't panic and start trying to find every possible problem representation."	Strategy 6: Avoid Goals "AVOID focusing on information that relates only to goals and steps to get to goals."

Table 2.5. Strategies Held to Influence the Application of Problem Construction, Information Encoding, Category Search and Specification, and Category Combination. (cont.)

Information Encoding	Category Combination
Strategy 1: All Information "Look at ALL of the information available that relates to the problem." Strategy 2: Important Features "Use important features of the problem to help you identify other important information." Strategy 3: Keyed Search "Use information you have to search for additional information." Strategy 4: Avoid Superficial Categories "Avoid selecting categories that focus on superficial features." Strategy 5: Avoid Perfectionism "Don't try to find a single perfect way to understand the problem." Strategy 6: Variety Criteria "Use a variety of standards to decide which categories to use."	Strategy 1: Prototypes "Look for examples, or 'prototypes,' that represent typical examples of the new idea you have." Strategy 2: Analogies "Remember to relate the information you have about a problem to something you already know about." Strategy 3: Ordinary/Unusual "Combine ordinary features in unusual ways OR unusual features in ordinary ways." Strategy 4: Elaboration "After you think of an idea, try to extend or elaborate it as much as you can." Strategy 5: Symbolism "Look for general or symbolic meanings of the information you have about a problem." Strategy 6: Avoid Oversimplification "Beware of explaining complex situations only in terms of simple relationships."

Once people completed this general background material, they were presented with the strategy-acquisition tasks. Here, the relevant instructional material described each strategy and its influence on people's creative problem-solving efforts. For problem construction, for example, satisficing and reframing were described, and it was shown how reframing helps problem solving and how satisficing hurts problem solving. Next, people were presented with a concrete illustration of how use of the strategy influenced performance on a "real-world" problem. Once subjects had worked through the material developed for a given strategy, they were presented with four questions on the material they had just read. These questions were intended to assess acquisition of knowledge about the particular strategy. If they answered three quarters of the questions correctly, they were allowed to go on to the next block of instruction. Otherwise, they were asked to work through this material again and then answer another set of questions. The average number of correct answers out of the total pool presented provided the subjects' final knowledge-acquisition score for each strategy.

To assess application of these strategies, subjects were presented with a two- or three-page description of current events in Russia and India. These current event descriptions were used as stimulus material, because they presented highly complex, ill-defined situations that could be used to develop problems bearing on several strategies. Once subjects had read this background material, they were presented with a series of four problems. These problems were generated by five psychologists to assess effective or ineffective application of a given strategy. In each problem, subjects were asked to show whether a certain course of action would help or hurt the government. They might, for example, with satisficing, be asked, "Would sending American farmers to Russia lead to increases in agricultural output?" with satisficing being indicated by an answer "yes," given the technology differences between Russian and American agriculture. After they had typed in their "yes/no" answers to each question, subjects were given feedback indicating why this was a good or poor answer with respect to the particular strategy. If subjects did not answer three of the four questions correctly, they were presented with three or four additional questions before they were allowed to move onto the next block of instruction. Again, the average number of correct answers provided to the pool of questions presented provided our primary measure of strategy application.

Due to the length of this training material, the subjects participating in a given study were asked to work through only two sets of training material. The 137 undergraduates who agreed to serve as subjects in our first study were asked to work through the exercises developed to assess acquisition and application of the strategies held to influence problem construction and information encoding using current events in Russia as the relevant stimulus material. The 112 undergraduates who participated in our second study were asked to use our description of current events in India as stimulus material when working through the exercises used to assess acquisition and application of the strategies involved in category selection and category combination.

In both studies, subjects were asked to complete a battery of reference measures before they began work on the strategy acquisition and strategy application material. These measures included the measures of each processing skill—problem construction, information encoding, category selection, and category combination—described earlier. These measures were used to assess how application of various strategies was related to the selection and application of appropriate content. Accordingly, problem construction, information encoding, category selection, and category combination were scored to reflect the use of content contributing to the production of original, high-quality solutions on creative problem-solving tasks. This rescoring of the skill measures was accomplished simply by taking a unit-weighted composite of the relevant content dimensions. Here, weights were assigned based on each dimension's correlations with the quality and originality scores derived from the two creative problem-solving tasks. Thus, for problem construction, scores for the use of high-quality approaches received a weight of +1 in forming this composite, while scores for the use of original goals received a weight of -1.

To provide more direct evidence bearing on how these strategies were related to performance on creative problem-solving tasks, subjects in both studies were also asked to work on a creative problem-solving task. This occurred after they had worked through the relevant strategy-assessment exercises. Here, subjects were asked to complete the Redmond et al. (1993) advertising problems, where they were to develop a market analysis, television advertisement, and magazine advertisement for a new product—the 3-D Holographic Television. Again, total scores reflecting the quality and originality of these products were obtained by summing three judges' average quality and originality ratings across the three products.

Problem Construction and Information Encoding

Table 2.6 presents the correlations between our measures reflecting acquisition and application of the problem-construction strategies and the measures reflecting the quality and originality of the products obtained from the advertising task. This table also presents the correlations between the strategy measure and performance on our measure

Table 2.6. Correlations Between Problem-Construction Strategies and Criterion Measures.

	Advertising Task		Managerial Task		Problem-Construction Measure	Information-Encoding Measure
	Quality	Originality	Quality	Originality		
Acquisition						
Don't stop with first choice	-.08	-.18	-.20	-.19	.08	-.05
Don't focus on goals	-.00	-.05	.09	.03	.12	-.01
Look for new information	-.03	-.07	.01	.09	-.13	-.06
Look for key information	.05	-.01	.35**	.33**	.08	.10
Look for analogs	.19	.13	.07	.15	.09	.02
Avoid exhaustive search	.24	.16	-.06	-.02	.15	.00
Application						
Don't stop with first choice	.22	.30**	.19	.28**	.21	.07
Don't focus on goals	.13	.18	.03	.00	.15	-.04
Look for new information	.25	.26**	.21	.27*	.23	.06
Look for key information	.09	-.03	.36**	.33**	.24	.20
Look for analogs	.05	.19	.03	.03	-.11	-.04
Avoid exhaustive search	-.00	.03	-.02	-.06	.15	-.00

* = $p < .10$
** = $p < .05$

of problem construction and information encoding. The correlations presented in Table 2.6 led to some compelling conclusions concerning the use of these strategies in working with relevant information.

The strategy-acquisition measures were not related to either our measures of problem-construction skills or performance on the advertising task. Thus, acquisition of knowledge about problem construction may not be crucial, except as it lays a foundation for subsequent application of problem-construction strategies. In fact, the correlations presented in Table 2.6 tend to support this proposition, at least in the sense that effective application of these strategy-application measures was positively related to our measure of skill application and creative problem solving. Effective application of all these strategies, except the use of analogies, was positively related to scores on our measure of problem-construction skills ($r = .20$). Furthermore, of these strategies, the tendency to avoid satisficing ($r = .26$) and a focus on specific goals ($r = .15$) as well an extended search for additional cues ($r = .25$), or new information, were positively related to the tendency to produce original, high-quality solutions on the creative problem-solving task. Thus, according to the earlier observations of Getzels and Csikszentmihalyi (1975, 1976) and Redmond et al. (1993), it appears that the use of strategies extending search (or inhibiting a superficial definition of the problem situation) contributes to creative thought and subsequent performance.

One question that might be raised about this general conclusion pertains to the potential existence of general response tendencies. More specifically, one might ask whether these relations really reflect strategies linked to problem construction because it is quite possible that these strategies reflect a general response orientation. Some evidence bearing on this issue may be obtained by considering the correlations between effective application of the problem-construction strategies and performance on our measure of encoding skills. As shown in Table 2.6, effective application of the problem-construction strategies was not related to performance on our measures of encoding skills. Thus, these strategies appear uniquely linked to problem construction.

Some additional support for the specificity of these strategies, or their linkage to effective application of a particular process, may be obtained by considering the correlations presented in Table 2.7. This table presents the correlations of acquisition and application of the encoding strategies with performance on our measures of problem-construction and encoding skills. In keeping with our foregoing observations, these correlations suggest that acquisition and application of the encoding strategies was more strongly related to performance on our measure of encoding skill ($r = .28$) than problem-construction skill ($r = .19$). This observation is based on the fact that

Table 2.7. Correlations Between Information-Encoding Strategies and Criterion Measures.

	Advertising Task		Managerial Task		Problem-Construction Measure	Information-Encoding Measure
	Quality	Originality	Quality	Originality		
Acquisition						
Look at all available information	.08	.03	.03	.07	.19	.12
Use important features	.14	.01	.22	.23	.04	.22
Look for key information	.44**	.23	.34**	.35**	.45**	.45**
Look for information on procedures	.06	-.11	.02	.02	.28*	.27*
Look for principles	.27*	.04	.60**	.51**	.22	.44**
Avoid focusing on goals	.03	-.00	.27*	.16	.04	.26*
Application						
Look at all available information	.07	-.01	.06	.03	.20	.22
Use important features	-.07	-.03	.23	.21	.13	.39**
Look for key information	.18	.10	.33**	.30**	.35**	.40**
Look for information on procedures	.13	.02	.34**	.24	.33**	.39**
Look for principles	.16	.13	.31**	.23	.08	.14
Avoid focusing on goals	.10	.09	.24	.11	.04	.09

* = $p < .10$
** = $p < .05$

the values contributing to these mean correlations are consistently larger for our measure of encoding skill than for that of problem-construction skill.

Table 2.7 also presents the correlations of the encoding strategies during acquisition and application with scores on our measure of encoding skills and our indices of solution quality and originality on the creative problem-solving task. Both acquisition and application of all of the encoding strategies were positively correlated with performance on our measure of encoding skill ($r = .28$). Strategy acquisition, however, was as strongly related to encoding skill ($r = .29$) as strategy application ($r = .27$), perhaps because encoding strategies require less experience and rely more on comprehension than problem-construction strategies. Regarding these strategies, however, one strategy in particular—a search for key diagnostic information ($r = .45$)—yielded particularly powerful relationships with encoding skill. Acquisition and application of this critical, evaluative search strategy also yielded the strongest relationship with the quality ($r = .44$) and originality ($r = .23$) of the solutions obtained on the creative problem-solving task. Apparently, search for key information is a particularly important influence on creative thought and subsequent idea generation.

Category Selection and Category Combination

Table 2.8 presents the correlations of the category-selection strategies with our measures of category selection and category combination and our measures of performance on the creative problem-solving task. As may be seen from the pattern of correlations, application of the category-selection strategies was more strongly related to performance on our measure of category-selection skill ($r = .17$) than to our measure of category-combination skill ($r = .05$). This observation is based on the fact that of these strategies, the application of four strategies seemed particularly important regarding performance on the category-selection measure. More specifically, the tendency to retain a variety of concepts ($r = .22$), retain related concepts ($r = .26$), avoid relying on one perfect category ($r = .35$), and avoid selecting categories based on superficial features ($r = .22$) all produced sizable positive relations. Apparently, selection strategies that result in the availability of multiple organized concepts contribute to category selection.

Given these findings regarding our measure of category-selection skills, the findings obtained when our indices of strategy acquisition and strategy application were correlated with our indices of performance on the advertising task were surprising. Here, it was found that acquisition ($r = -.20$) and application ($r = -.13$) of the cate-

Table 2.8. Correlations Between Category Search Strategies, Skill Measures, and Criterion Measures.

	Advertising Task		Category Search Measure	Category Combination Measure
	Quality	Originality		
Acquisition				
Use a variety of concepts	-.24	-.24	.08	.23
Search for related concepts	-.35**	-.27*	.01	.00
Search for general concepts	-.12	-.04	-.06	.26
Avoid superficial features	-.31*	-.34**	.14	.04
Avoid "perfect" solutions	-.13	-.20	-.18	-.04
Use multiple criteria	-.07	-.11	-.04	.38**
Application				
Use a variety of concepts	.15	.14	.22	-.04
Search for related concepts	-.18	-.17	.26	-.01
Search for general concepts	-.00	.07	-.01	-.00
Avoid superficial features	-.14	-.13	.22	.28
Avoid "perfect" solutions	-.37**	-.32**	.35**	.01
Use multiple criteria	-.35**	-.25	.00	.07

* = $p < .10$
** = $p < .05$

gory-selection strategies was negatively related to the quality and originality of solutions to the advertising problems. One explanation for this pattern of relations may be found in Simonton (1988, chap. 1, this volume). More specifically, any category-selection strategy, by limiting the range of potential combinations, may, to some extent, inhibit performance on creative problem-solving tasks, even if category selection may be necessary to make performance possible.

Category combination, because it provides a basis for the generation of new ideas, represents an important influence on creative thought. As indicated by Table 2.9, application of various strategies that might be used in people's combination-and-reorganization efforts was not related to performance on the creative problem-solving task ($r = -.04$). Strategy application, moreover, was not strongly related to performance on our measure of combination-and-reorganization skills ($r = -.02$), although it was related to performance on our measure of category-selection skill ($r = .17$). This pattern of results suggests that rigid application of even viable strate-

Table 2.9. Correlations Between Category Combination Strategies, Skill Measures, and Criterion Measures.

	Advertising Task Quality	Advertising Task Originality	Category Search Measure	Category Combination Measure
Acquisition				
Look for prototypes of a new idea	.10	.03	.07	.24
Try to think of analogies	.13	-.00	.23	.24
Look for different ways to combine	.25	.08	-.13	.13
Elaborate or extend any new idea	.25	.12	-.01	.01
Think of symbolic meaning in information	.27*	.22	.25	.04
Don't try to oversimplify	.09	-.04	-.05	-.00
Application				
Look for prototypes of a new idea	-.05	-.02	.33	-.12
Try to think of analogies	-.13	-.11	.17	.03
Look for different ways to combine	-.06	.01	.13	-.07
Elaborate or extend any new idea	-.12	-.09	.14	-.21
Think of symbolic meaning in information	.08	.04	.34**	.08
Don't try to oversimplify	.00	-.04	-.11	.16

* = $p < .10$
** = $p < .05$

gies may not contribute to people's combination-and-reorganization efforts, where substantial flexibility in the strategies being applied may be desirable (Jausovec, 1991).

Some support for this proposition may be obtained by considering the results obtained for our measures of strategy acquisition. Unlike strategy application, where people were given reinforcement for using certain strategies, strategy acquisition was concerned with understanding of alternative approaches. Acquisition of three of these strategies—use of prototypes, use of analogies, and looking for different ways to combine—were related to performance on our measure of combination skill ($r = .20$), but not category-selection skill ($r = .06$). More centrally, it was found that acquisition of all these strategies was positively related with the quality of solutions obtained from the advertising problem ($r = .18$). Here, acquisition of three strategies, in particular, appeared to be related to the quality of creative problem solutions: looking for different features to combine ($r = .25$), elaborating ideas emerging from a new combination ($r = .25$), and a search for metaphors or the symbolic implications of a category ($r = .27$). These findings are consistent with the earlier observations of Baughman and Mumford (in press), who found that feature search and mapping, and subsequent elaboration of new ideas, contributed to performance during combination-and-reorganization efforts. Furthermore, the use of metaphors is consistent with Mumford, Baughman, Maher et al.'s (1994) finding that the use of metaphors may be particularly important when people must combine diverse categories. Because the combination of more diverse categories is linked to the production of original, new ideas (Mobley et al., 1992), it is not surprising that an understanding of the role of metaphors, or symbolic information, was positively related ($r = .22$) to the generation of more original solutions on the advertising task.

DISCUSSION

These findings, concerning the strategies involved in people's combination-and-reorganization efforts, bring us back to the general model of creative problem solving proposed by Mumford et al. (1991). This model of creative problem solving is predicated on the assumption that the combination and reorganization of extant knowledge structures provides the substantive framework needed for the generation of new ideas. The results obtained in the present effort provide further support for this proposition. Not only were the products derived from people's combination-and-reorganization efforts strongly related to performance on two distinct creative problem-solving tasks. Additionally, the new features emerging from people's combination-and-reorganization efforts seemed particularly strongly related to the individual's ability to solve novel problems (Baughman & Mumford, 1995; Finke et al., 1992).

Although there is good reason to suspect that combination and reorganization might represent the central generative process underlying creative thought, this statement should not be taken to imply that it is the only process with which we should be concerned. As Mumford et al. (1991) pointed out, successful combination-and-reorganization efforts depend on the effective execution of several other processes. People must define the nature of the problem at hand and then acquire information about the problem situation. This information, furthermore, must be organized in terms of relevant concepts, and viable concepts must be identified even before we begin to combine and reorganize these concepts in our search for a new idea. Because the success of people's combination-and-reorganization efforts depends on the material provided by other processes, such as problem construction, information encoding, and category selection, one would expect that these processes would also influence people's performance on creative problem-solving tasks.

In fact, the results obtained in the studies suggest that all these processes do influence performance on creative problem-solving tasks. These processes, moreover, were related to creative performance on tasks drawn from two distinct domains. This point is important, because it suggests that these processes may provide the cross-domain framework needed to develop general theories of creativity and provide viable measures for assessing creative potential (Mumford & Gustafson, 1988). This conclusion is consistent with the notion that all creative efforts begin with an attempt to solve a novel problem. Thus, by focusing on the processes that allow people to identify, structure, and solve novel problems, it may prove possible to identify the general, cross-domain influences on creative performance. Until we understand how people go about applying these general processing capacities, it is unlikely that we will make much real progress in our attempts to understand creative thought (Baer, 1994).

The present set of studies was not intended to provide a complete and comprehensive answer to this question. Many issues that need to be addressed to answer this question were not and could not be considered in the present set of studies. To begin, these studies did not examine all of the processes identified by Mumford et al. (1991). Instead, we chose to focus on a few key processes: problem construction, information encoding, category selection, and category combination. Furthermore, no attempt was made in these studies to explicitly tease out the complex interactions among these processes implied by the sequential operation of these processes. Finally, this research does not speak to how these processes are applied by eminent individuals as they work through truly significant, "real-world," and, perhaps, world-shaking problems.

Also, however, we believe these studies have provided some important clues about how these processes are applied as people work through more routine kinds of novel problems. In their earlier work, Mumford, Reiter-Palmon, and Redmond (1994) suggested that all processes involve two distinct elements: First, there is the raw material or contents people use in working with a given process

(Holyoak, 1984). Second, there are the strategies or procedures used to transform and work with this raw material (Anderson, 1993; Greeno & Simon, 1988). The studies under consideration in the present effort suggest that people differ regarding both the contents being used and the strategies being applied, and that these differences in the contents and the strategies being used lead to differences in people's performance on creative problem-solving tasks.

Not only did these studies tell us something about the basic structure of process operation, they also provide some information about how these processing operations are applied. For example, it appears that multiple, different kinds of content elements may be considered in any given process. Problem construction, for example, may employ information about potential approaches and likely restrictions. Furthermore, several different strategies may be used in working with these content elements. In combination and reorganization, one might pull categories together to create a new category, either by searching for overlapping features or, alternatively, using metaphors.

Some strategies, of course, might be more appropriate when certain kinds of content elements are being applied. Furthermore, the correlations observed between the strategies and skill measures illustrate this point. Nonetheless, there is a need for further research intended to specify these content-strategy interactions in greater detail. Another implication of our findings concerning the use of multiple content elements and strategies pertains to the size of the resulting relationships. Under these conditions, no one kind of content and no one strategy will completely ensure effective application of a given process. Thus, each component is likely to yield only moderate correlations with overall performance. When, however, one aggregates over multiple strategies and contents, more powerful predictive relations are likely to be obtained. This point is nicely illustrated in a recent study by Mumford, Baughman, Supinski et al. (1994). They found that when one considers the different kinds of contents being used in different processes, the aggregate predictive relationships are quite powerful when used to account for performance on creative problem-solving tasks (i.e., yielding multiple correlations in the .60s).

Although any process might involve several content elements and a variety of strategies, evidently some content elements and strategies were more useful than others. In fact, the nature of the content elements and strategies related to creative performance paints a compelling picture of how people go about applying these processes in creative problem solving. Because creative problems tend to be ill-defined (Frederiksen, 1984), most theorists hold that creative efforts begin with an attempt to define the nature of the problem (Getzels & Csikszentmihalyi, 1975, 1976; Kay, 1991; Runco, 1994). Apparently, the use of original, unusual content elements does not contribute much to problem definition and subsequent performance, perhaps because what is called for is a sound, accurate structure within which the individual can work. The relations observed in the present effort suggest that this structure be defined by using an extended search of relevant representational elements to identify viable, high-quality approaches and potential restrictions on this approach. The tendency to define problems in terms of approaches and restrictions may prove particularly useful, because it would provide a flexible, but appropriate, framework guiding the application of subsequent processes, such as information encoding.

Given the need for ambiguity reduction in problem construction, it is not surprising that strategies and content elements leading to the development of a sound, general framework, even if it is not especially original, contributes to creative problem solving. The findings obtained for information encoding, although more surprising, are consistent with this theory. In encoding, more creative people used a search strategy that focused on the identification of key diagnostic facts. Indeed, people appeared to produce more creative solutions when this strategy led them to spend more time on relevant facts and relevant, but inconsistent, observations. Thus, encoding appears to represent a rather targeted, focused activity concerned with gathering relevant information. This includes information that is relevant but, in some way, does not fit with other observations, triggering the need to apply multiple relevant categories in problem solving.

In category selection, people must discover which particular concepts will be retained for use in problem solving. Here, the kinds of categories that appeared to contribute to creativity were those bearing on long-term goals of the problem-solving effort. Strategies that lead to the identification of multiple relevant categories appeared to contribute to the retention of these kinds of concepts. Thus, people who did not look for one perfect category and searched for multiple related categories appeared to evidence better category-selection skills. However, this distinctly consistent process appeared to limit the quality and originality of solutions in an immediate sense. By providing a more coherent set of concepts for subsequent combination-and-reorganization efforts, however, this process may make an indirect contribution to people's creative problem solving.

The results obtained for combination and reorganization suggest that the tendency to draw high-quality and original, new features from the new category resulting from people's combination-and-reorganization efforts was a key determinant of performance on creative problem-solving tasks. The identification of these emergent features, furthermore, might be helped by a flexible approach and the use of both feature-mapping and metaphorical strategies. This pattern of findings is consistent with earlier studies (Baughman & Mumford 1995; Finke et al., 1992). It does, however, represent something of a contrast to the findings obtained for the other processes: It is at this point, where a new idea is being generated, that originality is as important as quality, and more complex divergent thinking strategies, such as the use of metaphors, becomes relevant.

These observations not only paint a coherent picture describing how these processes contribute to creative thought, they also paint a picture that is not well-aligned with our stereotypical conceptions of creative problem solving. More specifically, we commonly assume that creative thought, particularly in the early stages of idea generation, is characterized by an open, free-ranging search for information and alternatives. The results obtained in the present effort, however, suggest that, even in the earliest phases of creative thought during problem construction and information encoding, people are engaging in a highly structured, rather directed set of activities. Such activities occur as people seek to define the problem, identify relevant information, and select appropriate categories for use in subsequent combination-and-reorganization efforts.

Although the targeted, perhaps evaluative, effort stands in contrast to some assumptions we commonly make about creative thought, it is consistent with what we know about the nature of the combination-and-reorganization process. Prior research by Mobley et al. (1992) shows that combination and reorganization represents a particularly challenging and demanding activity for most people. Furthermore, it is difficult to see how the new ideas emerging from people's combination-and-reorganization efforts will prove useful in addressing the problem at hand, unless the concepts being applied in combination and reorganization are directly relevant to the problem situation. Thus, the complex nature of combination-and-reorganization efforts, and the principles of cognitive economy, requires that individuals structure initial definition and information search, only retaining that information and those concepts necessary to understand the problem situation. Combination-and-reorganization efforts based on relevant categories and information are far more likely to result in the identification of new principles and ideas that lead to useful, new solutions. Put more directly, we have a situation where the cliché, "garbage in-garbage out," applies. People need to work with relevant, high-quality material in combination and reorganization if these efforts are to result in useful, new ideas.

One implication of these observations pertains to the role of critical or convergent thinking in the generation of new ideas. Traditional views of creative thought commonly hold that divergent processes precede convergent processes (Basadur, Wakabayashi, & Graen, 1990; Isaksen & Parnes, 1985). In more extreme views (Lindzey et al., 1978; Osborn, 1963), critical thought and evaluation can occur and serve any real purpose only after the individual has generated a new idea. Essentially, within this framework, critical thought serves primarily as a basis for idea evaluation.

The problem with this approach is that it ignores three questions that must be addressed for the combination-and-reorganization process to yield useful, new ideas: How should I structure the problem situation? What information should I look for? How should I organize this information before I attempt to put the pieces together? To answer all these questions, the individual must engage in critical thought, choosing the right approach, identifying crucial information, and gathering viable categories for organizing this information. Thus, critical thought precedes, and proceeds to, idea generation. By providing a structured set of concepts and observations to work with in combination and reorganization, critical thought may lay a necessary foundation for subsequent idea generation.

This conclusion might lead one to pose still another question: Critical thought certainly plays an important role in idea evaluation; however, it is quite possible that divergent thinking and the exploration of alternatives may also be needed in idea evaluation. The new ideas emerging from combination and reorganization represent fuzzy solutions that must be tried out and revised, if one is to arrive at a truly workable solution. In trying out new ideas, one must explore their potential implications and use the consequences associates with these implications as a basis for revising one's initial approach. A case in point, here, may be found in Mumford et al.'s (in press) study of organization leaders, where it was found that creative, high-performing leaders capable of solving novel organization problems used divergent thinking to identify restrictions on proposed new ideas and suggest requisite revision strategies. Thus, creative thinking may be called for after idea generation, just as critical thinking is required before initial idea generation.

Not only do these findings bring to question our traditional assumptions about the relationship between critical and creative thought, they suggest some changes in the kinds of interventions we use to develop creative potential. Quite often, our programs intended to develop creative potential explicitly seek to encourage exploration (Rose & Lin, 1984). Our findings do not argue against this approach in the sense that extended search, especially during problem construction, apparently contributes to the success of people's creative problem-solving efforts. On the other hand, our findings do suggest several other kinds of interventions that might contribute to idea generation and subsequent performance on creative problem-solving tasks. One might, for example, attempt to provide information about key diagnostics and provide well-organized, basic concepts that might be used to understand the kind of problems occurring in certain domains (Alexander et al., 1994; Mumford, Baughman, Costanza, Uhlman, & Connelly, 1993; Swanson, 1990; Ward et al., 1990). Alternatively, interventions might be devised that teach students how to apply certain strategies. Examples include the tendency to extend their search for ideas in problem construction and information encoding or the use of metaphors and feature mapping to combine categories. Finally, students might be taught to focus on approaches, rather than goals, in defining problems and shown how a search for useful approaches might be used to guide their subsequent problem-solving activities.

We suspect that many people, in considering these recommendations, will be taken aback. Are we really trying to "engineer" creativity? In one sense, this criticism is unimportant. Any attempt to understand human performance, including creative problem solving, will, more often than not, have as its goal the enhancement of performance. Certainly, any theory that leads to higher quality, more original problem solutions will have made a real contribution—one that increases, rather than limits, the individual's ability to express his or her potential.

At the root of this criticism, however, one finds a broader conceptual issue. In the romantic view, creativity is ultimately a mysterious phenomenon, the propensity of a few lucky individuals who have been touched by the gods. Within this framework, one is not likely to be optimistic about the potential for developing creative talent. Moreover, interventions of the sort described here that require the individual to focus on the problem at hand. They must identify key facts, requisite concepts, and viable approaches to the problem situation. This will be seen by some as a constraint on the unique gifts of these truly creative individuals. We would, however, argue that this view misses an important point: To be able to create something new through combination and reorganization, people must begin by identifying the right material to be combined and reorganized. The romantic view, one that loses sight of this basic point, is, in the end, likely to result in a limited, artificial understanding of the creative act. A case in point may be found in the distinction between critical and creative thought. A comprehensive understanding of creativity requires us to recognize the fact that both critical and creative thought are always in play as we grope toward the viable new problem solutions that are the basis for all innovation.

ACKNOWLEDGMENTS

We thank Elizabeth Supinski, David Costanza, and Victoria Threlfall for their contributions to this effort. Parts of this research were sponsored by a grant from the United States Army Research Institute for Behavioral and Social Sciences, Michael D. Mumford, Principal Investigator.

REFERENCES

Abra, J. (1994). Collaboration in creative work: An initiative for investigation. *Creativity Research Journal, 7*, 1-20.

Alexander, D. A., Ketton, T. L., White, S. H., Parsons, J. L., Cotropia, K. K., Liu, H. C., & Ackerman, C. M. (1994). Young children's solutions to realistic and fanciful story problems. *Journal of Creative Behavior, 28*, 89-106.

Alissa, I. (1972). Stimulus generalization and over-inclusion in normal and schizophrenic subjects. *Journal of Clinical Psychology, 34*, 182-186.

Amabile, T. M. (1983). The social psychology of creativity: A componential conceptualization. *Journal of Personality and Social Psychology, 45*, 357-376.

Anderson, J. R. (1993). Problem solving and learning. *American Psychologist, 48*, 35-44.

Arieti, S. (1976). *Creativity: The magic synthesis*. New York: Basic Books.

Baer, J. M. (1988). Long-term effects of creativity training with middle-school students. *Journal of Early Adolescence, 8*, 183-193.

Baer, J. (1994). Divergent thinking is not a general trait: A multidomain training experiment. *Creativity Research Journal, 7*, 35-46.

Basadur, M., Wakabayashi, M., & Graen, G. B. (1990). Individual problem solving styles and attitudes towards divergent thinking before and after training. *Creativity Research Journal, 3*, 22-32.

Baughman, W. A., & Mumford, M. D. (1995). Process analytic models of creative capacities: Operations involved in the combination and reorganization process. *Creativity Research Journal, 8*, 37-62.

Bradshaw, G. F., Gangley, P. W., & Simon, H. A. (1983). Studying scientific discovery by computer simulation. *Science, 222*, 971-975.

Carlson, W. B., & Gorman, M. E. (1992). A cognitive framework to understand technological creativity: Bell, Edison, and the telephone. In R. J. Weber & D. N. Perkins (Eds.), *Inventive minds:*

Creativity in technology (pp. 48-79). New York: Oxford University Press.

Chaffee, J. (1990). *Thinking critically*. Boston, MA: Houghton-Mifflin.

Chi, M. T. H., & Glaser, R. (1988). Expertise and problem solving. In M. T. H. Chi, R. Glaser, & M. Farr (Eds.), *The nature of expertise* (pp. 1-27). Hillsdale, NJ: Lawrence Erlbaum Associates.

Davidson, J. E., & Sternberg, R. J. (1984). The role of insight in intellectual giftedness. *Gifted Child Quarterly, 28,* 58-64.

Dillon, J. T. (1982). Problem finding and solving. *Journal of Creative Behavior, 16,* 97-111.

Domino, G. (1994). Assessment of creativity with the all: An empirical comparison of four scales. *Creativity Research Journal, 7,* 21-34.

Finke, R. A., Ward, T. B., & Smith, S. M. (1992). *Creative cognition: Theory, research, applications*. Cambridge, MA: MIT Press.

Frederiksen, R. (1984). Implications of cognitive theory for instruction in problem solving. *Review of Educational Research, 43,* 363-407.

Getzels, J. W., & Csikszentmihalyi, M. (1975). From problem solving to problem finding. In I. A. Taylor & J. W. Getzels (Eds.), *Perspectives in creativity* (pp. 90-116). Chicago, IL: Aldine.

Getzels, J. W., & Csikszentmihalyi, M. (1976). *The creative vision: A longitudinal study of problem finding in art*. New York: Wiley.

Ghiselin, B. (1963). Ultimate criteria for two levels of creativity. In C. W. Taylor & F. Barrow (Eds.), *Scientific creativity: Its recognition and development* (pp. 30-43). New York: Wiley.

Gick, M. L., & Holyoak, K. J. (1983). Schema induction and analogical transfer. *Cognitive Psychology, 15,* 1-38.

Greeno, J. G., & Simon, H. A. (1988). Problem solving and reasoning. In R. C. Atkinson, R. J. Herrnstein, G. Lindzey, & R. D. Luce (Eds.), *Stevens' handbook of experimental psychology* (pp. 589-672). Norwood, NJ: Ablex.

Gruber, H. E. (1988). The evolving system's approach to creative work. *Creativity Research Journal, 1,* 27-51.

Guilford, J. P. (1950). Creativity. *American Psychologist, 14,* 469-479.

Hennessey, B. A., & Amabile, T. M. (1988). The conditions of creativity. In R. J. Sternberg (Ed.), *The nature of creativity* (pp. 11-42). New York: Cambridge University Press.

Hogarth, R. M. (1986). *Decision making*. New York: Wiley.

Holyoak, K. J. (1984). Mental models in problem solving. In J. R. Anderson & K. M. Kosslyn (Eds.), *Tutorials in learning and memory* (pp. 193-218). New York: Freeman.

Hoover, S. M., & Feldhusen, J. F. (1990). The scientific hypothesis formulation ability of gifted ninth-grade students. *Journal of Educational Psychology, 82,* 838-848.

Isaksen, S. G., & Parnes, S. J. (1985). Curriculum planning for creative thinking and problem solving. *Journal of Creative Behavior, 19,* 1-29.

Jausovec, N. (1991). Flexible strategy use: A characteristic of gifted problem solving. *Creativity Research Journal, 4,* 349-366.

Kasof, J. (1995). Explaining creativity: The attributional perspective. *Creativity Research Journal, 8,* 311-366.

Kay, S. (1991). The figural problem solving and problem finding of professional and semiprofessional artists and nonartists. *Creativity Research Journal, 4,* 233-252.

Koestler, A. (1964). *The act of creation.* New York: Macmillan.

Kuhn, T. S. (1970). *The structure of scientific revolutions.* Chicago: University of Chicago Press.

Kulkarni, D., & Simon, H. A. (1988). The process of scientific discovery: The strategy of experimentation. *Cognitive Science, 12,* 139-175.

Lindzey, G., Hall, C. S., & Thompson, R. F. (1978). *Creative thinking and critical thinking.* New York: Worth.

Martinsen, O. (1993). Insight problems revisited: The influence of cognitive styles and experience on creative problem solving. *Creativity Research Journal, 6,* 435-447.

Mednick, S. A., & Mednick, M. T. (1967). *Examiners' manual: Remote-Associations Test.* Boston, MA: Houghton-Mifflin.

Mobley, M. I., Doares, L., & Mumford, M. D. (1992). Process analytic models of creative capacities: Evidence for the combination and reorganization process. *Creativity Research Journal, 5,* 125-156.

Mumford, M. D., Baughman, W. A., Costanza, D. P., Uhlman, C. E., & Connelly, M. S. (1993). Developing creative capacities: Implications of cognitive processing models. *Roeper Review: A Journal of Gifted Education, 16,* 16-21.

Mumford, M. D., Baughman, W. A., Maher, M. A., Costanza, D. P., & Supinski, E. P. (1994). *Process-based measures of creative problem-solving skills: Study IV. Category combination.* Manuscript submitted for publication.

Mumford, M. D., Baughman, W. A., Supinski, E. P., Costanza, D. P., & Threlfall, K. V. (1994). *Cognitive and metacognitive skill development: Alternative measures for predicting leadership potential* (Tech. Rep. No. MRI 93-2). Bethesda, MD: Management Research Institute, Inc.

Mumford, M. D., & Connelly, M. S. (1993). Cases of invention: A review of Weber and Perkins' *Inventive minds: Creativity in technology. Contemporary Psychology, 38,* 1210-1217.

Mumford, M. D., & Gustafson, S. B. (1988). Creativity syndrome: Integration, application, and innovation. *Psychological Bulletin, 103,* 27-43.

Mumford, M. D., Mobley, M. I., Uhlman, C. E., Reiter-Palmon, R., & Doares, L. (1991). Process analytic models of creative capacities. *Creativity Research Journal, 4*, 91-122.

Mumford, M. D., Reiter-Palmon, R., & Redmond, M. R. (1994). Problem construction and cognition: Applying problem representations in ill-defined domains. In M. A. Runco (Ed.), *Problem finding, problem solving, and creativity* (pp. 3-39). Norwood, NJ: Ablex.

Mumford, M. D., Zaccaro, S. J., Harding, F. D., & Fleishman, E. A. (in press). *The thinking leader: Developing creative leaders for a more complex world.* Mahwah, NJ: Lawrence Erlbaum Associates.

Nicholls, J. G. (1972). Creativity in the person who will never produce anything original and useful: The concept of creativity as a normally distributed trait. *American Psychologist, 27*, 717-727.

Novick, L. R. (1990). Representational transfer in problem solving. *Psychological Science, 1*, 128-132.

Okuda, S. M., Runco, M. A., & Berger, D. E. (1991). Creativity and the finding and solving of real-world problems. *Journal of Psychoeducational Assessment, 9*, 45-53.

Osborn, A. F. (1963). *Applied imagination.* New York: Scribner.

Owens, W. A. (1969). Cognitive, noncognitive, and environmental correlates of mechanical ingenuity. *Journal of Applied Psychology, 53*, 199-208.

Perkins, D. N. (1992). The topography of invention. In R. J. Weber & D. N. Perkins (Eds.), *Inventive minds: Creativity in technology* (pp. 238-250). New York: Oxford University Press.

Redmond, M. R., Mumford, M. D., & Teach, R. J. (1993). Putting creativity to work: Leader influences on subordinate creativity. *Organizational Behavior and Human Decision Processes, 55*, 120-151.

Rodgers, E. M., & Adhikarya, R. (1979). Diffusion of innovations: Up-to-date review and commentary. In D. Nimmo (Ed.), *Communication yearbook 3* (pp. 67-81). Brunswick, NJ: Transaction Books.

Rose, L. H., & Lin, H. T. (1984). A meta-analysis of long-term creativity training programs. *Journal of Creative Behavior, 18*, 11-22.

Rostan, S. M. (1994). Problem finding, problem solving, and cognitive controls: An empirical investigation of critically acclaimed productivity. *Creativity Research Journal, 7*, 97-111.

Rothenberg, A. (1986). Artistic creation as simulated by superimposed versus combined-composite visual images. *Journal of Personality and Social Psychology, 50*, 370-381.

Rothenberg, A., & Sobel, R. S. (1980). Creation of literary metaphors as simulated by superimposed versus separated visual images. *Journal of Mental Imagery, 4*, 77-91.

Rubenson, D. L., & Runco, M. A. (1992). The psycho-economic approach to creativity. *New Ideas in Psychology, 10,* 131-147.
Runco, M. A. (1991). The evaluative, valuative, and divergent thinking of children. *Journal of Creative Behavior, 25,* 311-314.
Runco, M. A. (1994). Conclusions concerning problem finding, problem solving, and creativity. In M. A. Runco (Ed.), *Problem finding, problem solving, and creativity* (pp. 271-290). Norwood, NJ: Ablex.
Runco, M. A., & Albert, R. S. (1985). The reliability and validity of ideational originality in the divergent thinking of academically gifted and nongifted children. *Educational and Psychological Measurement, 45,* 483-501.
Runco, M. A., & Chand, I. (1994). Problem finding, evaluative thinking, and creativity. In M. A. Runco (Ed.), *Problem finding, problem solving, and creativity* (pp. 40-76). Norwood, NJ: Ablex.
Shorris, E. A. (1981). *The oppressed middle: The politics of middle management.* New York: Anchor Press.
Simonton, D. K. (1988). Age and outstanding achievement: What do we know after a century of research? *Psychological Bulletin, 104,* 251-267.
Snow, R. E., & Lohman, D. R. (1984). Toward a theory of cognitive aptitude from learning from instruction. *Journal of Educational Psychology, 76,* 347-376.
Snow, R. E., & Swanson, J. (1992). Instructional psychology: Aptitude, adaptation, and assessment. *Annual Review of Psychology, 43,* 583-626.
Sobel, R. S., & Rothenberg, A. (1980). Artistic creation assimilated by superimposed versus separated visual images. *Journal of Personality and Social Psychology, 39,* 953-961.
Sternberg, R. J. (1986a). Synopsis of a triarchic theory of human intelligence. In S. H. Irvine & S. E. Newstead (Eds.), *Intelligence and cognition* (pp. 161-221). Dorrecht, Germany: Hijhoff.
Sternberg, R. J. (1986b). Toward a unified theory of human reasoning. *Intelligence, 10,* 281-314.
Sternberg, R. J. (1988). *The triarchic mind: A new theory of human intelligence.* New York: Viking.
Sternberg, R. J., & Lubart, F. I. (1991). An investment theory of creativity and its implications for development. *Human Development, 34,* 1-31.
Suler, J. R. (1980). Primary process thinking and creativity. *Psychological Bulletin, 88,* 144-165.
Swanson, H. L. (1990). Influence of metacognitive knowledge and aptitude on problem solving. *Journal of Educational Psychology, 82,* 306-314.

Walberg, H. J., & Stariha, W. E. (1992). Productive human capital: Learning, creativity, and eminence. *Creativity Research Journal, 5,* 323-340.

Ward, S. L., Byrnes, J. P., & Overton, W. F. (1990). Organization of knowledge and conditional reasoning. *Journal of Educational Psychology, 82,* 832-837.

3

IDEA EVALUATION, DIVERGENT THINKING, AND CREATIVITY

Mark A. Runco
California State University-Fullerton

Critical Creative Processes was conceived as a detailed argument that both divergence and convergence are involved in creative thinking. Divergence and related processes (e.g., lateral thinking) are often useful for creative thinking, but they do not operate alone. Divergence is most effective when it is coupled with convergent thinking, valuation, and discretion.

Although there are critical processes involved in creative thinking that are not easily tied to ideation, those are well covered in other chapters of this volume. Runco and Chand (1994) found relevant evaluative processes described in developmental, cognitive, and social psychological research. In this chapter, I focus on ideation and its relation with various kinds of evaluation. This relation, with the focus on ideation, receives sparce attention in other chapters in this volume.

I begin by outlining the premises of this line of work and by defending the use of ideational assessments. I then turn to a series of empirical studies of ideational evaluation. These studies cover parent and teacher evaluations of children's ideas, children's evaluations of their own ideas, evaluations of ideas given to realistic (in contrast to standard) problems, and comparisons of inter- and intrapersonal evaluations. In every case, the evaluation focuses on originality. Several other criteria are also studied, including creativity and popularity. The second of these has been included in the research because it is nearly the opposite of originality and it may be easier for judges (parents, teachers, children, or college students) to consider than originality. The studies reported herein are relevant to a wide variety of topics, including divergent thinking, creativity enhancement and facilitation, education, and parenting.

RATIONALE FOR IDEATION AND EVALUATION

The fundamental premise to this work is that ideation is an important process because ideas are used so often in people's lives. It is also important because creative work requires original ideation. Original ideation is not all there is to creativity, but it is an important part. It is also one of the first steps in creative work. Only interest may precede ideation. Very likely, an individual must have some interest before he or she even thinks about a topic or problem. Admittedly, there is some controversy over which comes first, emotion (which would include interest) or cognition (which would include ideation). Either way, ideation is one of the first things to happen in the creative process and is an important determinant of the success of that process. Effective solutions and useful innovations in every field begin with and depend on good ideas.

It may seem that there is no need for any defense of ideational research, but such a need may be more obvious if we recognize that ideational tendencies are typically identified and assessed with divergent thinking tests. Divergent thinking tests have many critics, and they could make the mistake of dismissing ideational research because they do not respect these tests.

This would be a mistake for several reasons. I say this with some certainty because there are data that support the use of divergent thinking tests. This is not to say that tests of divergent thinking are useful for studies of all kinds of creativity. Nor does it assume that divergent thinking is anywhere close to synonymous with creative thinking. Divergent thinking is, however, a useful estimate of the potential for creative thinking. It is useful because predictive validities are similar to those obtained by other kinds of assessments (Milgram, in press; Mraz & Runco, 1994; Torrance, 1968). They are, for the same reason, best viewed as estimates. And what is estimated? The best answer to this question is "creative potential." Performance on a divergent thinking test no more guarantees actual performance than profiles from commonly used personality inventories or scores from tests of intelligence.

Divergent thinking tests do have an advantage over these other inventories and tests: their reliance on ideas. A test of intelligence may give a reasonable estimate of how well an individual will do when faced with certain kinds of presented problems. It may, then, estimate problem-solving skills. This may be useful for many situations, but then again, there is more to life than problem solving! Studies of creativity show that problem finding is at least as important as problem solving, for example (Runco, 1994), and some kinds of creativity may be independent of problems. Self-expression, for example, is often a function of psychological health and not just a reaction to a problem (Runco, 1994). Ideas, on the other hand, are involved in most of people's day-to-day lives. Certainly, it depends on how *idea* is defined, but then again idea is a very popular idea and term. In recent work (Runco, in press), I reported that *idea* is the 490th most commonly used word in the English language, a fact that comes from a source checking more than 50,000 words (Kucera & Francis, 1967). I also reported an informal investigation showing how frequently the concept of *idea* is used in the social and behavioral sciences. The idea of ideas is extremely useful.

A second premise is that evaluation of some sort is always a part of ideation. Evaluation is inextricable from ideation, except for the random generation of ideas, and that rarely if ever happens—it isn't human. Humans are by nature selective. Only with experimental control can ideation and evaluation be separated. Such a separation, although artificial, allows us to better understand how ideas develop and can be best used.

Runco and Chad (1995) presented a model showing their separation. It describes the entire problem-solving process. It has two tiers, with three primary component on one tier and two secondary components on the other. The secondary components are essentially influences on the process. One represents information, which can be declarative (conceptual, factual) or procedural (strategic, tactical) and the other motivation (intrinsic and extrinsic). The primary components represent problem-finding, ideation, and evaluation. Problem finding may involve problem identification or problem definition (Runco, 1994). Ideation is well described by theories of divergent thinking (Guilford, 1968; Runco, 1991, 1992; Torrance, 1968) and involves fluency, originality, and flexibility. Evaluation in this model involves a critical process (determining what is wrong with a particular idea or solution) and *valuation* (determining what is right about an idea or solution). The latter is especially important for parents and teachers, for they may not at first grasp the logic of a child's idea; but to support that child's efforts they should put some effort into finding what is good and meaningful in that idea. They should valuate rather than evaluate.

The two-tier model of creative problem solving emphasizes interactions and recursions among the components. Ideation, for example, is probably a factor when defining problems as well as when solving them. Problem identification may lead to motivation as well as result from it. And surely evaluation provides feedback for ideation. The last of these is demonstrated in several of the empirical studies reviewed in the next section of this chapter.

EVALUATIONS OF CHILDREN'S IDEAS

Runco and Vega (1990) examined adults' evaluations of children's ideas. One motivation for this research was the possibility that slumps in creativity reflect social pressures placed on children by parents and teachers. Presumably this pressure is unintentional; parents and teachers may simply not recognize the value of children's ideas. As Elkind (1981) explained, children are "cognitive aliens," and this may make it exceedingly difficult to understand why they think what they think.

In Runco and Vega (1990) judgments were obtained from 123 adults (103 females, 17 males, with 3 not reporting gender) from child development classes of a large university. Of these adults, 36 were parents and 22 had teaching experience. Many of the participants were majoring in child development, whereas others were psychology majors or concentrating in another social science. The measures were developed from Instances, Uses, and Line Meanings divergent thinking tests. These had been administered to 240 children in an earlier investigation. Ideas from those children were placed on the measures given to the adults, and the adults were asked to rate each idea. The adults received three sets of 25 ideas for Instances, three sets of 25 ideas for Uses, and three sets of 25 ideas for Line Meanings. Each set of 25 ideas represented the ideas given by the children to one particular divergent thinking question.

The adults in the investigation rated each of the ideas on a 10-point scale. Detailed instructions were given before the adults completed the measures and were repeated, with slight changes in the wording, on each of the evaluative tests. One half of the group of adults was given instructions to rate the creativity of the ideas and the other half was to rate the popularity of the ideas. One group was informed that the ideas being rated were given by the children, and the other group was not so informed. The adults also were given two divergent thinking tasks: Instances and Line Meaning tasks. These were given before the evaluation tasks.

The instructions for the Instances evaluation were as follows:

> You may remember the Instances Games. Ideas given by a group of *children* are given on the attached pages. We would like you to tell us what you think of these ideas by circling one of the numbers next to each idea. Circle a high number (10, 9, or 8) for the *highly creative* ideas. Circle middle numbers (7, 6, 5, or 4) for the ideas that are somewhat or a little creative. Circle low numbers (1, 2, or 3) for the ideas that are *not at all creative*. Only circle one number for each idea, but try to use all of the numbers 1 through 10) for the entire list of 25 ideas. Here are two examples: To the "Move on Wheels" question, one of the ideas is, "Skateboard." If you think that this is an uncreative an idea, circle a low number, like a 2. A different idea to the "Move on Wheels" question is, "R2D2." If you think that is a *very* creative idea, circle a high number, like a 9 or 10.

Each example was accompanied by the 10-point scale, with a number circled.

The adults were randomly assigned to one of the four types of instructions (creative or popular, children or individual). The instructions just given varied such that one group saw the instrument with the word *individuals* instead of the word *children*. Others saw the term *popular* instead of the term *creative*.

Importantly, the scale was designed with 10 response options (instead of the more typical 5 or 7 Likert options) to allow participants to easily judge "how many children in a group of 10" would be likely to give each idea. For instance, if they thought perhaps 7 children in the group of 10, they were to circle the 7. An example page from the evaluation instrument is presented in Figure 3.1.

The results indicated that the evaluative measures were highly reliable (i.e., alphas of .92, .86, and .82). The evaluative measures also had reasonably high interest correlations (.87, .85, and .79), supporting their convergent validity. Perhaps more important was that the different sets of instruction elicited significantly different scores ($R = .92$, $p < .001$), with the popularity ratings being more accurate than the creativity ratings. This pattern held up for each of the three different divergent thinking tests as well ($Rs = .91$, .89, and .79, each $p < .001$). (Correlations coefficients are reported here, as they were in the original report, because the groups were compared and relationships examined with multiple regression techniques rather than t or F tests.) These coefficients might suggest that explicit instructions can be used to improve the accuracy of adults' evaluations.

Differences among the evaluative scores of parents, teachers, and other adults were surprisingly slight. In fact, gender, age, number of child development classes taken while a student, college major, and years of teaching experience were all unrelated to the

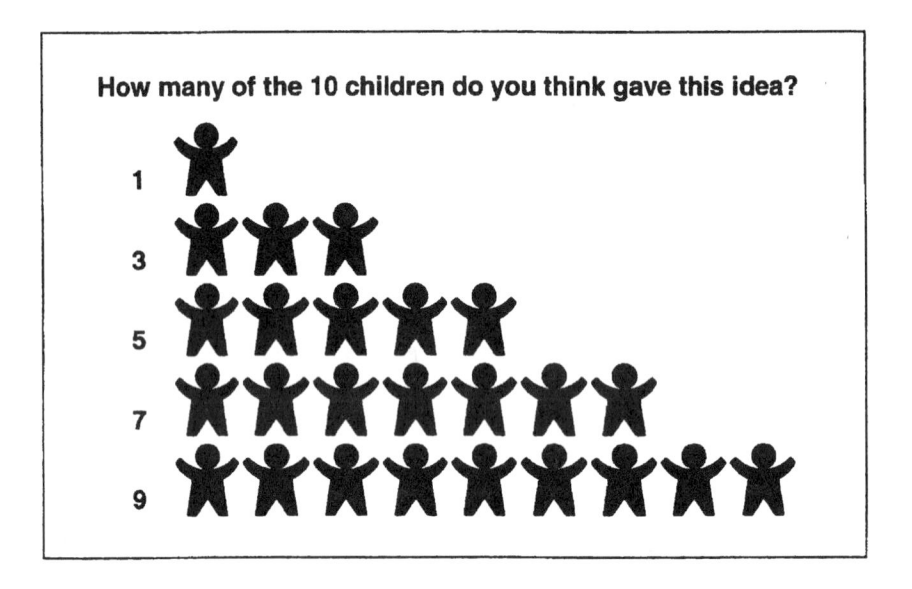

Figure 3.1a. Scale shown to subjects during originality evaluation

Figure 3.1b. Scale shown to subjects during preference evaluation

accuracy of evaluations. The notable exception was that parents with several children were more accurate than parents with few children (R = .45). This could be indicative of particular experience with children. Perhaps parents with several children have practice judging the likelihood that more than one child will think of a particular idea. ("Will they see through this, or will Tomas, Jane, and Zelda *all* realize what I am doing?")

A final significant result was that the evaluative accuracy of adults was significantly correlated with their own divergent thinking test scores (Rc = .52, p < .05). Surprisingly, this relation was strongest for the fluency scores (Rs = .31 and .28, both p < .05) rather than the originality scores. This relation does support the models of creative thinking that predict an interaction among the components of the creative process. It also suggests a practice effect whereby evaluative accuracy improves when the individual has many ideas to judge.

The differences between the accuracy judgments for creativity and popularity reflect the fact that the latter are more explicit and operational than the former. Recall that the instructions in the popularity condition asked the adults to "think of how many children in a group of 10 would think of each idea." This is much more operational than simply asking evaluators to consider the creativity of the ideas. *Creativity* may be too abstract a criterion. In an earlier study (Runco, 1989), I presented support for this interpretation. I found that when judging the artwork of children, professional artists disagreed more about *creativity* than *originality, technical skill,* and *aesthetic value.* In any case, the instructional differences suggests that explicit instructions might be used to improve the accuracy of adults' evaluations.

CHILDREN'S EVALUATIONS OF ORIGINALITY

Runco and Vega (1990) investigated adults' evaluations because those were presumed to influence the ideation of children. Children's ideation may, however, also change spontaneously and in a manner that is largely independent of the influence of parents, teachers, and particular experiences. I am not suggesting that the ontogeny of ideation is canalized and entirely independent of experience, but some of the changes may be maturational in a strict sense—genetically programmed and requiring very little nurturing for their expression.

The fourth-grade slump was once thought to occur because of experience. Ostensibly, by the fourth grade children had internalized all of the rules and expectations from the highly structured school system and began to think in a highly conventional fashion.

Now it seems likely that the fourth-grade slump is related to maturational processes that are manifest in children's play, rule use and games, language, and artwork, as well as their divergent thinking (Gardner, 1982; Rosenblatt & Winner, 1988; Runco, in press). The slump, when it occurs, may be tied to the same cognitive tendency that led Kohlberg (1987) to distinguish among preconventional, conventional, and postconventional moral reasoning. In a word, it may reflect *conventionality*. Just as popular ideas are by definition unoriginal, so too are conventional ideas unoriginal.

Previously (Runco, 1991), I examined the evaluative, valuative, and divergent thinking of children to determine if the accuracy with which they evaluate ideas for originality could be reliably assessed. A second objective of this investigation was to determine if there was an overlap between divergent thinking and a child's evaluative accuracy in this age group. This second objective is relevant to the issue of experience, for children might lack the experience generating ideas simply because they are young, and this might be apparent in a low correlation between ideation and evaluation. Granted, this is unlikely, in part because the children involved in the research must be old enough to respond to paper-and-pencil tests, and thus they will have a large amount of experience—not as much as adults, but relevant experience nonetheless. The low correlations would also be a surprise because, as previously mentioned, there may be maturational influences on evaluative accuracy. Maturational influences would not be entirely dependent on experience.

There were 107 children in this project, with 57 girls and 50 boys. Forty-two were in the fourth grade, 37 in the fifth, and 28 in the sixth. The average age of the children was 10 years and 5 months. The average WISC-R information test standard score (available for 77 of the children) was 17.6, which is nearly one standard deviation above the mean of 15.0 ($SD = 3.0$).

The evaluative measures administered to the children were much like those used in Runco and Vega (1991). The first test was based on the Instances divergent thinking test, the second on Uses, and the third on Line Meanings. The ideas contained in each of the tests were obtained from the 240 gifted, talented, and nongifted children mentioned earlier. The children in this particular study were, then, evaluating ideas given by other children. (It was an inter- rather than intrapersonal evaluation.) As was the case earlier, each subtest contained 25 items, and the children rated each on a 10-point scale.

Scores for these evaluation tasks were based on correlations between the ratings and the frequencies found in the previous study of 240 children. If a child in the evaluation study gave an idea a rating of "1," and that idea was in fact given by very few children in the earlier sample, the correlation (and the evaluation score based on the *r*) would be high. (Actually, it would be a *z* rather than an *r*. Coefficients were transformed with Fisher's *r-z*.) One of the randomly selected groups received the evaluation tasks with instructions asking them to rate each idea in terms of originality. The other group received instructions asking for ratings of popularity. The first group were asked to give high rating for creative ideas, low ratings to uncreative ideas, and moderate ratings to those ideas that were moderately creative. The second group was asked to give high ratings to popular ideas, low ratings to unpopular ideas, and moderate ratings to the moderately popular ideas. The subjects also took the three divergent thinking tests and were asked to give as many possible ideas.

The important findings of this particular study were that the evaluative abilities of school children were reliability assessed (α = .77), and that there was a moderate relation between divergent thinking and evaluative skill (Rc = .58; p = .08). A highly significant relation between ideation and evaluation was found in the analysis using only the fluency scores from Instances (R = .54; p = .02) and a marginal relation was found in the analysis using only originality from the Instances test (R = .49; p = .07). Apparently, divergent thinking and evaluative ability are not independent nor entirely interdependent but the degree of their relation varies among test format and among groups. Recall here that the relation was very clear in our earlier investigation (Runco & Vega, 1990) with adults. Recall also what was said about the possible impact of experience on that relation. Very importantly, the children who evaluated the ideas for popularity were much more accurate than those children who rated the ideas for creativity (R = .62; p < .0001). This difference confirmed what we (Runco & Vega, 1990) found with adults.

In Charles and Runco (in press), we more directly examined the possibility that the fourth-grade slump was a result of changes in how children evaluated their own ideas. We proposed that the fourth-grade slump might in part result from a change in evaluations, with children at that age devoting increased attention to the appropriateness of ideas. To the degree that original ideas are uncommon, they may be viewed as inappropriate, especially to an individual in the conventional stage. To a conventional individual, appropriateness might be defined in terms of social fit.

In Charles and Runco (in press), we relied on interpersonal evaluations given by third-, fourth-, and fifth-grade children. In addition to obtaining evaluation ratings, we asked children to explain why they evaluated the ideas in the manner they did. We preselected the ideas being rated to ensure that various levels of original and appropriateness were represented. The responses from an Instances test were scored for fluency, originality, appropriateness, and "cueing." The last of these was a precaution taken against the possibility that children could find ideas merely by scanning their immediate environment. Although that might be a useful strategy for boosting one's fluency score on a divergent thinking test, it tends to lower originality scores, at least if the respondents are completing the divergent thinking tasks in a group. Other examinees will see the same objects in the environment, and if several people write the same idea down, it will not be original. The use of cueing was justified by the research showing that the testing environment can influence ideation (Harrington, Block, & Block, 1987; Runco, Okuda, & Thurston, 1991; Ward, 1968). Harrington et al., for instance, defined high-quality ideas as absent from the testing environment.

It was reported (Charles & Runco, in press) that age was significantly correlated with evaluative accuracy. The actual coefficients indicated that the shared variance was only moderate, but the age-grade effects showed the statistically significant trend. Older children gave more accurate judgments about the originality of the ideas (see Fig. 3.1a), and their "preference judgments" (see Fig. 3.1b) showed them to like more popular (less original) ideas as they moved from the fourth to the fifth and then on to the sixth grades. Surprisingly, we did not find a fourth-grade slump in the divergent thinking of the school children.

If there was a clear slump when Torrance (1968) did his famous research on the fourth-grade slump, and then we (Charles & Runco, in press) found that children were not slumping, I might point to how "times have changed" and offer hypotheses about education and sunspots. Note, however, that I wrote "*if* Torrance (1968) found a clear slump." As a matter of fact, he found that 50% to 60% of the children in his samples showed a clear slump. That is far from 100%. A slump may be widely cited in part because it is consistent with other manifestations of increased conventionality at about the same age. Children's art becomes highly representational and less self-expressive, they stick to the rules in games, and they become more literal in their language. These conventional tendencies are not, however, indicative of ideation, so again the lack of the slump reported in Charles and Runco (in press) may not be all that much of a surprise.

EVALUATIONS OF APPROPRIATENESS AND ORIGINALITY

The assessment of judgments of appropriateness in Charles and Runco (in press) was in part justified by an earlier study (Runco & Charles, 1992). Information integration techniques were used in this particular study to assess the relations among originality, appropriateness, and creativity, with *ideational pools* used as stimuli. An ideational pool contains an examinee's were entire response output (Runco & Mraz, 1992). Here, the pools were constructed to allow clear contrasts of highly original and appropriate ideas. The highly original ideas were statistically uncommon. The appropriate ideas had been identified as such by trained judges. Thus, in Runco and Charles (1992), we were in a sense comparing objective originality and appropriateness scores with subjective originality and appropriateness ratings. Following information integration theory, the intent in this project was to determine the manner in which subjective judgments of originality and appropriateness were integrated in judgments of creativity. The secondary purpose was to examine relations between objective and subjective scores, and between objective and subjective appropriateness scores.

Seventy-one college students (50 females, 17 males, and 4 who did not report their gender) participated in this research. These students were in either an introductory psychology or a child development class. The average age of the students was 20.8 years. Six of the students were parents and 20 had some teaching experience. Each of the subjects was asked to sort different sets of cards. The sortings were then used as ratings, with all cards in one stack receiving the highest rating, the next stack receiving a rating one less, and so on. Each set contained nine cards, and each card (representing an ideational pool) contained eight ideas. Fluency of ideas was thereby held constant and could not influence judgments.

Most of the ideas on the cards were taken from an earlier study on divergent thinking (Runco & Albert, 1985). Three different versions of cards were developed. The first contained ideas that were either appropriate and original, or inappropriate and unoriginal (common). The second version contained ideas that were all inappropriate but varied in terms of the number of original and common ideas. The version of cards contained all original ideas but varied in the number of ideas that were appropriate and inappropriate. Three other tasks were administered (i.e., divergent thinking tasks, a preference for ideation survey, and a survey of demographics), in part as distractors between the various evaluations. Participants sorted the cards three times, each time using a different criterion: originality, appropriateness, and finally creativity. The sortings were taken to be indicative of ratings.

Originality ratings were relatively high when objective originality on the cards was high and appropriateness ratings were high when objective appropriateness increased. In all three sets of stimuli, subjective creativity ratings seemed most closely tied to ratings of originality. Increasing the number of original ideas on a card resulted in higher creativity ratings. Increasing the number of appropriate ideas, however, led to lower creativity ratings, even with originality held constant. These results suggest that original ideas do not need to be appropriate to be judged as creative and that appropriateness can inhibit judgments of creativity. These findings are contrary to those definitions of creativity that emphasis originality and appropriateness, but as we (Runco & Charles, 1992) pointed out, generalizations are limited. Appropriateness was objectively defined in very literal terms, and in actuality ideas can be metaphorically or literally appropriate (Runco, 1996).

EVALUATIONS OF IDEAS GIVEN TO REALISTIC TASKS

In Runco and Chand (1994), we employed a series of realistic tasks in our work on evaluative accuracy. Realistic tasks are unlike Uses, Similarities, and Instances tasks in that they contain situations that could be found in the natural environment. Here are the instructions:

> On the next few pages, we will describe a few problems that may occur at school and work. Your task is to first read about the problem and then try to write down as many solutions as you can for each problem. Here is an example: *Your favorite television show, L.A. Law, was on last night. You had so much fun watching it that you forgot to do your homework. You are about to go to school this morning when you realize that your homework is due in your first class. Uh-oh . . . what are you going to do?* For this problem, you could answer, "Tell the professor that you forgot to do your homework; try to do your homework in the car or bus on the way to school; ask your roommate, boyfriend, girlfriend, or classmate to help you finish you homework; do your homework tonight and turn it in the next time the class meets; or finish your homework first than show up late for class." There are many more answers to this problem, and all of them are legitimate.

This is a *presented problem divergent thinking task*. It provides a question about school and employment to examinees. *Discovered problems*, in contrast, allow examinees to generate problems that might occur in a given setting (work, school, home). A *discovered problem divergent thinking task* represents a combination of problem finding and divergent thinking. Participants are asked to look back on the problems they themselves generate about school and work and asked to choose one problem from each. They then choose the one problem that would allow them to generate the largest number of solutions.

Realistic problems have a strength and a weakness. The former reflects the fact that they may be more interesting than standard ideational tasks precisely because they are realistic. A respondent might not be interested in listing uses for a shoe, which is a task from the Uses test, but the respondent might be highly interested in solving a problem that could occur at school or work. The downside is that realistic tasks might be more constraining than standard Uses and Instances tasks. (Similarities is also somewhat constraining.) Presumably, the more open a divergent thinking task, the better. Realistic tasks often include constraints, albeit realistic ones.

One group of (randomly selected) participants received *explicit instructions* (see Harrington, 1975; Runco, 1986) with divergent thinking tasks. These stated "be creative" and "give only original responses." A creative idea was briefly defined in these instructions as original and worthwhile. An original idea was in turn defined as one that would be thought of by no one else. The divergent thinking tasks were scored for fluency and originality (i.e., uniqueness).

The participants first received the presented problems. After a distractor task (actually a questionnaire to collect demographics), participants received the problem-generation task. Explicit instructions reminded the one group to give only original responses. Responses from the problem-generation tasks were scored for originality and fluency. Unfortunately, only fluency scores could be calculated for the discovered problems. Because each participant worked with his or her own problem—problems they had themselves individually chosen—their ideas could not be compiled and compared to one another. Because it was impossible to objectively determine the uniqueness and originality of the ideas, it was also impossible to assess the accuracy of evaluations given on this task. Future research might use the available subjective scoring techniques (Hocevar, 1981) to determine the originality of ideas given to discovered problem divergent thinking tasks. Evaluative accuracies could then be determined.

Runco and Chand (1994) used three indices of evaluative accuracy. The first index indicated the number of ideas that were given a rating of 6 or 7 and that were in fact original. This was, then, an index of participants' accuracy specifically for judgments of original ideas. The second indicated the number of ideas that were given moderate ratings (3, 4, or 5) and were in fact moderately popular (not unique, but given by less than 10% of the sample). The third indicated the number of ideas given low ratings (1 or 2) that were indeed low in originality and relatively popular—that is, given by 10% or more of the sample of subjects.

The three indices were not intercorrelated (alphas = .05 for presented problems and .26 for problem generation tasks) but this was to be expected. This is why three different scores were defined. Certain tactics may be used when judging an idea of originality, whereas other tactics are more appropriate for judging popularity. Earlier research already demonstrated that there are significant differences between judgments of originality and judgments of popularity.

Regression analyses uncovered various relations between evaluative accuracy and ideation. The evaluative accuracy scores were significantly related to the production of original ideas on both the presented problems ($R = .61$; $p = .0001$) and the problem generation task ($R = .48$; $p = .0001$). There was, however, no indication that the explicit instructions influenced the accuracy of the evaluations.

The accuracy with with participants judged the ideas that were neither original nor highly popular was unrelated to both originality scores ($Rs < .24$). Evaluative accuracy when judging the popularity of ideas was also unrelated to both originality scores ($Rs < .10$). Again, there was little indication of any influence of the explicit instructions, although for the evaluations of moderate ideas (neither original nor popular) there was a marginal interaction ($R2$-change = .06; $p = .06$, $R = 35$; $p = .07$). This indicated that the judgments were slightly more accurate on this task when examinees received explicit instructions about originality on the problem-generation task.

It is still quite possible that explicit instructions could improve evaluative accuracies. The instructions that we tested (Runco & Chand, 1994) focused on ideation ("give ideas that no one else will think of") rather than judgment. The criteria for originality are the same but the wording might be changed so participants could more easily see the relevance to their judgments.

INTERPERSONAL EVALUATIONS OF IDEAS

In Runco and Smith (1992), inter- and intrapersonal evaluations of creative ideas were compared. The first objective of the study was simply to compare interpersonal evaluative accuracy and intrapersonal evaluative accuracy. There are many reasons to expect them to differ from one another. As described in Runco and Chand (1994), the individual is privy to a great deal of relevant information when he or she examines his or her own ideas—information that is unavailable to anyone else (for interpersonal evaluations). This may lead to predictable biases. The individual is, for example, less likely to judge an idea as original than someone else because he or she will be aware of the *associative history* of an idea. This just means that the individual may be aware of the associations that led to the particular idea and of other similar ideas that were considered. An idea being judged may not seem very unusual or novel compared to other ideas considered. This bias may be minimized if the individual is unaware of the associative history, or if he or she is working on a problem for some time and knows that solutions are difficult to come by. He or she may know that one idea is a winner because all the other ideas considered did not solve the problem.

Runco and Chand (1994) also drew from attibution theory to explain differences between inter- and intrapersonal evaluations of ideas. Summarizing our thinking, the individual who generates an idea is likely to be thinking about the problem and its context, whereas the judge is likely to focus his or her attention on the individual who gave the idea (rather than the context). This has been called the *divergent perspectives hypothesis*. It apparently applies to judgments of people as well as ideas.

The second objective in Runco and Smith (1992) was to compare originality with popularity in both the inter- and the intrapersonal judgments. The third objective was to compare two kinds of evaluations. The first was evaluation as defined throughout this chapter, which focuses on originality (or its antithesis, popularity). The second was an evaluative skill defined by the Structure of Intellect (SOI; Guilford, 1968; Meeker, 1980). The different evaluative skills were compared as a check of discriminant validity. The evaluative scores defined in this chapter are important only to the degree that they are independent of scores from other related assessments. If they were found to be related, there would be no need to develop and use the new evaluative measures. Scores from existing measures, including the SOI, would be sufficient.[1]

Runco and Smith (1992) administered three divergent thinking tests to 58 university students. The students represented various majors (business, communications, and psychology). The tests were Instances, Uses, and Pattern Meanings. Each student was to give as many ideas as possible for each of the questions. Responses were scored for their uniqueness and popularity. Each examinee had one uniqueness score and one popularity (nonunique) score for each test. Each also rated his or her own ideas on a 7-point scale. This was done with a red pencil (to minimize the chance of changing ideas) and only after all ideas were given. The Advanced SOI Test for Critical and Analytical Thinking (Meeker, 1980) was administered to check discriminant validity.

---

[1] This is the same issue of discriminant validity that motivated earlier work on divergent thinking (e.g., Getzels & Jackson, 1962; Wallach & Kogan, 1965). If divergent thinking scores were highly correlated with the IQ or another existing measure, there would be no need to use the divergent thinking tests. Performance on them could be predicted from those other measures.

The instructions for the intrapersonal evaluations read as follows:

> Now we would like you to look back at your own ideas on the three open-ended questions, and rate each to indicate its *creativity*. Use a colored pen (available at the desk) to write a number (between 1 and 7) next to each idea. Give high numbers (7 or 6) to your most creative ideas. Give low numbers (I or 2) to any of your ideas that are uncreative. Give middle numbers (3, 4, or 5) to ideas that are somewhat creative. *Do not add any new ideas to your list! Do not change any ideas, and do not erase any ideas!* If all of your ideas are *extremely* creative, you may give mostly 6s and 7s; but it is more likely that you will have some creative ideas, some only slightly creative, and some that most people would think of. You will probably want to use all of the numbers between one and seven.

Interpersonal evaluations were obtained with measures like those used in the earlier research.

The various measures were found to be acceptably reliable (Runco & Smith, 1992). Cronbach's alpha for the uniqueness scores of the interpersonal evaluation measure .67, and .64 for the popularity score. For the intrapersonal evaluations, the alpha for popularity was .61 and for uniqueness .50.

Further analyses confirmed that there was a significant difference between inter- and intrapersonal evaluative scores. This was especially true in a multivariate test [$F(1, 57) = 10.25$; $p = .002$]. The difference between the unique and popular evaluations was not significant, but there was a significant interaction, with subjects more accurate when rating the uniqueness of their own ideas than when rating them in terms of popularity, and even more accurate when rating ideas given by other people for popularity rather than uniqueness. This pattern of results held up even after covarying grade point average (GPA).

A canonical analysis indicated that the intrapersonal evaluation scores were significantly related to the divergent thinking scores ($Rc = .45$, $p = .016$), but the interpersonal scores were not. The intrapersonal creativity evaluation scores were marginally related to the divergent thinking uniqueness scores. Neither of the interpersonal scores was related to the corresponding (creativity or popularity) divergent thinking scores. Bivariate analyses indicated that for the interpersonal evaluations, uniqueness and popularity accuracy were unrelated to divergent thinking popularity scores. The uniqueness scores from the intrapersonal evaluation were unrelated to divergent thinking uniqueness scores, but popularity evaluative accuracy was related to the popularity scores from the divergent thinking tests ($r = .61$; $p < .001$).

A last set of analyses confirmed that the evaluative scores were unrelated to the SOI indices. The SOI indices were, however, correlated with the divergent thinking test scores, with *r*s above .25 for the uniqueness scores and above .28 for the popularity scores. GPA was significantly related to two of the SOI indices but unrelated to scores on the evaluative tasks and divergent thinking tests.

These results suggested that there is only a selective association between inter- and intrapersonal evaluative skills. The ratings of popularity on the interpersonal evaluation task reflected the highest level of accuracy, and ratings of the popularity on the intrapersonal task reflected the lowest. The results also suggest that there is a difference between evaluations of originality and evaluations of popularity, and they indicate that intrapersonal evaluative accuracy is related to divergent thinking. Interpersonal evaluative accuracy was unrelated to divergent thinking.

The nonsignificant correlations found with the SOI indices suggest that the evaluation of ideas may not depend on the skills assessed by the measures of more traditional critical thinking. I return to this issue in the discussion section of this chapter.

EVALUATIONS BY MANAGERS

In a previous study (Runco & Basadur, 1993), we reported what was essentially a pilot study of the evaluative skills of 35 managers. These managers represented lower and upper middle management in large international consumer goods marketing and sales companies. Their responsibilities included finance, manufacturing, operations, employee relations, distribution, marketing, and sales. They received training as part of this investigation. This 20-hour training was designed by Basadur (1994) and provided rationale and hands-on experience in what Basadur called the "complete problem solving process." This is an a modern application of the Osborn-Parnes Creative Problem Solving (CPS) theory. We collected data before and after training. We compared the pre- and posttraining data and correlated each with measures of attitudes and problem-solving style. The attitudes assessed were "preference for ideation," which was thought to be conducive to ideation and originality, and "preference for closure," which of course is likely to be inhibitive. The styles assessed, also developed by Basadur (1994), were described as follows:

> The generator process style favors learning (obtaining knowledge) by direct concrete experience, and using knowledge for ideation. Behaviorally, someone displaying the generator process style acts as an initiator, "absorbing diverse information and creating

diverse possibilities." The conceptualizer process style also favors using knowledge for ideation, but the knowledge is gained with detached abstract thinking. Unlike the generator process style, which is probably best early in the creative problem solving process (problem finding), the conceptualizer style probably contributes the most in the early or middle phases in formulating rather than discovering problems. The optimizer process style relies on detached, abstract thinking for obtaining knowledge, but tends to use knowledge for evaluation. Someone using an optimizer process style is therefore the most comfortable in the middle or later stages, developing solutions rather than finding or defining problems. Finally, the implementor process style prefers obtaining knowledge through direct concrete experience and using it for evaluation and is most comfortable in the last phase of creative problem solving, namely implementing solutions.

The ideation of the managers was assessed with four tasks. One was given before the training and one after. Instructions assured the managers of confidentiality and asked them to generate as many ideas as they could. Unlike all other divergent thinking reported in this chapter, because of practical constraints, there was a 2-minute time limit for each problem. These particular tasks were written by Basadur, who collaborated with senior management. The particular problems used were both a part of each participant's experience and an important part of their work. Each manager received one technical problem (e.g., how to reduce product damage) and one organizational problem (e.g., how to increase employee motivation). There were four problems, but each participant only received two. These were randomly selected, with counterbalancing to determine if the technical or organizational problems were given before or after training.

Evaluative skill was assessed by asking the participants to rate their own ideas on a scale ranging from 1 (*entirely unoriginal*) to 7 (*highly original*). Then, two evaluative scores were determined by calculating the number of original ideas that were accurately identified, and the number of original ideas rated incorrectly. For example, one point was earned for each original idea which was given a rating of 7, and one point was subtracted for each unoriginal idea given a 7. Both correct and incorrect identification scores were calculated in this way.

Analyses indicated that eight evaluation items (pre- and posttreatment for both problem-solving tasks, and both correct and incorrect identifications) were moderately reliable ($\alpha = .61$). As expected, the pre- and posttraining scores were significantly different, and this included both the correct-identification and incorrect-identification evaluation scores. A second analysis controlled for fluency scores, and here only the correct evaluations showed improvement with training. The incorrect-evaluation difference was no longer significantly different. The differences between pre- and posttraining in originality and fluency were statistically significant (and showed improvements!), as were the differences in the preference for divergence and the preference for closure. As expected, the last of these indicated a significant drop at posttraining. The fluency scores doubled as a result of the training, from a mean of 1.5 to 3.0, and originality scores increased from just under 12 to just under 20.

In Runco and Basadur (1993), we used analyses of partialed variance to determine if the pre-posttreatment differences in evaluation were moderated by the styles, divergent thinking, attitude indices. In the first, the evaluative skills scores were used as the dependent variable. The pretraining scores were regressed on the posttraining scores, followed by the style scores, the attitudinal scores, and the posttraining ideation scores. (The pretraining score was entered into the equation first, with the order of inclusion for the other predictors determined by their respective statistical tolerances.) When the correct-evaluation score was the dependent variable, the pretraining scores did not account for a significant proportion of variance of the posttraining scores. However, the total originality score was significantly related to the residual (which represented the posttraining variance not explained by the pretraining scores), as was the preference for divergence posttraining score, the Implementor style, and the total fluency score. The total of the explained variance (i.e., when all predictors were in the equation) was large and statistically significant ($R = .78$; $p < .001$). It appeared that there were individual differences in the impact of training. The impact of training on evaluative accuracy was moderated by by both style (i.e., Implementor) and ideational fluency. The impact of training on ideational originality was moderated by style (i.e., Conceptualizer) and the closure attitude. There was a negative correlation between premature convergence and originality.

Importantly, canonical analyses showed that the ideational originality and fluency indices were significantly related to the two correct-identification evaluative scores ($Rc = .78$). This seemed to reflect mostly the relation specifically between originality and the evaluative scores ($R = .76$). The fluency scores were unrelated to the evaluative scores. Originality accounted for twice the variance in the evaluation scores, as compared to fluency. This of course makes sense because examinees were asked to rate their ideas on the 7-point scale that had *entirely unoriginal* and *highly original* as anchors.

In Basadur, Runco, and Vega (in press), we extended this work with a larger sample and with more robust analytic techniques. We worked with 112 upper middle managers from a very large international consumer goods manufacturer. Managers of finance, operations, employee relations, manufacturing, and distribution were all represented. Each manager received 20 hours of Basadur's (1994) training in creative problem solving, which includes step-by-step practice and exercise of the various steps of creative thinking. Importantly, this training emphasized both convergent and divergent thinking. It also discussed the value of creativity, which presumably can influence the criteria individuals use when evaluating ideas and solutions.

Each manager received the 14-item measure of attitudes mentioned previously (see Runco & Basadur, 1993), along with four divergent thinking tasks, both before and after training. These tasks were defined in collaboration with senior managers of the same company, thus ensuring their realism. The tasks asked "How might we install our vending equipment accounts faster?" "How might we get in and out of markets faster?" "How might we make better decisions as a team?" "How might we communicate better as a team?" These were counterbalanced, some managers receiving the first or second question before training and some receiving those after training. (Subsequent analyses confirmed that the differences among tasks were not statistically significant.) Managers also evaluated the originality of their own ideas on a scale ranging from 1 (*entirely unoriginal*) to 7 (*highly original*). Managers also received Basadur's Creative Problem Solving Profile (CPSP), and Kirton's Adaptation Innovation (KAI) Inventory.

A multivariate analysis of variance indicated that training was very effective. Fluency scores increased (from an average of 9.1 to 13.4), as did originality scores (from 3.1 to 5.4). They also were significantly more accurate when judging originality. Their evaluations of unoriginal ideas (i.e., giving low ratings to ideas that were in fact unoriginal) did not change significantly. A causal model was generated, with weights that were almost entirely as expected. It confirmed, for example, that ideational skill—the generation of ideas—was strongly related to the accurate evaluation of ideas ($\beta = .74$). The Conceptualizer problem-solving style from the CPSP seemed to moderate the effects of training, for both ideation and evaluation; the Optimizer style seemed to moderate effects specifically for ideation; and the KAI moderated the effects on evaluation scores. Attitudes improved after training, in the sense that managers were more open to divergent thinking, but contrary to expectations these same attitudes did not moderate any training effects.

DISCUSSION

It is useful to summarize key findings from the research on ideation and evaluation.

- Popularity seems to be easier to judge than originality, at least for interpersonal evaluations. Runco and Smith (1992) found intrapersonal evaluations of popularity to be less accurate than evaluations of originality.
- Divergent thinking scores are significantly correlated with evaluation scores, although the strength of this relation varied in different age groups. It was strongest for adults (Runco & Vega, 1990).
- The evaluation tasks have demonstrated reliability, at least in terms of interitem (alpha) coefficients.
- There is some indication that the evaluation tasks have discriminant validity. Runco (1990), for example, found a negative correlation between the Information subest of the WISC-R and an evaluation task ($r = -.24$; $p < .05$). Runco and Smith (1992) reported nonsignificant correlations between inter- and intrapersonal evaluative accuracies and six SOI tests of evaluation. We also found evaluative accuracy to be independent of GPA.
- Numerous group differences were uncovered, although parents and teachers did not differ that much. Children in different age groups did differ (Charles & Runco, in press).
- Ideas judged to be creative must be original but need not be appropriate. Indeed, contrary to many definitions of creativity, appropriateness (literally defined) can inhibit judgments of creativity.

A number of methodological and statistical details were included in this chapter. The reason for this is that much of the research was exploring a new perspective on ideation and divergent thinking. The typical view is that critical thinking is unrelated to divergent ideation. The view propounded here is that a particular kind of evaluation is involved in ideation and is related to originality. This view was supported by the discriminant validity of the evaluation measures and by the relations between evaluation and scores on the divergent thinking tests.

This chapter shows the progression of the research on the evaluative component of the creative thinking process. The progress has been fairly significant, especially because the early efforts (e.g., Runco, 1991) were not entirely satisfactory. In particular, the scoring system used in the first few studies did not seem to fully capture participants' evaluative accuracy. Early evaluative accuracies were surprisingly low. It is no doubt difficult to judge ideas, especially with biases like those mentioned earlier in this chapter, so it could be that evaluative accuracies are indeed low. This could be a methodological artifact, however, which is one reason for the evolution of the the methodology and scoring systems.

The introductory section of this chapter foreshadowed the comparisons of judgments of originality with judgments of popularity. Popularity was examined because it was thought to be easier than originality for judges to use when evaluating ideas. This was demonstrated in several studies, and thus it seems that popularity should be targeted in efforts to enhance creative thinking—as an aspect of ideation or kind of idea to avoid. Popularity may be easier to explain and grasp, and as long as people are told that it is to be avoided (at least when originality and creativity are desired), the benefits may be the greatest.

Earlier, we (Runco & Smith, 1992) used Meeker's (1980) test of evaluation to check discriminant validity, but there are other ways to assess judgment. Watson and Glaser (1980) have a test of critical thinking (e.g., deduction, inference, and recognition of assumptions), for example. Then again, the SOI measure was thought to be the closest to the evaluation instruments, and thus the best test of discriminant validity. Other available measures do not focus on originality like the measures used in this chapter. On the other measures, examinees do not judge the correctness of solutions or the logic of an argument but instead determine the originality of ideas. Given its focus on originality, the assessments described throughout this chapter are more relevant to creativity. They also better test the componential theory of creativity that was presented in Runco and Chand (1995) and outlined earlier in this chapter.

The numerous significant correlations between ideation and evaluative accuracies might be indicative of practice and experience. Clearly, the individual who generates numerous ideas has more practice at and opportunity for judging ideas than does the person who tends to generate fewer ideas. The individual who habitually generates a large number of ideas may also eventually infer what constitutes good (or creative) ideas, and might additionally develop appropriate strategies for such judgments. If this interpretation of practice effects is accurate, there is all the more reason to provide students with opportunities to generate and evaluate ideas.

This raises a concern about brainstorming. Brainstorming is predicated on the idea that evaluation can be postponed. Evaluation may, however, be a useful part of ideation. Perhaps evaluation should be utilized rather than avoided. A recent review of brainstorming was provided by DeCock and Rickards (in press).

Future Research and Conclusion

Recall the earlier suggestion that future research could utilize subjective scoring techniques (Hocevar, 1981) to determine the originality of ideas given to discovered problem divergent thinking tasks. Evaluative accuracies for those tasks could then be determined. This would be interesting because very likely discovered problems require a type of evaluation. After all, examinees are asked to choose problems that would allow them to find numerous solutions. They are, then, asked to evaluate their ideas.

Similarly, we (Runco & Chand, 1994) proposed that explicit instructions have a significant effect precisely because they suggest apt evaluations to examinees. Certainly, they provide participants with the criteria that should be used when selecting which ideas should be explored and recorded. In this sense, all of the research on explicit instructions (e.g., Harrington, 1975; Runco, 1986) implies evaluations of ideas. We (Runco & Chand, 1994) did not find much of an effect of explicit instructions on evaluations, but these explicit instructions did not state anything about evaluations. We did mention originality but it was in the context of solving problems and generating ideas rather than as a means for improving judgments. Future research should test the impact of explicit instructions that are written specifically to facilitate evaluations of ideas.

Clearly, additional research on the "training" and facilitation of evaluation should be pursued. Explicit instructions might be used, and Basadur's (1994) complete program also showed promise. Recall here that one interpretation of the relation between ideation and evaluation involves experience: Individuals with more experience generating ideas are very likely better at evaluating them in part because they have more experience, and thus more realistic standards and more practiced skills. This implies that much could be accomplished with training. That might in turn improve the interrater agreement among judges in research relying on subjective evaluations of creative products or processes (e.g., Runco, 1989).

Research in progress is being conducted to further examine the discriminant validity of the evaluation measures and to examine predictive validity of the evaluative measures (Runco & Dow, 1999). As predicted by the componential model, what is most interesting will be the predictions using interactions among ideation and evaluation. Creative work in the natural environment requires both ideation and evaluation, and regression analyses will indicate the relative importance of the corresponding interaction.

Ideation has been empirical studied for nearly 50 years. In fact, Binet's early tests of mental abilities included tasks that required the generation of ideation and evaluation. The research reviewed in this chapter suggests that the evaluative component of creative thinking can be investigated, along with idea generation. The research reported in this chapter represents a series of investigations, but there is much room for further evolution of the methodologies and measures.

The term *evaluation* was used throughout this chapter to describe the convergent, critical process that is involved in creative thinking. This term—*evaluation*—was chosen to distinguish it from critical and convergent thinking. The processes that support original ideation are evaluative but not necessarily critical. Most striking is that the evaluation of ideas often requires that the individual judge for originality or creativity. Moreover, the requisite skills and tactics probably differ from those involved in traditional critical thinking. That is what the research reviewed herein confirmed—and it is in fact a good overview statement and conclusion for this chapter.

REFERENCES

Basadur, M. (1994). Managing the creative process in organizations. In M. A. Runco (Ed.), *Problem finding, problem solving, and creativity* (pp. 237-268). Norwood, NJ: Ablex.

Basadur, M., Runco, M. A., & Vega, L. (in press). Understanding how creative thinking skills, attitudes, and behaviors work together: A causal process model. *Journal of Creative Behavior*.

Charles, R., & Runco, M. A. (in press). Developmental trends in the evaluative and divergent thinking of children. *Creativity Research Journal*.

DeCock, C., & Rickards, T. (in press). In M. A. Runco (Ed.), *Creativity research handbook* (Vol. 2). Cresskill, NJ: Hampton Press.

Elkind, D. (1981). *Children and adolescence*. New York: Oxford University Press.

Gardner, H. (1988). *Journal of Aesthetic Education, 22*.

Getzels, J., & Jackson, P. (1962). *Creativity and intelligence: Explorations with gifted students*. New York: Wiley.

Guilford, J. P. (1968). *Creativity, intelligence and their educational implications*. San Diego, CA: EDITS.

Harrington, D. (1975). Effects of explicit instructions to "be creative" on the psychological meaning of divergent thinking test scores. *Journal of Personality, 43*, 434-454.

Harrington, D., Block, J., & Block, D. (1987). Testing aspects of Carl Rogers' theory. *Journal of Personality and Social Psychology, 52*, 851-856.

Hocevar, D. (1981). Measurement of creativity: Review and critique. *Journal of Personality Assessment, 45*, 450-464.

Kohlberg, L. (1987). The development of moral judgment and moral action. In L. Kohlberg (Ed.), *Child psychology and childhood education: A cognitive developmental view*. New York: Longman.

Kucera, H., & Francis, W. F. (1967). *Computational analysis of present-day American English*. Providence, RI: Brown University Press.

Meeker, M. (1980). *Learning to plan and make decisions: A structure of intellect evaluation sourcebook*. Vida, OR: SOI Systems.

Milgram, R. (in press). An idea whose time has come and gone? In M. A. Runco & R. S. Albert (Eds.), *Theories of creativity* (rev. ed.). Cresskill, NJ: Hampton Press.

Mraz, W., & Runco, M. A. (1994). Suicide ideation and creative problem solving. *Suicide and Life Threatening Behavior, 24*, 38-47.

Rosenblatt, E., & Winner, E. (1988). The art of children's drawings. *Journal of Aesthetic Education, 22*, 3-15.

Runco, M. A. (1986). Maximal performance on divergent thinking tests by gifted, talented, and nongifted children. *Psychology in the Schools, 23*, 308-315.

Runco, M. A. (1989). The creativity of children's art. *Child Study Journal, 19*, 177-189.

Runco, M. A. (1991). The evaluative, valuative, and divergent thinking of children. *Journal of Creative Behavior, 25*, 311-319.

Runco, M. A. (1992). Children's divergent thinking and creative ideation. *Developmental Review, 12*, 233-264.

Runco, M. A. (1994). Conclusions concerning problem finding, problem solving, and creativity. In M. A. Runco (Ed.), *Problem finding, problem solving, and creativity* (pp. 272-290). Norwood, NJ: Ablex.

Runco, M. A. (1996). Personal creativity: Definition and developmental issues. *New Directions for Child Development, 72*, 3-30.

Runco, M. A. (in press). The 4th grade slump in creativity. In M. A. Runco & S. Priztker (Eds.), *Encyclopedia of creativity*. San Diego, CA: Academic Press.

Runco, M. A., & Albert, R. S. (1985). The reliability and validity of ideational originality in the divergent thinking of academically gifted and nongifted children. *Educational and Psychological Measurement, 45*, 483-501.

Runco, M. A., & Basadur, M. (1993). Assessing ideational and evaluative skills and creative styles and attitudes. *Creativity and Innovation Management, 2*, 166-173.

Runco, M. A., & Chand, I. (1994). Problem finding, evaluative thinking, and creativity. In M. A. Runco (Ed.), *Problem finding, problem solving, and creativity* (pp. 40-76). Norwood, NJ: Ablex.

Runco, M. A., & Chand, I. (1995). Cognition and creativity. *Educational Psychology Review, 7*, 243-267.

Runco, M. A., & Charles, R. (1992). Judgments of originality and appropriateness as predictors of creativity. *Personality and Individual Differences, 15,* 537-546.

Runco, M. A., & Dow, G. (1999). *Assessing the accuracy of judgments of originality on three divergent thinking tests.* Submitted for publication.

Runco, M. A., & Mraz, W. (1992). Scoring divergent thinking tests using total ideational output and a creativity index. *Educational and Psychological Measurement, 52,* 213-221.

Runco, M. A., Okuda, S. M., & Thurston, B. J. (1991). Environmental cues and divergent thinking. In M. A. Runco (Ed.), *Divergent thinking* (pp. 79-85). Norwood, NJ: Ablex.

Runco, M. A., & Smith, W. R. (1992). Interpersonal and intrapersonal evaluations of creative ideas. *Personality and Individual Differences, 13,* 295-302.

Runco, M. A., & Vega, L. (1990). Evaluating the creativity of children's ideas. *Journal of Social Behavior and Personality, 5,* 439-452.

Torrance, E. P. (1968). A longitudinal examination of the fourth-grade slump in creativity. *Gifted Child Quarterly, 12,* 195-199.

Wallach, M. A., & Kogan, N. (1965). *Modes of thinking in young children.* New York: Holt, Rinehart & Winston.

Ward, W. C. (1968). Creativity in young children. *Child Development, 39,* 737-754.

Watson, G., & Glaser, E. M. (1980). *Critical thinking appraisal.* San Antonio, TX: Psychological Corporation.

4

CREATIVITY, PERSONALITY AND THE CONVERGENT-DIVERGENT CONTINUUM

H. J. Eysenck
University of London

CREATIVITY AND RIGOR—A FAMOUS DICHOTOMY

It is customary for philosophers, historians of science, psychologists, and others interested in the study of creativity to think in categorical, either-or terms reminiscent of Hegelian thesis-antithesis confrontation, but lacking the synthesis Hegel would have imposed as the terminal point of such an analysis. Such a categorical analysis of scientific behavior is apparent in Kuhn's (1957, 1970) theory of scientific revolutions. Kuhn contrasted *normal science* with *revolutionary science,* the former proceeding with problem-solving behavior within a widely accepted paradigm, whereas the latter sets out to change the paradigm. Such changes of paradigm are exemplified by the Copernican revolution, substituting a heliocentric universe for a percentric one; Lavoisier's overthrow of the *phlogiston* theory of heat; Einstein's theory of relativity; Plank's theory of *quantum mechanics*; and many others.

The notion of a paradigm has been criticized by Masterman (1970) as overly wide and undefined, and Kuhn (1970) amended his earlier conception by redefining it in terms of a *disciplinary matrix* and shared *exemplars.* A disciplinary matrix is a kind of scientific

Weltanschauung acquired implicitly through the educational process whereby one comes to be a licensed practitioner of the scientific discipline. This implicit acquisition occurs through the study of exemplars (i.e., examples identifying the ways the science's symbolic generalization [laws or theories] apply to phenomena). Such exemplars are furnished by textbooks and laboratory exercises, and occur in supervised research. It is this conditioning process that makes normal science so resistant to change. This resistance, so frequently observed and with hindsight so unreasonable (Milton, 1994), caused Kuhn to argue that there is nothing in common between the old and the new paradigm, and to add that one cannot scientifically decide between them because their very differences change the nature of admissible arguments. This notion that one cannot strictly evaluate the relative merits of old and new paradigms suggest a degree of subjectivity that is grossly exaggerated, as any historical study of such a "revolution" will show. Thus, the final success of the atomistic theory of matter was not determined subjectively, but in terms of hard experimental demonstrations that destroyed perfectly reasonable objections made by traditional, orthodox physicists (Brock, 1967; Knight, 1967; McGucken, 1969). Revolutionary theories are subject to much reasonable criticism when first formulated, and inevitably take time to establish their value.

Creativity is usually associated mainly with the achievements of the revolutionaries—Copernicus, Galileo, Einstein, Planck. This general notion derived from a study of the history of science is paralleled by a distinction often made by philosophers of science, namely between the *context of discovery*, on the one hand, and the *context of justification*, on the other. Philosophers of science, interested in scientific methodology, have usually been concerned entirely with the context of justification, leaving the context of discovery to psychologists (Schaffer, 1994). As Mickler (1974) pointed out, the sharp distinction of context of discovery from context of justification "is typically introduced to support the view that scientific methodology is concerned wholly with the justification of scientific ideas; how they are discovered is a matter for psychology, sociology and history" (p. 575). Here again we have a clear-cut categorization into two either-or camps: discovery versus justification, elaboration of new theories versus proof of the correctness of theories, with the former linked with creativity and other psychological mechanisms, the latter with procedures that might be reduced to the mechanical use of established methods (Suppe, 1974).

Finally, on the psychological side, is the contrast between convergent and divergent modes of thinking, together with tests designed to measure a person's ability to use either of these modes of thinking. The distinction is well known (Glover, Ronning, &

Reynolds, 1989) and widely accepted, and finds empirical support in a number of factorial studies (Carroll, 1993). Furthermore, the existence of a connection between creative behavior and divergent thinking has been established in several studies (Eysenck, 1994b). Convergent tests operate in a context of justification, with only one predetermined solution to reach, which lies within the range of normal problem solving; divergent tests operate in a context of discovery, with no predetermined paradigm—novel and previously unheard of solutions are not only admirable, but welcomed and praised. Thus, we have three parallel dichotomies, all related to the notion of creativity; scientific activity can be normal science, in the context of justification, and convergent, or it can be revolutionary, in the context of discovery, and divergent. The former is subject to specific rules, mechanical, and carried out in terms of given methodologies that can be stated by philosophers of science. The latter is creative, subject to no such rules, and falls into the field of psychology. The dichotomy outlined in the preceding paragraph is well illustrated in the joint work of two famous mathematicians, Ramanujan and Hardy (Kanigel, 1991).

Ramanujan was born in 1887, in Kumbakonam, a small Indian town on the sacred river Cauvery. He scarcely spoke during the first 3 years of his life; there were fears that he was dumb. He was an enormously self-willed child, and reacted very negatively to school when he was enrolled at the age of 5. "Even as a child, he was so self-directed that, it was fair to say, unless he was ready to do something on his own, in his own time, he was scarcely capable of doing it at all" (Kanigel, 1991, p. 13); school to him meant shackles to throw off, rather than keys to knowledge. He was solitary, lacked all interest in sport, but was fond of asking questions of a vaguely scientific nature. His father was a lowly clerk, working all day in a shop; he was essentially brought up by an intensely religious mother.

To say that Ramanujan excelled at mathematics would be an understatement. He not only excelled over his classmates but also his teachers. At a ceremony in 1904, Ramanujan was awarded the K. Rangenatha Rao prize for mathematics, the headmaster stating that he deserved higher than the maximum possible awards— Ramanujan, he said, was off the scale. His genius took flight when a book on mathematics came into his possession, G. S. Carr's *Synopsis of Elementary Results in Pure and Applied Mathematics*. It contained some 5,000 equations, and other mathematical facts— unsystematic, dealing with algebra, trigonometry, calculus, differential equations, analytical geometry—not a real synopsis, but rather a compendium. There was no method for arriving at formulas, or proving them in the book, so that Ramanujan had largely to fashion his own—which he did with delight.

Having discovered Carr, Ramanujan graduated from high school and entered Kumbakonams' Government College. He neglected all school subjects except mathematics, and thus he was left to do pretty well what he liked—it seems doubtful if his teachers could teach him anything. He failed English composition, and had his scholarship taken away. This began a long story of battling with the establishment, blind as always to true greatness, insisting on piddling rules made for mediocrity, and furious when faced with anything it could not understand. Ramanujan lost all his scholarship, he failed in school, he even lost students he was tutoring—his ever-original mind was not suited to rote-learning and traditional methods of doing things. Instead, he started to keep notebooks in which he would record ideas, proofs, theorems—anything that engaged his interest and stimulated his original and inventive genius. He kept up the habit of entrusting his ideas and findings to his notebooks throughout his troubled youth and even later; they were the spur for many excellent mathematicians to follow in his footsteps and prove his intuitive ideas.

In any case, for 5 years Ramanujan was left alone to pursue mathematics, receiving no guidance, no stimulation, no money except a few rupees earned from tutoring. College limited him, teachers could not evaluate his mathematics, and anything else he would not do—one can see their problem. He tried to interest the leading professional mathematicians in his work, but failed for the most part. What he had to show them was too novel, too unfamiliar, and additionally presented in unusual ways; they could not be bothered. Kanigel described in detail all the rejections, misapprehensions, and misconceptions Ramanujan encountered in his dealings with competent mathematicians; they simply could not deal with the novelty of his approach, the unusual methodology, and the exceptional fertility of his imagination. Above all, they failed to appreciate his intuition because of the lack of analytical proof; who was he to imagine he was right in his anticipation when there was no proof to show that his imagination was along the right lines (Mordell, 1941)?

Finally, in despair, Ramanujan wrote to G. H. Hardy, at the time the leading British mathematician, well known for his attempts to introduce continental ideas of rigor and proof into the somewhat sloppy mathematics current in England. In many ways, Hardy was the opposite of Ramanujan: widely read where Ramanujan was unfamiliar with classical and modern methods and developments; insistent on proof where Ramanujan was only interested in intuition; omniscient in academic subjects where Ramanujan was entirely ignorant.

In his letter, Ramanujan gave a brief outline of his life; he followed this with a statement that he could give meaning to negative values of the gamma function. He also disputed a mention contained in a mathematical pamphlet Hardy had written 3 years earlier. Finally, Ramaunjan enclosed a number of pages with some of his intuitive findings.

How would one expect the very embodiment of proof and rigor to react to the outpourings of the untutored, intuitive, entirely original, and incredibly creative Ramanujan? Hardy came from a lower middle-class family; his father was a shopkeeper, but the family emphasized intellect and learning. Hardy made his way to Winchester, one of England's leading public schools (for "public" read "private," of course!), and from there to Cambridge, through outstanding excellence and achievement. The letter he received, out of the blue, completely nonplussed him.

For Hardy, as Kanigel said, Ramanujan's pages of theorems were like an alien forest whose trees were familiar enough to call trees, yet so strange they seemed to come from another planet. Indeed, it was the strangeness of Ramanujan's theorems, not their brilliance, that struck Hardy first. Surely, this was yet another crank, he thought, and put the letter aside. However, what he had read gnawed at his imagination all day, and finally he decided to take the letter to Littlewood, a mathematical prodigy and friend of his. The whole story is brilliantly (and touchingly) told by Kanigel; fraud or genius, they asked themselves, and decided that genius was the only possible answer. All honor to Hardy and Littlewood for recognizing genius, even under the colorful disguise of this exotic Indian plant; other Cambridge mathematicians, like Baker and Hobson, had failed to respond to similar letters. Indeed, as Kanigel reported, "it is not just that he discerned genius in Ramanujan that stands to his credit today; it is that he battered down his own wall of skepticism to do so" (p. 171).

The rest of his short life (he died at 33), Ramanujan was to spend in Cambridge, working with Hardy, who tried to educate him in more rigorous ways and spent much time in attempting to prove (or disprove!) his theorems, and generally see to it that his genius was tethered to the advancement of modern mathematics. Ramanujan's tragic early death left a truly enormous amount of mathematical knowledge in the form of unproven theorems of the highest value, which were to provide many outstanding mathematicians with enough material for a life's work to prove, integrate with what was already known, and generally give it form and shape acceptable to orthodoxy. Ramanujan's standing may be illustrated by an interesting informal scale of natural mathematical ability constructed by Hardy, on which he gave himself a 25 and Littlewood a 30. To David Hilbert, the most eminent mathematician of his day, he gave an 80. To Ramanujan he gave 100! Yet, as Hardy (1940) said, "the limitations of his knowledge were as startling as its profundity."

Here was a man who could work out modular equations and theorems of complex multiplication, to orders unheard of, whose mastery of continued fractions was, on the formal side at any rate, beyond that of any mathematician in the world, who had found for himself the functional equation of the Zeta-function, and the dominant terms of many of the most famous problems in the analytic theory of numbers; and he had never heard of a doubly periodic function or of Cauchy's theorem, and had indeed but the vaguest idea of what a function of a complex variable was.

Together, Hardy and Ramanujan achieved what neither could have done alone; together they made an entry in the history of mathematics that will endure over time. But, as Bollobas (1988) observed, although Hardy furnished the technical skills needed to attack the problem,

> I believe Hardy was not the only mathematician who could have done it. Probably Mordel could have done it. Polya could have done it. I'm sure there are quite a few people who could have played Hardy's role. But Ramanujan's role in that particular partnership I don't think could have been played at the time by anybody else. (p. 78)

The greatest mathematicians—Gauss, Euler—of course combine the gifts of intuition and analysis; what makes Hardy and Ramanujan so interesting is precisely the one-sidedness of their gifts. Ramanujan without a doubt was a genius, but in the words of Mark Kac (1985), a Polish emigre mathematician, he was a "magician" rather than an "ordinary genius."

> An ordinary genius is a fellow that you and I would be just as good as, if we were only many times better. There is no mystery as to how his mind works. Once we understand what he has done, we feel certain that we, too, could have done it. It is different with the magicians. They are, to use mathematical jargon, in the orthogonal complement of where we are and the working of their minds is for all intents and purposes incomprehensible. Even after we understand what they have done, the process by which they have done it is completely dark. (p. 153)

This is another way to characterize the *intuitive* ("magician") as opposed to the *analytical* ("ordinary genius") scientist or mathematician (and probably, *ceteris paribus,* artist as well); we see the intuitive worker as intrinsically more "creative" just because the origins of his creativity are hidden in the unfamiliar cliffs and caves of the unconscious.

DICHOTOMY OR CONTINUUM

Hardy and Ramanujan are good examples of the traditional view of creativity and rigor as categorical and contrasted concepts—Hardy the convergent thinker, Ramanujan the divergent thinker. Yet what is so interesting is that both are *extremes,* with the great majority of mathematicians (and scientists generally) lying somewhere in between these extremes. I have mentioned Gauss and Euler; most of the great men whose lives and achievements are described in Bell's (1939) *Men of Mathematics* combine intuition and rigor to varying degrees. In other words, it is likely that we are dealing with a continuum on which Hardy and Ramanujan are located at opposite ends, the general distribution of mathematicians and scientists generally on that continuum is likely to be Gaussian—with perhaps a skew toward the Hardy end. Even the most creative must have a modicum of basic knowledge and rigor in his or her thinking; even the most orthodox and rigorous must use some degree of creative intuition to solve the complex formulae that confront him or her.

Thus, even convergent tests imply creativity, if of a low order, and even divergent tests imply ordinary association of ideas. Spearman (1923, 1927), in his attempts to discover the principles underlying ordinary intelligence (convergent), called these the "noegenetic principles" (i.e., novelty creating). Given that "a" is to "b" as "c" is to ? the answer is implied in the question, but is unknown to the solver; he or she is required to discover something new—new to him or her, if not to the person who constructed the problem. (Spearman argued the case persuasively.) Ramanujan discovered genuinely *new* theorems in his work, but he also "discovered" theorems already known to mathematicians. Would that make him any less "creative"? Cattell is credited with discovering the distinction between traits and states in personality study, but this was already discovered and explicitly formulated by Cicero 2,000 earlier (Eysenck, 1983). Cattell was unaware of Cicero's *Tusculan Disputations;* should he be credited with a creative innovation? Aristarchus had advanced a heliocentric theory 2,000 years before Copernicus; does that lessen the latter's claim to fame? Cattell and Copernicus worked out in detail the consequences of the creative intuition; does that make their work appear in the context of justification? There are many problems, often insoluble, that appear when a categorical distinction is made between the two extremes of convergent and divergent thinking.

Thus far the problem has been dealt with along *taxonomic* lines; perhaps a better understanding of it can be gained if a more *causal* analysis is pursued. Consider a well-known associationist theory of creativity, namely, the theory called by Campbell (1960) the "chance-configuration theory." According to this theory, which has recently been adopted and extended by Simonton (1988), the acquisition of new knowledge, and the solution of novel problems, require some means of producing *variation* by cognition, and it is argued that this variation, to be truly effective, must be fully *blind*. Blindness is defined in terms of variations being correlated to the environmental conditions, including the specific problem, under which the variations are generated (Campbell, 1974). As for the generality of these variations, Simonton preferred the adjective *chance*. (This theory, or something like it, was originally offered by Poincare, 1908.)

These heterogeneous variations are subjected to a constant selection process to retain only those that exhibit selective fit (i.e., those offering viable solutions to the problem at hand). Finally, the variations that have been selected must be preserved (i.e., there must be a proper retention mechanism) so that a successful variation can represent a permanent contribution to adaptive fitness. Thus, this manipulation of mental elements by a process of blind chance, issuing in a selection for problem-solving fitness, leads to configuration formation (i.e., stable permutations hanging together in a stable arrangement or patterned whole of interrelated parts). This very brief description fails to do justice to the extended discussion given by the authors of this theory, but it must suffice here.

A similar theory was developed independently and around the same time by Furneaux (1960). He postulated that the brain structure of any individual, P, includes a set of p^N neural elements that participate in problem-solving activities. The solution of a particular problem, h, of difficulty D, involves bringing into association a particular set, $D^N h$, of these elements; interconnected in some precise order. When problem h is first presented, single elements are first selected, at random, from the total pool p^N and examined to see whether any one of them, alone, constitutes the required solution. A device is postulated that carries out this examination—it must bring together the neural representation of the perceptual material embodying the problem, the rules according to which the problem has to be solved, and the particular organization of elements whose validity as a solution has to be examined. It must give rise to some sort of signal, which in the case of an acceptable organization will terminate the search process and will initiate the translation of the accepted neural organization into the activity that specifies the solution in behavioral terms. Alternatively, if the organization under examination proves to be unacceptable a signal must result that will lead to the continuation of the search process. This hypothetical device Furneaux called the *comparator*.

Furneaux went on to say that if $D = 1$, the comparator will reject each of the p^N trial solutions involving only a single element, and the search will then start for a pair of elements, which, when correctly interconnected, might constitute a valid solution. If $D = r$, then the comparator will reject in turn all the organizations involving from 1 to $(r - 1)$ elements. Speed of mental processing (i.e., time to solution) is an essential element of the theory, and Furneaux postulated that there will be a Time $T \sum_{r-1}^{1} E$ sec within which a solution cannot occur, where T = the time required for completing a single elementary operation within the search process, and $\sum_{r-1}^{1} E$ is the number of elementary operations involved in the search process up to the level of complexity $(r - 1)$. Similarly, after a time $T \sum_{r}^{1} E$ sec all possible organizations embodying r elements will have been examined, so that correct solutions to problems of difficulty r will always arise, within the period defined by the two limiting times $T \sum_{r-1}^{1} E$ and $T \sum_{r}^{1} E$. Extensions of the theory, possible objections, and empirical proof are dealt with in the original chapter. Critical discussions are found in Eysenck (1982, 1987, 1988, 1993), and an experimental test of the theory in Frearson, Eysenck, and Barrett (1990).

The similarities between the two theories are obvious. Both postulate a random-chance search process, leading to an organization-configuration that satisfies a comparator-selector. The major difference is that Furneaux dealt with intelligence, Campbell and Simonton with creativity! Thus, identical processes are postulated for intelligence and creativity, for convergent and divergent thinking. This surely suggests some degree of identity, or at least congruity. Many other psychologists (e.g., Newell, Shaw, & Simon, 1962) argued against any categorical separation, and we may hope to discover causal features in common to both.

The Problems of "Random Search"

Intuitively, the notion of chance-random-trial-and-error search does not dovetail well with the experience of reasoning and problem solving; what is characteristic of the process is the adoption of *heuristics* and strategies. As Newell et al. (1962) stated:

> We have seen that the success of a problem-solver who is confronted with a complex task rests primarily on his ability to select—correctly—a very small part of the total problem-solving maze for exploration. The processes that carry out this selection we call "heuristics." (p. 96)

The employment of heuristics and the strategies built thereon is found in both human and computer problem solvers, and, while retaining elements of random search, uses heuristic search techniques such as "recoding" (Miller, 1956) to simplify the choice and availability of elements from which to build a solution.

Blind search, as suggested by Campbell and Furneaux, is ruled out because it leads to a combinatorial explosion (Newell et al., 1962). A good example is choosing a move in chess. On the average, a chess player has a choice of 20 to 30 alternatives; these can be evaluated by considering the opponent's possible replies, one's own replies to his or hers, and so on. The tree of move sequences is tremendously large; considering just 5 move sequences for each player, with an average of 25 legal continuations at each stage, the set of such moves has above 10^{14} (100 million million) members. No wonder simple power-crunching computer chess players never did well, and were outclassed by machines using heuristic processes, strategies, and memory recall—just like humans!

Given this essential restriction of blind search to a not-so-blind search governed by heuristic guidelines, the Campbell-Furneaux model, particularly in the more testable form given by Furneaux (see Frearson et al, 1990), gives a good idea of the form such a model should take. But we are still confronted by the curious fact that similar models are labeled *creativity* in the one case, *intelligence* in the other. Can we discriminate theoretically and empirically between these two concepts?

THE ASSOCIATIONIST THEORY OF CREATIVITY

The answer to this query may be found in the theory put forward by Mednick (1962). All cognitive work, according to this theory, is done essentially by combining or associating ideas. Using the phrase *association test* as an example, Mednick argued that when a given word is used as a response to the first word that occurs to the tester, the response can be very close to the stimulus word (table-chair), or more remote (table-plate), or quite remote (table-shark). The remoteness of associated ideas is a characteristic of a given individual, and one may thus speak of the steepness of the *associative gradient*. The steeper the gradient, the more commonplace the resulting associations; the shallower the gradient, the more original, unusual, out-of-the-way the resulting association. Mednick also suggested that creativity is a function of the steepness of the associative gradient—the steeper the gradient, the more rigid, routine, ordinary the resulting thought process. The creative person has a shallow gradient, unusual responses, and abnormal reactions.

This theory has been very successful. Measures of the steepness of the gradient are reliable, and have been found to correlate quite significantly with independent estimates of the subjects' creativity (Eysenck, 1994b). The model requires one additional element, namely the size of the associationist pool. One can only produce associations that are already present in the subject's repertoire. Thus, Bousfield and Sedgwick (1944) found that in fluency tests (i.e., essentially multiple association tests) curves of output could be described by an exponential equation by an exponential equation: $n = C(1 - e^{-mt})$, where N is the number of associations produced up to a given time, t; C is the upper limit that the curve approaches asymptotically, presumably identifiable with the total supply of the kind of words called for by the instructions, while m is the rate of depletion of the supply of words, and e is the base of the natural logarithms. Applying this principle to an historical act of creativity, Darwin brought together the notion of diversity of offspring with that of Matthusian overproduction of offspring to produce the theory of evolution. This occurred after he had read Matthus; had he been ignorant of that work, he clearly could not have formed that association.

We are now somewhat nearer to a solution to our problem. The continuum we have postulated to exist between convergent and divergent thinking refers to the relative steepness of the associative gradient. Convergent thinking can proceed with the use of a steep associative gradient, because the class of relevant associations is already implicit in the statement of the problem. The more divergent the problem, the less clearly specified is the class of relevant associations. In science, it is often the very selection of the problem that is the most difficult part; and the most creative; this implies an almost complete absence of specification of the nature of the relevant associations. But this clearly constitutes a continuum; we are not dealing with a dichotomy, and the nature of the continuum is defined by the shape of the associative gradient. This, in turn, raises the all-important question of what determines the steepness of the associative gradient? I proceed to outline the answer I have suggested to this question (Eysenck, 1993, 1994a, 1994b).

CAUSES OF CREATIVITY

The way to answer to this question may be indicated by the fact that genius and creativity seem to be firmly connected with madness and psychopathology (Prentky, 1980; Richards, 1981, 1990). This well-established fact gives rise to a paradox; psychopathology is very apparent in creative people, but actual psychosis, particularly schizophrenia, has been found to suppress creativity, if anything. The answer, I suggest, lies in the postulation of a factor of *psychoticism* (Eysenck, 1992; Eysenck & Eysenck, 1976). This P factor is conceived of as a dispositional variable predisposing a person to psychotic illness if subjected to sufficient stress, and containing a combination of personality traits related to typical psychotic and pre-psychotic personalities. Figure 4.1 shows the concept in some detail, with P constituting the abscissa. P_A shows the increasing probability of a person having a psychotic breakdown as the P score increases. This general view gains credence from the fact that several researchers have produced evidence to show that nonpsychotic people in the schizophrenic *Erbkreis* are usually found to have high creativity (Eysenck, 1983).

This hypothesis can be tested by correlating P with scores on tests of creativity (divergent thinking), word association (unusual responses), Barron Welsh Art Scale (preference for complexity), and with real-life creativity in the arts; many such studies have given very positive results (Eysenck, 1993, 1994b; Goetz & Goetz, 1979a, 1979b). This leads to a search for an answer to the question: "What is it that links psychopathology and creativity?" The obvious answer, of course, is that cognitive behavior in both is characterized by a shallow associative gradient. Can we go beyond this descriptive answer and suggest a *causal* one? This is made possible by recent advances in the development of a general theory of schizophrenia that may throw light on the matter. It may be useful to start with a well-established theory, namely Cameron's notion of "overinclusion" (Cameron, 1947; Cameron & Margaret, 1950). Cameron believed that schizophrenics' concepts are overgeneralized. Schizophrenics are unable to maintain the normal conceptual boundaries, and incorporate into their concepts elements, some of them personal, which are merely associated with the concept, but are not an essential part of it. Cameron used the term *overinclusion* to describe this abnormality, and reported that in working on the Vygotsky test and a sentence-completion test, schizophrenics were unable to preserve the "conceptual boundaries" of the test. In solving a problem, the schizophrenic "included such a variety of categories at one time, that the specific problems became too extensive and too complex for a solution to be reached" (Cameron, 1938, p. 269). A fair number of experiments have been carried out to investigate this theory. These have been reviewed elsewhere (Payne, 1960; Payne, Matusek, & George, 1959).

Altruistic

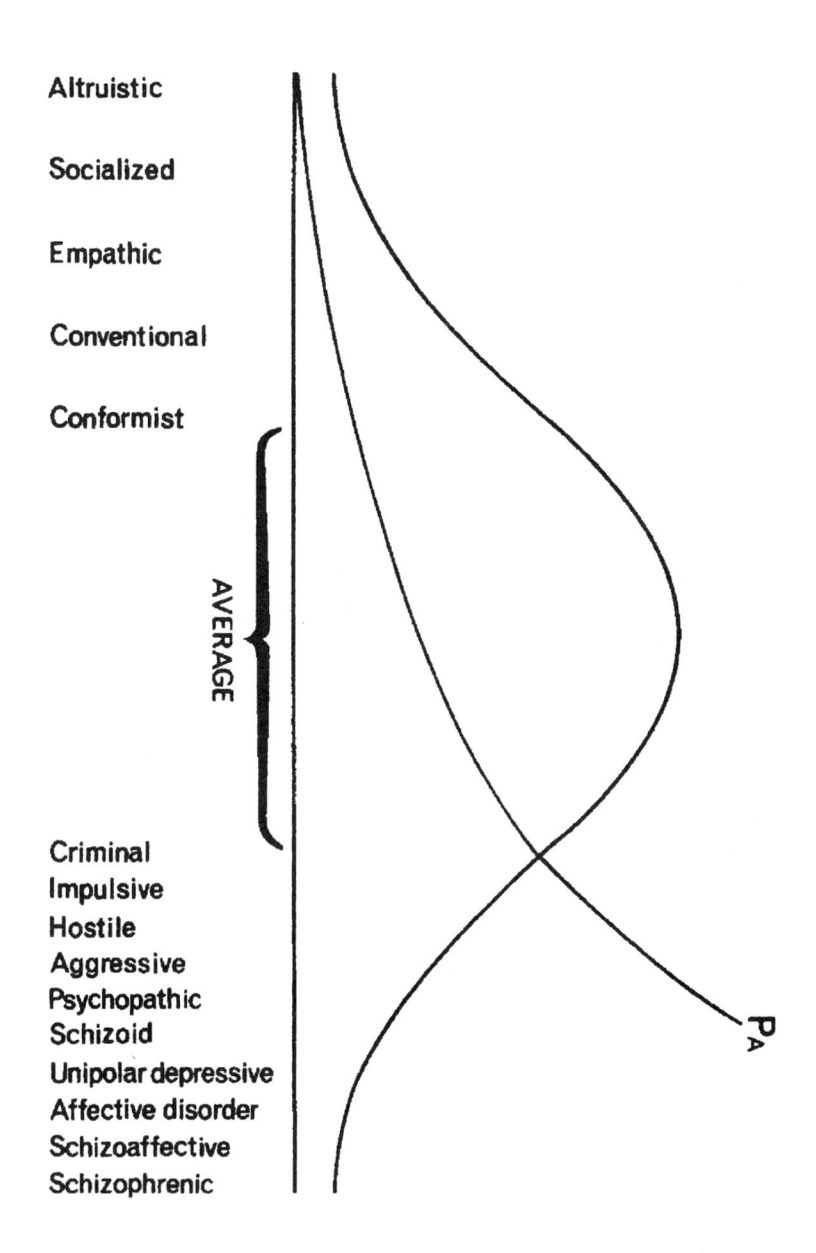

Socialized

Empathic

Conventional

Conformist

} AVERAGE

Criminal
Impulsive
Hostile
Aggressive
Psychopathic
Schizoid
Unipolar depressive
Affective disorder
Schizoaffective
Schizophrenic

P_A

Figure 4.1. Diagrammatic representation of the *psychoticism* continuum (abscissa). P_A denotes the probability or a person having a given score on psychoticism developing a genuine functional psychosis (Eysenck, 1994b)

Payne et al. (1959) suggested that it is possible to reformulate Cameron's theory of overinclusion in a slightly more general way so that a number of predictions follow from it. Concept formation can be regarded as largely the result of discrimination learning. When a child first hears a word in a certain context, the word is associated with the entire situation (stimulus compound). As the word is heard repeatedly, only certain aspects of the stimulus compound are reinforced. Gradually, the extraneous elements cease to evoke the response (the word), having become "inhibited" through lack of "reinforcement." The inhibition is in some sense an active process, as it suppresses a response that was formerly evoked by the stimulus. Overinclusive thinking may be the result of a disorder (failure) of the process whereby inhibition is built up to circumscribe and define the learned response (the word or concept). In short, it could be an extreme degree of stimulus generalization.

The same theory can be expressed in different terms. For its success, all purposeful behavior depends on the fact that some stimuli are attended to and some others are ignored. It is a well-known fact that when concentrating on one task, people usually are quite unaware of most stimuli irrelevant to the task. It is as if some filter mechanism cuts out or inhibits the stimuli, both internal and external, which are irrelevant to the task at hand, to allow the most efficient processing of incoming information. Overinclusive thinking might be the only aspect of a general breakdown of this filter mechanism.

A similar concept to overinclusion is that of *allusive thinking*, characteristic of many schizophrenics on object-sorting tests. McConaghy and Clancy (1968) demonstrated that this type of thinking existed widely in less exaggerated forms in the normal population, showed similar familial transmission in schizophrenics and nonschizophrenics, and was akin to creative thinking. Dykes and McGhie (1976) actually demonstrated that highly creative normals scored as highly allusive on the Lovibond object-sorting test, as did schizophrenics. The low creative normals tended to produce conventional, unoriginal sortings, whereas the highly creative normals and the schizophrenics tended to give an equal proportion of unusual sortings. "This supports strongly that a common thinking style may lead to a controlled usefulness in normals and an uncontrollable impairment in schizophrenics" (Woody & Claridge, 1977, p. 247).

What *measurable* agency can cause this cognitive inhibition that in normal people prevents loose, allusive overinclusiveness, and fails to do so in schizophrenics? A major candidate for the job is *latent inhibition* (LI; Lubow, 1989).

LI is defined by an experimental paradigm that requires, as a minimum, a two-stage procedure. The first stage involves stimulus *pre-exposure*; the to-be conditioned stimulus (CS) is exhibited without being followed by any unconditioned stimulus (UCS); this leads theoretically to the CS acquiring a negative salience; it signals a lack of consequences, and thus acquires inhibitory properties. The second stage, *acquisition,* has the CS being followed by an UCS, and it acquires the property of initiating the UC response (UCR). LI is shown by increasing difficulties of acquiring this property, as compared with lack of pre-exposure. With humans, there is a masking task during pre-exposure to the CS. For instance, the masking task might be the presentation of a series of syllable pairs orally, whereas the CS would be a white noise randomly superimposed on the syllable reproduction. The control group would be exposed only to the syllable pairs, without the white noise. In the test phase, the white noise is reinforced, and subjects given scores according to how soon they discover the rule linking CS with reinforcement. LI would be indicated by the group having the pre-exposure of the white noise discovering the rule later than the control group.

There are more complex, three-stage procedures (Lubow, 1989), but these complications are not crucial to the argument here. Clearly, the LI phenomenon involves cognitive elements; these are emphasized by Lubow (1989) in terms of his conditioned attention theory. According to this theory, nonreinforced pre-exposure to a stimulus retards subsequent conditioning to that stimulus because during such pre-exposure the subject learns not to attend to it. The theory is based on the use of attention as a hypothetical construct, with the properties of a Pavlovian response, and on the specification of reinforcement conditions that modify attention.

Does LI correlate negatively, as it should, with P? Several studies have shown that it does; high P scorers show little if any LI, whereas low P scorers show considerable LI. This may be taken even further. Theories of schizophrenia prominently involve *dopamine* (Gray, Feldon, Rawlins, Hemsley, & Smith, 1991); does P show a similar correlation? Gray, Pickering, and Gray (in press) have indeed found a substantial relationship of this kind, suggesting a causal sequence, rather like this:

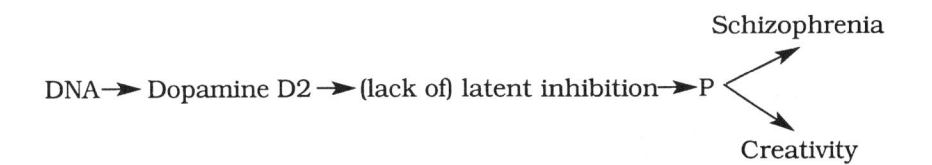

DNA➤ Dopamine D2 ➤ (lack of) latent inhibition➤P ⟨ Schizophrenia / Creativity

The alternatives implied by the two arrows at the right may be decided by the amount of stress experienced, quantitative differences in dopamine activity, or the presence of such positive personality factors as high ego strength (Barron & Harrington, 1981). There is, of course, still ample room for further research to determine answers to questions left open by this schematic design. I have only tried here to indicate the lines along which future clarification and development might proceed.

CONCLUSION

The evidence reviewed here suggests that the habit of discussing creativity in science in categorical terms—normal versus revolutionary science, context and discovery versus context of justification, convergent versus divergent tests—has little justification. Normal science is punctuated by minor revolutions, revolutions use methods of normal science to establish their novel conclusions. Einstein's revolution was adumbrated by Poincare, Lorentz, and others; it did not come out of the blue, but was a (major) step in a long continued development. Discovery is always linked with justification, and justification requires some degree of discovery in guiding the steps necessary to fulfill its function. Convergent tests, like divergent tests, require multiple associations of ideas; the two differ only in that in the one case only one of these is required and accepted, whereas in the other all are accepted. But the cognitive processes may not be entirely dissimilar. Psychologists making up convergent test items often find, to their dismay, that these are in fact divergent. Take an example:

> Which is the odd man out: Ankara   Berlin   Copenhagen
> Dachau   Moscow ?

The intention was to single out Moscow, as breaking the A-B-C-D sequence of initial letters. But some respondents answered *Dachau,* the only town not a capital. Others yet said *Copenhagen,* the only town not having six letters. Others again favored *Ankara,* the only town outside Europe. Clearly this *convergent* test may just as well be considered a *divergent* one.

    The major difference in all of these categorically separated concept pairs appears to lie in the steepness of the associate gradient characteristic of the individual, itself determined by his or her degree of LI which in turn is dependent on his or her level of dopamine. This clearly is a continuum; levels of dopamine, or degrees of LI, are not discontinuous in their distribution. Looking at extremes (e.g., Hardy-Ramanujan) may give the impression of discontinuity, but this is clearly a fallacy. Divergent tests may be more clearly designed to measure degrees of creativity-LI-dopamine, but they do not measure different cognitive mechanisms as compared with convergent tests. Both are concerned with associative processes, they differ in which aspects of these they concentrate on measuring. The major difference between the two concepts may lie on the personality side, but perhaps involve some pleiotropic genetic effect. It may be that the reception of true creativity by the mediocre majority is usually such that only a high-P personality can survive (Eysenck, 1994b). However that may be, it seems certain that future research into creativity must cease to be restricted to *correlational* methods and attempt to use *causal* models and analyses.

The concern I feel about the habit of contrasting convergent and divergent thinking as if they were categorically differentiated can be illustrated by reference to the origins of my own theory of creativity (Eysenck, 1994a). Can this be considered original? Looking simply at the references in the most recent *Handbook of Creativity* (Glover et al., 1989), and comparing them with my own book, there is much less overlap than one might have anticipated; there is no mention in the handbook of latent inhibition, negative priming, dopamine, psychoticism, eye-tracking, H2A B27, dichotic shadowing, backward masking, platelet monoamine oxydase, Kamin blocking, overinclusiveness, and many others. My theory follows traditional definitions of creativity by "bringing together" two sets of association hitherto kept separate—creativity and schizophrenia. Yet referring back to the Bousfield and Sedgwick (1944) formula, this "bisociation" was due to C rather than m, that is, to the store of knowledge rather than the rate of depletion of the store of ideas. As it happens, I had been a student of Spearman and of Burt, and hence familiar with the early work on fluency and creativity, as well as intelligence in general. I had also been given the task of introducing clinical psychology as a profession into Great Britain (Eysenck, 1990), and much of the work on the cognitive behavior of schizophrenia was done in my department, or by former students and colleagues (Frith, Gray, Claridge, Slade, Hemsley, Payne, Venables, and many others). Thus, the knowledge base (C), indispensable for effecting the bisociation, happened to be proved by accident, and required little m; indeed, lacking C, m could not have produced the combination. There is no obvious divergent thinking; given the fundaments, the conclusion is inevitable. It is the traditional *specialization* of knowledge in psychology that has kept the obvious association of these two fields of knowledge from becoming apparent. The emphasis on intuition and creativity as aspects of divergent thinking has tended to suppress the importance of a large knowledge base, and the associated convergent type of thinking.

REFERENCES

Barron, F., & Harrington, D. M. (1981). Creativity, intelligence, and personality. *Annual Review of Psychology, 32,* 439-476.
Bell, E. T. (1939). *Men of mathematics.* London: Camelot Press.
Bollobas, B. (1988, June). Ramanujan: A glimpse of his life and his mathematics. *Cambridge Review,* 76–80.
Bousfield, W., & Sedgwick, C. (1944). An analysis of sequences of restricted associative responses. *Journal of Genetic Psychology, 30,* 149-165.
Brock, W. H. (1967). *The atomic debate.* Leicester: Leicester University Press.
Cameron, N. (1938). Reasoning, repression, and communication in schizophrenics. *Psychological Monographs, 50,* 1-33.
Cameron, N. (1947). *The psychology of behaviour disorder.* Boston: Houghton Mifflin.
Cameron, N., & Margaret, A. (1950). Experimental studies in thinking: I. Scattered speech in the responses of normal subjects to incomplete sentences. *Journal of Experimental Psychology, 39,* 617-627.
Campbell, D. T. (1960). Blind variation and selective retention in creative thought as in other knowledge processes. *Psychological Review, 67,* 380-400.
Campbell, D.T. (1974). Unjustified variation and selective retention in scientific discovery. In F. J. Ayala & T. Dobzhansky (Eds.), *Studies in the philosophy of biology* (pp. 131-149). London: Macmillan.
Carroll, J. B. (1993). *Human cognitive abilities.* Cambridge: Cambridge University Press.
Dykes, M., & McGhie, A. (1976). A comparative study of attentional strategies of schizophrenia and highly normal subjects. *British Journal of Psychiatry, 128,* 50-56.
Eysenck, H. J. (1982). The roots of creativity: Cognitive ability or personality trait? *Roeper Review, 5,* 10-12.
Eysenck, H. J. (1983). Cicero and the state-trait theory of anxiety: Another case of delayed recognition. *American Psychologist, 38,* 114-115.
Eysenck, H. J. (1987). Personality and aging: An exploratory analysis. *Journal of Social Behavioral Psychology, 3,* 11-12.
Eysenck, H. J. (1988). The biological basis of intelligence. In S. H. Irvine & J. W. Berry (Eds.), *Human abilities in a cultural context* (pp. 87-104). New York: Cambridge University Press.
Eysenck, H. J. (1990). *Rebel with a cause.* London: W.H. Allen.
Eysenck, H. J. (1992). The definition and measurement of psychoticism. *Personality and Individual Differences, 13,* 757-785.

Eysenck, H. J. (1993). Creativity and personality: Suggestion for a theory. *Psychological Inquiry, 4,* 147-178.
Eysenck, H. J. (1994a). *Genius—The natural history of creativity.* Cambridge: Cambridge University Press.
Eysenck, H. J. (1994b). The measurement of creativity. In M. Boden (Ed.), *Dimensions of creativity* (pp. 199-242). London: MIT Press.
Eysenck, H. J., & Eysenck, S. B. G. (1976). *Psychoticism as a dimension of personality.* London: Hodder & Stoughton.
Frearson, W., Eysenck, H. J., & Barrett, P. T. (1990). The Furneaux model of human problem-solving: Its relationship to reaction time and intelligence. *Personality and Individual Differences, 11,* 239-257.
Furneaux, W. D. (1960). Intellectual abilities and problem-solving behaviour. In H. J. Eysenck (Ed.), *Handbook of abnormal psychology* (pp. 167-192). London: Pitman.
Glover, J. A., Ronning, R. R., & Reynolds, C. R. (Eds.). (1989). *Handbook of creativity.* New York: Plenum Press.
Goetz, K. O., & Goetz, K. (1979a). Personality characteristics of professional artists. *Perceptual and Motor Skills, 49,* 327-334.
Goetz, K. O., & Goetz, K. (1979b). Personality characteristics of successful artists. *Perceptual and Motor Skills, 49,* 919-924.
Gray, J. A., Feldon, J., Rawlins, J. P., Hemsley, D. R., & Smith, A. D. (1991). The neuropsychology of schizophrenia. *Behavioural and Brain Sciences, 14,* 1-84.
Gray, N., Pickering, A., & Gray, J. (in press). Psychoticism and dopamine D2 binding in the basal ganglia using single photon emission tomography. *Personality and Individual Differences.*
Hardy, G. H. (1940). *Ramanujan.* London: Cambridge University Press.
Kac, M. (1985). *Enigmas of chance.* New York: Harper & Row.
Kanigel, R. (1991). *The man who knew infinity: A life of the genius Ramanujan.* New York: Charles Scribner.
Knight, D. (1967). *Atoms and elements: A study of theories of matter in England in the nineteenth century.* London: Hutchinson.
Kuhn, T. S. (1957). *The Copernican revolution.* Cambridge, MA: Harvard University Press.
Kuhn, T. S. (1970). *The structure of scientific revolutions.* Chicago: University of Chicago Press.
Lubow, R. E. (1989). *Latent inhibition and condition of attention theory.* New York: Cambridge University Press.
Masterman, M. (1970). The nature of a paradigm. In I. Lakatos & S. Musgrave (Eds.), *Criticism of the growth of knowledge* (pp. 59-90). New York: Cambridge University Press.
McConaghy, W., & Clancy, M. (1968). Familial relationships of allusive thinking in university students and their parents. *British Journal of Psychiatry, 114,* 1079-1087.

McGucken, W. (1969). *Nineteenth century spectroscopy: Development of the understanding of spectra.* Baltimore, MD: Johns Hopkins University Press.

Mednick, S. A. (1962). The associative basis of the creative process. *Psychological Review, 69,* 220-232.

Miller, G. A. (1956). The magical number seven, plus or minus two: Some limits on our capacity for processing information. *Psychological Review, 63,* 81-97.

Milton, R. (1994). *Forbidden science.* London: Fourth Estate.

Mordell, L. J. (1941). Ramanujan. *Nature,* 1-18, 642-647.

Newell, A., Shaw, J. C., & Simon, H. A. (1962). The processes of creative thinking. In H. E. Gruber, G. Terrell, & M. Wertheimer (Eds.), *Contemporary approaches to creative thinking* (pp. 63-119). New York: Atherton Press.

Payne, R. W. (1960). Cognitive abnormalities. In H. J. Eysenck (Ed.), *Handbook of abnormal psychology.* London: Pitman.

Payne, R. W., Matusek, P., & George, E. I. (1959). An experimental study of schizophrenic thought disorder. *Journal of Mental Science, 105,* 627-652.

Poincare, H. (1908). *Science et methode* [Science and method]. Paris: Ernest Flaumarion.

Prentky, R. A. (1980). *Creativity and psychopathology: A neurocognitive perspective.* New York: Praeger.

Richards, R. L. (1981). Relationships between creativity and psychopathology: An evaluation and interpretation of the evidence. *Genetic Psychology Monographs, 103,* 261-324.

Richards, R. (1990). Everyday creativity, eminent creativity, and health: "Afterview" for CRJ special issues on creativity and health. *Creativity Research Journal, 3,* 300-326.

Schaffer, S. (1994). Making up discovery. In M. Boden (Ed.), *Dimensions of creativity* (pp. 13-52). London: The MIT Press.

Simonton, K. (1988). *Scientific genius.* New York: Cambridge University Press.

Spearman, L. (1923). *The nature of "intelligence" and the principles of cognition.* London: Macmillan.

Spearman, C. (1927). *The abilities of man.* London: Macmillan.

Woody, E., & Claridge, G. (1977). Psychoticism and thinking. *British Journal of Social and Clinical Psychology, 16,* 241-248.

5

CREATIVE INTERACTION: A CONCEPTUAL SCHEMA FOR THE PROCESS OF PRODUCING IDEAS AND JUDGING THE OUTCOMES

Edward Nęcka
Jagiellonian University

Evaluation and judgment undoubtedly constitute vital components of creativity because any creative output must meet the criteria of novelty and usefulness, or, to put it another way, the criteria of originality and appropriateness. In fact, the evaluative skills relevant to creativity may be viewed in several perspectives (Runco & Chand, 1994). First, there is a metacognitive factor, referring to the decision of whether the problem or topic is worth undertaking, and which mental operations may be appropriate to deal with it. Then, the novelty and usefulness of ideas produced by the creator must be examined, either by the creator him or herself or by the external critics. Here, the distinction between intrapersonal and interpersonal judgment holds. Finally, creative ideas usually need some elaboration, constructive criticism, and appreciation. This means that they should not only be evaluated but also "valuated" (Chand & Runco, 1992), and in particular improved and ameliorated before they are eventually accepted. Yet, evaluative skills and processes are not as widely recognized in the creativity literature as are divergent, or productive, skills and processes. Why is this so?

There are probably two main causes for this neglect. First, critical thinking skills seem less "exotic" than creative processes (Perkins, 1981). Criticism and judgment are skills that are commonly used and relatively well developed within the Western culture, whereas the production of ideas is perceived as something unusual, uncommon, and difficult. This implicit assumption may lead researchers to put more stress on functions that seem extraordinary, and therefore worth investigating. Second, the criteria of evaluation and judgment are highly domain-specific, particularly in reference to the appropriateness of the output. It happens that only few persons are competent enough to make a judgment. Consequently, it is not an easy task to carry out research on evaluation of the creative ideas, even though the consensual assessment technique is adopted.

In this chapter, I sketch a new conceptual schema for creative processes. Although the schema employs the notion of *interaction*, it has no specific connection to the so-called "interactionist" models of creativity (Amabile, 1983a, 1983b; Csikszentmihalyi, 1990; Necka, 1986; Simonton, 1988; Sternberg, 1988; Sternberg & Lubart, 1991; Urban, 1994). Here, the key notion of *interaction* applies to the inner processes of creative thought not to the confluence of a number of environmental, societal, motivational, and cognitive processes that—according to the interactional models—determine the emergence of the creative output. This does not mean that I neglect the importance of factors that transcend the mind of an individual creator. Neither do I ignore the fact that creativity is a multifactor phenomenon. I assume, however, that the creative idea is initially born and preliminarily judged within the boundaries outlined by the individual creator's mind. Even though many important factors contribute interactively to the final outcome, the act of creation will always be a private event. This assumption holds, in my opinion, both to the production of ideas and to their judgment, and any plausible theory of the creative process has to take it into account.

Before I sketch the interactionist schema for creative processes, I show the inappropriateness of the competing schema, the one that draws on the negative feedback paradigm. Next, the new conceptualization is presented, along with arguments concerning its suitability to account for creative processes. The chapter ends with suggestions of how the interactionist paradigm can be applied in order to describe and understand the role of critical thinking in creativity.

CREATIVE PROCESS AS A NEGATIVE FEEDBACK LOOP

Assuming that creative behavior is purposive in nature because it is directed to some differentiated states possessing the features of novelty and value, the temptation exists to apply the negative feedback paradigm to capture the essence of creativity. Specifically, the Test-Operate-Test-Exit (TOTE) schema (Miller, Galanter, & Pribram, 1960) should be applicable: In an attempt to hit a nail with the hammer, for instance, one must first check the position of the nail as well as the position of the hammer being held (test), then hit the nail with the hammer (operate), then check again (test), and finish, if the nail is in the proper position, or repeat the whole action, if it is not (exit). However, even the shallow attempt to compare hitting a nail with creative action shows that the negative feedback loop paradigm has important limitations.

First, any purposive behavior can start with the first check operation only if the goal is clearly stated. Otherwise, the checking phase is hard to perform because it relies on the comparison of the goal's parameters with the actual state of affairs. If the parameters are fuzzy, a comparison, if possible, is a matter of chance and guessing. And it is rarely the case in the field of creativity that a goal is clearly stated at the very beginning. Rather, it must be found, stated, and restated before one starts to pursue it according to the feedback principle (cf. Getzels & Csikszentmihalyi, 1975; Mackworth, 1965). While hitting a nail, an individual knows very clearly what he or she wants to do, whereas while writing a poem the individual often does not have much more than a vague idea of what a poem should be like. The same is true in the case of creating a new theory about which all that is known is that it should explain an aspect of reality in a sound, parsimonious, and testable way. Even in those specific cases where the goal is known and understood from the very beginning, as, for instance, when some commonly known scientific or technological problems are at issue, the need to restate a problem in a new way appears very often as soon as one begins to solve it. The vagueness of judgment criteria affects the second check operation as well, with the effect that one often makes premature evaluations concerning the question of whether the process has brought about any output complying with a goal's parameters. Metaphorically, it happens to be very difficult to check whether a nail is already hit or not.

Second, a goal in the creative process is by no means stable once stated, and even once restated. Rather, it evolves in the course of the process itself and, what is particularly important, due to the emerging outcomes of this process. Applying this principle to the nail-hitting example, it could be paradoxically stated that, if this activity were genuinely creative, it might appear that the goal is to make a hook of the nail instead of to hit it with the hammer. It seems as if the effects of goal-oriented behavior affected the goal itself and made it change to a great extent. If, when finished, a poem, a book, a theory—whatever—does not resemble its tentative sketch because the subsequently appearing ideas have forced on it a substantial change, this is the phenomenon to which I am referring. This is not to say that such a phenomenon must occur, but its probability seems to be so high that a model should treat it as a matter of principle rather than as an exception.

Third, the executive part of the TOTE loop, that is the operate component, is rarely available in its finite form from the beginning of a creative process. Rather, one must seek it and, if found, adapt it to the goal's requirements. Hitting a nail is a standard task for which there are well-learned performance habits. In creativity, habits, even though not useless altogether, are often not satisfactory, so one must work out essentially new ways of achieving a goal. It amounts to finding ways in which ideas, sculptures, paintings, technological appliances—whatever is necessary to fulfill a goal's requirements—are to be found. Moreover, even when found, they often need transformation and further elaboration, as they are unlikely to be accurate at the very moment they are found. This point of view complies with a classical definition of a problem situation as the one in which a solver does not know how to achieve a desired state of affairs (Duncker, 1945), although one should bear in mind that creativity is scarcely reducible to a problem-solving paradigm.

Indeed, the TOTE paradigm does not seem to model creative processes accurately unless one adds additional subloops for finding, stating, and restating a goal, as well as for the seeking operations (i.e., for generating ways in which a goal is to be achieved). But even though this could be done, the other two problems (i.e., vagueness of final judgment criteria and changes occurring in the goal itself) still remain. In particular, this paradigm is useless in accounting for a goal's changes. The reason is that the very nature of a negative feedback loop is to monitor the behavior of a system so that the final outcome exactly complies with some predetermined state of affairs. The hormonal system, for instance, cannot allow the level of insulin in the blood to be changed too much; the task of numerous feedback loops is to keep this level within thresholds predetermined by human physiology. In other words, a typical negative feedback loop, although purposive in nature, prevents changes instead of allowing them. The very purpose of a system behaving according to such a loop is to preserve the status quo despite adversities. This kind of paradigm is not applicable enough to an activity that may bring about outcomes that are completely different from those for which it was originally taken up.

What kind of schema would be more applicable to creativity, then? The traditional phase paradigm—preparation, ideation, illumination, verification—as hypothesized by Wallas (1926), Patrick (1937, 1938), and many others in some variations, is not better in this respect, if not worse because of its linearity. In other words, it does not stress the crucial fact of the creative processes' purposive nature. In the feedback paradigm, at least, a goal is imagined as controlling the process of ideation so that its outcome may fulfill a plan, whereas in the linear schema, a goal, once stated, does not participate in the subsequent phases because an idea is hypothesized as being judged in respect to its own value rather than to its fulfilling the goal's requirements. The competing circular model, as developed by Koberg and Bagnall (1976), that is, the repetition of the whole process due to the linkage between the verification stage and the new preparatory stage, amounts to pursuing a new goal after having accomplished the first one, instead of continually changing the same goal due to the properties of the emerging ideas. So, a new general schema is needed that would be able to account for the circumstances mentioned above. This new paradigm can be called *creative interaction*.

THE NATURE OF CREATIVE INTERACTION

Interaction is a process of continually and mutually affecting each other. The partners in interaction, with regard to creative processes, are (a) imagined and planned poems, symphonies, theories, inventions, ways of nursing infants or of dealing with stress—anything that someone wishes to achieve in a new and valuable way, and that will be called a *goal*; (b) ideas and voluntary movements (as in dancing, sculpting, playing the piano, and so on, but also in "regular" creative thinking if supported by manipulations and overt behavior) that people produce in response to the goal's requirements, and that will be called *tentative structures*. That a goal affects its tentative proposals is an obvious statement: Their very nature resides in fulfilling its needs, so they are sought as long as necessary and corrected as much as it is needed. Specifically, possible changes in a tentative amount to making it more valuable (e.g., more feasible, aesthetic, broad in scope) or more unusual (i.e., possessing a feature of novelty as compared to previously existed suggestions, if any). These two categories of change refer to the two definitional criteria of a creative outcome—value and novelty. The idea of tentative structures affecting their goal, on the other hand, requires deeper examination as it is by no means self-evident. We must state what kind of change a tentative structure may impose on a goal.

First of all, a tentative structure seems to be able to make a goal emerge. One may take up a creative activity not necessarily in response to a goal's requirements but prior to a goal's very existence. A pianist may begin to improvise tentatively at the keyboard without having any specific idea of what he or she wants to compose. Likewise, the first sketch of a drawing, or a single striking metaphor, may serve as the core of a future painting or of a would-be poem, respectively, although no specific idea of what the painting or the poem should be like yet exists. In such cases, a goal either does not exist before an action is taken up or it amounts to a vague wish to paint or to write something. The first tentative structure—a chord, a sketch, or a metaphor—serves here as a core around which a future goal, as well as its more elaborated tentative structures, crystallize. Or, the first tentative structure serves as a means by which the process is put into action and, as such, it need even not be present in the final outcome. Anyway, it need not be a goal that switches on the creative process. Rather, the process may be initiated itself and made emerge due to the first tentative structure being suggested.

Second, a tentative structure may make a goal either more precise or less precise. The first case is quite clear: Emerging tentative structures are likely to point out gaps and shortcomings in a goal as previously stated and thus facilitate its further elaboration toward greater consistency and precision. The second case is not so clear, although much more interesting. Imagine that a goal that is quite clearly stated cannot be satisfied by means of any appearing tentative structures, the latter being but faint and inadequate reflections of what a creator wishes to gain. The creator has at least two options here: to either put more precision on the goal's parameters (which reduces to the previous case) or to realize that some of these parameters are not necessary or even harmful because they channel his or her thought too much and thus deprive him or her of free speculation and imagining. The second option may incline the creator to make a goal less precise or to take away some of its parameters in order to make it perhaps more vague but easier to pursue and more likely to be achieved (cf. Kocowski, 1982). If it is very difficult to design a new type of bicycle, for instance, it might be much easier to think of some new types of nonmotorized recreational vehicles in general, not necessarily bicycles. Stating a goal in a more general and therefore less precise way is an efficient means to avoid some tacitly employed, although not necessarily sound, presuppositions concerning the nature of a goal. This principle is broadly applied by skillful problem solvers (Adams, 1978; Koberg & Bagnall, 1976). An interactional point of view suggests that it is these emerging tentative structures that make a problem solver deprive a goal of its precision, because of their inadequacy when applied to a goal as previously stated.

Third, a tentative structure may bring a goal into one's consciousness. This is to say that a goal's parameters, even though not stated explicitly at the conscious level of cognition, do happen to exist somehow in a quite precise form under this level. Behaviorally, this phenomenon elicits through one's disappointment concerning the tentative structure, the kind of feeling that implies some specific expectations one shows—without realizing it—toward the idea one seeks. If an author is disappointed about what he or she has written and says that "that's not it," it may be assumed that he or she knows quite well, or perhaps has a sense of, what "it" should be like. Otherwise, there would be no reason to reject the outcome with distaste. Such cases seem to happen quite frequently in the arts, particularly if a goal is of an emotional and subjective nature. An artist thus "knows" what the work should be like because these are his or her own emotional states that are to be expressed by means of a poem or a symphony. However, it is not easy to state such emotional goals in terms of conscious verbalization (Nisbett & Wilson, 1977). It is not until the first tentative structure is suggested, therefore, that disappointment and rejection—the proofs of previously existing parameters—do occur. As a consequence, a creator may realize what he or she is striving for because emerging tentative structures provide him or her with negative information of the kind that "that's not it." This is a very special way in which tentative structures may affect a goal and make it more elaborated at the conscious level.

Fourth, emerging tentative structures may show a goal's general inadequacy or ill-statement. This is not the case of more or less precision given to a goal; rather, a new goal is stated that differs in nature from the previous one, a phenomenon referred to in the problem-solving literature as *restatement* or *redefinition* of a problem at hand. Yet, this phenomenon should not be limited to redefinition, which implies only stating anew the same thing. What actually may take place amounts to taking up a completely new goal, the one that crystallizes during the creative interaction because the already produced tentative structures show the inadequacy of previously existing goals. Again, it is not until some tentative structures show a goal's inconsistency, or unrealistic nature, or futility, or whatever makes it not worth pursuing, that a creator decides to change the previously existing goal to a lesser or greater degree. In other words, it would be very difficult to realize that a goal needs changing without having made the tentative structures that show what is wrong in the statement of the goal. The latter may be assumed as thoroughly consistent and fully elaborated before one starts to pursue it, and only the series of faulty tentative structures makes it clear that an essential change is needed.

Fifth, a creator may abandon a goal because he or she realizes, by means of the tentative structures hitherto produced, that it would require too much time and effort, or too much risk, or would cause too much conflict with a creator's social milieu. This kind of motivation would not be typical to gigantic thinkers and artists of the highest devotion to their work, but less creative and less independent individuals may abandon creativity or take up more mundane tasks. The very special case of abandonment may occur when one realizes that pursuing a goal would bring him or her into conflict with believed values. Johannes Kepler, who allegedly said, "Who I am to violate the divine harmony of the celestial spheres?" provided the best example of such a conflict (although, fortunately, he did not abandon his work on the theory of solar system).

As can be seen, the scope of change that tentative structures may impose on a goal is large enough to call the whole process an interaction. What specifically occurs during creative interaction probably amounts to reducing the discrepancy between the parameters of a goal and those of a tentative structure. At the beginning of a creative process, a goal and a tentative structure—no matter which of them appears first—are not mutually compatible, that is, their parameters differ considerably from each other. They are bound to, by the way, if the process is to be called creative, because only some standard activities, as hitting a nail, for instance, show a great extent of compatibility between goals and means at the beginning of the process. As the process follows, which is a function of time, the degree of mutual compatibility becomes greater and greater, which is due to the goal's affecting its tentative structures as well as due to the tentative structures affecting subsequently emerging versions of a goal. The process ends when parameters of the final version of the goal are the same as parameters of the final tentative structure. At this point, both a goal and the final tentative structure form a unity that may be identified as a creative outcome as well.

There are several benefits of the proposed approach. First, it allows one to overcome the logically tempting, but psychologically not necessarily true, schema that a goal must be stated prior to the first idea's emergence. That the case may be reversed, or that an idea and a goal may emerge simultaneously, is rather difficult to state in terms of linear paradigms, whereas the present model deals with this problem easily. Pursuing a stable goal appears to be a special case rather than a principle of creativity.

Second, there is no need to hypothesize various stages in creative processes, such as logical, intuitive, and evaluative (Kaufmann, Fustier, & Drevet, 1970), or generative and evaluative (Guilford, 1967). It was always a point of disagreement between theoreticians to decide what kind of phases creative processes really comprise, and in which sequence. Besides, it was always clear that it is natural for creativity to go back to the preparatory phase in the middle of, for instance, generating ideas. This caused much confusion and put into question the very notion of phase as applied to creative processes. In the present model, there are no phases, which means that a process is imagined as homogenous in its interactive principle from its start to the end. And it seems easier now to refer to various kinds of mental processes (e.g., logical, generative, and so on) as operating at any moment of the creative process, instead of being alleged to phases understood in terms of the "earlier-later" paradigm.

Finally, the possibility of changing a goal to any extent and at any moment of a process is fully appreciated. Moreover, those changes are imagined as emerging from the inner forces of a process itself, that is, due to the hypothesized interaction between a goal and its tentative structures. In other words, creative processes are viewed here as self-steering in establishing and changing a goal pursued in the course of their occurrence. Needless to say, the interactive standpoint overcomes the "preserving the status quo" nature of the negative feedback paradigm.

For these reasons, the proposed model seems to describe creative processes in a logically more consistent and psychologically more valid way than do the competing paradigms. However, it would be but an empty schema if not completed by real psychological processes that perform the creative interaction between a goal and its tentative structures. Those processes, strategic as well as performative, are described in detail elsewhere (Necka, 1987). Now, it is necessary to show how the schema just sketched can be used in order to account for the role of judgment and critical thinking in creativity.

CREATIVE INTERACTION AND CRITICAL THINKING

As already been mentioned, the interactionist paradigm allows one to overcome the step-by-step approach proposed by many previous theories. It is particularly useful in reference to judgment and criticism. According to the stage theories of the creative process, an idea first must be produced in order to be assessed and judged. This general framework won its dominating position not only in theoretical considerations (see the previous section), but also in practical applications of creative thinking techniques, particularly brainstorming (Osborn, 1959). While adopting the interactionist approach, one does not need to distinguish between productive, imaginative, or divergent operations, on one hand, and reproductive, elaborative, or convergent operations, on the other. Rather, one has to admit that the creative process is basically homogeneous in its interactionist nature. Creation and evaluation are not two distinct stages or phases of the process; they are just two aspects of the same mental operation, which amounts to making the tentative structure and the goal be more adjusted to each other.

In fact, the schema of creative interaction draws on the Piagetian theory of intellectual development rather than on the linear models of thought. According to Piaget (1972), cognitive structures assimilate new information as long as they possess the potential to integrate the incoming new knowledge with already existing knowledge. When assimilation is not possible any longer, the cognitive structures have to accommodate and change themselves in order to be able to deal with new information. The dialectics of assimilation and accommodation are thus perceived as two aspects of every act of intelligence. In a sense, the creative interaction—as conceptualized in this chapter—is a very similar phenomenon. Every tentative structure has to accommodate to the goal, whereas the goal has to accommodate to the tentative structure. On the other hand, both partners of the interaction have to assimilate information that comes from the opposite side. As in the real dialogue, one has to absorb the partner's ideas, but—at the same time—one has the right to expect that his or her ideas will be taken into account. It means, however, that the creative interaction framework does not assume the significance of traditionally viewed judgment and evaluation in creative processes. Rather, the act of judgment and evaluation is assumed to take place in every instance of the appearance of a new tentative structure. Such structure has to be compared to the goal, and this kind of comparison requires evaluation and judgment. The outcome of the evaluation decides on the subsequent steps of the creative process.

According to the proposed conceptualization of the creative process, it is not ideas that are judged after being produced. Evaluation and judgment refers both to the tentative structure and to the goal, or—to put it in another way—it refers to the discrepancy between the goal and the tentative structure. Instead of the "produce first, judge afterward" schema, there is the continuous and practically never-ending process of making decisions whether a given tentative structure conforms to the goal, and how both partners have to be changed in order to make them more adequate and more compatible to each other. Such decisions and evaluations result, not in acceptance or rejections of ideas, but in changing the course and direction of the process. In particular, the results of evaluation of the discrepancy between the tentative structure and the goal may cause the following events:

1. The accommodation of the tentative structure into the goal's requirements.
2. The accommodation of the goal so that it might be closer to the tentative structure.

3. Abandoning of the goal and—possibly—emergence of the new one.
4. Realizing that a given tentative structure better suits the goal that was originally not realized or not taken into account.

Certainly, evaluation and judgment—perceived as the means to make the tentative structure and the goal more compatible to each other—constitute the very core of the creative process. If so, the real problem amounts to changing mental blocks in thinking about creativity, rather than in difficulties pertaining to the problem how to introduce evaluation and judgment into theories and research on creativity.

CONCLUSIONS

How can one defend the creative interaction framework against possible criticism? It is true that the suggested framework is highly speculative and needs empirical verification. However, it appears to describe the creative process in a suitable way, the more so if one concentrates on the evaluative aspects of creativity. According to the proposed schema, evaluation and judgment are just natural participants of the process, at least as natural as production of ideas. In fact, it is not necessary to speak about production and evaluation as separate functions, stages, or skills. The process consists of continual trials to make tentative structures and ensuing versions of the goal more compatible to each other. Therefore, evaluation is not a separate stage or function, but is the very core of what is associated with the notion of creativity.

The proposed schema also seems particularly suitable to deal with two particular aspects of creative judgment and evaluation: the role of metacognition and the importance of valuation. The metacognitive perspective refers to decisions due to which the goal has to be changed or even abandoned. It seems that the interactive point of view is particularly suitable to deal with such important moments of the creative processes, because the goal—as one of the partners of interaction—must be viewed as something susceptible to far-reaching changes, including its disappearance. The valuation perspective (Chand & Runco, 1992) refers to making an idea better than previously, and to improve it rather than just to accept or to reject it, which is connected with traditionally viewed evaluation. Valuation, as Runco and Chand defined it, seems much more typical for creativity than evaluation, and much more important. And the interactionist framework seems better prepared to deal with this problem than the competing models of creativity. This is because valuation may be redefined as the process of continuing the creative interaction, after the preliminary decision concerning the applicability of a given tentative structure has been already made. If a creator continues the interaction despite having reached the required level of compatibility between a tentative structure and the goal, it may result either in the statement of a new goal or in the production of a new tentative structure—a better one. This is just the process of creative valuation.

REFERENCES

Adams, J. L. (1978). *Conceptual blockbusting: A pleasurable guide to better problem solving.* New York: Norton.

Amabile, T. M. (1983a). *The social psychology of creativity.* New York: Springer-Verlag.

Amabile, T. M. (1983b). The social psychology of creativity: A componential conceptualization. *Journal of Personality and Social Psychology, 45,* 357-376.

Chand, I., & Runco, M. A. (1992). Problem finding skills as components in the creative process. *Personality and Individual Differences, 14,* 155-162.

Csikszentmihalyi, M. (1990). The domain of creativity. In M. A. Runco & R. S. Albert (Eds.), *Theories of creativity* (pp. 190-212). Newbury Park, CA: Sage.

Duncker, K. (1945). On problem solving. *Psychological Monographs, 58*(Whole No. 270).

Getzels, J. W., & Csikszentmihalyi, M. (1975). *The creative vision: A longitudinal study of problem finding in art.* New York: Wiley.

Guilford, J. P. (1967). *The nature of human intelligence.* New York: McGraw-Hill.

Kaufmann, A., Fustier, M., & Drevet, A. (1970). *L'inventique: Nouvelles methodes de creativite* [Inventics: New methods of creativity]. Paris: Entreprise Moderne d'Edition.

Koberg, D., & Bagnall, J. (1976). *The universal traveller: A soft-system guide to creativity, problem solving, and the process of reaching goals.* Los Altos, CA: Kaufmann.

Kocowski, T. (1982). *Potrzeby czlowieka. Koncepcja systemowa* [Human needs: A system approach]. Wroclaw: Ossolineum.

Mackworth, N. A. (1965). Originality. *American Psychologist, 20,* 51-66.

Miller, G. A., Galanter, E., & Pribram, K. H. (1960). *Plans and the structure of behavior.* New York: Holt.

Necka, E. (1986). On the nature of creative talent. In A. C. Cropley, K. K. Urban, H. Wagner, & W. Wieczerkowski (Eds.), *Giftedness: A continuing worldwide challenge* (pp. 131-140). New York: Trillium Press.

Necka, E. (1987). *Proces twórczy i jego ograniczenia* [Creative process and its obstacles]. Kraków: Wydawnictwo Uniwersytetu Jagiellonskiego [Jagiellonian University Press].

Nisbett, R. E., & Wilson, T. D. (1977). Telling more than we can know: Verbal reports on mental processes. *Psychological Review, 84,* 231-259.

Osborn, A. F. (1959). *Applied imagination.* New York: Charles Scribners.

Patrick, C. (1937). Creative thought in artists. *The Journal of Psychology, 4,* 35-73.

Patrick, C. (1938). Scientific thought. *The Journal of Psychology, 6,* 55-83.

Perkins, D. N. (1981). *The mind's best work.* Cambridge, MA: Harvard University Press.

Piaget, J. (1972). *The psychology of intelligence.* Totowa, NJ: Littlefield Adams.

Runco, M. A., & Chand, I. (1994). Problem finding, evaluative thinking, and creativity. In M. A. Runco (Ed.), *Problem finding, problem solving, and creativity* (pp. 40-76). Norwood, NJ: Ablex.

Simonton, D. K. (1988). *Scientific genius: A psychology of science.* New York: Cambridge University Press.

Sternberg, R. J. (1988). A three-facet model of creativity. In R. J. Sternberg (Ed.), *The nature of creativity. Contemporary psychological perspectives* (pp. 125-147). Cambridge: Cambridge University Press.

Sternberg, R. J., & Lubart, T. I. (1991). An investment theory of creativity and its development. *Human Development, 34,* 1-31.

Urban, K. K. (1994). Recent trends in creativity research and theory. In K. A. Heller & E. A. Hany (Eds.), *Competence and responsibility* (Vol. 2, pp. 55-67). Seattle: Hogrefe & Huber.

Wallas, G. (1926). *The art of thought.* New York: Harcourt.

6

EVALUATIVE THINKING, CREATIVITY, AND TASK SPECIFICITY: SEPARATING WHEAT FROM CHAFF IS NOT THE SAME AS FINDING NEEDLES IN HAYSTACKS

John Baer
Rider University

When she was younger, it seemed that my daughter Heather never saw an idea that she didn't like. I used to call her a "'Just say yes!' kind of kid" (until my wife cautioned that this might be sending the wrong kind of message about drugs). She liked every book she read and every movie she saw; she liked all her teachers, classmates, and neighbors; and she liked any idea that she, her friends, her family, or anyone else proposed.

This positive attitude did not always translate into action, of course. Although she would respond enthusiastically to the suggestion that she reorganize and clean up her room, she would usually get distracted by some other good idea along the way, and the room would remain in its normal chaotic condition.

Heather was an excellent divergent thinker. She loved any kind of divergent thinking exercise, she could think of a zillion uses for empty tin cans, and she was the star brainstormer of her elementary school's Odyssey of the Mind Creative Problem Solving team. She seemed to churn out ideas far faster than she could put them into action, and she left behind a trail of unfinished paintings, poems, and other projects (which became the raw materials for the almost organic mounds of debris that grew and metamorphosed on the floor of her room).

Heather's active imagination and her happy embrace of everything life had to offer made her a very charming girl, but it also got her into some difficulties. Ideas like walking across a barely frozen pond seemed just as viable to her as other interesting, but more carefully conceived, activities. When she was 8, we were able to dry her out and warm her up after she crashed through the ice and found herself waist deep in the frigid water below; but I sometimes worried what would happen as she got older and had the opportunity to conceive even more potentially dangerous activities.

Heather is 16 now, and I am pleased to report she has much better judgment than she did at 8. She may not carefully measure the distance, but she at least looks before leaping. She also is not quite as quick to come up with new ideas as she once was—at least, she doesn't articulate and act on as many ideas as she used to—but her ideas are often better, more workable, more worthy of her time and effort. And she manages to finish projects more often. (She even cleans her room from time to time.)

Heather may be something of an extreme case, but I believe many children develop in this manner. I suspect that it is because their judgment is generally not as good as their ability to come up with interesting ideas that we limit their freedom to make many important decisions for themselves. Heather is probably representative of most adolescents in the way she seems to be taming a very free-wheeling imagination and learning to take a somewhat more careful and thoughtful approach to life. But the change in Heather also exemplifies the interaction between divergent thinking and what I call (following Runco, 1993) *evaluative thinking* in this chapter. Both are necessary for creative performance, but only the former has received much attention in the creativity literature.

I do not really think that Heather is any less imaginative now than when she was 8. She may have simply learned to edit, at both conscious and unconscious levels, the stream of ideas that come to her. Is this a loss? Perhaps, but it is an even greater gain. Heather's skill at divergent thinking has become less obvious, but she is today much more creative than she was years ago. Creative in some areas, I should say: She is much more creative in painting than in poetry, much more creative in designing science experiments than in developing theories about number relationships, and much more creative in making collages than in sculpting, to cite just a few comparisons. Her creativity varies considerably from activity to activity. Perhaps it always did, but in the constant shower of ideas—most of which never moved off the drawing board—such differences in creativity across domains and tasks was less obvious.

Why have I taken the time to introduce Heather, and the manner in which her creative thinking has developed? Because I believe the ways she has changed over the past decade exemplify several important principles about creative thinking and its development, and these ideas are central to the themes explored in this chapter:

- Divergent thinking is only one part of creative thinking. The products of divergent thinking must in some way be evaluated (and often refined and re-evaluated in an ongoing, recursive process) as part of creative performance.
- Divergent thinking skills and evaluative thinking skills follow separate developmental trajectories.
- The development of evaluative thinking skills may influence one's divergent thinking, on both conscious and unconscious levels.
- Creativity, and its component skills of divergent and evaluative thinking, varies widely not only *between* individuals, but also *within* individuals. This includes both variation between broadly defined domains (such as art, science, and mathematics) and among tasks within each domain.

The four ideas listed here are the primary themes I develop, with special emphasis on the need to take a task-specific view of evaluative thinking. I have argued the same elsewhere in regard to divergent thinking (see Baer, 1991, 1993, 1994a, 1998). These themes are interwoven throughout the chapter rather than developed one at a time. The rest of the chapter is divided into four sections. In the first section, I look at several ways in which evaluative thinking—although called by different names—has been crucial in several important theories of creativity. This provides a framework for considering how evaluative thinking and divergent thinking work together to produce creative thinking. In the second section, I consider alternative ways to conceptualize evaluative thinking as a part of creativity and explain why I believe it prudent to distinguish evaluative thinking from what is often called convergent thinking. Having established a theoretical context and defined key terms, I then propose a task-specific theory of evaluative thinking, provide some experimental evidence for this task-specific approach, and explain the dangers of ignoring task specificity in evaluative thinking. In the concluding section, I discuss applications of a task-specific approach to evaluative thinking in creativity training and research.

A final proviso: In this chapter I talk about everyday, garden-variety creativity, the kind all individuals exhibit to one degree or another. The cognitive mechanisms underlying this kind of creativity may (or may not) be very different from the genius-level, paradigm-shifting creativity of which all individuals stand in awe. Although I doubt that radically different kinds of cognitive processes are involved in these two "types" of creativity (for reasons given later), the argument of this chapter was developed within the context of research and theories about everyday creative thinking processes. I leave it to those who have studied the works of genius to decide if or how my ideas might apply in that context.

TWO-STEP THEORIES OF CREATIVITY: DIVERGENT THINKING + EVALUATIVE THINKING = CREATIVE THINKING

Divergent thinking has been the most influential theory and metaphor in the creativity literature (Runco, 1993). However, many of the most influential theories of creativity have in fact given equal weight to evaluative processes, as is shown here. Unfortunately, these evaluative processes have often been ignored by those doing research or training using those same theories of creativity.

Even in the home of brainstorming—Buffalo's Creative Problem Solving (CPS) Institute, heir to Osborn's legacy—the Osborne-Parnes CPS model explicitly puts convergent or evaluative thinking on an equal footing with divergent thinking (see Figs. 6.1 and 6.2). At one of the CPS Institute's summer training programs I attended many years ago, Parnes stressed the equal importance of the two processes. He held up one of those collapsible coat racks (which look rather like the diagram part of Figure 6.1, although the coat racks are usually mounted horizontally) to illustrate the CPS model. At each step, he told us, we must both *diverge* to find many ideas and *converge* to select the best ideas. The two processes are inextricably linked. Pushing and pulling the device to make it shorter and longer (and the width of the diamonds larger and smaller), he stressed that the more we diverge, the more effort we must put into converging. The CPS model, although it involves several stages (and may involve much recursion), is based at every stage on this diverge-and-then-evaluate, two-step process.

Campbell's (1960) blind variation and selective retention theory of creativity is, in essence, a two-step model in which ideas are first produced and then judged. Campbell's theory is rooted in Darwin's theory of evolution, and his thinking echoes that of many

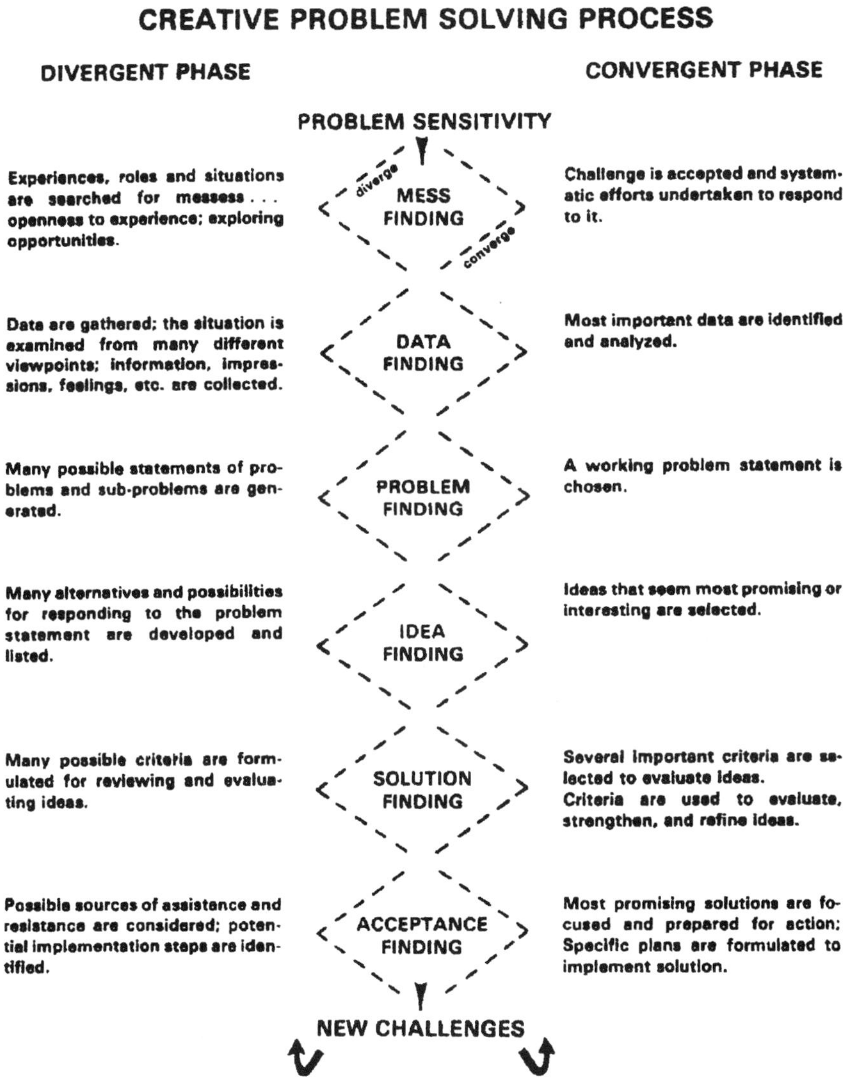

Evaluative Thinking 133

CREATIVE PROBLEM SOLVING PROCESS

DIVERGENT PHASE		**CONVERGENT PHASE**
PROBLEM SENSITIVITY
Experiences, roles and situations are searched for messes... openness to experience; exploring opportunities.	MESS FINDING	Challenge is accepted and systematic efforts undertaken to respond to it.
Data are gathered; the situation is examined from many different viewpoints; information, impressions, feelings, etc. are collected.	DATA FINDING	Most important data are identified and analyzed.
Many possible statements of problems and sub-problems are generated.	PROBLEM FINDING	A working problem statement is chosen.
Many alternatives and possibilities for responding to the problem statement are developed and listed.	IDEA FINDING	Ideas that seem most promising or interesting are selected.
Many possible criteria are formulated for reviewing and evaluating ideas.	SOLUTION FINDING	Several important criteria are selected to evaluate ideas. Criteria are used to evaluate, strengthen, and refine ideas.
Possible sources of assistance and resistance are considered; potential implementation steps are identified.	ACCEPTANCE FINDING	Most promising solutions are focused and prepared for action; Specific plans are formulated to implement solution.
NEW CHALLENGES

Figure 6.1. The Osborne-Parnes Creative Problem Solving Model

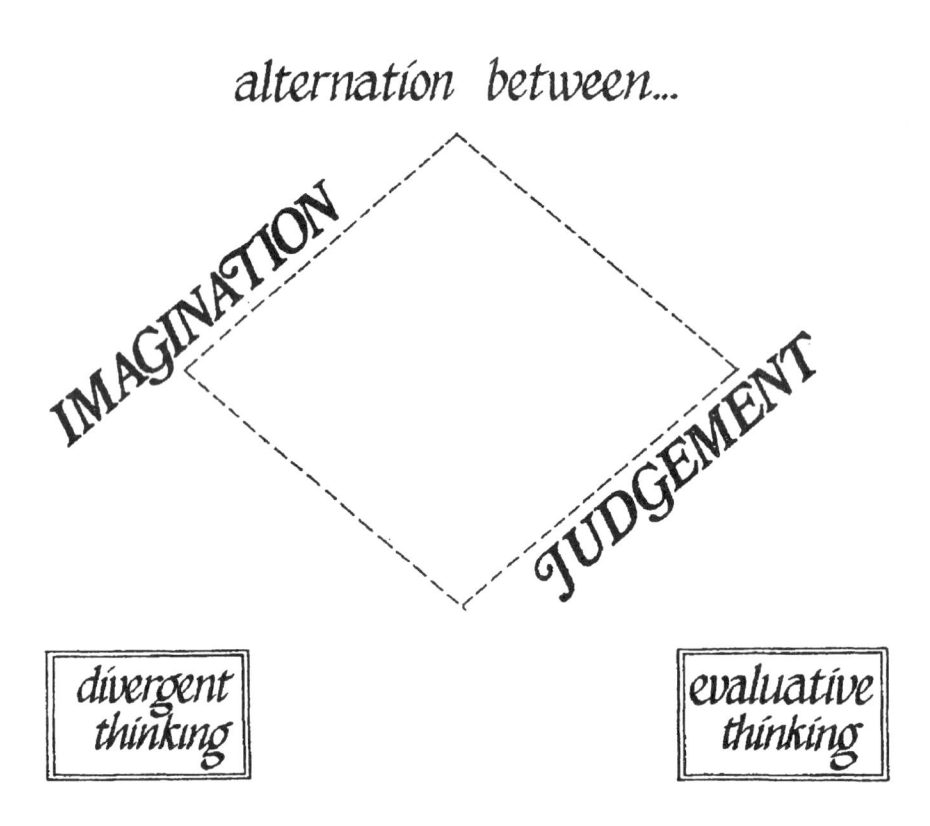

Figure 6.2. Divergent thinking + evaluative thinking = creativity

philosophers in the century between Darwin's (1859) publication of *On the Origin of Species* and Campbell's use of that work as the model for his own theory, as Campbell himself acknowledged (Campbell, 1960; Simonton, 1988). His theory emphasizes the importance of totally random, or "blind," variation, followed by selection of better ideas and their retention by the culture.

Simonton's (1988) chance configuration theory of creative thinking, which has its roots in Campbell's (1960) model, includes a similar two-step process in which the production of ideas is followed by judgment of those ideas. First, chance associations of mental elements result in what Simonton called *chance permutations*. Some of these chance permutations are selected as *configurations* on the basis of stability. Simonton called those chance permutations that are too unstable to be retained *aggregates*. The terms *configuration* and *aggregate* really represent a continuum, however, not a dichotomy. For any chance association, there is some probability between 0 and 1 that a stable configuration will result. Simonton explained at length what factors influence the formation of configurations. His theory of how some associations of mental elements come to be selected constitutes a theory of how evaluative thinking operates on the products of divergent thinking.

Note that like Campbell (1960), Simonton (1988) emphasized the random nature of the idea generation stage of his model. Also like Campbell, he posited a third stage, communication and acceptance, in which ideas are shared with and preserved by that community.

There is another recent theory of creativity that, like Campbell's (1960) and Simonton's (1988) theories, emphasizes a combination of idea generation and selection, but that does so in a way that works at an somewhat meta-theoretical level. That is, this theory—the work of Johnson-Laird (1987, 1988, 1993)—provides a framework within which one can think about any theory of creativity.

Johnson-Laird (1987, 1988, 1993) argued, from an information-processing viewpoint, for three kinds of creativity, which I call *real-time, standard two-stage,* and *paradigm-shifting* creativity. (Johnson-Laird referred to these three stages in different ways, depending on the point he was making; in his 1988 chapter he labeled them "Creation within a genre in real time," "Creation within a framework of stages, " and "Creation of new frameworks," respectively.)

Real-time (or, in computer jargon, "online") *creativity* refers to creative performance within some genre under time constraints that make performance spontaneous, with no opportunity for revision—as in jazz, modern dance, or other forms of improvisation; in everyday conversation; or in any kind of extemporaneous performance or problem-solving task (such as reacting to emergency situations). Because this kind of performance does not allow enough time for the generation of a wide range of alternative solutions and then a thoughtful selection among those candidate solutions, creative performance in real time requires tight constraints on the kinds of possible solutions that may be generated. Choice among candidate solutions in this model is essentially arbitrary, in Johnson-Laird's (1987, 1988, 1993) view, and therefore all the candidate solutions that are generated must meet the task constraints. This imposes significant limitations on the degree of variability that can be tolerated among the candidate solutions. Johnson-Laird likened this real-time model of creativity to Lamarck's theory of evolution because previous experience must guide the solution-generation process, rather than allowing an essentially random generation of ideas. This kind of real-time creative performance has received little attention in the creativity literature, making especially interesting Johnson-Laird's attempts to model it using computer programs that create improvised jazz bass lines.

Note that in real-time creativity, evaluation occurs *before* the production of ideas. Whatever constraints or evaluative standards apply are there at the outset (in most cases unconsciously, of course) to guide idea generation. This is a reversal of the more typical diverge-then-converge two-step process (e.g., Parnes, 1972).

Standard two-stage creativity refers to creative performance under conditions that allow time for evaluating and revising a variety of possible solutions. As in real-time creativity, the generation of possible solutions follows a set of criteria, but these are less strict than those needed in real-time performance. There are actually two sets of evaluative criteria, one to guide idea generation and a second for selecting among the ideas generated.

In the generation stage, the criteria for producing candidate solutions can be quite flexible, because unlike real-time creative performance, this standard two-stage model can tolerate the generation of solutions that do not meet minimal task constraints. The two stages of this model (generation of ideas and selection of solutions) allow more diversity in its initial generation stage because there is an opportunity at the next stage to reject unworkable solutions. This model thus allows a much wider range of possible solutions than the single-stage real-time model, in which the constraints on solution generation must be tight because there is no solution-evaluation stage prior to performance.

It is, of course, possible (and, I believe, quite reasonable) to think of the distinction between real-time and standard two-stage creative performances as a series of points along a continuum rather than as two discrete processes. The degree to which a performance is considered to allow standard two-stage processing depends on the nature of whatever limitations are placed on the second, evaluative stage. These variations in the time available for evaluating competing candidate solutions in turn allow varying degrees of flexibility or looseness in the criteria used to guide the generation of candidate solutions.

Note that the two stages in this model do not refer to divergent and evaluative thinking. As in real-time creative thinking, there are evaluative processes that precede divergent thinking. But in standard two-stage creative thinking, there are also evaluative processes that follow divergent thinking.

Paradigm-shifting creativity refers to creative performances that result in fundamental changes in the nature of the domain in which the creator is working—such as changes in the way the domain itself is conceptualized, or changes in the options available to those who later work and solve problems in that domain. In this kind of creativity, Johnson-Laird (1987, 1988, 1993) argued there can be no prior constraints on the kinds of candidate solutions that are generated. He, therefore, referred to this model as a "neo-Darwinian" process, and argued that "a neo-Darwinian procedure is the only mechanism available if there is no way in which the generative process can be guided by selective constraints" (Johnson-Laird, 1988, p. 218). This is an extreme case argument, however, because completely random idea generation would be a hopelessly time-consuming and wasteful enterprise. Johnson-Laird (1988) himself acknowledged that "the productive use of knowledge is a central part of genius" (p. 218) in the generation as well as the evaluation of ideas.

This paradigm-shifting model is much like Campbell's (1960) and Simonton's (1988) theories, both of which posit something like a random generative stage, the results of which are later evaluated. Simonton (1988), like Johnson-Laird (1988), was aware that true randomness at this stage is unlikely:

> Chance, after all, is a measure of ignorance, a gauge of the situation in which the number of causes is so immense as to defy identification. Though chance implies unpredictability, it does not necessitate total randomness. . . . We must merely insist that a large number of potential permutations exists, all with comparably low but nonzero probabilities. (p. 7)

This qualification pushes Simonton's theory somewhat closer to standard two-stage creativity.

The importance of Johnson-Laird's (1987, 1988, 1993) three-part meta-theoretical framework lies not so much in its ability to classify theories (although it can do that rather nicely), but in its ability to help reveal shared features among all theories of creativity. There are two key steps—idea generation and idea evaluation—that can interact in different ways to produce creative thinking. There are extreme cases in which evaluative thinking comes almost entirely after divergent thinking or all evaluative thinking precedes divergent thinking. However, in most creative thinking, evaluative thinking comes at both ends: before divergent thinking to guide the generation of ideas, and after divergent thinking to judge the quality of the ideas generated.

It should be emphasized that these evaluative and divergent thinking processes, and their interactions, occur at varying levels of consciousness, and to varying effect. The not-quite random nature of Simonton's (1988) chance permutations are surely made somewhat less random by what one knows (one's expertise in a field), including what one would consider a potentially workable idea. This is an example of how evaluative thinking can precede (and influence) divergent thinking.

It is important to note that the ways divergent and evaluative thinking processes interact can either help or hinder creativity. Likewise, the nature of this interaction can suit or fail to suit the task constraints. (Failure would thus be counterproductive.) For example, an individual might be very stringent in the criteria he or she imposes to limit idea generation because there is no time for later evaluation of ideas. This would be appropriate under the constraints of real-time creative thinking. However, the individual might also unnecessarily limit idea generation in situations that do not require strict time constraints, and thereby reduce the range of ideas and their likely creativity. Conversely, very loose limitations on idea generation may result in the serendipitous production of a very creative idea, or merely in the fruitless consideration of ideas that could have been safely censored before the fact by applying some limited evaluative standards prior to idea generation. Basadur (1995) looked at this issue in an interesting study in which he computed ratios of preferences for ideation (divergent thinking) and evaluation in problem solving. People working in areas that have relatively long time frames for action, such as researchers, were found to have a greater preference for ideation than people working in fields that typically require quicker action, such as sales persons. The latter group tended to prefer evaluation to ideation, which is consistent with the constraints of their work.

Does this make evaluative thinking more important than divergent thinking? There is (at least at present) no way to begin to answer this question, and it probably makes no sense even to try. Both are essential, and both are part of a continuous recursive process. Johnson-Laird's (1987, 1988, 1993) meta-theoretical analysis, as well as the theories of Campbell (1960) and Simonton (1988), serve as reminders, however, that neglecting evaluative thinking in favor of divergent thinking will severely limit our understanding of creativity.

EVALUATIVE, CRITICAL, OR CONVERGENT THINKING: WHAT'S IN A NAME?

Metaphors guide thinking. In his book, *Metaphors of Mind,* Sternberg (1990) demonstrated that the kinds of questions individuals ask about the mind determine the kinds of answers one gets. It is, in turn, the way one thinks about the nature of human intelligence—

the metaphors of mind—that determine the kinds of questions asked. Metaphors both drive and guide research and theories about the nature of human intelligence—and, as feminist philosophers of science have pointed out, everywhere in science (e.g., Fausto-Sterling, 1991; Harding, 1986; Nelson, 1990).

Runco (1993) suggested that the most common metaphor in creativity research is divergent thinking, and it is hard to imagine any other metaphor that has had anything like the influence of divergent thinking on creativity training and creativity theory as well (Baer, 1993). There are many aspects to creativity, of course, and divergence is not key to all of them. Johnson-Laird (1988) pointed out three such aspects when he noted that "creativity is like murder—both depend on motive, means, and opportunity" (p. 208). When it comes to motive, intrinsic motivation is perhaps the most important metaphor (Amabile, 1983). As for opportunity, there is no single dominant metaphor, although there is increasing interest in how different cultural milieu provide varying conditions for creative productivity (e.g., Csikszentmihalyi, 1988; Gardner, 1988; Simonton, 1988). But as far as the *means*—the skills one needs to be creative—the divergence metaphor has certainly been paramount.

Runco (1993) argued that "the metaphor for divergence has detracted from other important components of creativity. In particular, more emphasis should be placed on the evaluative, critical, and selective components of creative thought (and their interaction with divergent processes)" (p. 2). Runco also argued that "it is misleading and unrealistic to view convergence as opposed to divergence. They can and should work together" (p. 5).

I am in complete agreement that the divergence metaphor has been far too dominant in creativity research and theory, and that researchers need to understand better how evaluative processes interact with divergent ones to produce creative thinking (or, as some of the examples raised in the previous section show, how this interaction can sometimes *interfere* with creative thinking). But because metaphors are such powerful influences on thinking, one needs to be very careful how these nondivergent creative thinking processes are conceptualized.

As Runco (1993) pointed out, there is a temptation to use the convergence metaphor (as Parnes did effectively in the demonstration cited earlier). Both come from Guilford's (1967; Guilford & Hoepfner, 1971) structure of intellect (SOI) model. Convergence seems to provide a comfortable counterweight to divergence: Whereas divergent production refers to the solution of a problem requiring many different responses, convergent production is the solution of a problem with a single correct solution. But defined this way, the two do not actually interact at all. They are not even opposites, but rather mutually exclusive categories, like reptiles and mammals. They are parallel operations that come into play in different kinds of situations, at least on a theoretical level.

Of Guilford's (1967; Guilford & Hoepfner, 1971) five cognitive operations (cognition, memory, divergent production, convergent production, and evaluation), the one that seems to come closest to the kind of interaction with divergent thinking that is seen in creative thinking is evaluation. Evaluation involves making judgments and decisions based on logical criteria. The constraints that evaluative thinking, as conceptualized here as stage one of Johnson-Laird's (1987, 1988, 1993) standard two-stage model, put on divergent thinking need not be logical, of course, and they are often not consciously controlled. Nor, for that matter, must the evaluation of ideas that have been generated (in Stage 2 of the same model) be either logical or conscious. So evaluation, as defined by Guilford, is not exactly the kind of skill we are looking for either. But it does come much closer than convergence.

There is, of course, no need to choose one of Guilford's operations. *Critical thinking* could be used, but that term also has other associations than those in mind. To avoid this kind of misunderstanding, a new name could be invented for these nondivergent creative thinking skills that underlie creativity (or we might even give up trying to find a proper term and stick with the admittedly cumbersome "nondivergent creative thinking skills"), but this invites a different kind of misunderstanding. Each choice of term comes with its own set of drawbacks.

Must there be so much concern about what to call these nondivergent creative thinking skills? I think there must be, because of the power of metaphor in guiding thinking. There is still uncertainty as to what these skills are, or how they operate. If they are given labels now that suggest a certain kind of cognitive operation that is already familiar, it is likely to skew thinking, questions, theories, and research in the direction of that already familiar kind of cognitive operation. For this reason, I think the convergence metaphor is particularly problematic. Convergent thinking has been closely associated with the kind of "right answer" thinking that leads to high scores on IQ tests, which I doubt is at all the same as the thinking needed to guide and constrain divergent thinking or to judge among its products. The term *critical thinking* has been used in a wide variety of contexts and is probably less likely to have the specific connotations of convergent thinking; however, many programs to improve students' thinking skills by teaching them to do such things as "to support their opinions based on facts, definitions, concepts, and principles" (Gage & Berliner, 1992, p. 420) bear the name *critical thinking*. This, again, is not the kind of evaluative thinking that is important for creative thinking (at least I think it is not).

There is no one best term, and I have raised the issue not to propose that all other terms be dropped in favor of the one I prefer. Rather, I want to make the point that, although we may be sure that there are important evaluative skills involved in creative thinking, we don't really know much about them and therefore need to be careful not to make assumptions based on the words we use to describe them. Because it seems least problematic, I have followed Runco (1993) in using the term *evaluative* to describe this class of cognitive skills, but I believe this is a broad class of only loosely related skills. Part of what needs to be done is to learn how these skills differ from, and interact with, divergent thinking. Another is to understand how they differ from each other.

One distinction among these skills might be between those that precede and guide divergent thinking and those that follow and judge the products of divergent thinking (using the standard two-stage model as the guide). Perhaps as more is learned about these skills, separate terms will be needed to refer to these two different kinds of evaluative thinking. (Conversely, it may be found that they are similar, or even the same, cognitive operations.)

Research (Baer, 1991, 1992, 1994b, 1996; Runco, 1987, 1989) has shown that creative performance is task-specific, and I have argued elsewhere (Baer, 1993, 1994a, 1998) for a task-specific understanding of divergent thinking to explain this. It may be that evaluative thinking is also task-specific; that is, the kind of evaluative thinking that leads to creative performance on one task (e.g., writing stories) may be a different skill from the kind of evaluative thinking that leads to creative performance on some other task (e.g., writing poems). The two may seem similar, in that they perform similar functions in different task domains, and yet may be completely unrelated on a cognitive level. That is the argument of the next section.

I CAN FIND NEEDLES IN HAYSTACKS, SO WHY CAN'T I SEPARATE WHEAT FROM CHAFF? A TASK-SPECIFIC APPROACH TO EVALUATIVE THINKING

Many theorists have argued, in different ways, that intelligence is not a single ability but a series of several or even many abilities (see, e.g., Gardner, 1983; Guilford, 1967; Guilford & Hoepfner, 1971; Sternberg, 1990; Thurstone, 1938). Domain-general and domain-specific theories maintain, respectively, that intelligence is either a single, all-purpose kind of ability that is involved whenever we think about anything—a kind of central processing unit that handles cognitive tasks of any kind; or several abilities that are quite different from one another—not only in when they might be applied, but also in the kinds of cognitive operations involved in their operations.

As Karmiloff-Smith (1992) noted, "much depends, of course, on what one understands by 'domain'" (p. 6). Fodor's (1983) modularity thesis, for example, argues for very broad domains—for example, language and perception are handled by two different modules—with strict compartmentalization between domains. This compartmentalization includes information encapsulation (i.e., information used by one domain is not directly accessible by other domains). Fodor's fixed neural architecture is based on a hard-wired, innate brain structure.

Others allow more flexibility, both in the degree of genetic control of development and in regard to the possibility of information-sharing among domains. Gardner (1983), for example, posited seven "intelligences" that are demonstrated by such things as potential isolation by brain damage, the existence of autistic savants and prodigies, and evidence from psychological tasks and psychometric findings. Although there is significant genetic control over the development of these domain-specific intelligences, there is also room for "considerable plasticity and flexibility in human growth" (Gardner, 1983, p. 32). These intelligences are not totally independent, informationally encapsulated systems. Although Gardner stated that he has much "sympathy" for the positions of such modularity theorists as Fodor (1983), Gazzaniga (1985; Gazzaniga & Ledoux, 1978), and Pylyshyn (1980), Gardner nonetheless described his intelligences as merely "useful fictions—for discussing processes and abilities that (like all of life) are continuous with one another" (p. 70). Gardner also argued that "Nature brooks no sharp discontinuities" (p. 70) of the kind that modularity theories view as impregnable borders between domains, thus limiting his endorsement of a strict modularity stance.

One can, in fact, conceptualize cognitive development as domain-specific without adhering to any of the primary tenets of modularity. Karmiloff-Smith (1992) argued that "the storing and processing of information may be domain specific without being encapsulated, hard-wired, of fixed neural architecture, mandatory, and so forth" (p. 166). It is this more flexible, nonmodular view of domain specificity to which I refer next.

There is also disagreement among theories of domain specificity about the size of a domain. Both Fodor (1983) and Gardner (1983) conceptualized domains very broadly, whereas others (e.g., Baer, 1993; Gazzaniga, 1985; Karmiloff-Smith, 1992; Siegler, 1989) described them as more narrow, special-purpose constructs. Karmiloff-Smith's term for these very narrow domains is *microdomains* (in which she included such as skills as pronoun acquisition within the larger domain of language, or understanding of gravity within the larger domain of understanding physics), but she acknowledged that "the term 'microdomain-specific' [is] rather long-winded" (p. 141).

I prefer the term *task-specific*, but like *microdomain-specific*, this leaves undefined the exact bandwidth of each skill in question. Research in creativity (Baer, 1991, 1992, 1993, 1994a, 1994b, 1996; Runco, 1987, 1989) suggests that the skills underlying creativity performance, whatever they may be, are far less narrow than the seven intelligences proposed by Gardner (1983), but it is not clear the extent of this task specificity. Carey (1985, 1988) and Karmiloff-Smith (1992) presented evidence from a cognitive developmental perspective that suggests that knowledge reorganization—that is, how individuals take in information and construct from it their current understanding of the world—operates at a very task-specific level. Similarly, studies of transfer of learning, which show that it is often difficult for students to use knowledge or skills acquired in one context in other, even slightly different contexts (Johnson-Laird, 1983; Mayer, 1987; McCloskey, 1983; Woolfolk, 1993; Vye et al., 1988) point to a very narrow range of application of cognitive skills (although in the case of application in slightly different contexts, the narrow task specificity can often be overcome by direct instruction more easily than in the areas of knowledge reorganization and creativity).

The evidence for task specificity in creativity is largely correlational (Baer, 1993, 1998), although other approaches have also led researchers to question whether "there are any 'pan-artistic' skills that are called upon in all forms of art" (Winner, 1982, p. 388). A series of studies (Baer, 1991, 1992, 1993, 1994a, 1994b, 1996; Runco, 1987, 1989) has demonstrated near zero correlations between the creativity ratings of different kinds of creative products. In each case, expert judges, using Amabile's (1982) consensual assessment technique, rated the creativity of poems, art works, stories, and other creative products. This technique shows a high degree of interrater reliability; moreover, on a given task (such as writing poems or making collages), there is a high level of stability in individual levels of creativity, even after periods of up to 1 year (Baer, 1994c).

The creativity ratings of products in different domains (such as collages and poems) in a series of seven studies using individuals ranging in age from 7 to 40 years old hovered near zero (Baer, 1993). More surprising was the fact that even on tasks within the same domain (such as writing poetry, writing stories, and telling stories to go with a series of pictures, all of which would typically be considered part of the domain of language), the correlations were also near zero.

I have interpreted this elsewhere (Baer, 1993, 1994a, 1998) in terms of a task-specific theory of divergent thinking. In a training study (Baer, 1994a), subjects learned and practiced divergent thinking skills using standard kinds of divergent thinking exercises. The creative products (including poems, collages, short stories, original mathematical word problems, and spoken stories to go with a series of pictures) of subjects trained in divergent thinking received significantly higher creativity ratings than similar products by subjects who received a different kind of training not related to divergent thinking, thus demonstrating the importance of divergent thinking skill. However, even among those who received divergent thinking training, the correlations among ratings on different tasks were essentially zero. As the divergent thinking training involved a wide variety of contexts and types of exercises and thus provided practice in a wide variety of different divergent thinking skills, the no-correlation outcome was interpreted as evidence for a task-specific theory of divergent thinking. It appears, then, that there is not a single skill of divergent thinking; the evidence thus far questions the possibility of even broadly applicable domain-specific divergent thinking skills. Instead, there appear to be a wide range of distinct, narrowly task-specific divergent thinking skills.

What about the evaluative skills that contribute to creative performance? The evidence against domain-general evaluative thinking skills is the same as the evidence against domain-general divergent thinking skills. If there were domain-general evaluative thinking skills, then these should result in significant correlations among the creativity ratings on different products. But studies designed to find these correlations provided evidence that, to the contrary, the correlations among creativity ratings of different products, even those in the same general domain, were near zero (Baer, 1993, 1998). This evidence argues against the likelihood of there being any significantly important domain-general creative thinking skill. To the extent that evaluative thinking skills play an important role in creativity, as argued previously, then it appears that these evaluative skills are no doubt also task-specific.

What are these task-specific evaluative thinking skills? The exact identification of which skills influence what kinds of creativity awaits years of research and can be only speculative at this point. It should be remembered that, as with divergent thinking, evaluative thinking skills may appear very similar from the outside (in terms of the roles they play in cognition) and yet be very different on the inside (in terms of mind-brain functioning). Although it makes sense to group together evaluative thinking skills because they perform similar functions in different task domains, the cognitive operations involved may be largely unrelated to one another. This would limit the possibility of transfer—of successfully applying a skill that enhances creative thinking on one task on a different kind of task—and also explain the lack of correlations among creative products of different types.

Karmiloff-Smith (1992) pointed out that domain specificity can be partial, which helps explain why coaching and direct instruction aimed at promoting transfer can sometimes be successful (Mayer, 1987; Woolfolk, 1993; Vye et al., 1988) and why researchers need to attend to how task-specific and more general skills and knowledge interact (Siegler, 1989). Karmiloff-Smith also showed that domain specificity need not be innate, and that it may either increase or decrease with development.

It may be that, in the case of both divergent and evaluative thinking skills, it is possible to promote transfer so that skills used on one task may be brought to bear successfully on other, somewhat similar tasks. It is possible that through a process that Karmiloff-Smith (1992) called "representational redescription" one may come to have metacognitive access to these skills, and thus be able to deploy them more widely. Or it may be (as the evidence thus far seems to indicate; Baer, 1993, 1994a, 1994b, 1996) that the level of task specificity remains fairly constant both in the course of normal development and despite explicit training in divergent thinking. These questions await future research into the nature, development, and training of divergent and evaluative thinking skills.

Finally, it is important to emphasize that evaluative thinking skills in all likelihood follow their own developmental trajectories (Runco, 1991), which are at least partially independent of the development of divergent thinking skills. Runco (1991) and Runco and Smith (1992) demonstrated that there are modest correlations between divergent thinking skill and evaluative thinking skill; as the latter explain, "an individual who routinely thinks in a divergent fashion has more opportunities for practicing evaluations" (p. 301). A comparison of rates or order of development of these two kinds of creative thinking skills will be difficult to assess experimentally: There are no comparable units in which to measure and compare divergent thinking and evaluative thinking, and even if there were, the question of which divergent and evaluative thinking skills should be considered makes a meaningful comparison of an individual's levels of these skills at any point in time problematic. The anecdotal evidence with which this chapter opens suggests that the development of evaluative thinking tends to lag behind the development of divergent thinking, and Runco and Smith's explanation of how divergent thinking skill would lead to greater evaluative thinking skill as a result of practice also suggests that the development of divergent thinking skill would tend to precede the development of evaluative thinking skill. If so, this difference will have consequences for the kinds of training that it makes sense to do at different ages.

WHERE SHOULD WE GO FROM HERE?

It would be easier—although less interesting—if there were just one kind of divergent thinking, and one kind of evaluative thinking, and if these two skills combined in consistent ways to produce creative thinking. For those interested in improving creative performance, this would make the job simple and straightforward; and for those involved in creativity research and theory, there would not be that much work left to do.

As it stands, however, creativity researchers and theorists need not worry about running out of important and interesting topics to study. There is, first of all, work to be done replicating and extending studies about the generality of creativity across task domains, with special emphasis on looking for any developmental trends in the direction of either task specificity or domain generality.

To understand how evaluative thinking contributes to creative performance, researchers need to begin to isolate specific evaluative thinking skills that influence creativity in specific domains. Unfortunately, this will be rather slow and painstaking work, without even the guidance of a well-developed general construct of evaluative thinking. In the parallel pursuit of specific divergent thinking skills, researchers have a well-defined construct that, although incorrect when thought of as a general cognitive skill, is nonetheless a useful guide to discovering task-specific divergent thinking skills. The development of a general evaluative thinking construct, a goal toward which the chapters in this volume should make an important contribution, may help researchers working in a top-down direction to find specific evaluative thinking skills (Runco, chap. 3, this volume). Conversely, identification of specific evaluative thinking skills will undoubtedly help, in an inductive, bottom-up manner, in developing a more general evaluative thinking construct.

A two-level framework for thinking about evaluative thinking will probably be necessary. At the top will be a higher level, general evaluative thinking construct that describes similarities among the lower level, task-specific evaluative thinking skills. This construct and the similarities to which it directs attention will help in the identification of other task-specific evaluative thinking skills. However, the general construct must not lead to the assumption that there is actual similarity, or even overlap, at the level of cognitive operations among the various task-specific skills. This apparently mistaken assumption appears to have led to many misunderstandings in the area of divergent thinking (Baer, 1993, 1994d). There is no need to repeat this mistake in the area of evaluative thinking.

There is also the question of the course of development of evaluative thinking skills. This research area should include ascertaining the level of task specificity at different stages of development of these skills and whether task specificity increases or decreases in the course of development.

And finally, there is the question of how many general evaluative thinking constructs we need. Will one such construct be sufficient, or are there two very different kinds of evaluative thinking—one to guide and constrain divergent thinking before the fact, and another to evaluate the results of divergent thinking afterward? It seems likely that these will prove to be two very different kinds of skills. In any event, it seems prudent to proceed for the time being under the more cautious assumption that these two general varieties of evaluative thinking skills are more different than they are alike.

Those are questions for researchers and theorists. In the meantime, what guidance is available for those who wish to teach for more creative thinking? In particular, as much is not known yet about the nature of evaluative thinking skills, how can they be taught?

First, it would be wise simply not to ignore such skills, or to assume that they are the same as the one-right answer, convergent thinking skills tested on standard intelligence tests and reinforced regularly in most school programs. Psychometric techniques suggest there is little overlap between these convergent thinking skills (as measured by SOI measures and grade point average) and the creativity-relevant evaluative thinking skills one wishes to teach (Runco & Smith, 1992). The contexts for using evaluative thinking skills in the service of creative thinking are also quite different than the contexts in which convergent thinking skills are typically employed; therefore, even if one believed that there was some similarity between convergent and evaluative thinking at the level of cognitive operations, these creativity-relevant evaluative thinking skills would still need to be taught and practiced in appropriate creativity-relevant contexts.

Second, although the exact nature of these skills is not known, practice in using them can be provided. One important use of evaluative thinking, as described in the section on the standard two-stage model of creative thinking, is to evaluate the products of divergent thinking. Just as divergent thinking exercises are standard fare in creativity-training programs, so should be the evaluation of those ideas. Training that includes both divergent and evaluative thinking has been shown to lead to long-term improvement in creativity (Baer, 1988).

The issue of evaluation should lead researchers to be cautious, however. Amabile (1983) showed convincingly that the expectation that one's work will be evaluated lowers intrinsic motivation and creative performance. There need to be ways to practice evaluation that will not lessen creativity (which happens, I am guessing, by decreasing the amount of risk-taking one allows oneself in divergent thinking). Self-evaluation of one's own ideas, or any technique that avoids subjecting individual students' ideas to evaluation by others, should be stressed. Equally important, teachers need to teach students ways to overcome the negative effects of evaluation—that is, how to avoid losing intrinsic interest and "going extrinsic" in the face of evaluations of and rewards for our efforts (Hennessey & Zbikowski, 1993).

Creativity training, research, and theory have all been lopsided for many years, emphasizing divergent thinking at the expense of evaluative thinking. It appears that evaluative thinking may now begin to receive a more equal share of attention. It is to be hoped that the lessons of decades of research in divergent thinking—including both its successes and mistakes—can help make work in the area of evaluative thinking a most productive field of inquiry in the coming years.

ACKNOWLEDGMENTS

The ideas developed in this chapter owe a great intellectual debt to Mark Runco, first because many of them were stimulated by a paper he presented at the Wallace Symposium on Giftedness and Talent (Runco, 1993), and second because of his thoughtful editorial suggestions in response to my original manuscript.

REFERENCES

Amabile, T. M. (1982). Social psychology of creativity: A consensual assessment technique. *Journal of Personality and Social Psychology, 43,* 997-1013.

Amabile, T. M. (1983). *The social psychology of creativity.* New York: Springer-Verlag.

Baer, J. (1988). Long-term effects of creativity training with middle school students. *Journal of Early Adolescence, 8,* 183-193.

Baer, J. (1991). Generality of creativity across performance domains. *Creativity Research Journal, 4,* 23-39.

Baer, J. (1992, August). *Divergent thinking is not a general trait.* Paper presented at the annual meeting of the American Psychological Association, Washington, DC.

Baer, J. (1993). *Creativity and divergent thinking: A task-specific approach.* Hillsdale, NJ: Lawrence Erlbaum.
Baer, J. (1994a). Divergent thinking is not a general trait: A multi-domain training experiment. *Creativity Research Journal, 7,* 35-46.
Baer, J. (1994b). Generality of creativity across performance domains: A replication. *Perceptual and Motor Skills, 79,* 1217-1218.
Baer, J. (1994c). Performance assessments of creativity: Do they have long-term stability? *Roeper Review, 7*(1), 7-11.
Baer, J. (1994d). Why you shouldn't trust creativity tests. *Educational Leadership, 51*(4), 80-84.
Baer, J. (1996). The effects of task-specific divergent-thinking training. *Journal of Creative Behavior, 30,* 183-187.
Baer, J. (1998). The case for domain specificity in creativity. *Creativity Research Journal, 11,* 173-177.
Basadur, M. (1995). Optimal ideation-evaluation ratios. *Creativity Research Journal, 8,* 63-75.
Campbell, D. T. (1960). Blind variation and selective retention in creative thought as in other knowledge processes. *Psychological Review, 67,* 380-400.
Carey, S. (1985). *Conceptual change in childhood.* Cambridge, MA: MIT Press.
Carey, S. (1988). Conceptual differences between children and adults. *Mind and Language, 3,* 167-181.
Csikszentmihalyi, M. (1988). Society, culture, and person: A systems view of creativity. In R. J. Sternberg (Ed.), *The nature of creativity* (pp. 325-339). Cambridge, England: Cambridge University Press.
Darwin, C. (1859). *On the origin of species.* London: John Murray.
Fausto-Sterling, A. (1991). Race, gender, and science. *Transformations, 2*(2), 4-12.
Fodor, J. A. (1983). *The modularity of mind.* Cambridge, MA: MIT Press.
Gage, N. L., & Berliner, D. C. (1992). *Educational psychology* (5th ed.). Boston: Houghton Mifflin.
Gardner, H. (1983). *Frames of mind: The theory of multiple intelligences.* New York: Basic Books.
Gardner, H. (1988). Creative lives and creative works: A synthetic scientific approach. In R. J. Sternberg (Ed.), *The nature of creativity* (pp. 298-321). Cambridge, England: Cambridge University Press.
Gazzaniga, M. S. (1985). *The social brain: Discovering the networks of the mind.* New York: Basic Books.
Gazzaniga, M. S., & Ledoux, J. (1978). *The integrated mind.* New York: Plenum Press.

Guilford, J. P. (1967). *The nature of human intelligence.* New York: McGraw-Hill.
Guilford, J. P., & Hoepfner, R. (1971). *The analysis of intelligence.* New York: McGraw-Hill.
Harding, S. (1986). *The science question in feminism.* Ithaca, NY: Cornell University Press.
Hennessey, B. A., & Zbikowski, S. M. (1993). Immunizing children against the negative effects of reward: A further examination of intrinsic motivation training techniques. *Creativity Research Journal, 6,* 297-307
Johnson-Laird, P. N. (1983). *Mental models.* Cambridge, MA: Harvard University Press.
Johnson-Laird, P. N. (1987). Reasoning, imagining, and creating. *Bulletin of the British Psychological Society, 40,* 121-129.
Johnson-Laird, P. N. (1988). Freedom and constraint in creativity. In R. J. Sternberg (Ed.), *The nature of creativity* (pp. 202-219). Cambridge, England: Cambridge University Press.
Johnson-Laird, P. N. (1993). *Human and machine thinking.* Hillsdale, NJ: Lawrence Erlbaum Associates.
Karmiloff-Smith, A. (1992). *Beyond modularity: A developmental perspective on cognitive science.* Cambridge, MA: MIT Press.
Mayer, R. E. (1987). *Educational psychology: A cognitive approach.* Boston: Little, Brown.
McCloskey, M. (1983). Intuitive physics. *Scientific American, 248*(4), 122-130.
Nelson, L. H. (1990). *Who knows: From Quine to a feminist empiricism.* Philadelphia: Temple University Press.
Parnes, S. J. (1972). *Creativity: Unlocking human potential.* Buffalo, NY: D. O. K. Publishers.
Pylyshyn, Z. (1980). Computation and cognition: Issues in the foundations of cognitive science. *Behavioral and Brain Sciences, 3,* 111-169.
Runco, M. A. (1987). The generality of creative performance in gifted and nongifted children. *Gifted Child Quarterly, 31,* 121-125.
Runco, M. A. (1989). The creativity of children's art. *Child Study Journal, 19,* 177-190.
Runco, M. A. (1991). The evaluative, valuative, and divergent thinking of children. *Journal of Creative Behavior, 25,* 311-319.
Runco, M. A. (1993, May). *Giftedness as critical and creative thought.* Paper presented at the Wallace Symposium on Giftedness and Talent, Iowa City, IA.
Runco, M. A., & Smith, W. R. (1992). Interpersonal and intrapersonal evaluations of creative ideas. *Personality and Individual Differences, 13,* 295-302.

Siegler, R. S. (1989). How domain-general and domain-specific knowledge interact to produce strategy choices. *Merrill-Palmer Quarterly, 35*(1), 1-26.

Simonton, D. K. (1988). *Scientific genius: A psychology of science.* New York: Cambridge University Press.

Sternberg, R. J. (1990). *Metaphors of mind: Conceptions of the nature of human intelligence.* Cambridge, England: Cambridge University Press.

Thurstone, L. L. (1938). *Primary mental abilities.* Chicago: University of Chicago Press.

Vye, N. J., Declos, V. R., Burns, M. S., & Bransford, J. D. (1988). Teaching thinking and problem solving: Illustrations and issues. In R. J. Sternberg & E. E. Smith (Eds.), *The psychology of human thought* (pp. 337-365). Cambridge, England: Cambridge University Press.

Woolfolk, A. E. (1993). *Educational psychology* (5th ed.). Boston: Allyn & Bacon.

7

THE ROLE OF INTELLIGENCE IN CREATIVITY

Robert J. Sternberg
Yale University

Todd E. Lubart
University of Paris V

Are creative people always intelligent? Are intelligent people usually creative? What is the relation between creativity and intelligence? These are the questions addressed here. This chapter uses as its theoretical basis our own investment theory of creativity (Sternberg & Lubart, 1991, 1995) as well as the triarchic theory of human intelligence (Sternberg, 1985, 1997). The basic idea is that creative people, like good investors, buy low and sell high, but do so in the world of ideas. To come up with "low-selling" ideas that others do not yet appreciate, diverse parts of intelligence are needed (see also Sternberg & O'Hara, 1999).

First, we describe the synthetic part of intelligence, which is involved in generating new ideas. The questions here are: "What abilities are needed to come up with new insights and to redefine existing problems in new ways?" "What can be done to enhance the ability to come up with these insights?" Next, we discuss the analytic part of intelligence, which is responsible for basic problem-solving activities such as initially recognizing and structuring problems, and for evaluating the ideas that one generates during problem solving. The basic question here is: "How, in solving the problem, do individuals set up a problem, generate a strategy to solve it, and monitor progress, and how can these skills be enhanced to foster creativity?" Then, we discuss the practical part of intelligence, which is responsible for humans knowing which ideas are likely to be well received, and which ideas will lead to further good ideas. This part of intelligence is involved in deciding just what kinds of ideas people, including the person presenting the idea, will consider creative.

THE SYNTHETIC PART OF INTELLIGENCE: COMING UP WITH GOOD IDEAS

Measuring People's Ability to Redefine Problems

We mention here two of the types of measures we have used to assess the ability to cope with novelty by defining problems in unconventional ways. Both of them use a multiple-choice format, and both are timed, meaning that we record both speed and accuracy as people solve the problems.

The first kind of problem is called a *conceptual-projection* problem (Sternberg, 1982; Tetewsky & Sternberg, 1986). Consider how such a problem works. If one looks at an emerald or at fresh spring grass, one will notice that these objects have in common their color—green. Probably no one would question their color. Yet, there is no guarantee that the grass is actually green rather than "grue," meaning green until the year 3000 and blue thereafter. Similarly, although a sapphire or the sky on a cloudless spring morning both certainly appear blue, there is no guarantee that they are not actually "bleen," meaning blue until the year 3000 and green thereafter. (Both of these concepts are borrowed from Goodman [1955], formulator of the so-called "new riddle of induction," which raises the question of why it is that humans describe certain concepts in one way, such as green, rather than in another way, such as grue, when there is no strong evidence to favor one description over another.)

Now, it might be said, concepts such as *grue* and *bleen* are ridiculous, because if something has been, green every year up to now, there is no reason to expect that it won't continue to be green into the indefinite future. Similarly, if something has always been blue, it can be expected to stay that way. Suppose, however, that one had been brought up believing that emeralds truly are grue, and sapphires, bleen. Then it would be believable that up to now, emeralds have always been grue and sapphires have always been bleen, and moreover, that they can be expected to stay that way.

"Nonsense," one might say. *Grue* and *bleen* are complicated concepts, both of them involving changes (in the first case, from green to blue, in the second, from blue to green). One thing humans learn when at a very young age is that it is always better to go for the simpler rather than the complex explanation of something. Therefore, one should say that emeralds are green and sapphires, blue.

It turns out not to be so simple, however. Suppose an individual was brought up on a planet, say Kyron, where people learn that emeralds are grue and sapphires are bleen. Then, a Kyronese comes to the Earth for the first time and is introduced to the concepts of *green* and *blue*. These concepts seem strange at first, but finally the Kyronese understands. An object that is green is one that, in his conceptual system, is grue until the year 3000 and bleen thereafter; in contrast, an object that is blue is one that is bleen until the year 3000 and grue thereafter. Note that which set of concepts is more complicated, Earth people's or the Kyronians', depends on the conceptual system with which one starts. For humans, the Kyronians' system is more complicated, but for the Kyronians, the human system is more complicated! Think about it: A Kyronian would argue in favor of the simplicity of his or her concepts, just as humans would argue in favor of the simplicity of our concepts.

In other versions of the same type of problem, subjects learned some other interesting facts about the Planet Kyron, such as that there are four kinds of people: *twes*, who are born young and die young; *nels*, who are born old and die old; *bits*, who are born young and die old; and *deks*, who are born old and die young.

In both kinds of problems, people are given incomplete information and have to infer whether a given object is blue, green, grue, or bleen, in the case of the first type of problem, or a twe, nel, bit, or dek, in the case of the second type of problem. A few problems are illustrated in Figure 7.1.

Sternberg has formulated information-processing models for these problems that specify the mental processes people use to solve them from beginning to end. Sternberg also formulated mathematical models that enable the prediction and evaluation of each person's performance. In scoring performance on these kinds of problems, the overall speed of response and number correct can be examined. But more interesting are the scores for individual information-processing components. A component of this kind is an estimate of the time it takes the person to complete a single mental process. For example, one process would be the time it takes a person to encode (store in memory) a single word, such as "blue" or "green"; another process would be the time it takes the person to hit a response key, and so on.

156   *Sternberg and Lubart*

In these problems, you must predict states of the future from limited information.

On the planet Kyron, in a faraway galaxy, there are four kinds of unisex humanoids:

> A TWE is a Kyronian who is born a child and remains a child throughout its lifetime.
> A NEL is a Kyronian who is born an adult and remains an adult throughout its lifetime.
> A BIT is a Kyronian who is born a child and becomes an adult.
> A DEK is a Kyronian who is born an adult and becomes a child.

Your task will be to analyze two pieces of information about a particular Kyronian, and decide whether these two pieces of information describe a TWE, NEL, BIT, or DEK. The two pieces of information will be a description of the Kyronian in the year of its birth, 1979, and a description of the Kyronian 21 years later, in the year 2000. The description of the Kyronian in the year 1979 will appear on the left, and a picture of the same Kyronian in the year 2000 will appear on the right. Your task is to judge which of the three verbal descriptions correctly identifies the kind of Kyronian depicted in the verbal description and the picture.

There is one important thing for you to realize in this kind of problem. Because it is not possible to tell at birth whether the individual is a TWE or a BIT, on the one hand (because both appear as children), or a NEL or a DEK, on the other (because both appear as adults), the verbal description for 1979 can be counted on only to identify correctly the physical appearance of the Kyronian; it may or may not correctly predict the appearance of the Kyronian 21 years later. Consider the following example:

			A	B	C
NEL			NEL	BIT	DEK

The correct answer is NEL, because the Kyronian appears to be an adult in 1979, and appears to be an adult in 2000 as well. NEL, therefore, correctly predicted the Kyronian's physical appearance in 2000.

			A	B	C
(1)	BIT		BIT	DEK	TWE

Figure 7.1. The Kyronian problems (from Sternberg, 1986b)

Role of Intelligence 157

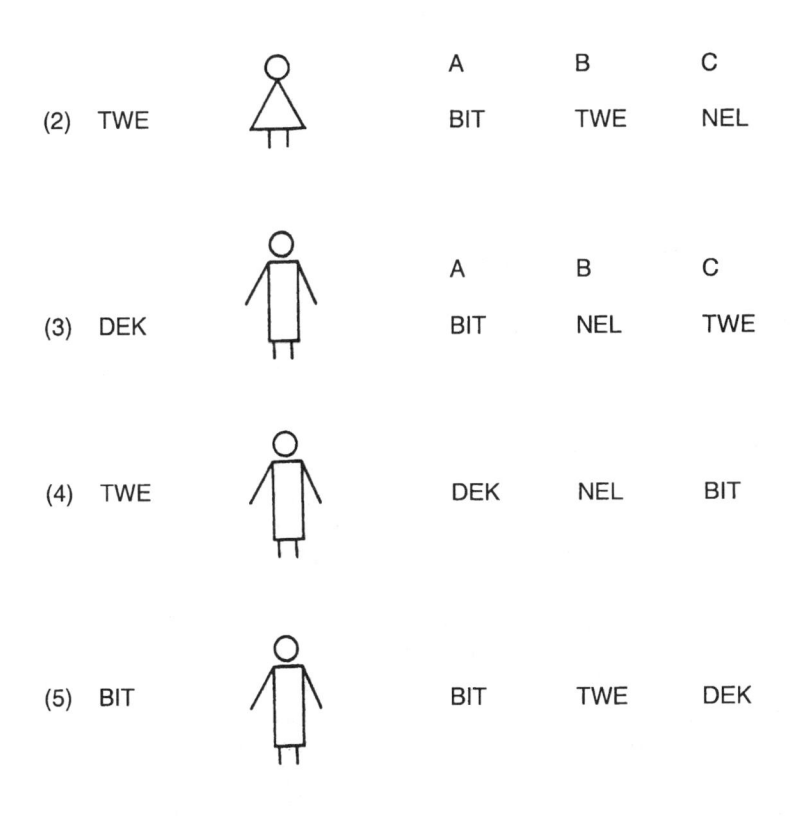

			A	B	C
(2)	TWE		BIT	TWE	NEL

			A	B	C
(3)	DEK		BIT	NEL	TWE

(4)	TWE		DEK	NEL	BIT

(5)	BIT		BIT	TWE	DEK

Answers to the Kyronian Problems

(1) C   (2) B   (3) B   (4) C   (5) A

Figure 7.1. The Kyronian problems (from Sternberg, 1986b) (cont'd.)

The crucial finding in this research is the information-processing component that best distinguishes more from less creative people. This component is the amount of time it takes a person to switch from "green-blue" thinking, on the one hand, to "grue-bleen" thinking, on the other, or back again. In other words, creative people are well able to transit between conventional and unconventional thinking. They find the transition relatively comfortable, and do it with ease. Less creative people, in contrast, even though they may have the facility to exercise with ease and even speed an array of more routine mental processes, find it difficult to transit between conventional and unconventional thinking. Many people who are "smart" in the sense of doing well in school or on conventional tests are in their element as long as they are reading the words of a problem or making simple comparisons; it is when they must think in terms of concepts that are truly novel to them that they have difficulty. In other words, they are fine with conventional problems based on conventional assumptions, but have more trouble with problems requiring unconventional assumptions and inferences.

A second type of problem used to assess people's abilities to think in unconventional ways is illustrated in Table 7.1. These problems are called *novel analogies* and, as can be imagined, these problems do not provide a particularly good measure of people's ability to think in unconventional ways. Standard analogies appear on a variety of intelligence and scholastic aptitude tests and generally measure conventional intellectual abilities. Standard verbal analogies, moreover, measure vocabulary and general information at least as much as they measure reasoning skill. Thus, someone who is a good reasoner may find verbal analogies relatively difficult if he or she does not recognize the meanings of the words in the analogies.

The analogies used here contained only fairly simple, common words. But they come with a twist; each analogy is preceded by a presupposition. The presupposition is counterfactual, meaning that it states something to be true that is not. Subjects are instructed to solve the analogies as though the presuppositions were true. Thus, if the presupposition were "Canaries play hopscotch," then the analogy would have to be solved as though this presupposition were indeed correct.

Again, there are fairly detailed information-processing models of how people solve these problems. There are also mathematical models that allow the analysis of an individual's score in terms of how long he or she takes on each processing component, and how accurate he or she is on that component.

What is found is that many of the best solvers of ordinary analogies find these novel analogies extremely difficult to solve. In other words, they just find it really hard to think in unconventional

Table 7.1. Novel Analogies.

In solving the analogies below, assume that the statement given before the analogy is true, whether or not it is actually true. Then solve the analogy taking this assumption into account.

(1) GOATS are robots.
    CHICKEN is to HATCHED as GOAT is to:
    BORN   FARM   BUILT   FACTORY

(2) NEEDLES are dull.
    THIMBLE is to BLUNT as NEEDLE is to:
    SHARP   SMOOTH   STAB   BRUISE

(3) PIGS climb fences.
    GOLDFISH is to BOWL as PIG is to:
    PEN   CAGE   DIRTY   GRACEFUL

(4) DIAMONDS are fruits.
    PEARL is to OYSTER as DIAMOND is to:
    MINE   TREE   RING   PIE

(5) TOASTERS write cookbooks.
    SPATULA is to UTENSIL as TOASTER is to:
    WRITER   APPLIANCE   BREAD   BOOK

(6) GHOSTS are athletes.
    WEREWOLF is to MONSTER as GHOST is to:
    DRAMA   SPIRIT   HAUNT   ACT

                ANSWERS TO NOVEL ANALOGIES

                (1) BUILT   (4) TREE
                (2) SMOOTH   (5) WRITER
                (3) CAGE   (6) SPIRIT

terms. So long as the analogy is based on the problem solver's ordinary knowledge of the world, solving an analogy is easy. But the uncreative problem solver has difficulty imagining any state of the world except the one to which he or she is accustomed. This is reminiscent of a well-known politician in Washington, who, after the demise of the Soviet empire, commented to the press that, as far as he was concerned, nothing had changed. The sad thing was that, for him, it was true. He just could not quite deal with a world in which the Soviet Union was no longer the monolithic enemy it always had been and—as Americans were brought up to believe—always would be.

Both of these kinds of problems are verbal, but it is possible to measure the ability to think in novel ways with other kinds of problems as well, such as quantitative ones. Figures 7.2 and 7.3 show two of the kinds of quantitative problems used that measure the ability to think in novel ways. In the first kind of problem, the *novel number matrix* problem, subjects are introduced to new symbols that substitute for numbers. They are then presented with numerical matrices that contain a mixture of conventional numbers and novel symbols. Subjects then have to fill in the missing entry in the number matrix.

In the second kind of problem, the *novel numerical-operations* problem, subjects are introduced to new mathematical operators they have never before encountered. For example, they may have to add two numbers if the first is less than the second, subtract the second number from the first if the second is less than the first, and multiply the two numbers if they are equal. Subjects then are given mathematical problems, such as those in Figure 7.3, to solve.

Once again, people who are good at solving conventional kinds of problems, in this case, mathematical problems, are not necessarily very good at solving these novel kinds of mathematical problems. To solve these problems, one needs not be a math whiz, but should to be able to let go of his or her conventional assumptions about the numbers and operations that are permissible when doing math.

Yet another kind of problem is figural, as shown in Figure 7.4. Subjects have to complete the figure series. The trick, however, is that the problems do not contain just a single row of figures, with each figure representing a continuation of a sequence from the last one. Rather, after the sequence is started, subjects are given a figure that has a different appearance. The subject needs to continue the series from this last figure—the one that has a different appearance from the previous ones in the series.

Role of Intelligence   161

DIRECTIONS

In each problem below, the numbers in the boxes go together in a certain way. The information below the boxes provides another way to show a certain number or numbers. Decide what number or symbol goes in the empty box.

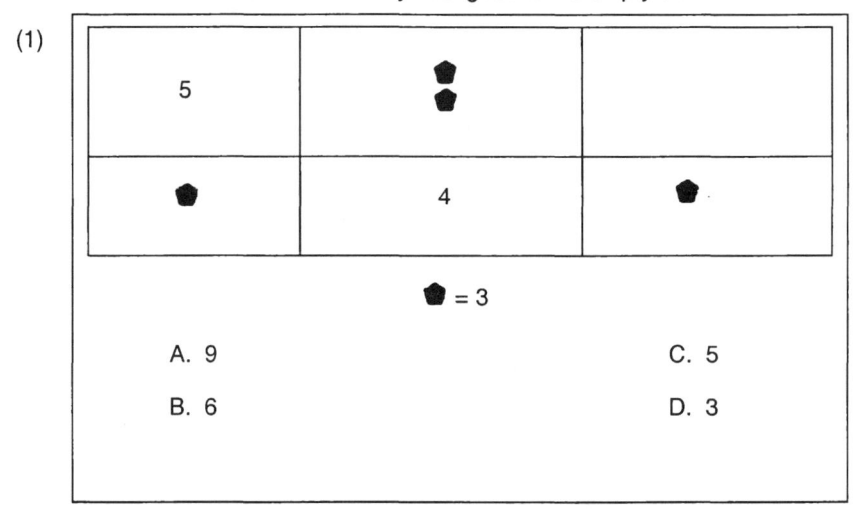

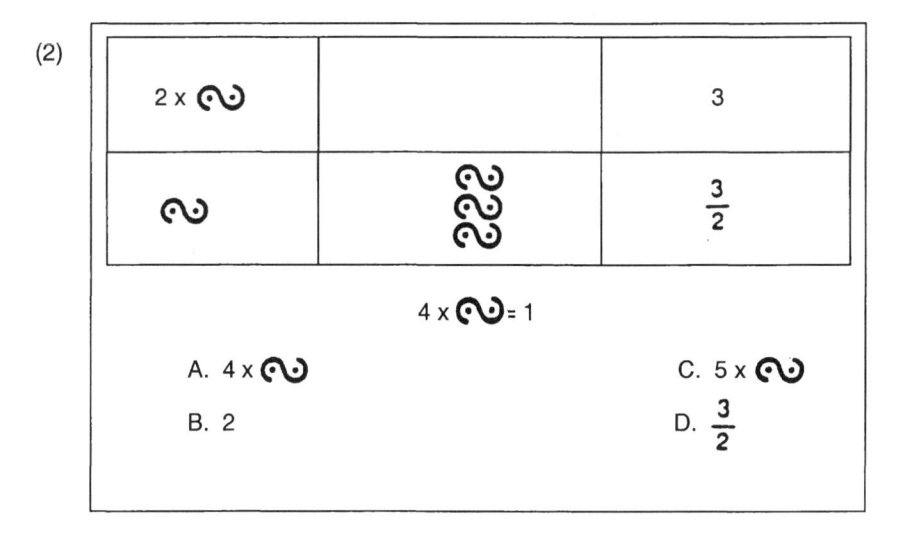

(1)

5	●●	
●	4	●

● = 3

A. 9   C. 5
B. 6   D. 3

(2)

2 × ∽		3
∽	∽∽∽	3/2

4 × ∽ = 1

A. 4 × ∽   C. 5 × ∽
B. 2   D. 3/2

Novel Number Matrix Answers

(1) C   (2) D

Figure 7.2. Novel number matrix

DIRECTIONS

In each problem below, you will employ unusual mathematical operations in order to reach the solution. There are two unusual operations: *graf* and *flix*. First, read how the operation is defined. Then, decide what is the correct answer to the question.

There is a new mathematical operation called *graf*. It is defined as follows:

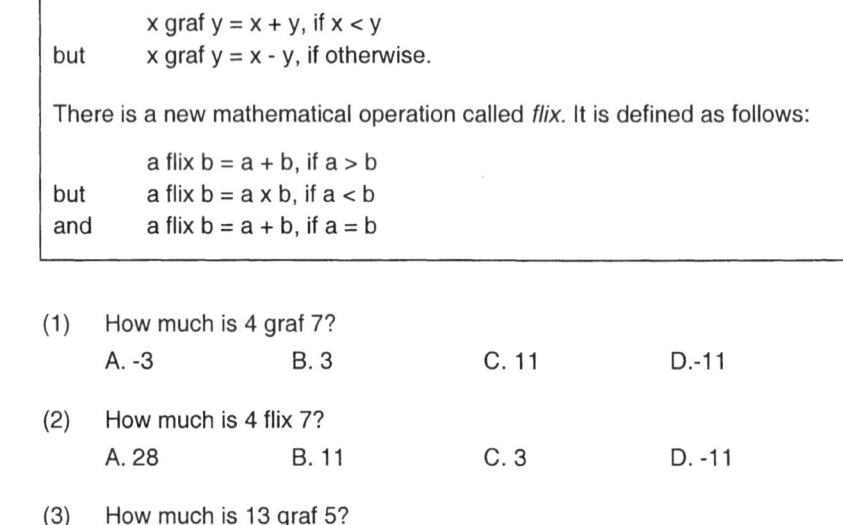

x graf y = x + y, if x < y
but   x graf y = x - y, if otherwise.

There is a new mathematical operation called *flix*. It is defined as follows:

a flix b = a + b, if a > b
but   a flix b = a x b, if a < b
and   a flix b = a + b, if a = b

---

(1) How much is 4 graf 7?
    A. -3   B. 3   C. 11   D. -11

(2) How much is 4 flix 7?
    A. 28   B. 11   C. 3   D. -11

(3) How much is 13 graf 5?
    A. 5   B. 18   C. 13   D. 8

(4) How much is 3 flix 7-1/2?
    A. 10-1/2   B. 21-1/2   C. 22-1/2   D. 4-1/2

Novel Numerical Operations Answers
(1) C   (2) A   (3) D   (4) C

Figure 7.3. Novel numerical operations

Role of Intelligence

DIRECTIONS

In each question, the shapes in the first row of boxes go together in a certain way to form a pattern. The second row of boxes follows the same pattern. Decide what shape goes in the empty box.

(1)

(2)

Figural Problem Answers

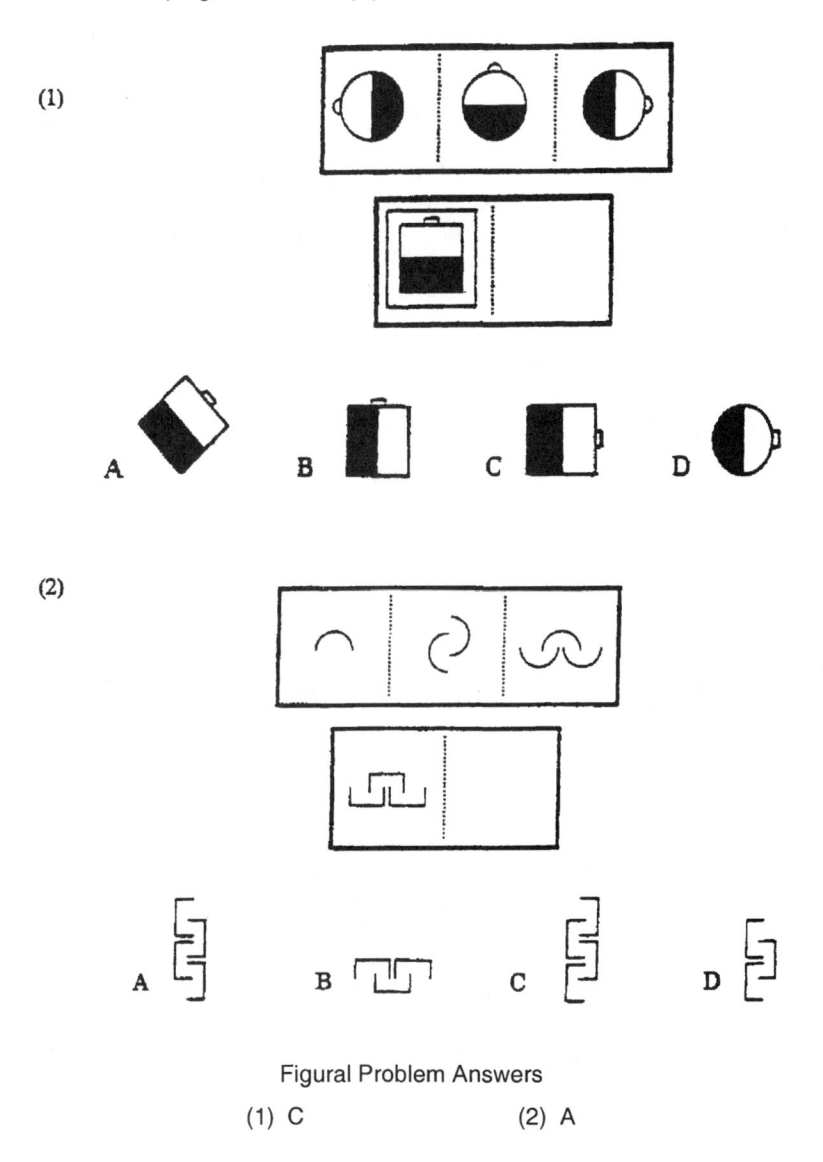

(1) C   (2) A

Figure 7.4. Figural problems

All of the problems described here are of the multiple-choice variety, where subjects are given a series of answer options and must choose the best one. But, it is important to measure subjects' abilities to think in novel ways using formats of testing that are not exclusively multiple-choice. Thus, essays are used that require subjects to think about problems that they probably have not thought about before, or at least to think about familiar problems in new ways. Table 7.2 gives some examples of some of the kinds of essays used previously with high school students.

In summary, a variety of different kinds of problems are used to measure people's ability to think in novel ways. In each case, conventional definitions of problems just do not work. A different kind of problem, however, the insight problem, is also used in order to measure specific information-processing abilities that may contribute to the redefinition of problems and to the solution of problems in novel ways. Insight and its measurement are discussed next.

Insight and Its Measurement

An insight is a new way of seeing something that usually feels as though it has occurred suddenly, and thus evokes a feeling of surprise, and often, delight. There are three basic kinds of insights that form the foundation of creative thinking: *selective-encoding, selective-*

Table 7.2. Essays.

DIRECTIONS

Write an essay in response to each of the following three questions.

(1) Many high schools now have police or security guards present in the building for security purposes. Analyze this issue: What are the advantages and disadvantages of having extra security people in the schools? Are you for or against this practice, and why?

(2) Suppose you are the student representative to a committee that has the power and the money to reform your school. Describe the ideal school that you would create. Include in your description any aspects of schools that you feel are important.

(3) Think of a problem that you are currently experiencing in real life. Briefly describe the problem, including how long it has been present and who else is involved (if anyone). Then describe three different practical things you could do to try to solve the problem.

comparison, and *selective-combination* insights. (For other views on insight, see Sternberg & Davidson, 1995.) These selective information processes can lead to problem redefinition (discussed previously) and to novel ideas for problem solution. In other words, these skills are an important part of the way that people buy low in the realm of ideas.

The first kind of insight is *selective-encoding insight*, which occurs when a person who is trying to learn something or to solve a problem sees the relevance to what he or she is doing of information whose relevance is not obvious. In other words, the person zeroes in on one or more critical pieces of information for the solution of a problem at hand.

A famous scientific example of a selective-encoding insight is Alexander Fleming's discovery of penicillin. Fleming was doing a laboratory experiment in which he was growing bacteria in a petri dish. The experiment went bad when bacteria infiltrated the petri dish, resulting in the growth of a mold. Most scientists, when their experiments go bad, curse their bad luck, and label the experiment a "pilot experiment." They then keep doing pilot experiments until they get the thing to work, at which point they label it the "real experiment."

Fleming was more observant than many scientists would have been. He noticed that the mold had killed the bacteria in the petri dish. And everyone knows how hard it is to kill bacteria. In noticing the bactericidal power of the mold, Fleming experienced a selective-encoding insight. His observation later led to the isolation of the critical antibiotic, penicillin, from the penicillium mold.

A selective-encoding insight was also at the heart of the discovery of super glue. Chemical researchers at a division of Eastman Kodak were searching for a heat-resistant material to cover aircraft cockpits. When one of the compounds was applied between two lenses to test the effect on light, the lenses would not come apart. The researcher who applied the compound was upset at the loss of expensive lenses but the supervisor, Harry Coover, saw things a different way. They had just discovered a powerful new adhesive.

Selective-encoding insights are not limited to scientific discoveries. Lawyers need selective-encoding insights in order to figure out the critical facts of a case. Often, clients are frustrated that the facts that seem important to them do not seem important to their lawyers. That's because lawyers know that cases often turn on minute points of law that clients would not even know existed. Doctors use selective-encoding insights when they are able to isolate the critical symptoms they will need in order to make a diagnosis. Business executives use selective-encoding insights when, confronted with a bewildering array of information, they realize that certain key facts are the ones that will enable them to make a decision that may have enormous financial implications for their company. Indeed, practically everyone needs selective-encoding insights at various points in their life. A spouse may use a selective-encoding insight in realizing that certain pieces of his or her partner's behavior don't seem quite right in the context of the way the partner has always behaved before. Of course, there are many other examples of selective-encoding insights.

The second kind of insight, *selective-comparison insights*, are used to figure out how information from the past can be brought to bear on the problems of the present. Such insights usually involve *analogical thinking*, in the sense that the person sees how something from the past is somehow analogous to something in the present. A famous selective-comparison insight was reported by Friedrich Kekulé in describing his discovery of the structure of benzene. Kekulé had been trying to discover the structure for some time without success. Then, one night, Kekulé had a dream in which he imagined a snake curling around and biting its tail. When Kekulé awoke, he realized that the snake curling around on itself was a visual metaphor for the structure of benzene—namely, a ring.

Selective-comparison insights, like the other kinds of insights, are useful in everyday life. The lawyer who realizes the relevance of a past precedent, or the relevance of prior information about the parties in a case, is having a selective-comparison insight. A business executive facing a tough decision who remembers a similar decision point in the past and an outcome that led to disastrous consequences is experiencing a selective-comparison insight. In all these cases, the past is brought to bear upon the present in a way that is nontrivial and nonobvious.

We call the third kind of insight a *selective-combination insight*. A person has a selective-combination insight when he or she sees how to fit together pieces of information whose connection is not obvious. For example, Charles Darwin's formulation of the theory of evolution was based at least in part on an insight of selective combination. The information available to Darwin also was available to many other scientists. They could equally well have come up with the theory, and one of them, Alfred Russell Wallace, eventually did. What Darwin saw was how to fit the disparate pieces of the puzzle together.

Louis Comfort Tiffany revolutionized the art of stained glass in the 19th century when he selectively combined English Stourbridge glass, the work of Emile Galle, and his own traditional knowledge of producing glass windows. He created Favrile Glass and used its natural color gradations and texture variations to make his glass windows, lamps, and other products. Tiffany also combined the cames (grooved strips that hold the glass segments together) with the stained glass itself in a new way. For example, he would vary the width or texture of the cames and use them to depict tree branches or other integral parts of his stained-glass window compositions.

Selective-combination insights, like selective-encoding insights, are critical in everyday life. A concrete example is the formulation of a creative recipe. With guests coming, the cook has to figure out how to make a good-tasting dish out of the available ingredients. A spouse may use a selective-combination insight to figure out that the pieces of the partner's behavior that don't add up all fit together to suggest that more is going on in the partner's life than meets the eye. A teacher can make a creative curriculum through a selective combination of students' interests, materials, and assignments. For example, a woman taught remedial high school English to 12th-grade students who had previously failed. In a typical class, she might have students read a newspaper article on an issue of interest (such as gun control), learn vocabulary based on the article, and write a letter to the editor about the issue. The effectiveness of this strategy—combining diverse materials with the students' own interests—was such that her lesson plans easily held the students' attention. In business, entrepreneurs essentially engage in selective combinations. They bring together disparate parties who fit each other's needs and create new ventures.

Insight abilities, like the ability to define problems in novel ways, can be measured. Table 7.3 shows some examples of insight problems we have used (e.g., Sternberg & Davidson, 1982) to measure these abilities.

This study of insight problems has reminded us at times of just how modest we, as investigators, need to be about our own insight abilities. For one thing, we have had many subjects solve problems that we ourselves have been unable to solve. For another, we sometimes encounter surprises even when we can solve the problems.

Consider an example of a well-known insight problem given as an example of a good problem for measuring intelligence in an article published in the *American Scientist* (Sternberg, 1986a). The problem was the so-called "water lilies" problem:

> At the beginning of the summer, there is one water lily on a lake. The water lilies double in area every 24 hours. At the end of 60 days, the lake is completely covered by water lilies. On what day is the lake half-covered?

The "correct" answer is "Day 59," because if the water lilies double in area every 24 hours, and if the lake is completely covered with water lilies after 60 days, then one day before, on Day 59, the lake will be half covered. About 1 month after the article was pub-

Table 7.3. Arithmetical and Logical Insight Problems.

(1) You are at a party of truth-tellers and liars. The truth-tellers always tell the truth, and the liars always lie. You meet a new friend. He tells you that he just heard a conversation in which a girl said she was a liar. Is your new friend a liar or a truth-teller?

(2) A recipe calls for four cups of water. You have only a three-cup container and a five-cup container. How can you measure out exactly four cups of water using only these containers?

(3) In the Thompson family, there are five brothers, and each brother has one sister. If you count Mrs. Thompson, how many females are in the Thompson family?

(4) Susan gets in her car in Boston and drives toward New York City, averaging 50 miles per hour. Twenty minutes later, Ellen gets in her car in New York City and starts driving toward Boston, averaging 60 miles per hour. Both women take the same route, which extends 220 miles between the two cities. Which car is nearer to Boston when they meet?

(5) A bottle of wine cost $10. The wine was worth $9 more than the bottle. How much was the bottle worth?

Note. The insight problems are from Sternberg (1986b).

Answers to Arithmetical and Logical Insight Problems

(1) Your new friend is clearly a liar. If the girl about whom the friend was talking were a truth-teller, she would have said that she was a truth-teller. If she were a liar, she would have said that she was a truth-teller also. Thus, regardless of whether the girl were a truth-teller or a liar, she would have said that she was a truth teller. Since your friend said that she said she was a liar, your friend must be lying, and hence must be a liar.

(2) Fill the five-cup container with water. Pour as much of the contents as you can into the three-cup container. Now spill out the contents that you just poured into the three-cup container. You now have two cups in the five-cup container. Pour the contents of the five-cup container into the three-cup container. Now fill the five-cup container again. Pour as much of the contents of the five-cup container as you can into the three-cup container. This container will take only one cup. You now have four cups left in the five-cup container.

(3) Two. The only females in the family are the mother and her one daughter, who is the sister to each of her brothers.

(4) Each car is the same distance from Boston when they meet, as the cars are immediately next to each other.

(5) 50¢.

lished, the author received a page-and-a-half, singled-spaced typewritten letter from a famous aerodynamic designer. In the letter, the designer proved that if life-size water lilies really doubled in area every 24 hours, at the end of 60 days, the world would be almost completely covered with water lilies. Oh, well: It is certainly an alternative perspective on the problem! We have found, as have so many testers before, that sometimes the people tested are more insightful than those doing the testing!

Many different kinds of problems have been used to measure insight above and beyond those we used in our own research (Kotovsky, Hayes, & Simon, 1985).

Educational and Practical Implications

Our discussion of the failure of testers to recognize the superior insight abilities of some of their subjects suggests one important implication of creativity for education. Teachers and other evaluators need to be sensitive to the fact that sometimes their students will see things that they themselves do not see. One of the worst things that a teacher can do is to close off all possible solutions to a problem other than his or her own, and assume that if a student disagrees with the teacher's view on a problem, the student must be wrong. In our experience, this kind of closed-mindedness occurs much more often than anyone would like.

This phenomenon is not limited to the schools. In business as well, management often tends to see a certain problem in a certain way, or to define itself in a certain way. For example, in the 1970s one could go to a department store and find a dazzling selection of brands of typewriters. But on going to a department store now and looking at the typewriter section, chances are that, if one is able to find typewriters, there will be just one or at most two brands. The companies that defined themselves as making typewriters, and especially manual typewriters, have, for the most part, folded. Companies that defined themselves more broadly—as making word-processing devices of one kind or another, for example—stayed around longer as the manual typewriter market declined. But one company, known for its word processors, eventually hit the financial straits. Those companies that defined themselves even more broadly—as making computational devices that include machines that process words—have had more success. To stay successful in a rapidly changing world, a company has to keep redefining itself in order to succeed.

In their everyday lives, too, people need to keep redefining themselves. There was a time when people would start in one job at the beginning of their work life and change jobs perhaps once or twice for the rest of their career. These days, people change more frequently, in part because companies come and go so quickly. But even people who stay in the same nominal job, often change what they actually do in the job in very little time. For example, if one looks at what a secretary does today, versus what a secretary did 15 or 20 years ago, it will be clear that the job has changed enormously. Many secretaries now use computers for various functions on the job. Computer skills have become a must for the more highly skilled among them. Twenty years ago, only a very small fraction of secretaries would have even known the first thing about a computer. Moreover, there was no reason why they should have known more—computers were not yet being used in their jobs. The same, of course, can be said for the executives for whom they work, many of whom have themselves had to learn how to use personal computers.

We believe that it is important in the schools, as well as on the job, to be on the lookout for people with unusual creative intelligence. In our own work, we have put this principle into practice. Recently, Sternberg and Clinkenbeard (1995) ran a summer program at Yale for 60 gifted high school students. Usually, "gifted" means "high IQ," or "high grade point average." But we identified our gifted students in a different way.

We gave program applicants problems based on the triarchic conception of intelligence. One third of the problems required creative intellectual abilities, measured by the kinds of problems just described. One third required analytic abilities, and another third, practical abilities, which are discussed later. In order to ensure that the test was as fair as possible to all of the students who took it, we also used different kinds of test items. In particular, for each of the analytic, creative, and practical abilities, one fourth were multiple-choice verbal items; one fourth were multiple-choice quantitative items; one fourth were multiple-choice figural items; and one fourth were essay items. Thus, students with different kinds of talents (e.g., more verbally oriented, or more mathematically oriented) would be equally favored by the test.

As a result of the testing, we had three categories of students: high-analytics, high-creatives, and high-practicals. Basically, people were identified as "high" in an ability if their standardized score (score that ranks them relative to other people) in a given ability was statistically substantially higher than their scores in the other abilities. In the 1992 summer program, comprising 60 students, these were the only categories selected for inclusion in the program. In the 1993 summer program, comprising more than 200 students, we had two additional identified groups: a balanced gifted group (roughly equally high in all three ability areas) and an above average "control" group (students high in the various abilities but not scoring high enough to be identified as gifted in any of the abilities.)

Students were then streamed into one of several sections of a college-level, advanced placement (AP) introductory psychology course. Because all the students were entering high school juniors and seniors, this course presented a challenge of high magnitude. The 1992 summer program had three sections: analytic, creative, and practical. The 1993 summer program had an additional section: traditional (see Sternberg, Ferrari, Clinkenbeard, & Grigorenko, 1996; Sternberg, Grigorenko, Ferrari, & Clinkenbeard, 1999). Because students were assigned to sections at random (with the constraint that each section have the same number of students), they were somewhat more likely to be in a section that did not correspond to their own strength than to be in one that did. For example, in the 1992 summer program, the high-creative student had only a one in three chance of being placed in the creatively oriented course (and a one in three chance of being in the analytic course, and one in three for the practical one).

The analytic section of the course emphasized the development of skills such as analyzing theories, comparing theories, critiquing experiments, and the like. The creative section emphasized coming up with original ideas for theories, experiments, and the like. The practical section emphasized the use of psychology and psychological principles in everyday life. The traditional section emphasized learning of the basic facts of the discipline.

All students were also assessed in four different ways: for basic recall of the course material (the traditional emphasis in educational testing), for analysis of course material, for creative use of course material, and for practical use of course material. Examples of the kinds of questions we used are shown in Table 7.4. The same kinds of questioning strategies could be applied in any field: Instructors can ask students either to remember material, analyze material, creatively use the material and go beyond it, or think about the practical implications of the material.

Most importantly from the standpoint of this book, students who were identified as creatively gifted, who were placed in a section of the introductory psychology course that emphasized creative thinking, and who were then assessed in ways that allowed them to use creative thinking, excelled on these measures beyond the performance of the other groups. High-practical students also did particularly well on the practical assessments when they had been placed in a section that emphasized practical thinking.

These results show the benefit of matching instruction and assessment of students with their triarchic ability pattern. Obviously, we are not saying that students should learn and be tested only in a way that matches their ability pattern. But we are saying that we believe that there are a lot of creative students out there

Table 7.4. Summer Program Assessment Questions.

Basic Recall:

You have recently accepted a job selling raffle tickets. You will be paid $5 for every 10 tickets you sell regardless of whether it takes you 10 minutes or 10 days to sell them. What kind of reinforcement schedule are you being paid on?

    a. variable interval
    b. fixed interval
    c. variable ratio
    d. fixed ratio

Vygotsky's idea of the zone of proximal development implies that researchers should change the way children are tested. Which of the following changes in testing would Vygotsky recommend?

    a. more items on every test
    b. giving hints to students
    c. taking points off for guessing
    d. giving more essay questions than multiple choice items

Analytic:

Compare the theory of constructive perception with the theory of direct perception. Briefly describe each theory, and then evaluate each theory for strengths and weaknesses. Compare and contrast the theories with one another. Finally, make an argument for why you think one is a "better" account of perception than the other.

Creative:

Based on everything you have learned in this course, come up with your own theory of intelligence. You should at least address the following questions, but feel free to go beyond them as well: What is intelligence? How is it acquired? Is it fluid or fixed? What are the factors that influence someone's intellectual capabilities? You can draw on theories from the readings, but be sure that your theory adds something new to the existing literature. Also be sure to state what is distinctive about your theory and to explain the advantages of your theory over other theories.

Practical:

You are a clinical psychologist who follows the school of behaviorism and who utilizes the principles of learning theory in doing therapy with clients. A man comes to you and wants you to help him give up smoking. What processes might you try to aid him in this endeavor? How successful do you think your treatment would be and why?

who are withering on the vine because the way they are taught and assessed does not give them a chance to express their gifts. Creative students are not going to show their extraordinary strengths in a course that requires them to memorize a textbook.

The results for the high-analytic students were a surprise, although not necessarily a disappointment. We expected, of course, that the high-analytic students would do best when placed in a section that emphasized analytic teaching and learning, and then when assessed with tests that measured analytic thinking. Instead, the high-analytic students were the worst of the lot, no matter how they were taught, and no matter how they were assessed. In other words, it didn't matter how they were taught—they still didn't do well!

At first we were baffled by these results, but their meaning quickly became clear when we identified who the high-analytic students were and talked to their course instructors about them. The high-analytic students were basically the ones who had always been identified as gifted throughout their schooling. They were the traditional high-IQ students, the ones who were fully aware of their own abilities and whose schools were fully aware as well. These were students who had, throughout most if not all of their studies, learned that they could get away with relatively little effort. For the most part, they had never been really seriously challenged; they were students who could get top marks doing a minimum of work. They came to our summer program, therefore, expecting that once again they could breeze by without working very hard. They discovered, probably for the first time in their lives, that they were wrong!

They were the lucky ones. Most such students do not discover that the days of being top performers without working end after high school. We have taught any number of students who come to college as freshmen, expecting that they will get by without working and then discovering, often too late, that they are wrong. The summer psychology students had the advantage that they were given the opportunity to learn the lesson sooner rather than later.

Our goal in the summer program was to teach subject matter to high school students in a way that emphasized analytic, creative, or practical thinking. In another program for upper elementary school students, Davidson and Sternberg attempted to show that creative-insightful thinking could be directly taught, even to very young children (Davidson & Sternberg, 1984). A 5-week program was devised that taught students how to solve insight problems of the kinds described earlier (e.g., the water-lilies problem). More examples of problems we used are shown in Table 7.5.

Students were instructed in the processes of selective encoding, selective combination, and selective comparison, in a variety of domains, including the mathematical, as shown previously.

Table 7.5. Insight Problems.

(1) If you have black socks and brown socks in your drawer, mixed in the ratio of 4 to 5, how many socks will you have to take out to make sure of having a pair of the same color?

(2) A farmer has 17 sheep. All but 9 broke through a hole in the fence and wandered away. How many were left?

(3) A farmer buys 100 animals for $100. Cows are $10 each, sheep are $3 each, and pigs are 50¢ each. How much did he pay for 5 cows?

(4) Suppose you have two pencils, a good one and a cheap one. The good one cost $1 more than the cheap one. You spent $1.10 for both pencils. How much did the cheap one cost?

(5) If there are 12 one-cent stamps in a dozen, how many two-cent stamps are there in a dozen?

Answers to Insight Problems

(1) Three
(2) Nine
(3) $50
(4) 5¢
(5) 12

Instruction was in the context of science, verbal, and other types of problems. Students in this program included both those who had been identified as gifted by their schools and those who had not been so identified.

We found that after 5 weeks, students identified as gifted and those not so identified both improved significantly in their ability to solve various kinds of insight problems. The rate of improvement for the two groups was roughly the same, so that although students in both groups benefited, there was still a mean difference between groups at the end of the program. Neither this program nor any other simply wipes out individual differences. But the results clearly showed that insightful thinking can be taught, at least to some degree.

There was one other result worthy of mention. When we initially gave the insightful thinking tests, we found them to be modest predictors of who had been classified as "gifted." Quite a few children identified as gifted were not particularly adept at solving the insight problems, whereas many other children not identified as gifted were quite adept at solving these problems. In other words, whatever criteria the school was using to identify children as gifted, insightful thinking did not seem to be among them. We believe that the same could be said for many, and probably most, other schools as well. Once again, the creatively gifted are often those most at risk for having talents that are neither appreciated nor often even recognized in the context of the school.

Presently, we, together with Wendy Williams and a team from Harvard University, are putting the finishing touches on the development of a program for upper elementary and middle-school students called Creative Intelligence for Schools. The goal of this program is to help children develop the creative skills that often start to languish as they advance through the school system. The program is based on the investment theory of creativity described in this volume, and will serve to put into practice the ideas that are discussed in this and subsequent chapters.

Our own practical interests are not limited to the context of the school. We also currently have a research program for developing creative leadership skills. We give our students case studies such as that shown in Table 7.6 as a basis for learning how to handle leadership challenges creatively. Through these case studies, leaders learn the skills needed to supervise in new and productive ways. For a number of years, Richard Wagner, Wendy Williams, and Robert Sternberg studied the practical intelligence of managers. The research was in many respects quite successful, producing a theory and a resulting test that could predict success in management about twice as well as a conventional intelligence test (see Williams & Sternberg, in press). But in this work, something was unsettled: We were assessing the ability of people to adapt to their environments, but not the ability of people to shape these environments—to turn the environments into what they wanted them to be. More and more, we began to see that the people who really made the difference in corporate America were not necessarily just the highly competent managers, but the real leaders who shaped the way their companies operated. So we have recently become interested in the creative side of management—the leadership side—believing that in the world of business as in our schools, we cannot afford to squander what we believe to be our most precious human resource—creativity.

THE ANALYTIC PART OF INTELLIGENCE: THE BASICS OF PROBLEM SOLVING

There is a natural tendency to pit synthetic ability against analytic ability, or "right-hemisphere" thinking against "left-hemisphere"

Table 2.6. Creative Leadership Skills.

Your goal is to make sure your guidance is communicated accurately to all levels of the organization. In the past, information has been lost or distorted as it has filtered down the organizational chart, resulting in misunderstandings and hard feelings on the part of some employees. You have reason to believe that someone down the line is purposely holding back and distorting information for his own ends, but you are not sure who it is. What might you do to find out, and then what should you do if you are able to identify the individual?

---

thinking. But this dichotomy, like most dichotomies, is overstated. With respect to synthetic and analytic abilities, people are not really one thing or another, but some combination of both.

Creativity requires not only coming up with ideas, but knowing when a problem exists to start with, how to define the problem, how to allocate resources to solve the problem, and how to evaluate the value of potential solutions—knowing which ideas are the good ones. Renzulli (1986), and many others as well, have proposed that to be creative, one needs some minimum threshold of analytic ability. But most scholars, including Renzulli, believe that the threshold is not terribly high. An individual does not have to be an IQ star to be creative.

The relation between intelligence and creativity is often reported in terms of IQ scores. These scores represent a standardized metric for comparing people. The population average IQ is defined as 100 with scores typically ranging between 70 (low intelligence) and 130 (high intelligence). IQ can be measured by several different intelligence tests. These tests focus on analytic ability.

There are three basic findings concerning IQ and creativity (Barron & Harrington, 1981; Lubart, 1994). First, creative people tend to show above average scores, often above 120. Second, the correlation between IQ and creativity varies across studies from weak and slightly negative to moderately strong and positive. Third, the typical correlations tend to be approximately equal to .20. Thus, creativity is weakly related to, but by no means the same as, intelligence. After an IQ of 120, intelligence does not seem to matter much to further increases in creativity.

There are several possible explanations for these observed results. Consistent with the ideas of intelligence expressed here, there is the "measurement" explanation: IQ tests vary on the specific abilities, but another test could measure less-relevant abilities. This leads to a range of observed correlations between creativity and IQ. In general, IQ tests measure at least some relevant abilities, leading creative people to show elevated average test scores.

In terms of broader theory, another explanation concerns the importance of multiple resources for creativity: Only part of the variability in creativity can be accounted for by intellectual processes. Other resources such as a risk-taking personality, task-focused motivation, and supportive environment play a role.

Creativity researchers have proposed three further explanations for the observed IQ-creativity connection. One is a "diminishing returns" hypothesis (Hayes, 1989). Beyond an above average level, intellectual skills benefit creativity less and less. The second is the "certification" hypothesis (Hayes, 1989). Intelligence provides access (e.g., completing an advanced degree) to fields that offer the most opportunities and rewards for creativity. The third is a statistical reason. Research samples vary on the extent to which an adequate range of intelligence and creativity occurs (Haensly & Reynolds, 1989). These differences affect the observed correlations.

Attention is now turned to the analytic skills that are basic to solving any problem. Even if one is going to solve a problem in a mundane way, these skills are still needed. However, each ability can also be used to facilitate a buy-low approach to a problem.

Problem Recognition and Definition

The first basic analytic skill is recognizing there is a problem to solve. To detect a problem situation, one must be willing to acknowledge that a problem may exist. Many a close relationship founders on people's unwillingness even to acknowledge that anything possibly could be wrong. Many businesses fail for the same reason.

How did a country like the United States, which was once financially solvent and the powerhouse of world economies, end up with such an outrageous national debt? By having a problem and failing to recognize it until it was too late. One might even say the same of the Communist system and its collapse. The problems that led to the collapse of the Soviet empire existed for a long time, but the government did not admit to them. Many problems could be solved easily if they were recognized early on. But people often duck their heads in the sand, and by the time they take them out, the problem is out of hand.

The second half of realizing a problem exists is figuring out exactly what it is. That's what problem definition is all about. Earlier, we discussed redefining problems. Problem definition is what occurs beforehand: A problem cannot be redefined until there is an initial definition.

In a study with 31 art students, Getzels and Csikszentmihalyi (1976) provided a set of objects and asked the artists-in-training to use some or all of the objects to make a drawing. The general task was defined but the artistic problem that could be the basis of a composition was completely open. The researchers observed the students' behavior as they worked. The students who ended up producing original drawings—as judged by art critics—spent more time formulating their compositions. This differential attention of the highly original students to problem formulation was also seen in the large number of objects that they explored and manipulated before settling on a still-life arrangement. Furthermore, the highly original students were more prone to redefine the nature of their compositions as they worked—in other words, they did not feel locked into one view, a concept we discussed earlier in this chapter in the section on problem redefinition.

Deciding on How Mentally to Represent Information About a Problem

How one mentally represents information can have a major effect on how it is solved, and even on whether it is solved. The following problem about a monk seeking study and contemplation illustrates what we mean (see also Sternberg, 1986b).

> A monk wishes to pursue study and contemplation in a retreat at the top of a mountain (see Fig. 7.5). The monk starts climbing the mountain at 7 a.m. and arrives at the top of the mountain at 5 p.m. of the same day. During the course of his ascent, he travels at variable speeds, and takes a break for lunch. He spends the evening in study and contemplation. The next day, the monk starts his descent at 7 a.m. again, along the same route. Normally, his descent would be faster than his ascent, but because he is tired and afraid of tripping and hurting himself, he descends the mountain slowly, not arriving at the bottom until 5 p.m. of the day after he started his ascent. Must there be a point on the mountain that the monk passes at exactly the same time of day on the two successive days of his ascent and descent? Why?

Tough problem. But the problem is much easier if represented in a way that is somewhat different from the way people usually represent it. The answer, by the way, is that yes, it is necessarily the case that the monk must pass through exactly the same point (or altitude) on the mountain at corresponding times on the days of his ascent and descent. The problem becomes much easier to conceptualize if, rather than imagining the same monk climbing the mountain one day and going down the mountain the next, one imagines two different monks, one ascending and the other descending the mountain on the same day. It may be assumed that the monks start and finish at the same time, although this assumption is not necessary for solution of the problem. Note that this re-representation of the problem, shown in Figure 7.6, does not change the nature of the problem nor the solution, but simply makes the problem easier to solve.

Role of Intelligence 179

Figure 7.5. The monk problem

Figure 7.6. Solution to the monk problem

Related to strategy selection is resource allocation. One of the resources that each person has to allocate is time. How much time should be devoted to completing various projects or parts of each project? Sternberg (1981) found that more intelligent people tend to spend relatively more time on global, up-front planning for how they are going to solve a problem, but relatively less time on local, along-the-way planning, whereas less intelligent people do just the opposite. The less intelligent just plunge into the problem without thinking about it much, whereas the more intelligent give it a lot of thought before acting on it. Creative thinking requires time, and people who are always putting out fires often do not have the time to think about anything in a very creative fashion. To be creative, it is often necessary to permit extra time on a task in order to search for more novel solutions.

We believe that the allocation of resources is an issue of paramount importance not only at the individual level, but also at the corporate and national levels. Many people agree that industry in this country is losing the strong scientific and technological edge it once had. There may be many reasons why this would be so, but one is almost certainly the relatively small amount of money that is being allocated to research and development, particularly when there is a long time line until the anticipated payoff.

Whereas Japanese companies think in time frames of 10, 20, 30 years, and more, U.S. companies often seem to think only in terms of immediate payoffs. Basic research usually does not have an immediate payoff. Neither do many of the fundamental changes that can be made in the restructuring of a company. But the long-term payoffs may be much greater than those born out of short-term investments. If, as a society, America wants to retain its edge, it will be necessary to think in terms of a much longer time frame than that which now seems comfortable.

Formulating a Strategy and Allocating Resources for Solving a Problem

Having figured out and represented what the problem is, one needs to decide how to solve it. It is necessary to analyze the available alternatives and to choose the path that will allow achievement of the goal. Buying low can involve strategy selection, if one decides to choose a strategy that is novel and that is not what everyone else is doing or would do.

Formulating an optimal strategy is sometimes a matter of knowing what questions to ask. Take what would seem to be one of the most routine of life chores: refinancing a home mortgage in times of low interest rates. How the person refinancing formulates his or her strategy for doing so may greatly affect the ultimate outcome.

With regard to creative work, the use of divergent versus convergent thinking may be an especially important part of strategy selection. Divergent thinking refers to the generation of ideas from given information with an emphasis on the variety of new ideas (Brown, 1989). For example, if one is writing a poem, listing all the ideas he or she can for topics would be a case of divergent thinking. Numerous studies, including longitudinal ones, show a positive relationship (often .20 > rs > .30) between divergent thinking and creative performance (Barron & Harrington, 1981; Torrance, 1979, 1988). We suggest that people who engage in divergent thinking as part of their problem-solving strategy have an advantage. Divergent thinking provides a range of alternatives to work with and helps a person move beyond the first acceptable idea that comes to mind. These initial ideas, generally, are readily available to many people—to pursue them would be buying high. A convergent thinking strategy—trying to find "the" one answer—is typically emphasized in schoolhouse problems. This strategy, when alternated with a divergent one, may be optimal because people will be both providing lots of ideas and continually refocusing back toward their goal. Our observations of Yale undergraduates in experiments on creativity suggest that the less creative students tend to have a purely convergent strategy—which leads them to generate only one idea that "solves" the problem, but, as noted earlier, tends to be a mundane solution.

Notice how a correct analysis of a problem, followed by a creative re-representation of that problem, can greatly facilitate problem solution. Other researchers (Kotovsky et al., 1985) have used a Tower of Hanoi problem that requires the problem solver to move a set of discs from one peg to another following specified rules. Research with various representations of this problem shows that people's average time to solve the problem can vary by a factor of eight, depending on the specific way the problem is represented. Certain representations make the problem rules easier to learn and use.

The importance of problem representations is not limited to what might seem like academic problems. People who use spreadsheet programs use them not because they provide unique information that could be obtained in no other way, but because they represent information in a way that makes it relatively easy to see the consequences of various decisions. Similarly, different word-processing programs for personal computers all accomplish about the same thing in the end—what differs is how they represent information to the user, and how much they facilitate the task of writing via their form of representation. The enormous success of the Apple Macintosh computer has been precisely because of its representing information in a user-friendly way that people can understand.

There is probably little that can be done with a Macintosh that cannot be done with another processing system. The difference is in ease of representation.

The importance of representation applies in the world of the school as well. For example, we teach statistical courses to our students. Math is difficult for students in large part because of the difficulty students have in knowing how to represent mathematical information. Many mathematical techniques can be represented either algebraically or geometrically. That is, they can be represented as a series of equations or as a set of geometric forms in a two- (or more-) dimensional space. When we teach math ourselves, we try to use both representations, realizing that some students respond better to one representation, others to the other representation.

Monitoring and Evaluating Problem Solving

When most adults were children, teachers used to give timed tests of arithmetic computation problems. The idea was that the best student was the first one done. There is a problem with this mentality: It encourages people to rush through what they are doing, often without thinking about what it is they are doing, and then to rush to turn in the work when they are done, without even checking it first.

A teacher once gave one of us and his classmates a somewhat difficult problem involving the computation of change for $5. Some of the students came up with negative answers. The fact that the answers made no sense (what is "negative change"?) escaped the students; they turned in their papers anyway. Markman (1979) conducted research on children's detection of blatant contradictions in texts they read, and similarly, has discovered that, for the most part, children do not even notice the contradictions.

Creative work almost always is fraught with errors along the way. Ben Shahn (1964), an American artist, described the need for an "inner critic," saying that even "when a painting is merely in the visionary stage, the inner critic has already begun stamping upon it. . . . 'Your idea is underdeveloped' says the inner critic. 'You must find an image in which the feeling is embedded'. . . . Now find that image" (p. 20). Poincaré (1921), a mathematician, wrote that the mind acts like a sieve, separating good from bad ideas. Unless the creators analyze and correct their errors as they are on the route to finishing their work, they are sure to produce work that is less than the best of which they are capable.

Indeed, if one looks at the original drafts of writers and poets, extensive editing is evident. The rough draft of Walt Whitman's poem, "Come Said My Soul," indicates that the first line originally read, "Go, said his soul to a poet, write me such songs."

However, Whitman disliked the second part of the line and tried "such verse write." He crossed out this second attempt and tried "go write such songs." In the end, the poem opened: "Come, said my Soul, Such verses for my Body let us write (for we are one)" (Mitgang, 1984, p. 21).

In summary, we have argued that although the synthetic aspect of intelligence is certainly the most important to creative work, the analytic aspect is important too. To do the most creative work, one must analyze problems well, and often, analyze his or her own problem-solving efforts, too.

THE PRACTICAL PART OF INTELLIGENCE: MAKING GOOD IDEAS WORK

In thinking about creativity, individuals often fail to deal with the practical part. The practical part, however, is important, even in academic situations! Where does the practical part enter?

First, it is one thing to find a problem or an idea interesting. It is another to have a sense of whether anyone else will find it interesting. For example, no matter how creative an experiment someone designs to show that people remember two-syllable words better than they remember four-syllable words, few people are likely to be interested. Good choice of problems requires not only taking one's own interests into account, but the interests of others. Is it a problem that anyone in the world besides the individual is likely to find of interest? If not, his or her work is not likely to be recognized as creative.

We say "not likely" because, if there is no interest, the individual still has one other option available: to try to interest others. A point made previously with regard to Alexander Fleming, and one that we see repeatedly in the history of creative thought, is that sometimes creative people recognize the importance of a problem, whereas others don't or just aren't ready to see it. The creative person may thereby find him or herself spending a lot of time convincing others that the problem is worth studying, or that his or her approach to the problem is one that people should listen to. This is the problem that one of us faced when he gave his first colloquium at the Educational Testing Service: how to convince a basically hostile audience that it should pay attention and listen to what is about to be said.

It might seem slightly "dirty" to raise issues such as these. After all, what do they have to do with creativity? Actually, a lot. Because creativity is socially constructed—creative work is creative by virtue of people designating it as such—we can't speak of creativity outside of a social context. What is creative to one group of people may not be to another. It's a small wonder that people spend so much time speaking to and writing for the already converted. Politicians talk to their supporters; physicists spend most of their time talking to physicists. It is much harder, however, to convince a crowd that does not share your presuppositions of the value of what you do. Yet, the greatest payoff, ultimately, is often in reaching out to the unconvinced, not just to those who are already likely to believe anything you say.

What we are suggesting, and what may seem offensive to some, is that there is a "sales" aspect to creativity. When examining how people get from "buying low" to "selling high," there will almost always be a middle period in which people are not just coming up with good ideas, but actively trying to convince other people of the worth of these ideas. Everyone would like to believe that good ideas just sell themselves, but they rarely do.

No one knows how hard it is to sell good ideas or products better than do perfume manufacturers. Which is why they spend millions of dollars hiring creative marketing talent, and also why the lion's share of the cost of perfume is for marketing, not for the product itself. Most perfumes smell pretty good. But the creativity that went into creating the fragrance is only the first step in selling it. Perfumes sell at least as much on image, including the design of the model, as they do on the actual scents. A delightful scent is likely to have only limited success, or to fail outright, unless it is creatively—and aggressively—marketed.

Of course, the case is even tougher with products such as gasoline. Basically, it probably makes little difference what brand one buys, or even if it is a generic brand, which is often purchased from the major oil companies any way. Thus, the quality of the marketing campaign may dwarf in importance the quality of the gasoline itself.

We would like to think that great ideas in science, literature, art, or music are different from perfume, and certainly from gasoline. To an extent, of course, they are. We are in no position to argue whether the creativity that goes into making a spectacular scent is any less than that which goes into making a spectacular sculpture. It is hard to compare apples and oranges, but much harder to compare perfumes and sculptures. What they have in common, however, is the need to appeal to people. Even in the rarefied fields of science such as physics, it is not enough just to have ideas—physicists have to know how to convince others of their worth. We have talked to people in many fields, and without exception they agree that there are some in their fields whose ideas have won much more acceptance than they deserve because of the quality of the sales job, whereas there are others whose ideas have won less acceptance than they deserve because they are not well packaged.

Although there is no easy formula for successfully selling an idea, several factors should be considered (LeBoeuf, 1980; McCormack, 1984). Some things that can help to sell a new idea are (a) giving a high-quality presentation of the idea; (b) networking to find key people who may be interested in the idea or helpful in some way; (c) knowing the market, where the idea could fit in, and whether the timing is right; (d) creating a need for the idea (emphasizing problems with the status quo and pointing out the benefits of the idea); and (e) looking at the idea from the "buyer's" point of view—understanding the image that is being projected and what the idea means to the potential buyer.

The need for practical intelligence in creativity goes beyond just selling the work. It also involves knowing how to interpret and act on the reactions the work receives. For example, people in many fields apply for funding in order to do the creative work that they wish to do. There are grants in all the sciences, in the humanities, in the arts, and so on. When scientists, artists, and others apply for grants, their proposals are usually critiqued, and the critiques returned to the proposers. Part of the practical intelligence of creativity is knowing how to react to these critiques. It is knowing that if one is buying low, one is bound to encounter criticism, and the individual has to be sure to separate the profound and useful criticism from the empty and useless. It is knowing how to take the comments of others and use them in a way that makes the ideas or product better, and not just a rehash of what other people have done before and may well want to see again.

In conclusion, to be creative involves three aspects of intelligence: the synthetic part of coming up with ideas; the analytic part of recognizing them, structuring them, allocating resources, and evaluating the quality of ideas; and the practical part of knowing how to promote and refine ideas, based on critiques received from others.

ACKNOWLEDGMENTS

The work reported herein was supported under the Javits Act program (Grant #R206R950001) as administered by the Office of Educational Research and Improvement, U.S. Department of Education. The findings and opinions expressed in this report do not reflect the positions or policies of the Office of Educational Research and Improvement or the U.S. Department of Education.

REFERENCES

Barron, F., & Harrington, D. M. (1981). Creativity, intelligence, and personality. *Annual Review of Psychology, 32*, 439-476.

Brown, R. T. (1989). Creativity: What are we to measure? In J. A. Glover, R. R. Ronning, & C. R. Reynolds (Eds.), *Handbook of creativity* (pp. 3-32). New York: Plenum.

Davidson, J. E., & Sternberg, R. J. (1984). The role of insight in intellectual giftedness. *Gifted Child Quarterly, 28*, 58-64.

Getzels, J. W., & Csikszentmihalyi, M. (1976). *The creative vision: A longitudinal study of problem finding in art.* New York: Wiley.

Goodman, N. (1955). *Fact, fiction, and forecast.* Cambridge, MA: Harvard University Press.

Haensly, P. A., & Reynolds, C. R. (1989). Creativity and intelligence. In J. A. Glover, R. R. Ronning, & C. R. Reynolds (Eds.), *Handbook of creativity* (pp. 111-132). New York: Plenum Press.

Hayes, J. R. (1989). Cognitive processes in creativity. In J. A. Glover, R. R. Ronning, & C. R. Reynolds (Eds.), *Handbook of creativity* (pp. 135-146). New York: Plenum.

Kotovsky K., Hayes, J. R., & Simon, H. A. (1985). Why are some problems hard? Evidence from Tower of Hanoi. *Cognitive Psychology, 17*, 248-294.

LeBoeuf, M. (1980) *Imagineering.* New York: Berkley Books.

Lubart, T. I. (1994). Creativity. In E. C. Carterette & M. P. Friedman (General Eds.) and R. J. Sternberg (Vol. Ed.), *Thinking and problem solving* (Vol. 12, pp. 290-332). New York: Academic Press.

Markman, E. M. (1979). Realizing that you don't understand: Elementary school children's awareness of inconsistencies. *Child Development, 50*, 643-655.

McCormack, M. H. (1984). *What they don't teach you at Harvard Business School.* New York: Bantam Books.

Mitgang, H. (1984, January 3). Library displays the poet's search for perfection. *New York Times*, p. 21.

Poincaré, H. (1921). *The foundations of science.* New York: Science Press.

Renzulli, J. S. (1986). The three-ring conception of giftedness: A developmental model for creative productivity. In R. J. Sternberg & J. E. Davidson (Eds.), *Conceptions of giftedness* (pp. 53-92). New York: Cambridge University Press.

Shahn, B. (1964). The biography of a painting. In V. Thomas (Ed.), *Creativity in the arts* (pp. 13-34). Englewood Cliffs, NJ: Prentice-Hall.

Sternberg, R. J. (1981). Intelligence and nonentrenchment. *Journal of Educational Psychology, 73*, 1-16.

Sternberg, R. J. (Ed.). (1982). *Handbook of human intelligence.* New York: Cambridge University Press.
Sternberg, R. J. (1985). *Beyond IQ: A triarchic theory of human intelligence.* New York: Cambridge University Press.
Sternberg, R. J. (1986a). Inside intelligence. *American Scientist, 74,* 137-143.
Sternberg, R. J. (1986b). *Intelligence applied: Understanding and increasing your intellectual skills.* San Diego, CA: Harcourt Brace Jovanovich.
Sternberg, R. J. (1997). *Successful intelligence.* New York: Plume.
Sternberg, R. J., & Clinkenbeard, P. R. (1995). A triarchic model of identifying, teaching, and assessing gifted children. *Roeper Review, 17,* 255-260.
Sternberg, R. J., & Davidson, J. E. (1982). The mind of the puzzler. *Psychology Today, 16,* 37-44.
Sternberg, R. J., & Davidson, J. E. (Eds.). (1995). *The nature of insight.* Cambridge, MA: MIT Press.
Sternberg, R. J., Ferrari, M., Clinkenbeard, P. R., & Grigorenko, E. L. (1996). Identification, instruction, and assessment of gifted children. A construct validation of a triarchic model. *Gifted Child Quarterly, 40,* 129-137.
Sternberg, R. J., Grigorenko, E. L., Ferrari, M., & Clinkenbeard, P. R. (1999). A triarchic analysis of an aptitude-treatment interaction. *European Journal of Psychological Assessment, 15,* 1-11.
Sternberg, R. J., & Lubart, T. I. (1991). An investment theory of creativity and its development. *Human Development, 34,* 1-31.
Sternberg, R. J., & Lubart, T. I. (1995). *Defying the crowd: Cultivating creativity in a culture of conformity.* New York: Free Press.
Sternberg, R. J., & O'Hara, L. (1999). Creativity and intelligence. In R. J. Sternberg (Ed.), *Handbook of creativity* (pp. 251-272). New York: Cambridge University Press.
Tetewsky, S. J., & Sternberg, R. J. (1986). Conceptual and lexical determinants of nonentrenched thinking. *Journal of Memory and Language, 25,* 202-225.
Torrance, E. P. (1979). *The search for Satori and creativity.* New York: Creative Education Foundation.
Torrance, E. P. (1988). The nature of creativity as manifest in its testing. In R. J. Sternberg (Ed.), *The nature of creativity: Contemporary psychological perspectives* (pp. 43-75). New York: Cambridge University Press.
Williams, W. M., & Sternberg, R. J. (in press). *Success acts for managers.* Mahwah, NJ: Lawrence Erlbaum Associates.

8

THINKING CRITICALLY ABOUT CREATIVE THINKING

Diane F. Halpern
California State University-San Bernardino

It is one of the few topics on which almost everyone can agree: Americans need to improve their ability to think clearly. In order to achieve this objective, U.S. schools and universities must instruct their students in the science, art, and practice of *critical thinking*, the term that has become the buzz word that denotes good thinking—thinking that relies on an examination of evidence, a weighing of the reasons that support conclusions, an understanding of probabilities, a consideration of goals and a variety of ways to satisfy them. It is the rallying cry of both liberals and conservatives as they search for answers to society's most pressing problems. How else can one understand the fact that both the Bush and Clinton administrations supported the same set of college-level educational goals that focused on critical thinking? It must be that both sides of U.S. politics believe that their party is sure to attract converts when more people learn to think critically. Although the encouragement of good thinking is a worthy goal at all levels of education, and age-appropriate critical thinking guidelines have been suggested for primary and secondary school students (e.g., Herrnstein, Nickerson, de Sanchez, & Swets, 1986), I restrict my discussion of critical thinking to college-level issues because it is the area that I know best.

One of the goals for college-level instruction that was identified by the National Educational Goals Panel in its Goals 2000 (educational goals for the year 2000) concerns the need to have a college-educated populace with the ability to think: "By the Year 2000, the proportion of college graduates who demonstrate an advanced ability to think critically, communicate effectively, and solve problems will increase substantially" (National Education Goals Panel, 1991, p. 237). The experts who comprise the National Education Goals Panel recognized the need to produce college graduates who can think critically as essential for America's successful "competition in a global economy and exercise the rights and responsibilities of citizenship" (National Education Goals Panel, 1991, p. 237). The recommendations of the elite members of the Goals Panel were based on a thoughtful analysis of what educated adults will need to know and be able to do as America enters a new millennium. These spokespersons for the educational needs of America have been strangely silent about education designed to enhance creative thinking and about the need for an educated citizenry that can think in ways that are creative as well as critical.

Creativity has never been given the attention it deserves in standard educational settings. Although educators generally agree that creativity is important, few ever design curricula or present lessons with this goal in mind (Mack, 1987). The benign neglect of creative thinking as an educational goal is not a recent phenomenon. More than three decades ago, Lowenfeld (1962) called creativity "education's stepchild," a fact that was as true as the 20th century came to a close as it was in the free-wheeling decade of the 1960s. There are a number of reasons why creative thinking has been absent from the national agenda for improved thinking skills. One likely reason involves the problem of defining and classifying thinking skills. Is creative thinking a subset of critical thinking or is it a "different animal" that operates independent from those processes that define critical thinking? In this chapter, I discuss the often fuzzy relation between these two aspects of cognition, with special emphasis on the implications for the education of adults who can think critically and creatively.

WORKING DEFINITIONS AND DEFINITIONS THAT WORK

The question of the relation between creative and critical thinking is a matter of definition. Whether critical or creative thinking is a subset of the other, whether they are essentially identical or wholly different, depends on how these constructs are defined and, most importantly, who gets to do the defining. Consider these definitions that represent a consensus of expert opinions in the fields of cognitive psychology and philosophy (e.g., Angelo & Cross, 1993; Facione, 1991; Halpern, 1996, 1998; Moore & Parker, 1995; Nickerson, 1986; Weisberg, 1993):

> *Critical thinking*: the use of those cognitive skills or strategies that increase the probability of a desirable outcome. Thinking that is purposeful, reasonable, and goal-directed.
>
> *Creative thinking*: Thinking that leads to an outcome that is novel (or unusual) and appropriate (or good).

As seen in these two definitions, critical and creative thinking are complementary processes that are not identical, but are similar. Creative thinking requires that the outcome be novel; whereas, there is no need for novelty in the definition of critical thinking, although novel responses are not excluded from this definition. Some theorists have restricted the definition of critical thinking so that it involves only the judgment and applicability of possible actions (e.g., carefully thinking about whether to "accept, reject or suspend judgment about a claim" [Moore & Parker, 1995, p. 4]). This sort of restriction omits the generation of possible solutions to a problem from the domain of critical thinking, but I believe that it is not a useful way of categorizing cognitive process. The evaluation and application phases can also involve novel and appropriate thinking, so creativity cannot be separated from critical thinking. Possible relations and degrees of overlap between these two constructs are shown in Figure 8.1.

As shown in Figure 8.1, these definitions eliminate the possibilities that critical and creative thinking are either wholly different or identical. Furthermore, critical thinking is a more inclusive concept than creative thinking; therefore, critical thinking cannot be conceptualized as a subset of creative thinking. Given that there is considerable overlap in thinking that is categorized as critical or creative, it seems likely that much of what is known about each of them should be applicable to the other. For example, if one were to conclude that either critical thinking or creative thinking can be enhanced with specific instruction, it would be likely that this conclusion could be generalized, at least in part, to the other. Similarly, if one were to conclude that everyone is capable of either creative or critical thought, then this conclusion should apply to the other construct as well. If there is a great deal of overlap or similarity in these processes, then generalizations from one to the other can be made with greater certainty than if there is little overlap or similarity between these two constructs.

192 Halpern

A. Two separate circles symbolize the possibility that creative and critical thinking are totally different constructs.

B. A single circle is used to depict the possibility that creative and critical thinking are identical constructs.

C. This is a schematic to represent the possibility that creative thinking is a subset of critical thinking. The differences in the size of the two circles represent the extent to which the two constructs overlap.

D. In this set of diagrams, creative and critical thinking overlap, but each has discrete or unshared aspects.

Domain of Critical Thinking

Domain of Creative Thinking

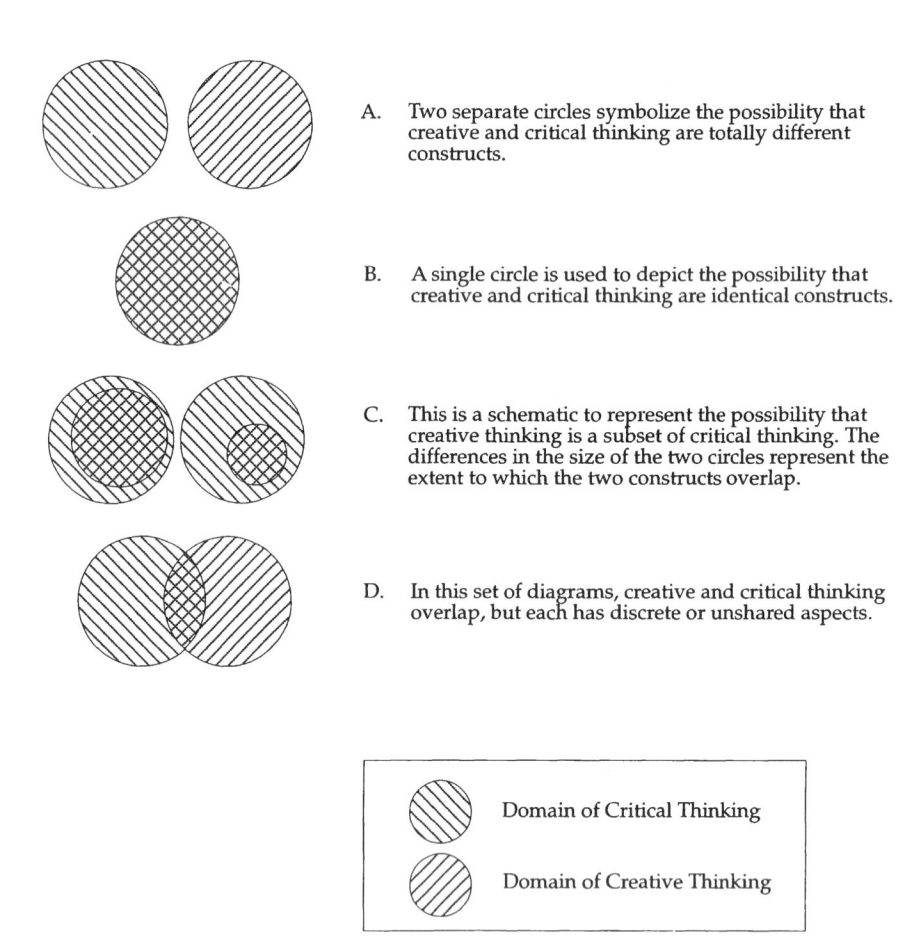

Figure 8.1. Circle diagrams that represent possible relation between creative and critical thinking. The similarities between these two constructs are shown by the extent to which the two circles overlap. The possible relations range between two wholly different constructs, as shown in the top figures (A) to identical constructs as show in the second figure (B). It is concluded that A and B depictions are incorrect, and the relationship between creative and critical thinking is closer to those diagrams in C and D.

A Skills Taxonomy

Instruction designed to enhance thinking of any sort is predicated on two underlying assumptions: (a) there are clearly identifiable and definable thinking skills (or strategies or dispositions—something that can be learned) which students can be taught to recognize and apply appropriately; and (b) if recognized and applied, the students will be more effective thinkers. Creative thinking requires a good (or appropriate) outcome; whereas critical thinking requires only the increased likelihood of a good (or appropriate) outcome. Creative thinking also requires that the outcome be uncommon—although the process that is used to arrive at a novel outcome can be quite ordinary. Both Perkins (1985) and Weisberg (1993) described how ordinary processes of transfer can lead to extraordinarily creative outcomes. Thus, creative thinking is defined solely by its end product, not the process that went into it; critical thinking is defined by its process that bears only a probabilistic relation to its end product.

By definition, it is possible to use the skills of critical thinking and arrive at an outcome that is not desirable. The selection of an appropriate action in a given situation bears only a probabilistic relationship to a desired goal. There are several possible scenarios in which this could happen. For example, suppose that an individual has a dread disease and will probably die within 6 months. In addition, there is a surgical operation that is safe and effective 99% of the time. As a critical thinker, the individual would probably decide to go ahead with the surgery. He or she also could die on the operating table. This is an example where the thinking may have been perfectly appropriate, but the outcome was disastrous. The definition of creative thinking solely depends on the result of the thinking process; the definition of critical thinking allows for the possibility that the result may be catastrophic, yet the thinking that went into the decision could be perfectly sound.

The similarities and differences between these two concepts are most clearly seen in the specific skills that are targeted in instructional programs that are designed to enhance them. I provide here a taxonomy for categorizing and understanding the skills that are often targeted for instruction in critical and creative thinking courses. Several different taxonomies of thinking skills are also possible, and a legitimate case can be made for alternative groupings or for adding other skills and deleting some of those that are listed. For other taxonomies, see Speedie, Treffinger, and Houtz (1976) or Fuller (1982). This categorization is not meant to be the definitive list of critical thinking skills. Rather, it is proposed as a concrete starting place for the task of identifying and organizing what we want college graduates to know and be able to do so that they can compete and cooperate in the world's marketplace and function as effective citizens in a complex democratic community. In other words, it is based on a belief about the skills and attitudes that America and the world will need from the citizens of the 21st century.

Following are the five category headings for organizing college-level thinking skills:

Verbal Reasoning Skills. The skills listed under this rubric include those that are needed to comprehend and defend against the persuasive techniques that are embedded in everyday language (also known as natural language). Thinking and language are closely tied constructs, and the skills listed here recognize the reciprocal relation between language and thought in which an individual's thoughts determine the language used to express them, and the language that is used shapes the thoughts.

Creative thinking, like critical thinking, also requires the use of verbal reasoning skills because language is so intimately tied to thought that it can direct thought in novel ways. For example, shifts between abstract and concrete language can serve as a spur to creative thinking, and the generation of analogies that are adapted from distant domains of knowledge is frequently identified as the keystone of creative thought (Halpern, 1987). This is just one example where the distinction between critical and creative thinking blurs. When discussing arguments with the metaphor of war, is one thinking creatively or critically (Lakoff & Johnson, 1980)? Many topics rely on metaphors selected from distant domains for the exchange of ideas, showing that these constructs are not easily separated in many real-world settings.

Argument Analysis Skills. An argument is a set of statements with at least one conclusion and one reason that supports the conclusion (Halpern, in press). In real-life settings, arguments are complex with reasons that run counter to the conclusion, stated and unstated assumptions, irrelevant information, and intermediate steps. Arguments are found in commercials, political speeches, textbooks, and anywhere else where reasons are presented in an attempt to get the reader or listener to believe that the conclusion is true. The skills of identifying conclusions, rating the quality of reasons, and determining the overall strength of an argument are a common part of most college-level thinking skills courses.

Creativity operates in argument analysis via the types of reasons that are considered and the possibility that the same set of reasons can support multiple conclusions. Creative ideas often involve "noticing" information that others had regarded as irrelevant or the ability to incorporate anomalous data into a unified theory. Creative thinking about arguments can lead to novel conclusions and novel reasons and counter-reasons. The way one retrieves and applies knowledge can range from relatively rote (e.g., 2 + 2 = ?) to truly novel, but there is no clear line that shows a dichotomy between these two extremes.

Skills in Thinking as Hypothesis Testing. The rationale for including this category of skills in a thinking course is that much of day-to-day thinking is like the scientific method of hypothesis testing. In many everyday interactions, people function like intuitive scientists in order to explain, predict, and control the events in their life. The skills used in thinking as hypothesis testing are the same ones used in scientific reasoning—the accumulation of observations, formulation of beliefs or hypotheses and the use of the information collected to decide if it confirms or disconfirms the hypotheses.

The scientific process of hypothesis testing is open to creative interpretations at every step ranging from the selection of what is worth studying to deciding what and whom to observe and what to conclude. Alternative explanations are the lifeblood of creative breakthroughs in every field of human endeavor.

Using Likelihood and Uncertainty. Because very few events in life can be known with certainty, the correct use of probability and likelihood plays a critical role in almost every decision. Huff's (1954) tiny, popular book *How To Lie With Statistics* is still widely quoted because it explains how easy it is to mislead someone who does not understand basic concepts in probability. The critical thinking skills that are subsumed under this heading are an important dimension of a college-level thinking taxonomy.

Creative use of probability is essential in many domains of knowledge. An unusual co-occurrence of two events can lead to the revolutionary set-breaking advances, if an individual is able to recognize it. Conversely, the more common tendency to attribute the co-occurrence of two or more unusual events (such as a phone call from an old friend one was just thinking about or being dealt a royal flush in a poker game) to a supernatural force instead of recognizing the probabilistic nature of events is a great detriment to finding appropriate explanations.

Decision-Making and Problem-Solving Skills. In some sense, all of the thinking skills are used to make decisions and solve problems, but the ones that are included here involve the finding of problems, generation and selection of alternatives, and judging among the alternatives. Many of these skills are especially useful in quantitative reasoning problems, but they are broadly applicable in almost any example that can be dreamed-up.

Decision making and problem solving are the more usual metaphors for the process of creativity, but as shown here, unusual and good outcomes can involve any of these five thinking skills categories. The creative aspect is usually identified as the generation of novel alternatives, but as I indicated earlier, creative thinking can operate at any of the stages.

Taken together, these five categories (sometimes referred to as macroabilities) define a workable model of critical and creative thinking. They have the benefit of focusing on skills that are teachable and generalizable and would, therefore, help to bridge the gap between thinking skills that can be taught in college and those skills that are needed in the workplace. The thinking skills that are classified within these broad categories are presented in Table 8.1. An extended discussion that provides examples and more precise definitions can be found in Halpern (1994, 1996).

Attitudinal and Motivational Propensities

With apologies to President Clinton and his campaign staff, one way to summarize the process of creative and critical thinking is with the phrase, "It's the attitude, stupid!" Critical and creative thinking are more than the successful use of a particular skill in an appropriate context. It is also an attitude or disposition to recognize when a skill is needed and the willingness to apply it. There is an important distinction between what people can do and what they actually do in real-world contexts. Motivation and time on task are at least as important as skill in creating creative thinkers. Following are some of the dispositions or attitudes of creative and critical thinkers.

Willingness to Engage in and Persist at a Complex Task. Good thinking is hard work. It requires diligent persistence, a trait that is central to academic success and most other success in life. In the jargon of cognitive psychology, tasks that require critical and creative thinking have a high mental workload. A critical and creative thinker must be willing to expend the mental energy that is required to begin and complete the task. Thanks to the careful work of Csikszentmihalyi and his colleagues (e.g., Rathunde & Csikszentmihalyi, 1993), it is known that undivided interest in an area is predictive of high-level talent in the future. Good thinkers put in the time and effort to achieve their goal—in fact, it is often difficult to get them to move on to other activities. There is an engrossing, positive affect to intense engagement in a task that needs to be recognized and fostered.

Willingness to Plan. Psychologists call this the ability to inhibit action. A planful approach requires individuals to check their

Table 8.1. College-Level Thinking Skills.[a]

Categorization of Skills

1. Verbal Reasoning Skills

   a. Recognizing and defending against the inappropriate use of emotional and misleading language (e.g., labeling, name-calling, ambiguity, vagueness, hedging, euphemism, bureaucratese, and arguments by etymology [original word use])
   b. Detecting the misuse of definitions and reification
   c. Understanding the use of framing with leading questions, negation, and marked words to bias the reader
   d. Using analogies appropriately, which includes examining the nature of the similarity relationship and its connection to the conclusion
   e. Employing questioning and paraphrase as a skill for comprehension of text and oral language (i.e., recognizing main ideas)
   f. Producing and using a graphic representation of information provided in prose form

2. Argument Analysis Skills

   a. Identifying premises (reasons), counterarguments, and conclusions
   b. Reasoning with "if-then" statements (which includes avoiding the fallacies of affirming the consequence and denying the antecedent)
   c. Judging the credibility of an information source
   d. Judging the consistency, relevance to the conclusion, and adequacy in the way premises support a conclusion
   e. Understanding the differences among opinion, reasoned judgment, and fact
   f. Recognizing and avoiding common fallacies such as straw person, appeals to ignorance, slippery slope, false dichotomy, guilt by association, and arguments against the person.

3. Skills in Thinking as Hypothesis Testing

   a. Recognizing the need for and using operational definitions
   b. Understanding the need to isolate and control variables in order to make strong causal claims
   c. Checking for adequate sample size and possible bias in sampling when a generalization is made
   d. Being able to describe the relation between any two variables as positive, negative, or unrelated
   e. Understanding the limits of correlation reasoning
   f. Seeking converging evidence to increase confidence in a conclusion
   g. Considering the relative "badness" of different sorts of errors
   h. Solving problems with proportional and combinatorial (systematic combinations) reasoning

Table 8.1. College-Level Thinking Skills.[a] (cont'd.)

Categorization of Skills

    i. Determining how self-fulfilling prophecies could be responsible for experimental results and everyday observations

4. Using Likelihood and Uncertainty

    a. Recognizing regression to the mean
    b. Understanding and avoiding conjunction errors
    c. Utilizing base rates to make predictions
    d. Understanding the limits of extrapolation
    e. Adjusting risk assessments to account for the cumulative nature of probabilistic events

5. Decision-Making and Problem-Solving Skills

    a. Listing alternatives and considering the pros and cons of each
    b. Restating the problem to consider different sorts of alternatives and different goals
    c. Recognizing the bias in hindsight analyses
    d. Seeking information to reduce uncertainty
    e. Recognizing decisions based on entrapment
    f. Producing graphs, diagrams, hierarchical trees, matrices, and models as solutions aids
    g. Understanding how worldviews can constrain the problem-solving process
    h. Using numerous strategies in solving problems including means-ends analysis, working backward, simplification, analogies, brain storming, contradiction, and trial-and-error

[a]Skills have been excerpted from Halpern (1994).

impulsivity and engage in intermediate tasks such as seeking additional information, organizing facts, and generating qualitatively different alternatives. The willingness to plan must become a habitual approach that is applied in many different contexts. The willingness to plan is especially needed if the outcome is to meet the two criteria of creativity. People tend to respond in well-worn ways to familiar situations; creative thinking requires that the usual response be held in abeyance to allow additional possibilities emerge. This concept is close to the idea of delaying gratification. The payoffs may be lie somewhere in an uncertain future, but the effort must be made in the present.

Flexibility or Open-Mindedness. An attitude of flexibility is marked with the willingness to consider new options, try things a new way, reconsider old problems. It is the disposition to seek creative solutions. It is the antithesis of the rigidity and dogmatism that is characteristic of a "closed mind." An attitude of "that's the way we've always done it," or "if it ain't broke, don't fix it," is diametrically opposed to the type of attitude that is needed for creativity. The ability to think flexibly has been part of the literature on creative thinking for decades (Gordon, 1976).

Willingness to Self-Correct. This refers to the willingness to learn from errors instead of becoming defensive about them. Individuals with the willingness to self-correct are able to utilize feedback and recognize the factors that led to an error. In order to improve the thinking process, ineffective strategies and automatic responses need to be recognized and abandoned. Anyone who takes chances, does things in an unusual way, recognizes something that no one else sees, will make mistakes. In fact, Simonton (1984, chap. 1, this volume) found that creative people make more mistakes and have more good ideas because they have more ideas, overall, than their less creative counterparts. Failure and the willingness to learn from it is an important component of the creative endeavor.

Being Mindful. Psychologists call this trait *metacognition* or *metacognitive monitoring.* It is the tendency to monitor one's comprehension and progress toward a goal. Creative and critical thinkers develop the habit of self-conscious concern for and evaluation of the thinking process. They are able to control the thinking process because they have knowledge about what they know and don't know and what they have to do to learn more. In order to pose thoughtful questions, the question asker must know what gaps in knowledge need to be filled and how to fill them. In order to be mindful, one must fight against a tendency to respond and act in stereotyped, rote ways—ways that are opposite to the novel responding that defines creativity (Langer, 1989).

Consensus-Seeking. Committee and group structures are most often the norm in the world of work. Good thinkers need to be disposed to ways in which consensus can be achieved. Consensus-seekers will need not only high-level communication skills, but they will also need to find ways to compromise and to achieve agreement. Without this disposition, even the most brilliant thinkers will find that they cannot convert thoughts to actions. Consensus seeking is not meant to imply conformity; rather it requires the ability to persuade others that a particular response is the right one in a particular situation.

Taken together, these six traits are characteristic of a creative and critical thinking attitude or disposition.

A PROBLEM-SOLVING FRAMEWORK

In considering the shared components between critical and creative thinking, it is useful to view the thinking process as solving a problem. Other metaphors are possible, but a spatial problem provides a concrete way to visualize the elements that comprise the thinking process. A problem exists when there is a "gap" or obstacle between the current state (where the problem solver is) and the goal (where the problem solver wants to be). The problem lies in finding a way to get from the current state to the goal.

An example is useful in understanding how this spatial metaphor can provide a workable framework for critical and creative thinking. For example, imagine an individual who is unhappy with her marriage. The goal is a marriage in which she is happy, and the current state is a marriage that is not the same as the goal. If the hapless heroine in this story wants a happy marriage, she will have to find a way to get from where she is—in a marriage that does not make her happy—to where she wants to be—happily married. But, in real life, the elements or components of a problem, known as the problem space, are highly complex because a "happy marriage" is multidimensional (good conversation, physical intimacy, comfortable relationship, etc.), and there are many possible routes to the "happy marriage." The problem also involves the way in which she defines the goal. She could seek ways to make her current marriage "good" or find another spouse who meets her criteria. In real life, the way she operationally defines a good marriage drastically changes the type of solution she decides to seek. What about trying to fix what she believes to be wrong with her current marriage? Is this a realistic goal for this hypothetical wife? If she redefines the goal or generates solutions in ways that are novel and appropriate (e.g., finds a friend to satisfy her need for conversation, or joins a commune, or makes changes in herself that alter her husband's behavior), then she has engaged in creative thinking. If this woman solves the problem by common methods, such as divorce, then the solution, even if good, is not particularly creative.

The evaluation of various types of options that she generates is both a critical and creative act, as is the identification and use of available information and resources. In most settings, it is impossible to disentangle the creative and critical aspects of thinking. The same problem-solving framework can be applied in any context as a way of analyzing the component processes. Consider great advances in science or mathematics or breakthroughs in dance or other art forms. The goal can be defined and routes to the goal explored. If there are multiple possible goals or solution results, evaluation is an important part of the process. When the definition of the goal or the solution strategy is novel, then the act is creative.

A creative response is not always the best. Suppose that one needs to find the area of a rectangle. If there is a simple, well-learned formula (length times height) that can be used in a fairly rote and automatic way to solve this problem, there is no need to discover an alternative solution, although most people believe that there is value in the thinking process because something may be learned that will be useful at some time in the future when ready-made, automatic solutions are not available.

For those who are interested in the educational implications of critical and creative thinking, the important issue centers around the evidence concerning specific educational experiences that can result in better thinking students.

TEACHABLE COMPONENTS OF CRITICAL AND CREATIVE THOUGHT

One of the advantages of a problem-solving metaphor for thinking is that it allows for the isolation of distinct stages in what is really a continuous and recursive process. Most of the attempts to improve thinking rely on the identification of components of the thinking process, instruction that is designed to improve the component, and then training to "put thinking together again." One way to think about these components is to conceptualize them as small cognitive processes that undergird thinking. For example, generation of possible solutions is an important part of many programs. Techniques like brainstorming, listing features, noting positive and negative aspects, listing all of the terms that come to mind, are all designed to increase the number of alternatives that are generated. The underlying rationale is that the more alternatives that are generated, the more likely someone is to generate a good alternative.

Making novel connections is another component of problem solving that is targeted in some educational programs. This is the idea behind techniques that employ concept mapping and the use of computer-based hypertext that allows for links among concepts. The deliberate use of alternative points of view (e.g., think about the problem from the perspective of an atom in a molecule, etc.), making novel combinations, and instruction in using analogies can be grouped here. The idea is to find remote links, parallel structures, and new ways of organizing information in the belief that this will lead to new ideas that are of high quality.

The most systematic instruction centers on the evaluation of alternative routes to the goal and the evaluation of the goal state. How can one determine when to stop writing or drawing? When is a picture finished? Is it good enough? Is it good? There are several systematic worksheet methods for deciding which of several alternatives is a good way of satisfying a goal.

Instruction in thinking is poorest in the area of recognizing that there is a problem and its close relative, reframing the goal so that it appears different from its original form. For example, I just learned about a new type of shoe that is a sandal and a sneaker. The idea is so simple and so obvious—a simple combination—why didn't I (or you) think it up? I never considered the "problem" of shoes as they exist now. Once it is pointed out to me, it is "easy" to see that this is just one example of finding problems where the rest of use don't see them.

Can Critical Thinking be Improved?

The simple answer to this question is, "yes, of course." There is nothing in the definition that would preclude the possibility of improvement if an individual is provided with appropriate instruction. The ability to think clearly and well is not a fixed quantity, nor is it impervious to experience. Logically, people can learn, at least some of the skills that comprise critical thinking such as the propensity and skill needed to consider whether there is evidence or good reasoning that support a conclusion. People can learn to recognize common thinking errors such as failures to consider regression to the mean or the use of emotional language designed to sway public opinion. Although these are discrete sorts of examples, they can be combined for an overall improvement in thinking.

There is also a considerable body of empirical evidence to support the conclusion that critical thinking can be enhanced with appropriate instruction that is designed specifically for this purpose. Numerous reviews of the literature support this belief: "Our results show that, contrary to much contemporary theorizing about reasoning, highly general inferential rules can be taught and that the quality of people's everyday reasoning can be improved" (Lehman & Nisbett, 1993, p. 354).

It also seems clear that improvements in the ability to think clearly are not an automatic by-product of education. Improvement in the ability to think critically and creatively seems to transfer to novel situations when the instruction is designed to foster transfer. Instruction that is specifically designed to improve thinking and to ensure that these skills are transferred and used in a variety of settings is needed. This conclusion is summed up well by Adams (1989) who concluded her review of the literature with these thoughts: "students . . . genuinely profit from instruction on thinking and that, for maximum impact, such instruction should be introduced as a course in itself—separate from regular curricula" (p. 72). The improvement of thinking is not something that is automatic or easy, but it is possible to learn thinking skills that are used in appropriate real-world settings (Adams, 1989; de Sanchez, in press; Nisbett, 1993).

Can Creative Thinking Be Improved?

The improvement of creative thinking could mean an increase in the number of creative outcomes or an outcome that is extremely creative, by this I mean an outcome that is more unusual or more appropriate than other less creative outcomes. It seems that both types of enhancements (more outcomes that are creative and outcomes that are more creative) are possible results of creativity training. Reviews of the literature on creativity training support the idea that creative thinking can be enhanced in both ways with appropriate instruction. Consider this cautious conclusion from a review of research: "an interpretation of the results [provides] modest support for the hypotheses that divergent thinking training improved creative performance seems warranted" (Baer, 1993, p. 74).

The research literature on both critical and creative thinking is huge. Not surprisingly, there are reports of null results, but numerous carefully designed studies show that, at least some educational programs, can help students improve in their ability to think critically and creatively and that this accomplished best when courses are specifically designed to promote transfer.

THE PROBLEM OF DOMAIN SPECIFICITY

Are there generally creative people? Can we find anyone who is a creative cook, dancer, physicist, author, and artist? Of course not, especially if strict standards are used to determine which meals, dances, physics problems, books, and paintings are novel and good. The critical element in creative and critical thinking is an extensive network of knowledge in some domain of knowledge. There is no substitute for knowledge. It is not possible to think critically or creatively when the individual knows very little about some area. For example, if one does not know very much about the events that occurred during World War II, one cannot think about this war creatively (e.g., suggesting novel causes of events) or critically (e.g., understanding how

Hitler was able to persuade millions of people to operate factories of death). In the jargon of cognitive psychology, the state of affairs in which little is known in some domain is described as consisting of skimpy and unconnected knowledge structures.

There is also a skills component to most creative actions, and some portion of the skills component is due to natural abilities. The great creative dancer has an extensive knowledge of dance forms and the ability to execute great dance moves. One would not expect a prima donna or jazz musician or great rapper to solve problems in astronomy or to write a creative poem. It would be silly to argue whether knowledge or thinking skills is more important—both are needed.

KNOWLEDGE NETWORKS

I like to visualize all of an individual's knowledge as a large jungle gym, which looks like a child's climbing toy with multiple connections from which children hang and swing. As more knowledge is gained about some area (e.g., video games, rocket science, African history), more "arms" are attached to this jungle gym of knowledge. In this way, experts build larger structures of knowledge about their topic of expertise than novices. Experts also arrange their knowledge components in ways that make access easy. When what one knows about one area of knowledge is connected to what he or she knows about some other area of knowledge, it is easy to make connections between them. The ability to make unusual connections is part of the creative process. Think about the creative (unusual and good) connections that some inventor came on when thinking about a good way to close bottles of glue. This unsung hero thought about other "good closures" that he or she had seen, and voila—a glue top that closes with the same principles as the anus was designed. (You can think of this the next time you use LePage's glue.)

There are numerous studies that compare expert and novice approaches to a variety of problems (e.g., Glaser, 1992). The expert not only has more information available in memory; he or she also has it organized so that it can be used easily and has more connections to other knowledge structures that are stored in memory.

Tickling Memory

No matter what the problem is, memory must be tickled. By this I mean that the thinker must be able to access and use information that is in memory. All of us have had the frustrating experience of walking away from an exam or a game show with a blank paper or empty pocket only to realize that we knew the "winning" answer, but just "didn't think of it when it was needed." Information must be accessible when it is needed, or else it is of little or no good. The creative and critical thinker "remembers" a good response that the rest of us don't think of. One "trick" is to find ways to learn information so that it can be remembered with appropriate retrieval cues (e.g., examples of good closing devices).

Imagine the problem of transportation before the automobile was invented. Creative thinkers recognized that there was a problem, even when other people could not imagine that anything was "wrong" with travel by horse or train. Creative people also "remembered" that it might be possible to make an engine that could move people seated in some sort of vehicle. The idea of a horseless carriage was ludicrous to most people at that time. They knew that an engine could never replace the horse, after all, we would need paved roads, repair centers, gasoline stations, and other "ridiculous" and widespread changes in order to make the horseless carriage a useful invention. There is no end to the list of possible problems that creative individuals could "notice" and then "remember" a possible solution that the rest of us never saw or remembered. How about an alternative to the road-clogging, air-polluting automobile that was has taken over most of the world since the turn of the last century? Creative thinkers, are you working on this?

TOWARD TOMORROW

The list of problems that urgently need solutions is depressingly long. Can an education that incorporates all that we know about critical and creative thinking result in a world in which many of these problems are solved? I think so. First, we need to recognize what the problems are. My personal list includes all sorts of prejudice, world hunger, poverty, diseases, wars, mental illness, the frailty associated with aging, and other types of human suffering. I am certain that creative readers can name many more. We know that colleges can provide instruction that improves creative and critical thinking. Why can't we apply the collective talent, knowledge, and thinking power of our most educated citizens to finding solutions to these problems? To naysayers, who believe that the problems of the 21st century are too big to tackle or cannot imagine relief from some of the pain of living, I remind them of a comment made by Bishop Desmond Tutu, a central figure in reforms in South Africa. He responded to his critics with instructions on how to eat an elephant—a mouthful at a time. Similarly, other major and seemingly intractable problems can be discovered and improved by encouraging high quality and innovative thinking in today's college students. As we sit in the shadow of the nuclear bomb, as much of the world's forests are being destroyed, as war rages in many places on earth, it seems that our very existence depends on it.

REFERENCES

Adams, M. J. (1989). Thinking skills curricula: Their promise and progress. *Educational Psychologist, 24*, 25-77.

Angelo, T. A., & Cross, K. P. (1993). *Classroom assessment techniques* (2nd ed.). San Francisco: Jossey-Bass.

Baer, J. (1993). *Creativity and divergent thinking.* Hillsdale, NJ: Lawrence Erlbaum Associates.

de Sanchez, M. (1995). Using critical thinking principles as a guide to college-level instruction. In D. F. Halpern & S. G. Nummedal (Eds.), Psychologists teach critical thinking [Special Issue]. *Teaching of Psychology, 22*, 72-74.

Facione, P. (1991, August). *Testing college-level critical thinking skills.* Paper presented at the 11th annual International Conference on Critical Thinking and Educational Reform, Sonoma, CA.

Fuller, R. G. (Ed.). (1982). *Piagetian programs in higher education.* Lincoln: University of Nebraska.

Glaser, R. (1992). Expert knowledge and processes of thinking. In D. F. Halpern (Ed.), *Enhancing thinking skills in the sciences and mathematics* (pp. 63-76). Hillsdale, NJ: Lawrence Erlbaum Associates.

Gordon, W. J. J. (1976). Metaphor and invention. In A. Rothenberg & C. R. Hausman (Eds.), *The creativity question.* Durham, NC: Duke University Press.

Halpern, D. F. (1987). Analogies as a critical thinking skill. In D. Berger, K. Pezdek, & W. Banks (Eds.), *Applications of cognitive psychology: Computing and education* (pp. 75-86). Hillsdale, NJ: Lawrence Erlbaum Associates.

Halpern, D. F. (1993). Assessing the effectiveness of critical thinking instruction. *Journal of General Education, 42*, 238-254.

Halpern, D. F. (1994). A national assessment of critical thinking skills in adults: Taking steps toward the goal. In A. Greenwood (Ed.), *The national assessment of college student learning: Identification of the skills to be taught, learned, and assessed* (pp. 24-64). Washington, DC: U.S. Department of Education, National Center for Education Statistics.

Halpern, D. F. (1996). *Thought and knowledge: An introduction to critical thinking* (3rd ed.). Hillsdale, NJ: Lawrence Erlbaum Associates.

Herrnstein, R. J., Nickerson, R. S., de Sanchez, M., & Swets, J. A. (1986). Teaching thinking skills. *American Psychologist, 41,* 1279-1289.
Huff, D. (1954). *How to lie with statistics.* New York: Norton.
Lakoff, G., & Johnson, M. (1980). *Metaphors we live by.* Chicago: University of Chicago.
Langer, E. J. (1989). *Mindfulness.* Reading, MA: Addison-Wesley.
Lehman, D. R., & Nisbett, R. E. (1993). A longitudinal study of the effects of undergraduate training on reasoning. In R. E. Nisbett (Ed.), *Rules for reasoning* (pp. 340-357). Hillsdale, NJ: Lawrence Erlbaum Associates.
Lowenfeld, V. (1962). Creativity: Education's stepchild. In S. J. Parnes & H. F. Harding (Eds.), *A source book for creative thinking.* New York: Charles Scribner's Sons.
Mack, R. W. (1987). Are methods of enhancing creativity being taught in teacher education programs as perceived by teacher educators and student teachers? *Journal of Creative Behavior, 21,* 22-33.
Moore, B. N., & Parker, R. (1992). *Critical thinking* (3rd ed.). Mountain View, CA: Mayfield.
National Education Goals Panel. (1991). *The national education goals report.* Washington, DC: U.S. Government Printing Office.
Nickerson, R. (1986).*Reflections on reasoning.* Hillsdale, NJ: Lawrence Erlbaum Associates.
Nisbett, R. E. (Ed.). (1993). *Rules for reasoning.* Hillsdale, NJ: Lawrence Erlbaum Associates.
Perkins, D. N. (1985). What creative thinking is. In A. Costa (Ed.), *Developing minds: A resource book for teaching thinking* (pp. 58-61). Alexandria, VA: Association for Supervision and Curriculum Development.
Rathunde, K., & Csikszentmihalyi, M. (1993). Undivided interest and growth in talent: A longitudinal study of adolescents. *Journal of Youth and Adolescence, 22,* 385-405.
Simonton, D. K. (1984). *Genius, creativity, and leadership.* Cambridge, MA: Harvard University Press.
Speedie, S., Treffinger, D. T., & Houtz, J. C. (1976). Classification and evaluation of problem-solving tasks. *Contemporary Educational Psychology, 1,* 52-75.
Weisberg, R.W. (1993). *Creativity: Beyond the myth of genius.* New York: Freeman.

9

CREATIVE ATTRIBUTIONAL SELF-TALK

Thomas E. Heinzen
William Paterson University

Evaluation of one's creative efforts presents most people with a highly personal interpretive dilemma: How to explain the "findings"? Two factors seem to figure prominently in the interpretive mix: Who did the finding and what did they find? How well one resolves the interpretive dilemmas influences consequent creativity because the "who" and the "what" of evaluation conspire to activate existing schemas—one's habitual ways of thinking. Some of these habitual cognitions support creativity; others do not. More significantly, at least for the social psychology of creativity and the development of personal creativity, such cognitive schemas are amenable to retraining: People can learn to think creatively in response to evaluation. Consequently, this chapter asserts that the "trainable" individual difference that determines whether evaluation will facilitate or inhibit one's creativity is a difference with a therapeutic twist: attributional self-talk.

At first glance, the creativity literature regarding evaluation appears to contradict existing social psychological literature regarding the effects of evaluation on performance (including creative performance). On one hand, self-evaluation of one's own creative efforts seems necessary for ongoing creativity. But both real and implied evaluation by others leads to evaluation apprehension that is likely to inhibit creativity. This seems to suggest that the resolution of this apparent contradiction in the literature lies in the source of evaluation (self or others). But this chapter also proposes that the self-other distinction is simply an artifact of cognitive attribution biases.

A more likely cause of the differential effects of evaluation (suggested by the attribution literature) is not who does the evaluating but how individuals explain to themselves why the conclusions of a particular evaluation of their work came out the way it did (or in the case of an anticipated evaluation, why the evaluation might come out in a certain way). Knowing who does the evaluating simply engages individuals' attribution biases and promotes one explanation over another, usually at the expense of accuracy. For example, the actor-observer bias (Jones & Nisbett, 1971) unites with the self-serving bias (Brown & Rogers, 1991; Miller & Ross, 1975) to predict that individuals, as the creators being evaluated, will tend to explain harsh evaluations by others as being caused by situational forces or the evaluator's inability to appreciate the work, but "critical" evaluations by individuals themselves as perceptive and constructive. In general, one's attribution biases lead the individual to infer more validity to his or her own evaluations than to the evaluations of his or her work made by most other people.

A VERBAL REPORT

Because the role of verbal reports as a "window to the mind" is once again receiving recognition as an occasionally valid means of data collection (Crutcher, 1994; Payne, 1994; Wilson, 1994), I offer a brief report that might clarify how the effects of evaluation on creativity are shaped by attributional self-talk. In this case, the situation presents an apparently positive evaluation by others. It is particularly seductive because a positive evaluation is far more appealing and potentially distracting than a negative evaluation.

I recently received a memo from the college's director of institutional research curiously headed "Positive Comments from the Senior Survey." The memo noted that "Students were asked to identify one course that they believed would have a lasting impact on them and to describe why they thought the course was so successful. Although students were not asked for the name of the faculty member, in some cases they provided it." Attached to the memo were three very flattering comments that graduating seniors had said about me. This appears to be a very positive evaluation that might reinforce my own classroom creativity.

Now my initial reaction in terms of self-talk was appreciation for the recognition, in the form of "Isn't this nice? I wonder who wrote these comments?" This was followed quite quickly by an impulse to "file this away for promotion." But as I explained this evaluation by others to myself, I thought "I wonder if there were any negative comments about me in the survey, and who might be seeing them, and how many such negative comments might there be?" I also wondered to myself "Did other faculty members tend to get more positive comments than I, or fewer such comments?" followed by some rather self-righteous and mean-spirited thoughts, such as "I bet so and so didn't get any positive comments!" Finally, I found myself trying to explain why students would make such comments (I concluded, with blatantly self-serving modesty, that "They were just sincere descriptions of a very useful course") and why the director of institutional research had chosen this form of feedback to the faculty (I hypothesized that "She's a psychologist and knows that reinforcers generally work better than punishers" vs. "The administration is leaning on her for more accountability evaluation measures and she's setting us up for a new attack on academic freedom").

The entire process of my own self-talk fairly reeked of my allowing automatic cognitions whose effect is likely to inhibit classroom creativity, if any actually existed in the first place. My self-talk of feeling appreciated might reinforce creativity, but only if I perceive that being creative in the classroom was the element of my teaching to which the students were actually responding. Even feeling appreciated can nourish an array of subtly creativity-distracting cognitions, such as "I really prefer to please and entertain students so they will say more nice things about me rather than to teach them difficult material," especially if I am nursing a pathological need for approval from others. My impulse to file positive evaluations away for promotion has similarly distracting potential effects on any creativity because not only does reward tend to undermine creativity (Amabile, 1983), but the undermining appears to be accomplished in part by offering a mental distraction that is appealing. Promotion implies more money and prestige and the thought of such things is likely to consume significant mental energy as I imagine what I will do with all that money (?!) and prestige (?!)—and mental energy spent on such imaginings is mental energy that is no longer available for creativity. All of this self-talk occurred in the space of seconds, but I also found myself indulgently rereading the repeated praises of myself by three students.

Attribution research applied to creativity is clarifying that attributional (explanatory) biases, most of which lead individuals to inaccurate and self-serving conclusions (Heinzen, 1994; Kasof, 1994), affect both one's evaluation of and one's ability to produce creative products. My own response to a positive evaluation represents a very common self-serving bias in which positive outcomes are attributed to the self and negative outcomes are ignored or attributed to circumstances.

Attributional self-talk (over which individuals fortunately have some measure of control) determines the effects of evaluation on creativity. I can (and do) tell myself that

> These comments are a limited sample; I'm glad if I am sometimes doing something right but there is a great deal about my teaching that I am not hearing about that I just don't know about. I also know that there are whole chunks of good material I just haven't really taken the time to learn properly, partly because I know I can entertain and tapdance my way through certain sections. The best thing for me to do, if I wish to become more creative in the classroom, is to focus on learning more, enjoy my teaching, and allow myself some measure of spontaneity rather than pleasing students because enjoyment and spontaneity are more strongly associated with creativity than trying to please others—and I enjoy being creative.

By practicing such rational, creative self-talk one can inhibit creativity-undermining attributions and facilitate creativity-enhancing attributions—even in the face of distracting evaluations by others.

CONTRADICTING LITERATURES: DOES EVALUATION FACILITATE OR INHIBIT?

The idea that evaluation facilitates performance, including creative performance, is familiar within social psychology, even though it sometimes appears under alternative names and topics. For example, the experience of failure provides rather obvious evaluative feedback. The "need for achievement" and "fear of failure" literatures (see Birney, Burdick, & Teevan, 1969; McClelland, Atkinson, Clark, & Lowell, 1953) identified early on that individuals who fear failing tend to make decisions that avoid specific, evaluative feedback by choosing either extremely simple tasks (failure is highly unlikely in a simple task) or exceedingly difficult tasks (failure is relatively acceptable because the difficult task was such a "long shot" anyway). By contrast, individuals high in the need for achievement tolerate failure, not for its own sake, but because failure provides specific and rapid information about the current boundaries of their abilities.

A great deal of the creativity literature also indicates that creative individuals, like those low in fear of failure and high in need for achievement, also avoid either simplistic or "self-handicapping" strategies and spontaneously seek some form of meaningful evaluation of their work. In fact, evaluation appears to be an inherent part of the creative process at intrapersonal, interpersonal, and social levels of creativity. At an intrapersonal level, Harrington (1990) concurred with MacKinnon's (1962) earlier intuition that evaluation is included as a necessary component of the internal creative process. At an interpersonal level, Runco's (1991) study of the evaluative role in creative thinking among children demonstrated that the evaluative component was particularly susceptible to instructions that prompted children to be concerned with how others would evaluate their creative ideas. Children evaluated their own work more accurately when pressed to hazard a guess about how others would evaluate their work (suggesting, among other things, a strong self-serving bias when self-evaluating for creativity). Csikszentmihalyi (1990) expanded the importance of evaluation to a social level by asserting that artists such as Rembrandt are recognized as creative only by dint of the comparative evaluations of art historians. So evaluation, in fascinatingly diverse forms, appears to be a frequent and perhaps necessary component for creativity.

All of this suggests a nice, tidy coherence within the theoretical and experimental literature regarding the facilitative effects of evaluation on creativity. But not surprisingly, the emerging social psychology of creativity unites with some other streams of equally well-established social psychological research to force individuals to think more deeply about the beneficial effects of evaluation. At a more vivid level, who among those claiming to be practicing researchers really believes that their personal creativity reliably increases as a result of evaluations by the assorted administrators in their lives who point out their shortcomings or praise their accomplishments? My guess is that the main effect of their feedback is distraction, and only occasionally encouragement. When they provide money, space, and time, individuals (hopefully) acknowledge and appreciate their efforts. But when they try to tell individuals how to do their jobs because they, as evaluators, presumably know better . . .

Two streams of research in social psychology persuade me that the effects of evaluation often are less than beneficial, and may include elements that are likely to undermine creativity. The first comes from the social facilitation and evaluation apprehension literature and the second directly from creativity studies by Amabile and her colleagues. The process of reconciling this literature with the literature just described will hopefully prove to be a tangible benefit with both clinical and research applications.

The social facilitation effect occurs when the performance of a dominant response is increased in the presence of an audience but inhibited if the response is more difficult (Zajonc, 1965). That is why a cure for such maladaptive behaviors as anxiety attacks, stage fright, and social phobia is practice—until the difficult behavior becomes a dominant one. Evaluation apprehension remains the key explanation for the social facilitation phenomenon because it reliably inhibits the performance of difficult tasks (such as behaving creatively) but reliably facilitates the performance of well-learned tasks.

Although evaluation apprehension is not the only explanation for the social facilitation effect, it remains a compatible rather than a competing explanation. For example, Sanders (1981) offered a simple distraction explanation in which trying to perform well on a difficult task (such as one requiring creativity) was more difficult in the presence of others because their mere presence is mentally distracting, even if it is not in an evaluative context; performance on an easy task increased because people try harder, perhaps since there is someone there to impress. The presence of others often implies some level of evaluation that makes difficult tasks more difficult and easier tasks even easier to perform.

The other research stream that supports the notion that evaluation undermines creativity emerges more directly from Amabile's (1983) experiments that note that evaluation-related variables such as reward and other factors that distract one's attentional resources or undermine intrinsic motivation all work to damage one's potential creativity. This fits quite nicely with the characteristics of flow described by Csikszentmihalyi (1975) as a key ingredient in creative productions. Any factor, including evaluation, that inhibits flow will inhibit creativity. Evaluation that feeds flow enhances creativity; evaluation that impedes flow inhibits creativity. So the issue of evaluation can be approached armed with two contradictory literatures—and the challenge either to reconcile the positions or to create a crucial experiment capable of disavowing the claims of one or both positions.

DEPRESSIVE ATTRIBUTIONS AND CREATIVITY

Who is doing the evaluating (self vs. others) tends to promote different attributions about why creativity did or did not occur. When one attributes the cause of creativity, or the lack of it, to him or herself rather to others or to circumstances, those attributions have affective and behavioral consequences. For example, when I self-evaluate my contributions to the scientific understanding of creativity, I may conclude that I am making significant advances, moderate contributions, or engaging in trivial activity. But because I am self-evaluating, whatever I conclude implies that I retain the power to adjust my future activities in a more productive way, and that I accept responsibility for my choices even if I am at the end of my career or at the end of a chapter in my career.

However, in keeping with the literature regarding attributional styles that lead to depression (Dykman & Abramson, 1990), I might experience learned helplessness or even more clinically dangerous hopelessness. Depression is likely to result if I determine that I have failed to make a meaningful contribution, and if I make attributions that (a) failure is due to some permanent condition within me, (b) I similarly fail at other endeavors, and (c) I always have and probably always will continue to fail at being creative. In other words, how I explain the cause of my personal level of creativity to myself will influence future creativity (and mental health).

Changing the attributions that lead to depression should reduce depression and increase creative potential. For example, if I still conclude that I have failed to be creative, but that (a) my failure is due to a cause external to myself, and (b) I am sometimes creative at other endeavors, then I am likely to conclude that (c) it is probable that I will be creative again sometime in the future. This more optimistic attribution bias leads to creativity-related behavioral consequences such perseverance and circumvention (Heinzen, 1994) while reducing a sense of learned helplessness and hopelessness. Different attributions regarding past and present creativity have differential effects on future creativity.

It is worth noting that conceptually this approach does not endorse the painfully romantic notion that depressive pathology is necessary for creativity. Depression is not creative; it is depressing. Any related creativity more plausibly emerges as an enhanced byproduct of a contrast effect that leads individuals to make globally positive attributions (even when they are not justified) when evaluating ourselves, just as employers err in evaluating an average job applicant as "excellent" if the applicant is interviewed just after a truly "poor" candidate (Wexley, Sanders, & Yukl, 1973). But then it is the stark contrast of feeling well as compared to experiencing depression that promotes o creativity, rather than the depression itself—and depression is only one of several emotional states (albeit a common and powerful one) capable of producing such contrast effects.

CHANGING ATTRIBUTIONAL SELF-TALK IS HARD WORK!

Individuals can, with effort, exercise some measure of control over their normally spontaneous attributional processes: They can change their schemas. Becoming aware of their own attributional processes sometimes represents a clinical activity, but it is one with a fairly respectable, research-affirming basis. In addition to straightforward self-reflection, cognitive therapists have demonstrated a variety of techniques that help individuals to become aware of the ways in which they explain the causes (and consequences) of behavior to themselves (Beck, 1976; Dryden, 1986; Ellis, 1984, Maultsby & Ellis, 1974). Whichever technique proves to be most effective, what emerges is a recognition that the cause of behavior has less to do with external events (such as being evaluated) than the way individuals explain the causes of those events to themselves. Individuals' attributional processes, that is, the way they talk to themselves, determines whether evaluations will lead to higher or lower levels of creative activity.

If the basic propositions of this chapter are accurate, then individuals can influence themselves to become more creative by choosing to engage in creative self-talk. However, as cognitive therapists clearly indicate (Ellis, 1984), transforming one's own habitually destructive (noncreative) self-talk is likely to require considerable effort. Amabile (1990), in a somewhat similar vein, asserted that "It may, in fact, be true that undermining creativity is much easier than stimulating it. But that is no reason not to try" (p. 73).

Amabile proposed that highly creative people have found ways to minimize the effects of forces that normally undermine intrinsic motivation necessary for creativity. They may cognitively reframe their inclinations for biased attributions in ways that reduce the seductive effects of positive evaluations, glean the benefits from negative evaluations, reduce the distraction potential of external evaluations, and rationally process both self-evaluations and evaluations by others in the service of their own creativity. Evaluation occurs in so many diverse forms that an array of self-talk strategies is probably necessary to maintain creativity.

Amabile (1990) offered the experience of both creative film producers and creative scientists to buttress her argument that some as yet unnamed individual difference was capable of minimizing the effects of distracting external forces such as success. She represented one version of the creative individual difference in attributional self-talk in this way: "I am well aware of my strong intrinsic interest in my work, and that can't be easily shaken; I certainly enjoy the benefits of wealth, fame, and critical acclaim, *but I place all that secondary to my own passion for what I do*" (p. 73, italics added). More significantly, she and her colleagues have been able to demonstrate that such attributional self-talk could be encouraged in others by presenting individuals with role models who demonstrate rational, creativity-enhancing attributional self-talk (Hennessey, Amabile, & Martinage, 1991). Making intrinsic motivation salient through role-modeled self-talk helps "immunize" individuals at risk for having their creativity undermined. Creativity is encouraged by consciously claiming that (a) one's own intrinsic passion is the source of creative energy; and (b) evaluations by others, especially pleasing evaluations, are potentially harmful.

CREATIVE RESOLUTIONS TO FOUR EVALUATION DILEMMAS

Unfortunately, positive evaluations by others are not the only kind of evaluation to which individuals are subjected. As noted in Figure 9.1, four combinations of evaluation circumstances exist that might affect creativity-related attributions: positive self-evaluations accompanied by positive evaluations by others; positive self-evaluations accompanied by negative evaluations by others; negative self-evaluations accompanied by positive evaluations by others; and negative self evaluations accompanied by negative evaluations by others. Although other individual differences also affect the degree to which each person will be influenced in each situation, each circumstance promotes particular attributional schemas and consequent interpretive dilemmas.

Evaluation by Others

	+	−
+	Cell I "C'est Moi!" versus "Flow"	Cell II "The Wild Good Chase" versus "The Pioneer"
−	Cell III "Missed Opportunities" versus "Institutionalize Creativity"	Cell IV "Learned Helplessness" versus "A New Strategy"

Evaluation by Self

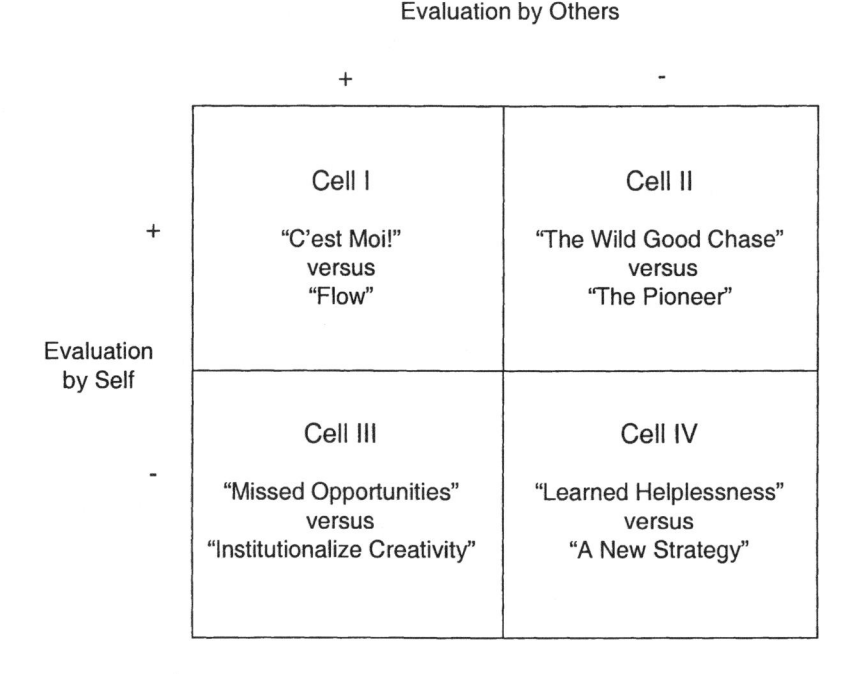

Figure 9.1. Four evaluation dilemmas affecting creativity

Each evaluation circumstance presents a particular opportunity to interpret the evaluation in a way likely to augment creativity, but is accompanied by a simultaneous cognitive threat to one's creativity. In general, the creative interpretations require cognitive effort and self discipline, whereas the contrasting threats tend to engage automatic cognitive schemas. Consequently, each circumstance implies a different cognitive challenge for persons wishing to nourish their creativity. How well individuals each resolve the tension between such opportunities and threats, attributionally, will contribute to determining how creatively they emerge from each evaluation circumstance.

For example, the evaluation dilemma described in Cell I threatens individuals seductively because it inspires the least critical and most self-serving attributions. The person reasons "Creativity is in my personality; afterall, others agree with me that I am extremely creative." The effects of this evaluation circumstance can be harmful. Anecdotally, sports writers sometimes accuse athletes whose outstanding performance has declined of "having read their own press clippings." Because it is pleasant to find one's own positive self evaluation warmly confirmed by others, attributions threaten to undermine existing creativity because the individual is not encouraged to be critical. The danger is succinctly expressed in the horrifyingly humorous song sung by Camelot's handsome Sir Lancelot: "C'est Moi!" On the other hand, individuals in Cell I may be enjoying a once in a lifetime opportunity, engaging in a Csikszentmihalyi-like "flow" of creativity. The trick is to remain creative in the face of distracting public acclaim.

Creative self-talk can resolve the dilemma between "C'est Moi! " and "flow" by exercising rational restraint and appreciation for this situation. For example, a person in Cell I might take Amabile's warning to heart, and process this evaluation circumstance by telling him or herself that "currently, my creativity is being appreciated by others. I certainly hope it will continue to be l appreciated, but if it is not, I choose to value my own creativity while paying attention to valid criticism when it is offered. Although I enjoy the recognition, I place that secondary to my passion."

Although it is initially more effortful to maintain cognitive control rather than to yield to flattery and the various seductions of public acclaim, it is significantly less effortful than trying to regain the quicksilver of cognitive creativity after it has slipped away.

Cell II poses a different kind of evaluation dilemma. It threatens creativity by encouraging attributions that will discount others' input. The person reasons "Creativity is in my personality, but others don't seem to recognize that fact, so it must be something about them that is dull or insensitive." The threat to one's creativity in this circumstance seems to be that a quixotic idealist pursues an increasingly ludicrous "wild goose chase" that he or she can eloquently justify only to him or herself. But the accompanying opportunity seems to be one with a pedigree across a variety of disciplines: the "pioneer." Creativity often does require independence of thought, a discounting of the opinions of others, and a determination to continue even when the weight of public or peer opinion goes against what may be just a timid intuition.

Rationally healthy, creativity-enhancing attributional self-talk can resolve the dilemma between the wild goose chase and the pioneer. When one believes that he or she is "really on to something" but realizes that others clearly are not in agreement, creativity-enhancing attributional self-talk might sound something like this:

> I recognize that I am going out on a limb and that I may be unappreciated by others, so I will do my best not to overindulge in the role of the unappreciated genius. Such feelings represent a distraction from my real passion. Solitary genius does exist, but my being solitary does not mean that I am a genius; so I will try to consider criticism by others as having potential value.

The role of the "unappreciated genius" represents a social script (similar, perhaps, to "the mad professor" and "the lone ranger") that Schank and Abelson (1977) described as knowledge structures that provide ready explanations for automatic behaviors (see also Ross, Amabile, & Steinmetz, 1977). It seems probable that individuals who endeavor to be creative may have particular scripts which, based on stereotypes of what it means to be creative, present unique attributional threats. Once again, it is initially more effortful to resist the easily acquired, temporarily self-serving script than it is to talk to oneself about evaluation in a way that is likely to preserve and enhance creativity.

Cell III represents an evaluation situation that threatens creativity in a somewhat unusual way. If individuals become overly focused on their own negative self-evaluations, even when others around them continuously offer reassurance that their creative work has value and is being well received, they may miss opportunities to develop or apply their work that may not conveniently reappear when they may want the work again later. Others are cheering the creativity, but the individuals remain personally unconvinced. This circumstance suggests that the creator is willing to engage in self-criticism, and refuses to be seduced by the positive evaluations of others—what others have identified as a generally creative response to evaluation. But although such false modesty may be becoming, it is distracting and can lead to "missed opportunities." And the accompanying opportunity is that, although the individuals are being well received, they have opportunities to obtain significant resources that can help "institutionalize creativity." There are, indeed, organizations that do a better job of maintaining creativity than others (Heinzen, 1994) and folk wisdom in this situation asserts that one should "strike while the iron is hot."

Consequently, creativity-enhancing attributional self-talk can resolve the dilemma between the threat of missed opportunities and the opportunity to institutionalize creativity by telling oneself the following:

> I don't really like the distraction of public appearances, book tours, or having to take the time to write for grant money—and I am not persuaded that my work is as great as other people say it is—but tangible resources can help support creativity and I prefer to think of the long term benefits of expanding this creative activity in addition to enjoying the immediate pleasures of engaging in current creativity. Afterall, these opportunities may not reappear and I don't want to look back at the present circumstance as a lost opportunity.

When one self-evaluates his or her own work more negatively than do others, one may be (a) more perceptive; (b) taking his or her own unique talents for granted; or (c) overly self-critical or engaging in a false modesty. Whatever the explanation for this particular evaluation dilemma, they all lead to the individual not taking action or seizing opportunities that may not come again.

Finally, Cell IV represents a discouraging situation in which both the individual and others agree that creativity has not been realized or enjoyed. This threatens to promote attributions that may pose a clinical concern if creativity is valued and the individual internalizes and globalizes the causes of the poor evaluation. A curious, companion danger is that if learned helplessness has developed, creative success is just a step away but will not be realized due to a lack of perseverance and a generalizing discouragement. The accompanying opportunity is an opportunity for change. Because there exists a universal opinion that one's present path is not productive, one may as well see the handwriting on the wall, and adopt a "new strategy." Consequently, creativity-enhancing attributional self-talk can help to resolve the dilemma between learned helplessness and a new strategy.

For example, I know a couple who together devoted the early and middle portions of their adult lives to acting, but finally concluded that they did not enjoy the combination of grit, luck, and raw talent necessary for a long-term successful career. She became a school teacher; he became a fairly successful salesperson. They greatly prefer their present lives to the unrelenting battle to "make it" in the acting world. Ironically, my sense is that they are living more creative lives now than before; they are certainly much happier. In a paraphrase of conversations with them, I can report they (eventually) explained negative evaluations of their creativity in a healthy, creativity-enhancing way: "We were competent but not overly gifted; we were hard working but not sufficiently mean or willing to compromise; and we were often unlucky and often became discouraged at our bad luck."

Their attributions were rationally honest and recognized the significant role of chance in the acting business. They refused to internalize or globalize negative evaluations and, creatively, changed their lives so that they now provide their children with both an appreciation for good theater and for the difficulties in producing good theater.

SUMMARY

Each of the four different evaluation circumstances described here promotes different attributions regarding creativity. Individuals' attribution biases lead them to explain evaluations of their creativity in ways that influence consequent creativity. The fundamental attribution error is so named because it is so common and seems to be associated with so many other attribution errors. It refers to one's tendency to explain outcomes as being caused by people (who are vivid, memorable, and attract attention) rather than circumstances (which are often abstract, complex, and do not attract one's attention; Jones, 1979; Ross, 1977). Because there is none as vivid and memorable to one's self as one's self, individuals often engage in the fundamental attribution error as they seek to explain their own creativity. Consequently, when the treasured creative process or product is evaluated by both the individual and by others, the individual attributes more validity to his or her own judgment and tends to disregard the validity of the judgments of others, who are clearly less capable of appreciating one's own creative efforts.

However, rational and creative self-talk can minimize one's own biases (which, ironically, appear to be aimed at protecting one's self-esteem) and encourage creativity. Telling oneself that "others may be able to perceive things I am unable to perceive, even about my own work; therefore, I sometimes will consider their opinions," is not only true, but also helpful at producing better work. Indeed, it is at the heart of the scientific peer review system, which for all its faults has created significant amounts of memorable, valuable, trustworthy science. But it is also creatively rational to admit that "I may have an insight or a methodology which others simply do not comprehend; having considered the evaluations of others, I still choose to forge ahead in what I believe is a promising direction."

Cognitive therapies already exist that allow individuals to become more aware of their automatic attributional cognitive processes. Most therapies, although they usually make theoretically casual statements regarding creativity, like to claim creativity as a consequence of their interventions. This chapter asserts that individuals can employ attribution theory to encourage creativity-enhancing or creativity-undermining cognitions, both therapeutically and for reasons of personal and organizational development. More specifically, scientific evidence is beginning to develop that indicates that individuals can immunize themselves against the effects of commonly destructive influences on creativity through role modeling appropriate cognitions. Consequently, the opportunities to measurably and meaningfully influence the nurturing of creativity are increasing. This chapter attributes such practical growth within creativity research to the rapidly developing social psychology of creativity.

REFERENCES

Amabile, T. M. (1983). *The social psychology of creativity*. New York: Springer-Verlag.

Amabile, T. M. (1990). Within you, without you: The social psychology of creativity and beyond. In M. A. Runco & R. S. Albert (Eds.), *Theories of creativity* (pp. 61-91). Newbury Park, CA: Sage.

Beck, A. T. (1976). *Cognitive therapy and the emotional disorders*. New York: International Universities Press.

Birney, R. C., Burdick, H., & Teevan, R. C. (1969). *Fear of failure*. New York: Van Nostrand-Reinhold.

Brown, J. D., & Rogers, R. J. (1991). Self-serving attributions: The role of physiological arousal. *Personality and Social Psychology Bulletin, 17*, 501-506.

Crutcher, R. J. (1994). Telling what we know: The use of verbal report methodologies in psychological research. *Psychological Science, 5*(5), 241.

Csikszentmihalyi, M. (1975). *Beyond boredom and anxiety*. San Francisco: Jossey-Bass.

Csikszentmihalyi, M. (1990). The domain of creativity. In M. A. Runco & R. S. Albert (Eds.), *Theories of creativity*. Newbury Park, CA: Sage.

Dryden, W. (1986). Language and meaning in RET. *Journal of Rational-Emotive Therapy, 7*, 3-27.

Dykman, B. M., & Abramson, L. Y. (1990). Contributions of basic research to the cognitive theories of depression. *Personality and Social Psychology Bulletin, 16*(1), 42-57.

Ellis, A. (1984). *How to maintain and enhance your rational-emotive therapy gains.* New York: Institute for Rational-Emotive Therapy.

Harrington, D. M. (1990). The ecology of human creativity: A psychological perspective. In M. A. Runco & R. S. Albert (Eds.), *Theories of creativity.* Newbury Park, CA: Sage.

Heinzen, T. E. (1994). *Everyday frustration and creativity in government.* Norwood, NJ: Ablex.

Hennessey, B. A., Amabile, T. M., & Martinage, M. (1989). Immunizing children against the negative effects of reward. *Contemporary Educational Psychology, 14*(3), 212-227.

Jones, E. E. (1979). The rocky road from acts to dispositions. *American Psychologist, 34,* 107-117.

Jones, E. E., & Nisbett, R. E. (1971). *The actor and the observer: Divergent perceptions of the causes of behavior.* Morristown, NJ: General Learning Press.

Kasof, J. (1995). Explaining creativity: The attributional perspective. *Creativity Research Journal, 8*(4), 311-366.

MacKinnon, D. W. (1962). The nature and nurture of creative talent. *American Psychologist, 17,* 484-495.

McClelland, D. C., Atkinson, J., Clark, R., & Lowell, E. (1953). *The achievement motive.* New York: Appleton-Century-Crofts.

Maultsby, M. C., Jr., & Ellis, A. (1974). *Techniques for using rational-emotive imagery.* New York: Institute for Rational-Emotive Therapy.

Miller, D. T., & Ross, M. (1975). Self-serving biases in attribution of causality: Fact or fiction? *Psychological Bulletin, 82,* 313-325.

Payne, J. W. (1994). Thinking aloud: Insights into information processing. *Psychological Science, 5*(5), 241-248.

Ross, L. (1977). The intuitive psychologist and his shortcomings: Distortions in the attribution process. In L. Berkowitz (Ed.), *Advances in experimental social psychology* (Vol. 10, pp. 173-220). San Diego, CA: Academic Press.

Ross, L., Amabile, T. M., & Steinmetz, J. L. (1977). Social roles, social control, and biases in social-perception processes. *Journal of Personality and Social Psychology, 35,* 484-494.

Runco, M. A. (1991). The evaluative, valuative, and divergent thinking of children. *The Journal of Creative Behavior, 25*(4), 311-319.

Sanders, G. S. (1981). Driven by distraction: An integrative review of social facilitation theory and research. *Journal of Experimental Social Psychology, 17,* 227-251.

Schank, R. C., & Abelson, R. P (1977). *Scripts, plans, goals and understanding.* Hillsdale, NJ: Lawrence Erlbaum Associates.

Wexley, K. N., Sanders, R. E., & Yukl, G. A. (1973). Training interviewers to eliminate contrast effects in employment interviews. *Journal of Applied Psychology, 57,* 233-236.

Wilson, T. D. (1994). The proper protocol: Validity and completeness of verbal reports. *Psychological Science, 5*(5), 249-252.

Zajonc, R. B. (1965). Social facilitation. *Science, 149,* 269-274.

10

PRAGMATIC PSYCHOLINGUISTICS AS A FRAMEWORK FOR THE EVALUATION OF CREATIVITY

Albert N. Katz
The University of Western Ontario

Creativity is generally accepted as a psychological phenomenon separable from other related mental phenomena, such as intelligence and wisdom (see Sternberg, 1985). In fact, the word *creative* is ranked among the 5% of the most commonly used words in the English language (Kucera & Francis, 1967). The use of the term is ubiquitous. Recently, at a parent-teacher meeting, I heard one such use: A teacher described a student as being "quite creative." That same morning, I was reading about an ongoing court case in Toronto involving an artist: Experts such as psychiatrists and writers were being called to testify to the creative artistic worth on what some allege are pornographic depictions of children. And at work, sitting on promotion and tenure committees, the creativity of other professor are evaluated. In what way is creativity discussed in these various ways the same and in what ways do they differ?

In this chapter, I suggest a framework for addressing this issue, which arises from the literature in pragmatic psycholinguistics. The approach is based on the concept that communication is inherently ambiguous and meaning is context-determined. Rules of communication permit coherence to be achieved within this noisy environment. These rules necessitate the communicator to have a mental model of the world and to make inferences about the mental model held by the audience to which the communication is directed. I argue that this approach is applicable to how researchers study creativity. I also argue that the same principles might underlie both interpersonal judgments of creativity (of the sort just discussed) and intrapersonal evaluations, such as occurs during the creative process itself.

THE TRADITIONAL APPROACHES TO THE STUDY OF CREATIVITY

In the zeal to create a science of creativity, researchers have adopted an objective perspective: Creativity has to be measurable and, consequently, the definition of creativity has depended on interpersonal verifiable criteria. These criteria have, like Janus, two faces: one that looks inward at the characteristics of the creative person, such as those features that distinguish the creative from those of lesser creativity, and a second face that looks outward at the products generated by the creative person and the impact of these products on the person's environment and the recognition of the creativity presented. Research strategies for examining the psychological properties of the "creative" person (i.e., the inner face) have usually been parasitic on identifying characteristics of the output of that person (i.e., the outer face).

Galton (1869), for instance, and later more sophisticated analyses (e.g., Simonton, 1984) make the assumption that one can identify creative people on the basis of archival data. The truly creative are those who produce high impact work, and this impact will be reflected in public recognition, such as the number of dedicated pages in an encyclopedia, the number of biographies, and the like. By these criteria, of course, the teacher described earlier would have no grounds for calling one of her charges creative.

Other common research strategies are similarly outward looking, although in principle can accommodate the teacher: identifying highly creative people on the basis of expert panels (e.g., MacKinnon, 1975) or on the basis of tests that purport to measure creativity (e.g., Hocevar & Bachelor, 1989). The first approach, employing an expert panel, thrusts the problem of defining creativity (as it does with Galton's technique) into the heads of experts without clarifying the basis on which experts make their decisions. And experts themselves might differ in lawful ways. For instance, Taylor, Smith, and Ghiselin (1963) showed that subjective ratings of creativity given by experts are often unrelated to objective measures of creative productivity. More importantly, the tacit knowledge used in identifying creative people differed as a function of relationship: Coworkers identified different people than did supervisors who, in turn, differed from heads of laboratories. If creativity is in the eye of the (expert) observer, it pays to be attentive to the relationship of the expert and who he or she is judging.

The second approach, using test scores, may appear to have an advantage over the use of experts because the criteria for selection are overt test scores, and not covertly held beliefs. This advantage is largely illusionary, however, because most tests are based on tacit (expert-driven) theories of creativity and are often validated by subjective ratings (e.g., Mednick, 1962; Torrance, 1974; Welsh, 1975). Moreover, as Nicholls (1972) pointed out, the general failure of these tests to select people who satisfy "expert" nomination indicates, at the least, that the criteria implicit in creativity tests differ from the criteria used by experts.

The common research strategies noted here depend on expert-driven models of creativity. That is, experts define what creativity means, and then employ measurement techniques to isolate people who possess these characteristics. The danger is that, in principle, the expert definitions and the people who are characterized by these definitions could be at variance with what the term means to the people using the concept. I argue here that the basis for creating a science of creativity should start with an in-depth understanding of the inward-looking face of creativity: the concept as used both in everyday language and in the language of specialized domains. I argue further that pragmatic principles of language can be used to help unravel how the concept is used in these contexts. These principles lead to the unavoidable conclusion that the inward and outward faces of creativity are intrinsically and inextricably linked. Finally, I attempt to examine studies, most of which were done for other purposes, within this general framework.

CREATIVITY AND THE PRAGMATICS OF SPEECH

Consider the following two sentences:

1. Do you think John Smith is the most creative person in our department?
2. Do you think John Smith is the most intelligent person in our department?

A standard test of reference in language studies is whether one can replace one word for another without changing meaning. As applied to Questions 1 and 2, the term *creative* would be synonymous with the term *intelligent* if the terms could be used interchangeably. Most individuals would, I think, argue that the two are not synonymous.

But how do we decide that John Smith meets the criteria described in Question 1? In essence, the question reduces to what some have labeled the *communication game*. The rules of the game are simple. The observer has access to a set of people or activities performed by a set of people. The observer's task is to choose, from that set, the person (or activity) that meets given criteria, such as those implied in Question 1. The observer's choice must be constrained by the theory or mental model he or she holds about creativity. The pragmatic approach would argue that the meaning of the term *creative* held by the observer is not static, but depends on the context in which it is placed. One aspect of the context is the communication milieu: In essence, one may ask the question, "Creative to whom"? Thus one's choices will be constrained by the mental model one holds and the mental model one believes is being held by the audience (or judges). As applied to the problem of Critical Processes, the claim is that our outward judgment of creativity is based on inward-based (and largely implicitly held) mental models. I argue further that the person (or activity) chosen would shift if the criteria were changed to those described in Statement 2, indicating different mental models underlie individuals' conceptualization and use of the terms *creative* and *intelligent*.

From the perspective of a pragmatist, the question of interest is in identifying the conditions or contexts under which a speaker uses the term *creative,* in lieu of another word (such as *intelligent*) in communication. The extreme freedom to frame human communications suggests a high probability that the presented message is not received in the way intended. Pragmatists argue that the inherent ambiguity in speech is mitigated by rules that govern communication.

Grice (1975) and others (e.g., Norman & Rumelhart, 1975) outlined the tacit rules that govern communication. Later theorists attempted alternative approaches (e.g., Clark & Marshall, 1981; Sperber & Wilson, 1986); the differences between these approaches are of minor importance here because there is general agreement that the overriding principle is that of cooperation: Participants work as if they have a contract in which each partner contributes to communication in appropriate ways.

The alternative theoretical approaches differ in the rules that are suggested to implement the cooperative principle. The following rules, taken from various sources, are exemplary. Grice (1975), for example, argued that the terms of the contract are such that each participant should say only as much as is needed to be informative (maxim of quantity), should say only is true (maxim of quality), should make one's contribution relevant to the context (maxim of relation), and should say it politely, briefly, and to the point (maxim of manner). To this list, Norman and Rumelhart (1975; also see for an elaborated exposition, Clark & Marshall, 1981) added that the terms of the contract imply sensitivity by the speaker to the knowledge and beliefs held by the audience (inasmuch as one must infer and respond to these characteristics of the audience). Finally, Norman and Rumelhart and others argued that the speaker can intentionally violate these rules, but to maintain the cooperative principle must explicitly mark any such violation of the contract. With respect to this last point, assume that someone utters the following statement: "John Smith is the most creative person in class" and intends it to be sarcastic. Under this condition, the contract states that the speaker has to provide hints that the principles of politeness and quality are being violated. In Kreuz (1996) and Katz (1996) some of these hints were offered.

The pragmatic approach to language thus suggests that use of the term *creativity* will be made when a speaker or writer *believes* that the term is relevant, informative, and unambiguous to his or her audience. Thus, one should be able to capture the essence of the use of the term *creativity* by isolating the contexts in which it is uttered, and in isolating the conceptual structure of the term that the speaker assumes is shared with his or her audience. Context is especially important from a pragmatic perspective because the meaning assigned to a term cannot be defined unambiguously; meaning is assigned with reference to the situation in which it is employed (see Givon, 1989).

An example follows of how a pragmatic language-based analysis might apply to one aspect of creativity research. Barron and Harrington (1981), in a review of creativity research, indicated that the identification of core personality traits shared by creative people was one of the most exciting facets of modern research into creativity. Various so-called creative personality trait-based scales have emerged over the years and, given that the scales have shown to be correlated with one another, one can argue that the traits shared in common by these scales reflect a consensus on the mental model that underlies understanding of the creative person.

The most extensive of these scales was developed by Harrison Gough and can be used for demonstrative purposes. Gough's (1979) scale is based on an extremely large sample ($N = 1,701$) of highly creative people from 12 separate fields studied during assessments completed at the Institute of Personality and Research (IPAR) in Berkeley. The participants were all highly effective people who had been nominated by experts and, at IPAR, were rated along a set of dimensions. One assessment instrument was the adjective checklist, a list of 300 adjectives from which both the creative participants and judges chose adjectives descriptive of the person. Participant and judge alike knew that they had been nominated for creative performance in their fields of study. In any event, 30 adjectives were shown to be good predictors of judged creativity: 18 traits were positively correlated with creativity ratings (capable, clever, confident, egotistical, humorous, individualistic, informal, insightful, intelligent, interests wide, inventive, original, reflective, resourceful, self confident, sexy, snobbish, and unconventional) and 12 traits were negatively correlated (affected, cautious, commonplace, conservative, conventional, dissatisfied, honest, interest narrow, mannerly, sincere, submissive, and suspicious). Thus, in general, the creative person being studied (and the external judge) is more likely to describe him or herself (the creative participant) with labels such as being unconventional or inventive, and is likely to reject labels such as honest and suspicious.

But what do these core traits reflect? They are reliable and good discriminators. On one hand, it could be argued that they represent the "meaning" of the term *creativity*; a pragmatist, on the other hand, would argue that the meaning of the term is not fixed but is context-sensitive. I argue, from a pragmatic perspective, that in order to understand these ratings, one has to understand the communicative context in which these terms were generated, and the relationship of the people in communication with one another.

The creative personality scale consists of highly creative (and largely publicly acknowledged) people invited to an assessment, interacting with skilled investigators familiar with the creative achievements of their sample. If, in this context, one asks people to describe one another, the cooperative principle should come into play (e.g., rules such as only communicating what is needed, no more or no less). If everyone knows that the person being rated is creative then the terms reflecting the underlying mental model of the person as a creator may not be informative or relevant to the communication of new, unknown facts. The analogous situation arises when someone is asked to describe his or her spouse: Presumably terms like human or female would be unlikely candidates for use because these characteristics will be presupposed; yet, arguably these characteristics are central to the person being described. As applied to the Gough, and similar scales, the argument would be that many of the so-called core creative personality may not reflect the mental model underlying the creative person and would presumably reflect some ancillary (but shared) information that would be new. Such information might be about interpersonal style or characteristics associated with how the person has responded to social recognition.

Naturally, research is required to test the hypothesis just made. The point is that a pragmatic orientation to the questions of creativity forces researchers to make central the problem of context and knowledge assumed by different participants in a communicative interaction.

CREATIVITY AND COMMON GROUND

Common ground is the knowledge the speaker assumes that he or she shares with the audience (Clark & Marshall, 1981). This knowledge interacts with the Gricean principles stated earlier inasmuch as it is the database, often unstated in the discourse itself, that underlies use of the principles. In fact, common ground—or in Clark and Marshall's (1981) terms, mutual belief—depends on the speaker assuming that he or she shares a context with the audience that will permit recovery of the intended meaning. Of most interest here is common ground based on stored knowledge of the world that the speaker assumes about the audience, and that the speaker uses to guide communication. Empirical investigations have confirmed the presence and use of common ground based on this principle (see Gerrig & Littman, 1990).

As applied here, this principle would assume that a person who employs the term *creative,* as in Question 1, has an internalized mental model about the meaning of the term *creative* and a mental model of what the term means to the audience to which it is directed. Common ground is based on the assumption that the mental model presupposed by the speaker about the audience is consensual, that is, shared by the typical participant in the community to whom the term is being addressed.

In principle, one should be able to find evidence for shared meaning in studies that are analogues to the communication game: Participants are asked to choose (or generate) according to the criterion of "being creative." In the ideal study, one cannot define what the term means for the participant because correspondence must depend on each member of the audience using his or her own mental model, and not one imposed from "above" (such as by experts). The measurement instrument itself also has to be relatively open-ended because more formal measurement implicitly defines the mental model for the audience; I argue that providing rating scales or a fixed set of adjectives from which to choose serves the role of providing an expert-driven mental model for the participant.

Analyzing studies using the logic of the communication game, with the caveats just suggested, does provide evidence for a consensually shared mental model of what it means to be creative.

Consider, for instance, Amabile's (1983) research program. In a set of studies, Amabile asked participants to produce a product (such as figural art or poetry). She then had the products rated along a set of dimensions. Of interest here are the ratings of creativity, defined as follows: "Using *your own subjective definition of creativity*, the degree to which the design is creative" (p. 43, italics added; also see p. 52). Note that Amabile did not impose a definition on her participants, most of whom could be considered to be from knowledgeable to expert in the domains being studied. From the perspective of a pragmatist, the result of most interest is the agreement on what constitutes creative activity: Reliability values all are over .70, and go as high as .93 (see Amabile, pp. 50, 56).

Other researchers have employed variants of what Runco (e.g., 1989) labeled *social validation methodology*. In this procedure, one sample freely describes characteristics of creativity, and a second sample rates these characteristics along some dimensions of interest. For instance, Sternberg (1985), in an extensive set of studies, asked both expert and novice participants to generate behaviors that were characteristic of an ideally creative person. As with Amabile, no definition was imposed on what was meant by being creative. A second group rated behaviors that were listed more than once. Ratings, on a 9-point scale, were of the degree to which the behavior was characteristic of an ideal creative person, once again leaving the definition of creative to the mental model of the participant. The ratings were, as with Amabile, highly reliable (ranging from .81 to .93) and did not differ for experts and laypersons. Equally impressive agreements were found with teachers asked to rate traits common to creative children (see Runco, 1984, 1987).

Katz and Thompson (1993) asked layperson participants to generate specific acts performed by the most creative people who they knew personally. A second set of laypersons rated each act, along a 7-point scale, to the degree that the act was a good example of what they thought creativity was. Reliability of these ratings was high: (r = .92). Another group of participants who were presented examples of these acts were asked to describe the acts in any way they wished; the concept *creative* was not even mentioned. The likelihood that creative was applied to an act varied directly with how good an example of the concept it had been rated (r = .65). This last finding is especially noteworthy because, from the perspective of communication, the free choice of the term *creative* presupposes that participants would recognize the label as informative, relevant, and the like or, to use the metaphor of the communication game, should be able to choose the appropriate act, just given that description.

Taken together, these and other data are a clear indication that, at least in U.S. culture, people share common ground with respect to the term, *being creative*. In the contexts studied, when participants use the term they have a clear mental model of the concept that one intends to communicate, and an expectation that the audience will share that mental model as well. And, at least on one level, the expectations are met inasmuch as the concordance rates are reasonably high. I argue later that coherence (such as achieving agreement that John Smith is creative) can emerge even if different features of the mental model are aroused in different people.

THE COMMUNICATION GAME AND CREATIVITY: INSTRUCTIONS

Consider the communication game again. Now the rules are changed slightly. Without access to any other information, participants were asked to "be creative." In essence, they are asked to display their mental model of creativity. Because, as previously argued, humans share common ground with respect to the concept, it should be expected that, following the cooperative principle, the recipient of the message will act in an appropriate manner. If performance is different under the "be creative" set (relative to the standard instructions) then it is clear that the instructions engaged a mental model of what creativity means to the participant.

The ideal study would be one in which the only information given to the participant are conveyed in instructions to act creatively. Unfortunately, there are few studies that meet this ideal. One such study employed the use of empirically keyed adjective checklist data from which "creative personality scales" are derived, such as the Gough scale described earlier (Domino, 1970; Gough, 1979). These scales were based on adjectives that discriminated the (self- and the expert-defined) creative group from comparison samples. There is some data indicating that creative people (defined by test score performance) tend to see these terms as central to their self-concept (Katz, 1987). Of interest here is the finding by Ironson and Davis (1979) that people instructed to "be creative" choose more of the ostensible creative traits relative to the number chosen under the usual, neutral instructional set. To the extent these terms reflect a mental model of creativity, the pragmatic approach to these data would lead to the argument that so-called creative and less creative people share the same mental model about what it means to be creative, but only the former wish to display themselves in those terms.

Similar findings can be found when other (purported) creativity tests are employed. Harrington (1975), Katz and Poag (1979), Runco and Okuda (1991), and others have all shown that divergent thinking scores can be shown to increase in the direction of greater creativity when explicit instructions are given to "be creative." Creativity, in this case, is defined variously by the number of ideas produced, originality of these ideas, and the different categories employed. In these studies, additional information is given defining what creativity could mean, so the effects are not as clear an indication of the mental model used naturally by participants, and may reflect a willingness to adopt the audiences' definition of the term. Nonetheless, the effects parallel those found with the adjective checklist data: One can show increases in the number, type, and originality of responses when appropriately instructed to be creative, and this effect is largest with low-scoring participants (see Runco, 1990). It appears as if high scorers "spontaneously" communicate or display themselves according to a certain mental model of creativity, whereas low scorers know what the model is, and can act accordingly, but opt not to do so.

Taken together, these instruction-manipulation studies suggest that an important aspect in the analysis of creativity should be a shift away from "knowing how" procedural explanations toward explanations based on "knowing when." In line with pragmatic theorizing, creativity and its expression are not fixed or static, but are dependent in part on contextual constraints, such as expectations imposed from an audience. The question of interest should be why some people choose to display themselves in terms of the mental model underlying the "creative person," whereas others (even those who know what that model is) do not choose to do so.

THE MENTAL MODEL OF CREATIVITY

In the previous sections the aim has been to show that common ground exists with respect to the concept of creativity, and that context, operationalized by linguistic instruction, can engage the concept even in people who do not demonstrate it spontaneously. In this section, I describe studies that attempt to identify characteristics of the mental model.

In Katz and Giacommelli (1982), we utilized a technique found in psycholinguistic research (see Fillenbaum & Rapoport, 1971). In this tradition, participants are given a number of terms representing a well-defined semantic domain (such as kin terms) and are asked to freely sort these words into as many piles as they wish, with words in a pile reflecting those that share a common meaning that is distinct from the meaning of the words in the other piles. Hierarchical clustering analysis is then employed to uncover the underlying characteristic of the organization of the items. In our case, we employed items that came from the adjective checklist that could describe either creative or more mundane problem solving. Moreover, using the logic of instructional set previously described, half our participants were asked to make their sorting as related to people who are being creative; the other half received neutral instructions.

The findings were intriguing. Under the "creative" instructions, fewer piles were used relative to the more general neutral case, suggesting that the mental model underlying creative thinking was more specified than that underlying problem-solving activities in general.

The hierarchical clustering analysis indicated that some clusters were shared by the mental models underlying both creative and more normal problem solving: being clever (e.g., imaginative, innovative), being hardworking, (e.g., conscientious, persevering), being systematic (e.g., logical, methodical), being flexible (e.g., flexible, versatile), and being unusual (e.g., bizarre). The more interesting differences emerge with the instructional set because from a pragmatic perspective, these differences reflect subtleties in the mental models used for conceptualization and communication. Under the standard instructions, a cluster was found that was not present in the creative-salient instruction case: being negative (e.g., critical, intolerant). And there was a cluster found under creative but not standard instructions: being cognitively open (e.g., appreciative, sensitive). Thus, relative to other high-level problem solving, the mental model underlying creative activity has openness to experience and a rejection of negative evaluation as central components. To my knowledge, there is no other study available in which instructions and concepts relevant to creativity were examined simultaneously. The pragmatic approach suggested here argues for the need of additional studies of this sort, with larger and better selected item pools.

Most of the studies examining the nature of the mental model comes from the social validation studies described earlier. The first phase involves generating output characteristics of creativity. I used the data from these studies to demonstrate that common ground exists with respect to the mental model of creativity. The second phase involves examination of some of the properties of the generated items. In most cases, participants are asked to rate the generated output along a set of dimensions.

In Amabile (1983), the first phase involved the generation of a figural design or of a haiku poem. These artistic productions were rated on a set of dimensions by judges with varying degrees of expertise in the domain being studied. A fairly large number of different ratings were taken, varying along quite different aspects of the stimuli; representative ratings of the artistic output included novel use of materials, neatness, and silliness, whereas the verbal productions were rated on dimensions such as novelty of word choice, grammar, and emotionality. For both types of output, ratings of technical goodness (e.g., neatness, balance) was separable from ratings that expressed nontechnical aspects of the output. And it was the nontechnical factor that was most related to the mental model underlying creativity, represented by dimensions such as novelty, spontaneity, liking, and variability. At the least, these data suggest that the mental model of creativity emphasizes characteristics other than those found in effective, competent performance.

Runco (1989), using parents as judges, identified 25 traits related to parental judgments of children's creativity. These traits were found to group into three clusters: intellectual traits (e.g., clever, varied interests), attitudinal predispositions (e.g., independent, dreamy), and motivational characteristics (e.g., adventurous, spontaneous). Sternberg (1985), through the use of multidimensional scaling techniques, isolated eight characteristics of the mental model of the ideal creative person. These characteristics, along with a descriptive phrase are as follows: nonentrenchment (impulsive), high in integration and intellectuality (grasps abstract ideas), aesthetic taste and imagination (has good taste), decisional skill and flexibility (can change directions), perspicacity (questions social norms), drive for accomplishment and recognition (is motivated by goals), inquisitiveness (is inquisitive), and intuition (is intuitive). In Katz and Thompson (1993), we demonstrated that the people who performed an everyday act considered to be creative (e.g., "developed a pictorial means of communication for a person who could not speak") was more likely to be described in terms that refer to aesthetic taste and imagination, integration and intellectuality, and drive for recognition and accomplishment than was a person who performed an everyday act rated as less creative (e.g.,"dyed hair an unusual color"). People who performed high and low creative acts were not seen to differ on dimensions such as perspicacity or decisional skill and flexibility. An implication of this finding is discussed later.

In summary, then, what is known about the mental model of creativity? First, it appears to be multidimensional. However, the studies reviewed here do not permit an unambiguous statement regarding the number nor the nature of the dimensions involved. At the least, dimensions involving intellectual, motivational, and personality characteristics are implicated. Also implicated are dimensions that map more easily onto the novelty of output and those that map more readily onto technical competence of the output. And many of these dimensions can be further subdivided, but again with little agreement across studies. For instance, Gough's (1979) 30 core personality characteristics differ considerably from Domino's (1970)

59 core characteristics; the dimension of negative evaluation identified in Katz and Giacommelli (1982) does not have a ready counterpart in Sternberg's (1985) work, and so on. Second, it appears some of these dimensions are shared with other cognitive domains, such as those required for everyday problem solving. In Katz and Giacommelli (1982), we noted considerable overlap in the categories used to organize problem solving in general from those that emphasized creative cognitions. In a similar vein, Sternberg (1985) noted that the scaling of the ideal creative person overlapped moderately with that obtained with the ideal intelligent person, and very little with the scaling based on the ideal wise person. I speculate later on some of the ways that the various dimensions might work in everyday communication.

The conclusions made here must be offered with some caution. First, in many of the studies just reviewed, judges were provided with a set of scales on which to make their ratings. Unfortunately, from the pragmatic perspective, the rating scales themselves often are "expert-defined," and thus may not be an exhaustive listing or (arguably) even central properties of the mental model underlying creativity. The scaling procedures employed in Sternberg (1985) and in Katz and Giacommelli (1982) were open-ended and let the participants impose their own structure on the material and, as such, were more likely to reflect the mental model used spontaneously and naturally by the judges. More studies of this type are required, with a larger sample of stimuli relevant to creativity, and with scaling based on both expert and novice judges.

The second caution is a repeat of the caveat made earlier. A pragmatic approach is, by definition, highly context-sensitive. The person communicating engages his or her own mental model and the model he or she assumes of the audience to which the communication is directed. When dimensions are provided for ratings, this almost certainly acts as a context in which to understand the goals and intent of the audience, and, as such, will lead to appropriate production on the part of the person providing the ratings. Thus, findings that technical and nontechnical aspects of production are separable, and that creativity is especially related to the nontechnical component cannot be taken as evidence that the nontechnical factors are not part of the mental model underlying performance because these findings might just reflect a presupposition (assumed to be shared with the audience) that creative output must be technically sound, and hence would not be relevant to communicate. What is required are studies that disentangle information assumed to be known to the audience from "new" information that one is attempting to communicate.

CREATIVITY AND CONTEXT

We are left with a puzzle. On the one hand, there is evidence, reviewed here, that people share common ground with respect to the mental model of creativity: There is good interrater reliability on what constitutes creative output. On the other hand, there is evidence, also reviewed previously, that, across studies, different dimensions appear to underlie what people mean by the term *creativity*. How is coherence (i.e., agreement in making judgments) achieved in the midst of such variability in the expressed nature of the mental model adopted?

The answer I propose to this puzzle lies in the contextual nature of communication. The pragmatic approach to language is based on the idea that meaning is not fixed, but is context-sensitive. From this perspective, judgments about creativity are not based on a static, all-or-nothing model in which each and every feature of creativity must be activated before creativity is recognized. Instead, the model has to be one in which sufficient (but not exhaustive) concordance is reached between participants in communications. The specific features activated in part will depend on contextual factors and on individual differences among the participants.

The preceding argument depends on accepting the notion that creativity is context-specific. Taken to its logical conclusion, the argument would be that judgments of creativity will shift with changes in one's context, in domains of interest, and from person to person. These shifts must, nonetheless, make contact with some commonality shared across contexts, domains, and people, otherwise coherence would not occur (and communication not be possible).

The distinction between an immutable fixed conceptualization of creativity and one that is highly context-specific is demonstrated in Fine (1983). Fine analyzed reactions to art forgeries. An art forgery is a piece of art, purportedly created by an acknowledged master, that is subsequently uncovered to be done in recent years by someone who has passed it off as the work of the master. Note that forgeries are not reproductions or copies of other work, but are rather "new" pieces in the distinctive style, with the aesthetic, associated with the master. Some art forgeries have been bought and displayed in major museums, after extensive research by reputable experts in the field. So, at one level, the art has to be technically and stylistically convincing. Moreover, as Fine pointed out, forgeries are often viewed as being creative, when understood to be the work of the master. After the forgery is uncovered, however, a transformation takes place: The creativity inherent in the art and in the person who produced it are denigrated. What has changed is not the "creative" output itself, but the historical, motivational, and economic context in which the output is interpreted. Csikszentmihalyi (1990) made a similar point when he noted that the work of artists and scientists often is appreciated and understood differently during their lifetime than after death.

Art forgeries are, of course, special cases involving the reputation of experts and the potential loss of huge amounts of money. However, a pragmatic approach to creativity would lead to the argument that context is just as important in everyday instances of creativity, such as that expressed by the teacher noted at the beginning of this chapter.

In an earlier study (Katz & Thompson, 1993), we initially had university-level students think of creative people that they knew personally and then asked them to generate acts or behaviors that these people performed that "reflect or exemplify" their creativity. Another sample rated each act to the degree to which it was prototypical of their concept of being creative. Thus, a pool of everyday acts deemed to be prototypical and nonprototypical of creativity was obtained. An example of a prototypical (good example) of an everyday creative act is: "wrote a children's story" and an atypical (poor example) act is: "built the world's largest slide rule."

Are prototypical and atypical acts contextually sensitive (i.e., the evaluation of the level of creativity dependent on who, when, and how they were created) or are they contextually insensitive (i.e., the act is a display of creativity or not, regardless of contextual information)? To answer this question, information about the person performing the act was provided. In half of the cases, the person was described in terms consistent with either the aestheticism, intellectuality, and motivational dimension of the creative person identified by Sternberg (1985). The other half of the sample received information that was the opposite of this description. An example of an atypical act, performed by a person described in terms reserved for someone who exhibits a high drive for accomplishment and recognition would be:

> Anne enjoys working on projects from which others will benefit. She realizes a special sense of accomplishment after she has completed a job well done, and she feels especially well rewarded when others take time to recognize her contributions.
> ANNE BUILT THE WORLD'S LARGEST SLIDE RULE

The acts were subsequently rated on a 7-point scale along a creative-uncreative dimension, where creativity was not defined for the participant. This scale was embedded within a set of 22 scales. Four findings are especially important.

First, acts deemed typical of creativity out of context were not rated as more creative when performed by a person described in terms consistent with the mental model of the ideal creative person. Acts deemed atypical were not rated as less creative when performed by a person described in terms that rejected the mental model. These findings suggest that the participants implicitly generate the mental model of the creative person when presented the acts in the absence of any "new" information about who performed the act. From a pragmatic perspective, the participant is, in effect, asking him or herself, "What type of person would perform this act?" and some acts are more likely than others to engage the creative person mental model.

Second, acts deemed typical of creativity (out of context) were denigrated and rated as significantly less creative when performed by a person who did not conform to the mental model. This finding is, of course, an analog of the art forgery findings just described. Our understanding of expressed creativity depends not only on the product itself, but also on the context or ecology in which embedded. Third, acts that out of context are perceived as atypical of creativity were rated as significantly more creative when performed by a person who conforms to the mental model of the ideal creative person. These data reinforce the contextual effects described earlier but now indicate that context can boost one's evaluation of creativity, even for sub-par products!

Finally, the dimensions of the mental model manipulated here differed in their susceptibility to context information: Manipulating aesthetic aspects of the model had the greatest effect and manipulating drive for recognition and acknowledgment the least. From the pragmatic perspective, it could be argued that the participant, receiving the person-information, would reason that the information is being given to maximize communication, that is, it should be relevant and informative to the task at hand. In Katz and Thompson (1993), at least, the most informative information appears to be that involving aesthetic knowledge of the performer.

The argument made earlier stated that the mental model underlying creativity is multidimensional. I argue that context about a person not only supports (or refutes) the mental model, but can also serve to emphasize different dimensions. For instance, Rossman and Gollob (1975) manipulated information about the personality, abilities, and biographical information. This information was provided to participants, either separately or as a combined package, and judges were asked, based on this information, to evaluate each person with respect to degree of creativity or intelligence. There was an overlap in intelligence and creativity ratings, indicating, as argued previously, that the mental model of creativity overlaps with that of intelligence. However, and of more importance here, the ratings were reliably different: One could account for creativity ratings even when the effects of intelligence was partialled out. Moreover, different information was used to predict creativity and intelligence. Personality information (being adventurous, clever, independent, unconventional) predicted judged creativity, whereas ability information (such as vocabulary and school performance) predicted intelligence.

These data indicate the dynamic interaction of communication. The mental model of creativity provides coherence to the dialogue between the creator and his or her audience such that the creative product informs the audience and the audience influences the nature of the product. The multidimensional nature of the mental model provides for the flexibility in defining the aspects of creativity most relevant to the context at hand. For instance, in some contexts the person doing the act might be of most importance, such as demonstrated in art forgeries, or in our earlier research (Katz & Thompson, 1993). In other contexts the act, and not the person, might be of greater importance, such as occurs when later evaluation boosts the importance given to a person, such as occurred with the artist Rembrandt or the genetic work of Mendel. From the pragmatic perspective outlined here, the questions of interest are in isolating salient domains and, within each domain, the dimensions of creativity that are important.

By a domain, I mean a context that is likely to engage the mental model of creativity, (i.e., contexts in which one is likely to use that term as an appropriate descriptor). Each domain has its own grammar, its rules of procedure, and of acceptable output. As such, there is set of behaviors that would be considered appropriate and vary in prototypicality for each domain. Milgram (1990), for instance, distinguished between three domains relevant to considering creativity in children: the family, the school, and the community. From the perspective taken here, the concept of *creativity* could differ in the degree to which it is central to functioning in the specific domain. Moreover, different dimensions of the concept might play different roles within each domain. Creativity might, for instance, be more central to the grammar of an artistic domain than a school domain and, within the artistic domain, personality features might be less salient than might be the case in the school domain.

Scaling of creativity and featural prototypicality within different domains is theoretically possible, at least for what I label as *highly conventionalized domains*, such as the arts, science, and academic settings. These domains act in a manner similar to well-defined problem spaces inasmuch as domain-specific rules of procedure accord the mental model of creativity a central role.

Scaling would, at best, only give an approximation of the characteristics of importance. It must be kept in mind that, even within highly conventionalized domains, the dimensions of importance are not static. As such, the communicator's mental model might differ in important ways from that of his or her audience. The failure to find a high correspondence in identifying creativity for laboratory supervisors relative to co-workers (Taylor et al., 1963) or between teachers and parents (Runco, 1989) as indications that the rules of procedure within a domain (such as work or school contexts) implicate differences in the mental models of the partners in communication.

Whatever the nature of these differences, they must be relatively modest otherwise communication would be completely disrupted. There is a common core to the various domain-specific mental models of creativity, and within a domain, there is set of dimensions that are especially important, as determined by the rules of procedure for that domain. These assumptions are based on the fairly high agreement in what constitutes creativity across domains and levels of expertise (Amabile, 1983; Gough, 1979; Sternberg, 1985). Failures to find correspondence in conjunction with coherence in dialogue within domains suggest two possibilities.

The first possibility is that within a domain there is general consensus on the dimensions of importance; what differs is the *interpretation* given these dimensions. For instance, supervisors and co-workers might both agree that having wide interests is salient to the domain of science. Yet, from the supervisor's perspective that dimension might be seen as disruptive and contrary to productive output, whereas the co-worker might see the same domain as a resource for novel ideas (see Kirton, 1976). As another example, novices and experts within a domain might agree on a salient dimension but employ different comparison groups: A science teacher might compare the novelty of an idea with respect to that produced by other students, whereas a scientist might limit the comparison group to the productions of an elite group who have made significant impact in a field. Thus, coherence is achieved because the participants in communication recognize "novelty" as a feature of the common ground, the differences that emerge are due to what the shared feature means to different people. Consistent with this argument is a finding reported by Runco (1989). He identified seven traits that both parents and teachers agreed were important to creativity, yet the correlation between teachers and parents on ratings of the degree with which this trait was expressed by a child accounted for 10% to 15% of common variance.

A second (and not mutually exclusive) possibility is that access to the (shared) mental model proceeds in a polymorphous fashion (cf. Hampton, 1979). The idea here is that the mental model consists of a set of dimensions and that activation of the mental model will occur if a sufficient number of these dimensions are activated. Thus, in principle, two people in communication might be sampling from the same set of dimensions, but the specific instances being considered are largely (or, in the extreme case, completely) different. Communication coherence is maintained because the same mental model is employed; misunderstanding arises because different aspects of the mental model are salient to different people in the communication. Consistent with this possibility is the finding in Katz and Thompson (1993) that only three of Sternberg's (1985) dimensions mapped onto judgments of everyday instances of creativity and, in Runco (1989), only 7 (out of 25 traits) were chosen as exemplifying creativity by both teachers and parents.

Cross-cutting domain differences, there are individual differences. Some of my earlier research (Katz, 1984) illustrates some of the individual differences that might come into play. I demonstrated that, given a set of creativity tests, reliable patterns of performance distinguished different groups of undergraduate students. For instance, there is a group of people who could generate many ideas to figural stimuli but who performed poorly on finding a convergent response and a separate group of people who prefer simple stimuli and perform extremely well on tests of closure. These differences were similar to some of the differences in work style described for research scientists by Gough and Woodward (1960); the first group was labeled *initiators* and the second group *estheticians.* In a second study (Katz, 1984), I showed that the people who demonstrated these different patterns of performance also demonstrated personality differences similar to those described by Gough and Woodward: The initiators described themselves as serious, intellectually driven, adaptable, and somewhat arrogant, whereas the estheticians described themselves as moody, self-critical, quickly bored, and restless.

Finally, I applied this work to an eminent group of Canadian researchers: fellows of the Academy of Science, Royal Society of Canada. Fifty-nine members of the academy completed a set of work style and personality questionnaires. Of importance here, one could predict the work style these creative researchers reported about themselves (such as whether they described themselves in terms reserved for initiators or estheticians) on the basis of personality scales and test performance scores developed on undergraduate students.

These data indicate that there are individual differences in cognitive style that cross-cut domains. One could be an esthetician in science or in arts and, I argue, such a person would value aesthetic dimensions of creativity within each of these domains. The testable question of interest is whether these differences in style are reflected, even within a domain, in the arousal of different aspects of a shared mental model. When evaluating creativity does an initiator think of aspects of production (e.g., originality), whereas an esthetician thinks more of aesthetic aspects (elegance of solution, for instance)? From a polymorphous perspective, it does not matter whether different aspects are aroused as long as the dimensions that are aroused activate the same mental model (i.e., creativity). Nonetheless, at a more microscopic level of analysis, coherence is achieved at the cost to agreement in meaning.

This discussion was based on conventionalized domains in which creativity is accorded an important role. Almost all research in creativity comes from analysis of performance in these conventionalized domains. But what about other domains, such as sports or doing housework? Some psycholinguistic models would suggest that other domains could be described in terms of the creative mental model by metaphoric extension. That is, if one can map the mental model of creativity appropriate to a conventional domain onto a novel domain, then the prediction would be that the conceptualization of creativity would become less restrictive. There are models on how such domain mapping occurs (Katz, 1989; Trick & Katz, 1986).

Predicting which domains are likely to be described in terms currently dedicated to more conventionalized domains necessitates scaling various domains for similarity. For instance, one might argue that goal achievement, rules of inquiry, and the like are important in the domain of science. If one could find a domain similar (but not too similar) along these dimensions, then the argument would be that metaphoric extension could obtain. So if an individual feels that the sentences "Sport is a science" or "Science is an art" are apt metaphors, then the argument would be that athletes could be described in terms now reserved for artists, scientists and the like. In fact, such metaphoric extension might be occurring currently. In sports, one often hears of soccer plays as being creative, yet that term is seldom employed for plays in U.S. or Canadian football. Csikszentmihalyi (1990) pointed out that some have also applied the term to synchronized swimming. I suggest that the two mechanisms described here for communication within a domain might also be applicable across domains: Coherence is achieved polymorphously or by shading the meaning of core characteristics of the mental model.

PRAGMATICS AND INTRAINDIVIDUAL JUDGMENTS: SOME HYPOTHESES

The previous discussion has emphasized the interpersonal aspects of creativity inherent in language as a tool for communication. However, language is also considered to have intrapersonal cognitive effects, such as forming the basis for one's conceptualizations of the world (Katz, Cacciari, Gibbs, & Turner, 1998; Lakoff & Johnson,

1980). The discussion of mental models has assumed a close relation between the communication and conceptual aspects of language. In this final section, I speculate that the interpersonal pragmatic principle discussed throughout should have also an influence on intrapersonal judgments of creativity.

Although the literature on intrapersonal creativity evaluation is small, there are some intriguing findings that deserve explanation. First, evaluations of inter- and intrapersonal creativity are only moderately related (see Johnson & Jennings, 1963; Johnson, Parrott, & Stratton, 1968; Runco & Smith, 1992). Second, one can train participants to improve the quality of intrapersonal creativity evaluations; quality being determined by expert raters (Johnson et al., 1968). Moreover, the improvement in evaluating one's own ideas has been shown to transfer between different tasks (Stratton, Parrott, & Johnson, 1970).

The pragmatic tact taken in this chapter suggests a research paradigm with which to address the issue of intrapersonal evaluation, and suggests some explanations for the three findings just outlined. When a person is engaged in the process of creating, the actions are intentional because he or she is working toward a specific goal. In most cases, the intention behind the action is to display and subject the output to social evaluation. As such, the creative individual is concerned with communicating to some potential audience, and to this audience the act should meet Gricean-type principles: It should tell the audience something new in a relevant and appropriate way. What meets these criteria, of course, depends on the envisioned audience. The audience might be as large as a paying public. It could be smaller, as directed to a select critical group of experts or, in the smallest case, the audience will be oneself, and the act be evaluated to the extent that it says well what one is attempting to communicate. Thus, as with interpersonal evaluation, intraindividual evaluation depends on the use of one's own mental models and its interactions with the mental model assumed of the specific audience of import.

This analysis is that intrapersonal evaluation should (like interpersonal evaluation) be context-sensitive, flexible, and dependent, to some extent, on the ultimate audience to which it is directed. This analysis suggests the following type of social validation study; to my knowledge no such study yet has been conducted. First, participants (including those involved in creative activities) should be asked to list characteristics of creativity for a person who wants to participate in creative activities that will be personally satisfying or accepted by the paying public or appreciated by the avantgarde critic. The argument would be that different features would be generated for these different contexts. One could then obtain ratings as to the importance of each characteristic. Following the logic just described, instructional manipulations of this sort should provide some insights into the mental model of creativity assumed by the creative individual about different audiences.

The research proposed here should also provide insight into a component of the intrapersonal evaluative question. The hypothesis is that self-evaluation depends on the specific audience of importance. Thus, another testable idea is that participants who generate ideas should evaluate the creativity of their own ideas differently depending on the audience to which the idea is directed. For instance, participants could be asked to rate the creativity of their ideas as they believe the paying public (or, in another condition, the avant-garde experts) would rate them. The argument is that different ideas should be chosen as being creative, and that the chosen ideas should be related in a principled way to the mental models they assume about the target audience. Naturally, if one were to get ratings from the target audiences, one would also obtain information on the accuracy with which the creating person can infer the (average) mental model of the audience.

The pragmatic perspective also suggests an explanation for the three findings about intrapersonal evaluation described at the beginning of this section. The improved "quality" in rating one's ideas and transfer of these improved ratings across tasks would indicate merely that participants have been made aware of the audience (and the associated mental model) to which their output is being directed for evaluation. In a manner analogous to the "be creative" instructions described for the interpersonal case given previously, the increased correspondence and transfer effects described earlier might reflect a willingness to adopt the mental model assumed about the audience rather than a change in conceptualization (i.e., the creator may not change his or her beliefs, but instead give the audience what it wants).

In a similar way, the moderate correlations between inter- and intrapersonal evaluation of creativity might, in part, be due to "noise" created by uncertainty over the audience to whom the output should be considered creative. Presumably, one could boost the correlations by reducing uncertainty such as should be obtained if participants were asked to choose the ideas they thought would be considered creative by avant-garde experts, and then compare those responses to the judgments made by the expert group.

A second possibility for the moderate relations between intra- and interpersonal evaluation has been discussed earlier within the context of interpersonal evaluation: The mental models underlying creativity defined either intrapersonal or interpersonal might be related polymorphously or along dimensions for which the meaning about a shared dimension differs for the creative performer and that consensually adopted by the external judge. This possibility has some clear testable predictions.

In an earlier study (Katz, 1984), I demonstrated several different cognitive styles in creative activity (e.g., between estheticians and initiators). From the pragmatic approach suggested here, one prediction is that, when participants with different creative styles are asked to evaluate the creative goodness of their own products (and in which, explicitly or implicitly, they are the audience), they will employ dimensions that differ as a function of their style. Estheticians should consider the elegance or completeness of what they have produced, whereas initiators should evaluate aspects of production, such as the originality or number of possible solutions. These type of differences should also be found in interpersonal evaluations.

Consideration of individual differences also should have implications for the implementation of intrapersonal evaluations in the context of interpersonal feedback. In real-world creative pursuits, judgments of the worth of one's ideas are not independent of interpersonal judgments passed by significant others on works in progress. When do creative people incorporate the comments of their critics, and when do they reject them? The pragmatic approach taken here suggests a framework in which this question can be approached. And several hypotheses are suggested. It could be argued that the more similar the creative person perceives the audience to be on salient dimensions of the creative model, the more receptive the creator will be to critical input. For instance, if the aim of an author is to express him or herself in a specific way (see Helson, 1973), then he or she should be more receptive to a critic who shares that dimension relative to the reception given to someone who writes in a different mode. Moreover, my earlier (Katz, 1984) cognitive style research suggests that some people will be more resistant to external input, regardless of context. For instance the *artificer* type has a personality that can be described by terms such *obliging, tactful,* and *steady.* One prediction is that people who exhibit this cognitive style would be more likely to be influenced by external evaluation than those who exhibit some other cognitive styles, such as the *methodologist* (who rejects convention) or the *esthetician* (who is rebellious and nontrusting).

SUMMARY

The aim of this chapter was to provide a framework for considering issues in the evaluation—both interpersonal and intrapersonal—of creativity. The framework, developed from the perspective of a pragmatic psycholinguistics, is context-specific and assumes an interaction of a creative person with the audience to which he or she is attempting to communicate. The rules of this communication are such that participants in communication must share common ground with respect to a mental model about creativity. Such commonality can exist even if different features are aroused or if the features have different meaning to different people. From the perspective taken here, emphasis must be given to better understanding the domains in which creativity is expressed, and the contexts that permit coherence to occur when different features, or different meaning of these features, are aroused.

ACKNOWLEDGMENT

The writing of this chapter and the research from my laboratory reported within was supported by a grant from the Natural Science and Engineering Research Council of Canada (NSERC A7040).

REFERENCES

Amabile, T. (1983). *The social psychology of creativity*. New York: Springer-Verlag.

Barron, F., & Harrington, D. (1981). Creativity, intelligence, and personality In M. Rosenzweig & L. Porter (Eds.), *Annual review of psychology* (Vol. 32, pp. 439-476). Palo Alto, CA: Annual Reviews.

Clark, H., & Marshall, C. (1981). Definite reference and mutual knowledge. In A. Joshi, B. Webber, & I. Sag (Eds.), *Elements of discourse understanding* (pp. 10-63). Cambridge: Cambridge University Press.

Csikszentmihalyi, M. (1990). The domain of creativity. In M. A. Runco & R. S. Albert (Eds.), *Theories of creativity* (pp. 190-212). Newbury Park, CA: Sage.

Domino, G. (1970). Identification of potentially creative persons from the adjective check list. *Journal of Consulting and Clinical Psychology, 35,* 48-51.

Fillenbaum, S., & Rapoport, A. (1971). *Structures in the subjective lexicon*. New York: Academic Press.

Fine, G. (1983). Cheating history: The rhetorics of art forgery. *Empirical Studies of the Arts, 1,* 74-93.

Galton, F. (1869). *Hereditary genius*. New York: MacMillan.

Gerrig, R., & Littman, M. (1990). Disambiguation by community membership. *Memory and Cognition, 18,* 331-338.

Givon, T. (1989). *Mind, code and context.* Hillsdale, NJ: Lawrence Erlbaum Associates.

Gough, H. (1979). A creative personality scale for the adjective check list. *Journal of Personality and Social Psychology, 37,* 1398-1405.

Gough, H., & Woodward, D. (1960). Stylistic variations among professional research scientists. *Journal of Psychology, 49,* 87-93.

Grice, H. (1975). Logic and conversation. In P. Cole & J. Morgan (Eds.), *Syntax and semantics, Vol. 3: Speech acts* (pp. 41-58). New York: Seminar Press.

Hampton, J. (1979). Polymorphous concepts in semantic memory. *Journal of Verbal Learning and Verbal Behaviour, 18,* 441-461.

Harrington, D. (1975). Effects of explicit instructions to "be creative" on the psychological meaning of divergent thinking test scores. *Journal of Personality, 43,* 434-454.

Helson, R. (1973). The heroic, the comic and the tender: Patterns of literary fantasy and their authors. *Journal of Personality, 41,* 163-184.

Hocevar, D., & Bachelor, P. (1989). A taxonomy and critique of measurements used in the study of creativity. In J. Glover, R. Ronning, & C. Reynolds (Eds.), *Handbook of creativity* (pp. 53-75). New York: Plenum.

Ironson, G., & Davis, G. (1979). Faking high or low creativity scores on the adjective check list. *Journal of Creative Behaviour, 13,* 139-145.

Johnson, D., & Jennings, J. (1963). Serial analysis of three problem-solving processes. *Journal of Psychology, 56,* 43-52.

Johnson, D., Parrott, G., & Stratton, R. (1968). Production and judgment of solutions to five problems. *Journal of Educational Psychology, 59* (Monograph Supplement No. 6).

Katz, A. (1984). Creative styles: Relating tests of creativity to the work pattern of scientists. *Personality and Individual Differences, 5,* 281-292.

Katz, A. (1987). Self-reference in the encoding of creative-relevant traits. *Journal of Personality, 55,* 97-120.

Katz, A. (1989). On choosing the vehicles of metaphors: Referential concreteness, semantic distances, and individual differences. *Journal of Memory and Language, 28,* 486-499.

Katz, A. (1996). On interpreting statements as metaphor or irony: Contextual heuristics and cognitive consequences. In J. Mio & A. Katz (Eds.), *Metaphor: Implications and applications* (pp. 1-22). Hillsdale, NJ: Lawrence Erlbaum Associates.

Katz, A., Cacciari, C., Gibbs, R., & Turner, M. (1998). *Figurative language and thought.* New York: Oxford University Press.

Katz, A., & Giacommelli, L. (1982). The subjective nature of creativity judgments. *Bulletin of the Psychonomics Society, 20,* 17-20.

Katz, A., & Poag, J. (1979). Sex differences in instructions to "be creative" on divergent and nondivergent test scores. *Journal of Personality, 47*, 518-530.

Katz, A., & Thompson, M. (1993). On judging creativity: By one's acts shall ye be known (and vice versa). *Creativity Research Journal, 6*, 345-364.

Kirton, M. (1976). Adaptors and innovators: A description and measure. *Journal of Applied Psychology, 61*, 622-629.

Kreuz, R. (1996). The use of verbal irony: Cues and constraints. In J. Mio & A. Katz (Eds.), *Metaphor: Implications and applications* (pp. 23-38). Hillsdale, NJ: Lawrence Erlbaum Associates.

Kucera, H., & Francis, W. (1967). *Computational analysis of present day American English.* Providence, RI: Brown University Press.

Lakoff, G., & Johnson, M. (1980). *Metaphors we live by.* Chicago: University of Chicago Press.

MacKinnon, D. (1975). IPAR's contribution to the conceptualization and study of creativity. In I. Taylor & J. Getzels (Eds.), *Perspectives in creativity* (pp. 60-89). Chicago: Aldine.

Mednick, S. (1962). The associative basis of the creative process. *Psychological Review, 69*, 220-232.

Milgram, R. (1990). Creativity: An idea whose time has come and gone? In M. A. Runco & R. S. Albert (Eds.), *Theories of creativity* (pp. 215-233). Newbury Park, CA: Sage.

Nicholls, J. (1972). Creativity in the person who will never produce anything original and useful. *American Psychologist, 27*, 717-727.

Norman, D., & Rumelhart, D. (1975). *Explorations in cognition.* San Francisco: Freeman.

Rossman, B., & Gollob, H. (1975). Comparison of social judgments of creativity and intelligence. *Journal of Personality and Social Psychology, 31*, 271-281.

Runco, M. A. (1984). Teachers' judgments of creativity and social validation of divergent thinking tests. *Perceptual and Motor Skills, 59*, 711-717.

Runco, M. A. (1987). Interrater agreement on a socially valid measure of students' creativity. *Psychological Reports, 61*, 1009-1010.

Runco, M. A. (1989). Parents' and teachers ratings of the creativity of children. *Journal of Social Behaviour and Personality, 4*, 73-83.

Runco, M. A. (1990). Implicit theories and ideational creativity. In M. A. Runco & R. S. Albert (Eds.), *Theories of creativity* (pp. 234-252). Newbury Park, CA: Sage.

Runco, M. A., & Okuda, S. (1991). The instructional enhancement of the flexibility and originality scores of divergent thinking tests. *Applied Cognitive Psychology, 5*, 435-441.

Runco, M., & Smith, W. (1992). Interpersonal and intrapersonal evaluations of creative ideas. *Personality and Individual Differences, 13*, 295-302.

Simonton, D. (1984). *Genius, creativity and leadership.* Cambridge, MA: Harvard University Press.

Sperber, D., & Wilson, D. (1986). *Relevance: Communication and cognition.* Oxford: Blackwell.

Sternberg, R. (1985). Implicit theories of intelligence, creativity and wisdom. *Journal of Personality and Social Psychology, 49*, 607-627.

Stratton, R., Parrott, G., & Johnson, D. (1970). Transfer of judgment training to production and judgment of solutions on a verbal problem. *Journal of Educational Psychology, 61*, 15-23.

Taylor, C., Smith, W., & Ghiselin, B. (1963). The creative and other contributions of one sample of research scientists. In C. Taylor & F. Barron (Eds.), *Scientific creativity: Its recognition and development* (pp. 53-76). New York: Wiley.

Torrance, P. (1974). *Torrance tests of creative thinking: Norms technical manual.* Lexington, MA: Personnel Press.

Trick, L., & Katz, A. (1986). The domain interaction approach to metaphor processing: Relating individual differences and metaphor characteristics. *Metaphor and Symbolic Activity, 1*, 145-169.

Welsh, G. (1975). *Creativity and intelligence: A personality approach.* Chapel Hill: Institute for Research in Social Science, University of North Carolina.

11

THE DEVELOPMENT OF CREATIVE THINKING AND CRITICAL REFLECTION: LESSONS FROM EVERYDAY PROBLEM FINDING

John F. Wakefield
University of North Alabama

When Piaget (1911/1977) was about 15 years old, he wrote a short preface to one of his earliest articles, providing an example of development in his own thinking. In this preface, he indicated that he had earlier taken certain "ill-defined specimens" of freshwater shellfish to an expert malacologist to ask his opinion about their classification. Piaget subsequently used the problems posed by these specimens to develop a new classification scheme for these and other species of freshwater shellfish, an insightful act. In this short preface a relation is apparent between what might be called *expertise* and *problem finding*. Piaget's choice of problem indicated the progression of his thought beyond the cognitive operations represented by expert classification of species according to an existing scheme.

This episode illustrates the possibility that problem finding is involved in the development of thinking. Problem finding has long been thought to be close to the heart of originality in science and the arts (e.g., Getzels & Csikszentmihalyi, 1976; Macworth, 1965;

Souriau, 1881; Wakefield, 1992). What this chapter explores is the thesis that problem finding (an element of creative thinking) develops understanding.

The task of identifying just how problem finding is involved in cognitive development requires a brief description of *complementarity* in development (Wakefield, 1996), or how stage and phase theories are being combined to describe cognitive development more fully than either type of theory alone has described it in the past. After looking at complementarity in development, the role of problem finding during stage transitions, and everyday problem finding in mathematics, the chapter turns to educational implications of everyday problem finding, particularly for the development of creative thinking. Finally, the chapter concludes with a consideration of the place of creative thinking in a curriculum that includes critical reflection.

COMPLEMENTARITY THEORY: PHASES WITHIN STAGES OF DEVELOPMENT

Piaget (1969) offered the best stage theory of cognitive development, although many psychologists now believe this theory to be inaccurate in some ways. Every student who has taken an undergraduate psychology course can recite the sequence of developmental stages in Piaget's theory: sensorimotor, preoperational, concrete operational, and formal operational. These stages were named after the modes of adaptation or development that they reflect. During infancy, adaptation is thought to occur through the sensory and motor systems; during early childhood, it occurs through prelogical use of symbols (including development of vocabulary and graphic representations); during middle childhood, it occurs through logically interrelating objects and events in experience; and during adolescence, through the distinction of logical relationships from experience (such as in the form-content distinction).

Insight is gained into this theory by understanding that the same French word that means "stage" (étage) also means "floor." Although Piaget frequently used biological metaphors, his root metaphor for cognitive development appears to be the construction of a multistoried building. Each floor represents a developmental plateau, on which the acquisition of knowledge is more common than fundamentally new understanding. Between stages are transitions (staircases) to a new stage. These transitions involve fundamental changes in understanding.

Viewed in terms of skill development, each stage represents a period of skill consolidation. Learning theorists generally acknowledge the process of skill consolidation to entail three phases (Anderson, 1995). In the cognitive or novice phase, learning involves acquisition of facts and rules. Rules, for example, might include steps in some problem solving procedure. In the associative or intermediate phase, learning involves knowledge compilation or practice. Awareness of rules and facts diminishes as they take the form of condition-action statements ("If [condition], then [action]"). Verbalization often drops out, and performance of the skill becomes smoother than in the cognitive phase. In the autonomous or expert phase, learning involves fine tuning of performance, with little or no awareness of facts and rules. Short-term memory space is freed for other uses.

This description of skill learning is sometimes used to replace Piagetian stages, but it has proven inadequate to explain age effects. Although it is true that young children resemble novices or beginners, that elementary age children resemble intermediates in understanding and skill, and that adolescents are comparative experts, several experiments designed to highlight expert-novice differences among children at different ages have found age effects that cannot be explained through expert-novice differences alone.

For example, German researchers divided groups of students in Grades 3, 5, and 7 into experts and novices based on their knowledge of soccer rules (Schneider, Korkel, & Weinert, 1989). They further divided them into low and high aptitude groups, resulting in 12 groups of subjects in all. The researchers played a tape-recorded story about the participation of a young soccer player in an important match, then tested the students' recall of and inference from what they had heard.

What they found was, in part, to be expected from prior research on expert-novice differences. Experts at each grade level performed better on the cognitive skill tests than the novices at the same grade level (for both high and low ability groups). What expert-novice differences could not account for was the finding that older novices (Grade 7) outperformed younger experts (Grade 3). The effects of age on both memory and inference were significant apart from the effects of experience.

Other researchers have found qualitative differences in the thinking of experts at different ages. In one study (Means & Voss, 1985), younger subjects (from Grades 2, 3, and 5) and older subjects (from Grades 7, 9, and college) were each separated into experts and novices based on the number of times they had seen the films *Star Wars* and *The Empire Strikes Back*. (Novices had seen each movie at least once, but a combination of both movies no more than three times.) Subjects were questioned about basic actions and goals in the movies.

The results bear some similarity to those from the soccer study. Although experts remembered more basic actions than novices, older novices stated high goals in the movies about 10% more frequently than did younger experts. Furthermore, older experts stated high goals about 30% more frequently than did younger experts. These results suggested that older novices and experts both processed information more deeply than did younger experts. The source of the deeper processing by older children was not discussed, but it is reasonable to associate it with developmental differences in thinking.

Phases of learning appear to be folded within each stage of development. This broad interpretation of what happens during cognitive development is consistent with neo-Piagetian conceptualizations of progressive change in specific skills. Case (1993), for example, described the development of cognitive skills as a staircase. The staircase for each skill consists of three phases of learning folded within each of four stages of skill development. The stages represent the influence of natural limitations on short-term memory. Phases within each stage represent ascending levels of proficiency, or the influence of skill practice on development. These phases can be labeled according to commonly accepted terms—*beginning*, *intermediate*, and *advanced*. The folding of phases of learning within each stage of development results in complementarity between nature and nurture in skill development.

THE ROLE OF PROBLEM FINDING IN STAGE TRANSITIONS

What goes on during stage transitions is of greater interest for the study of creative thinking than what goes on during stage plateaus. The phases of learning that represent skill development on a given plateau primarily involve knowledge compilation, practice of procedures, and the solving of well-defined problems. This is what Piaget called *assimilation*. Assimilation peaks in the middle of each stage of development, and probably accounts for an accelerated period of skill acquisition, as measured by tests that contain well-defined problems. Skills appear to improve faster during the intermediate phase of acquisition than they do either in the beginning or in the advanced phase because of practice conditions, which generally involve isolation of skills, well-defined problems, and feedback. If one takes a broad view of the U.S. educational system, it is evident that the system is set up to optimize learning under such conditions. Skills are isolated through separation of subject areas and curriculum objectives; well-defined problems are all that most textbooks and supplementary exercises contain; and feedback is systematic in terms of evaluation.

By way of contrast, skill acquisition between Piagetian stages (or during stage transitions) is laborious and slow. It does not involve skill consolidation through intensive practice, but exploration of ill-defined problems, or what in terms of problem solving is called *problem finding*. These transition periods are more closely related to what Piaget called *accommodation*. Accommodation peaks between stages of development, and the U.S. educational system is generally less well adapted to it. Adaptations should include an integrated curriculum; ill-defined problems that are found in experience; and unpressured exploration or discovery. Although some or all of these conditions are present in some classrooms, they are entirely absent in others, even at grade levels during which transitions might be expected to occur.

The example from Piaget's early adolescence, during the transition between concrete and formal operations, illustrates the kind of mental activity to expect during stage transitions. To sort a collection of shells, Piaget first had to learn a routine procedure for classifying shellfish according to an existing scheme (a concrete operation). This is the type of task that might be learned in school. Piaget implied that this procedure was learned from Dr. Paul Godet, "my reverend master," who published a classification scheme in 1907 (when Piaget was 11 years old). This scheme was insufficient to assimilate certain ill-defined specimens. As a consequence, these specimens could not be meaningfully understood except as ill-defined. Piaget perceived that the problem lay not in the classification of these specimens according to an existing scheme, but in the classification scheme itself, which was an impediment to understanding. The goal of understanding the ill-defined specimens could only be achieved through the invention of a new scheme. This goal required consideration of the formal requirements of a classification system—considerations that necessarily accompanied Piaget's invention of a new way to classify *Limnaea*. Classification of this type of freshwater shellfish represented a breakthrough problem to formal operations.

Thinking about the limitations of current understanding is a slow, laborious, and probably quite personal endeavor. Ill-defined problems cannot be solved quickly. Hurrying children through them may create developmental discontinuities in understanding, ultimately developing inert or fragile knowledge. Transitions between stages in the development of any skill must occur under conditions that permit unpressured exploration and the invention of new understanding. Only under such conditions can stage transitions occur, and continuity of understanding be preserved.

EVERYDAY AND EXPERT PROBLEM FINDING IN MATHEMATICS

Some progress toward understanding the role of problem finding in education has recently been made in research on "sense-making" in mathematics by children. The term *everyday problem finding* is now often used to describe sense-making in mathematics. For example, Resnick, Bill, Lesgold, and Leer (1991) developed a year-long program for at-risk first and second graders that emphasized teaching children to find everyday arithmetic problems as part of their homework. Even more recently, experiments have been conducted with average fifth-grade students to teach everyday problem finding in the context of solving story problems (Winograd, 1993). The impetus for both these and other efforts to teach everyday problem finding have been the *Curriculum and Evaluation Standards for School Mathematics* of the National Council of Teachers of Mathematics (1989). These standards mandate teaching everyday problem finding in Kindergarten through Grade 4, and problem formulation skills in upper elementary and secondary grades.

What has been discovered in these studies is intriguing. First, children tend to improve their mathematical understanding. Participation in the year-long program for at-risk students increased their mathematics achievement from the 25th to the 70th percentile on standardized tests. Second, the ambitious attempts of fifth graders to formulate problems have revealed specific strategies for problem finding. The best story problems, for example, seem to come from the experience of the students. Students identified with their own problems. This finding confirms and extends to a younger age group the hypothesis that problem finding is personal in nature (Wakefield, 1994). It is a personal act, even in science and mathematics. Almost all students also invented problems so difficult that they did not always have the skills to solve them. This finding suggests that students considered problem finding as a way of making sense of situations. If this interpretation is correct, these results confirm that problem *finding* is more closely related to accommodation than to assimilation (or practice).

Both of these studies were conducted with students near the ages that Piaget identified with stage transitions. What can they reveal about how problem finding and creative thinking develop? They demonstrate that everyday and expert problem finding are developmentally related. Problem finding seems to bridge the gap between expertise at some current stage or level of functioning and novice functioning at a "higher" stage or level. Expert problem finding of the kind commonly associated with high-level creativity may only represent an extension of sense-making beyond what is commonly understood in a given domain at a given time. Einstein once said that "To raise new questions, new possibilities, to regard old questions from a new angle, requires creative imagination and marks real advance in science" (Einstein & Infeld, 1938, p. 92). This disposition on the part of the creative scientist reflects the disposition of a normal child to make sense of or know (in a deep sense) the world around him or her. It also reveals something about creative thinking by children.

Creative thinking is essentially developmental. It is a vehicle to develop new understanding for both the individual and society. Making sense of the world about one as a child is foundational to creative thinking as an adult.

Other psychologists have reached this insight. Resnick (1987) suggested that one cause for the failure of mathematical understanding to develop may be that as students, many individuals do not link the rule systems that they master with more intuitive and personal knowledge of mathematics. They adopt knowledge rather than develop their understanding. As a consequence, when they become experts, they are not likely to develop knowledge beyond expertise and make creative contributions. They have no curiosity about mathematics or mathematical insights. A reasonable focus of educational research, then, is on ways to link early mathematics instructions with intuitive math concepts that children already have (Leinhardt, 1988) so that sense-making can link up with formal instruction in the early elementary grades. This research focuses on the prelogical to concrete logic transition, which as Piaget (1969) noted, occurs about the time most children begin receiving formal instruction in school.

CURRICULA WHICH DEVELOP CREATIVE THINKING

So far, this chapter has examined developmental theory and research on everyday problem finding in order to present a background for the focus of the rest of this chapter, which is education. The essential lesson for education from developmental theory and research on everyday problem finding is that problem finding is developmental. What develops is understanding of the world around an individual (accommodation). This lesson is as true of art as it is of mathematics and science. The question, "How do we develop creative thinking?" is inextricably intertwined with the prerequisite question, "How do we develop understanding?"

A point of departure is Whitehead's (1929) observation that mental development proceeds in cycles, beginning and ending with exploration, but with practice or "precision" established in the middle. As Gardner (1989) pointed out, this sequence is acted out often enough in education to produce some highly creative thinkers in the United States. Cultures that emphasize initial imitation and practice can produce higher literacy rates, but they also produce fewer creative thinkers. U.S. schools generally enact a cyclical curriculum, if only inconsistently and in its broadest outlines.

For example, many early childhood educators have formulated "developmentally appropriate practices" for children through age 8 (Bredekamp, 1987). The impetus for this move was a collection of reports in the 1980s that discovered misguided efforts to accelerate development among preschoolers. Some of the misguided efforts were associated with drill-and-practice (precision teaching) programs. Researchers pointed out the risks, and the need for a curriculum that emphasized learner-initiated activity as opposed to teacher-initiated activity. The foundation of developmentally appropriate practices was constructivism, the same general approach as developed by Piaget.

What I point out here is that repetition, in itself, is not developmentally inappropriate for young children. Young children repeat or rehearse a great deal, but they differ from older children in the form that repetition or rehearsal takes. The practicing of young children is self-initiated, even if only to ask a teacher or parent to reread a book, or to spend a lengthy period of time practicing pouring liquids at the water table. As Piaget (1969) pointed out, the imaginative play of young children is almost pure assimilation—or practice.

Consequently, imaginative play by children does not necessarily involve creative thinking. Its function is often quite the opposite: to practice and proceduralize skills. If one searches for a period of *creative* activity, it is much more likely to be found at the beginning or at the end of early childhood than in the middle, which is a period filled with examples of self-initiated practice. If early childhood learning is viewed in this light, it is much more likely that creative acts can be identified than if it is simply assumed that all imaginative or self-initiated activities are inherently creative. Viewing the period between 3 and 5 years of age, which Erikson (1982) called the "play years," as a period of skill consolidation is less romantic than viewing it as extremely creative, but it also is more realistic.

What kinds of skills are being developed during early childhood? Apart from physical and social skills, they include cognitive skills, such as rudimentary forms of logic. In the 1970s, researchers discovered the assumption that preschoolers cannot think logically was mistaken. Even neo-Piagetian researchers have revised downward the age associated with the prelogical-logical transition. How far down in age should it be revised? This is an unresolved question, but its exploration is important for curriculum development.

Studies of reasoning in preschoolers have found that a rudimentary form of logical understanding is acquired very early. This form of deduction is consistent with experience and requires that sufficient information be supplied to draw a conclusion. A typical problem in conditional logic that most 4-year-olds can solve is as follows:

> If this is Room 9, then it is the bathroom.
> This is Room 9.
> Is it the bathroom?

By the school years, the rate of acquisition in this skill is already decelerating (O'Brien & Shapiro, 1968). Research with 4- and 5-year-olds (Hawkins, Pea, Glick, & Scribner, 1984) indicates that this skill is well established by 5 years of age, and it may extend to fantasy or hypothetical material that is not consistent with experience ("Pogs wear blue boots. Tom is a pog. Does Tom wear blue boots?"). Unfortunately, age of initial acquisition has not been studied, but it seems to be as early as 2 or 3 years of age.

Researchers can hypothesize this age from learning curves that have been constructed for the entire developmental period. Thurstone (1955, cited in Guilford, 1967), for example, found deductive reasoning to be acquired during the developmental period in a very distinctive S-shaped curve, with acceleration at the age of 4, rather stable improvement until about 11, then a subsequent deceleration until adulthood. This information supports the hypotheses that (a) age 4 marks a phase of rapid skill acquisition, in contrast to ages 3 and 5; and (b) ages 11 and 12 mark a period of slowed skill acquisition, in contrast to immediately preceding and following ages.

As can be recalled, rapid skill acquisition—as measured by tests that contain well-defined problems—is probably an effect of practice, not of problem finding. Problem finding generally *precedes* rapid skill acquisition, identifying ages 2 or 3 as the transition period for most children. It is clear from the research that ages 4 and 5 are too late—the skill is already well established by then. Preschool curricula, then, can include practice in logic of the simple type just described, as long as the practice is initiated by the child rather than by the adult. Self-initiated practice might take the form of simple games or play with manipulatives that involve simple logical tasks.

What does not develop for many children during the preschool years is the ability to use rule systems on demand—the kind of task posed by reading, writing, and arithmetic. This ability to apply logic on demand appears to require more working memory than the use of discrete symbols or rudimentary forms of logic. It also requires sense-making at a new level of difficulty. To read with understanding, to write to communicate, and to compute the answer to a well-specified problem, are all goals that require the development of new understanding, not just practice of skills.

For this reason, the early elementary school years should be a time of problem finding. Progress in specific skills can be expected to be relatively slow while enormous strides are made in understanding their use. Everyday problem finding should be at a peak. The whole-language movement in education (Goodman, 1986) is doing much to increase educators' awareness of how important integrated learning is to develop academic skills during this transition. Similarly, the re-emergence of the project approach (Katz & Chard, 1989) has emphasized student-generated questions in the early elementary years.

What is critical during this transition is that teachers respect the initiative of the learner while they introduce learners to academic skills, rather than scaffold learning to achieve curriculum objectives in a way that does not respect the initiative of the learner. Transition periods need to be just that—transitions. Teachers need to be vigilant because many recent discussions of scaffolding—even by scholars—ignore the intentions of the learner, which were part of the original concept of scaffolding (Bruner, 1975; Searle, 1984; Vygotsky, 1978).

Proponents of outcomes-based education (OBE), for example, are quick to hop on scaffolding as a relevant teaching technique to implement a curriculum, but their concept of the scaffolding is not the same as the one developed from Vygotsky (1978). The intentions of the learner (and many teachers) are ignored when OBE planning decisions are made. Cognitive skills can be scaffolded to preserve problem finding and sense-making, but only if the intentions of the learner are respected.

By 9 or 10 years of age, children can often profit from more structured forms of practice to consolidate skills. Even in first grade, worksheets are not inappropriate for some students who have begun to master particular skills. Worksheets (or their electronic counterpart in drill-and-practice programs) are designed to isolate skills, provide practice, and supply feedback. They always involve well-defined problems and an emphasis on problem solving rather than problem finding.

This emphasis helps consolidate a skill, but the overall context needs to remain one of meaningful development rather than rote rehearsal. If a skill is decontextualized for the purpose of practice, it also needs to be exercised in context, so that its significance to the learner remains clear. Otherwise, children wind up practicing skills just for the grade that they receive on practice exercises and begin to adopt the grade—rather than skill improvement—as a rationale for learning.

This middle period of rapid improvement in the fluency of a skill is associated with a decline in creative thinking in the fourth grade. Scholars from Torrance (1962) to Gardner (1982) have identified this decline, associating it with the difficulty of the curriculum, the uncreative way in which it is taught, or a period of realism in the thinking of children.

Is such a decline natural? I believe that to a certain extent it is. This is an age associated with precision in thinking. What is problematic is not the decline, but the failure of creative thinking to emerge afterward. If mental development follows cycles, creative thinking should emerge in a periodic way, but often it does not. This failure may be the result of instruction in the fourth or fifth grade (when a child is age 9 or 10), but I am inclined to associate it with developmental discontinuities created by inadequate instruction much earlier—in the first and second grade (or when a child is age 6 or 7). Fragile or inert knowledge developed during the early transition period may result in the inhibition of creative thinking during the later one. What can be lost in the early transition—an urge to make sense of everything that is learned—may be gone forever, even putting children at risk for school failure.

By 11 or 12, the rate in acquisition of deductive reasoning slows as many children enter a new stage of reasoning. A fair amount of research indicates that they acquire formal or systematic reasoning slowly at first, followed by a phase of accelerated acquisition at the ages of 13 and 14 (Kuhn & Ho, 1977; Markovits, Schleifer, & Fortier, 1989; Overton, Ward, Novek, Black, & O'Brien, 1987; Roberge & Paulus, 1971; Ward & Overton, 1990). This observation leads to the inference that ages 11 and 12 are associated with ill-defined problems and a creative phase in the thinking of some, if not all children.

At least some curricula have acknowledged this period of transition. The discovery science curricula of the 1960s, for example, focused on this age group, but as implemented, these curricula did not always respect the intentions of the learner in scaffolding the development of understanding. Guided discovery science texts, for example, presented well-defined problems and limited student participation to confirmatory activities (Shulman & Tamir, 1973). They developed scientific process skills (such as measuring and recording data), but not creative thinking.

Other problems of discovery curricula lay in the very concept of a curriculum based on age-related differences in development. Individual differences in cognitive skills are quite large by Grade 6. More apt sixth graders, for example, might be ready to develop formal reasoning, but not all students are. Scaffolding for less apt students can rob them of the opportunity to participate in discovery, unless such scaffolding respects their intentions as learners.

Piaget believed the adolescent transition to be prolonged from 11 to about 15, but the research cited earlier indicates a period of accelerated skill acquisition beginning at about age 13. Acceleration in the development of a skill is usually identified with practice (or the intermediate phase of learning)—not with problem finding or creative thinking.

This period of acceleration in skill acquisition is accompanied by declines in creative thinking, which like earlier declines, have been explained in different ways by different scholars. Many educators have identified the early adolescent decline in creative thinking with peer pressure and conformity. Once again, however, this decline seems natural to me as new thinking skills enter their "precision" or intermediate phase of development. They are being practiced and consolidated. Schools seem to cater to this development through isolation of skills, well-defined practice problems, and evaluative feedback. What does not seem natural is the irreversibility of the decline in creative thinking after early adolescence. Here, I join in the concerns of many educators for what happened earlier, during the transition to adolescence. Somewhere in this transition, sense-making was lost, so that algebra became a set of formulae to memorize, history became a series of dates, and literature became merely an exercise in reading comprehension.

The overwhelming lesson of everyday problem finding for curriculum development is the importance of sense-making, particularly during transition periods. Educators want children to make sense at other times too, but the key to making sense at other times appears to be making sense of transitional experiences. If students do not make sense of these experiences, what can they do but rely on earlier forms of understanding, which are inadequate for many complex tasks? As a result, they act when they should reflect, memorize when they should think things through, and are bound by what is rather than consider the possibilities. In short, they become incapable of creative thought whenever they fail to "make sense."

INDIVIDUAL DIFFERENCES IN CREATIVE THINKING

So far, I have discussed very broadly, the curriculum and cycles of cognitive development. What about individual differences in creative thinking? A return to the concept of developmental appropriateness reveals that it distinguishes age-appropriate from individually appropriate practices (Bredekamp, 1987). There are always individual differences that confound age-related curricula, but if one begins with the idea that curriculum is not what is written in some guide, but what is actually taught, the problem of individual differences becomes much more solvable.

Written curricula should represent cycles in the development of thinking, but so should the plans of a teacher on any given day, or with any given child. Exercises should be flexible enough to work toward problem finding, for example, rather than beginning with it. Scaffolding of this form is particularly useful for children who have mastered problem solving of a particular type, and are ready for a challenge. Some kindergartners or fifth graders, for example, might find this type of exercise a challenge that brings with it new understandings.

Individual differences in any skill are profound and quickly outrun any effort to keep all children at the same age involved in the same kind of mental activity. This applies to problem finding as well as it does to any other activity. As a result, different tasks need to be available for children of the same age. Curriculum guides commonly recognize this situation by providing "enrichment activities," but there are also different roles in any project, and different criteria for evaluation that should be applied, when individual differences in creative thinking enter the picture.

Teachers of exceptional children (both gifted learners and children with disabilities) recognize that instruction needs to be adapted to the individual rather than the individual to instruction. Readiness to learn is highly individual, and damage can be done to a child's disposition to learn if a teacher assumes that all children should progress at the same rate. This assumption leads many teachers to prefer using able learners as peer tutors rather than address their individual needs as learners. Peer tutoring has practical advantages for some able learners (who can benefit by helping others) as well as the teacher and less able learners, but I am not sure that it leads the able learner to develop understanding in the sense that has been described here. It provides an efficient means to occupy all students in the same activity, but why not free able learners to explore the limitations of their skills through some kind of contractual arrangement? To me, individualized projects seem to be a more profitable use of most of their talents than tutoring, which may benefit some able learners, but is better addressed through voluntary parental (and student) involvement than through conscripting students wholesale into the role of tutor.

Individual departures from the curriculum for able learners might take the form of creative projects, but at other times they should take the form of opportunities to practice skills that other children have not acquired yet, or are just beginning to acquire. Creative projects might involve acquiring new knowledge (the initial phase of learning), or they might involve going beyond expertise to develop a product of value to other learners, and that on completion, can be shared with them. Sometimes departures should take the form of opportunities simply to practice a skill that other learners are just beginning to acquire, or have not acquired yet. Consolidation of a skill is no less important than its initial development. Creative projects and even routine practice may require a special location (such as the library or music room) or special equipment (such as access to computers or multimedia), but it does not necessarily require extended isolation from the rest of the class, or abandonment of the standard curriculum.

A CURRICULUM FOR CREATIVE THINKING AND CRITICAL REFLECTION

Although the consideration of problem finding helps to identify transition periods when children might be expected to be creative, it does not address the question of the place of creative thinking in relation to the scope of problems, that is, whether they be narrow or broad in their implications. As revealed here, the development of expertise has implications for the *depth* of a question, but what about its *breadth*? This question involves consideration of at least three different arenas of the problematic, and how creative thinking develops in these different arenas.

Following Habermas (1974), Van Manen (1977) distinguished three arenas of the problematic that he labeled *technical, practical,* and *critical.* These arenas are like concentric circles of widening scope, so that the smallest arena might be said to lie within the next largest arena, and this arena within the largest of the three. The smallest arena is often described as technical, because within this scope, reflection focuses on creating new means to attain given goals. Its focus tends to be on problem solving. Most problems put to students in school, for example, are of a technical nature.

The middle arena is often described as practical, because reflection focuses on congruence between social practices and personal values. It tends to balance problem solving with problem finding. Relatively few problems of this nature are currently encountered by students, because such encounters involve questioning whether an activity or practice is worthwhile. Putting choices before students, however, would raise issues of congruence between activities and personal values.

The widest arena of the problematic is often described as critical because it focuses on moral or ethical issues. Its focus tends to be on what Freire (1993) called *problematizing.* Considered from this perspective, critical reflection involves problem finding of the widest scope. Very few students are ever challenged to reflect on the social values implied by personal practices.

I need to point out here that critical reflection is a special application of what is sometimes referred to as *critical thinking*. Critical thinking skills (such as clarification of a question, judging credibility of support, and use of criteria to judge the adequacy of a solution) are to philosophy largely what problem finding and solving skills are to psychology (Quellmalz, 1987), but critical reflection applies these skills to the relations between practice and what is considered to be moral or ethical in a culture. Critical reflection involves asking questions such as "What do my practices say about my assumptions, values, and beliefs?" "What views of power do they embody?" or "Whose interests seem to be served by my activities?" This application of critical thinking broadens inquiry and the scope of problem solving. Instead of asking, "Is the problem solved effectively?" (technical reflection) or "Do I value the problem-solving activity?" (practical reflection), the learner using critical reflection might ask "What good does this activity serve?" or *cui bono*? ("for whose advantage is it?").

To help students raise questions of this nature is essentially to propose that the general curriculum have a moral dimension, not in terms of the indoctrination of moral values, but in terms of moral reasoning about actions. The moral dimension of development was not ignored by Piaget, and a brief exploration of the relation between creative thinking and critical reflection leads to a reconsideration of his ideas.

Piaget (1948), of course, discriminated between at least two stages of moral reasoning: the morality of constraint in which a child assumed that authority (or a rigorous equality) was just, and the morality of cooperation, which was formed out of reciprocal relationships between the child and others. The development of the morality of cooperation occurs in late childhood—about the time that formal operations are said to begin to develop. The relevant question here is, are children before this age of 11 or 12 capable of critical reflection?

This question deserves study in light of what has been proposed about the development of creative thinking. If creative thinking develops through stages, children may need time and opportunity to work through developmental prerequisites to critical reflection. It may be more expedient to limit reflection on the elementary level to the technical and practical arenas. Thus, an elementary teacher might scaffold discussions to set or attain academic or social goals (which include the objectives represented by classroom rules), but refrain from asking students to consider wider issues. Wider considerations might be more profitably addressed at the secondary level, when children appear to become capable of this type of thinking.

Despite developmental limitations on critical reflection, the development of sense-making should probably follow the same course in the moral domain as in academic subjects, that is, going through phases within stages. Even in early childhood, everyday social problems of preschoolers or kindergartners can be used to promote moral development. When young children encounter everyday social problems (e.g., involving a failure to participate, share, or take turns), they might be asked by the teacher to clarify their goal and develop a strategy to achieve it. This technique, which is known as social problem solving, can be practiced so the young child becomes proficient at solving everyday social problems (Shure, 1993).

As they enter elementary school, children should be challenged to relate rules to their own needs, discovering that rules and strategies must be formulated to meet these needs (practical reflection). Glasser (1990) wrote about this innovative mode of classroom management, describing five needs that should be met in the course of developing rules and strategies: Survival, love, power, fun, and freedom. In Glasser's approach, problem solving with students enables them to establish a congruence between what they need as individuals and as a group, often beginning with everyday problems that involve the need for a rule or the failure to follow a rule.

Critical reflection or problematizing, however, might be more profitably developed as part of the upper elementary and secondary school curriculum. Reflecting critically about the relationships of social practices to moral and ethical standards should not focus on developing strategies to attain social goals but begin with "everyday problematizing." If philosophy is taught as a subject, it might address everyday ethical dilemmas—such as those encountered in daily school life—as early sixth or seventh grade, then focus on more systematic instruction in ethics in eighth grade and high school (cf. Lipman, 1988). Students might be expected to improve in critical reflection as they are challenged to raise questions about the relation of social practices to ethical norms or standards in a variety of contexts over a prolonged period. In short, practice (with feedback) can be expected to make students more proficient at critical reflection, once critical reflection has developed as a form of everyday problem finding.

The failure to develop critical reflection in stages, each of which is founded in everyday problem finding, results in a moral knowledge that is fragile or inert. In this respect, knowledge of what is good is similar to knowledge of mathematics. It must be constructed to make sense to the knower. Failure to construct moral knowledge through everyday problem finding can result in rote memorization of rules, imitation without understanding, or thoughtless conformity.

Moral knowledge cannot be constructed by rationality in isolation, however, because it is founded on shared norms or standards. Piaget (1948) identified mutual respect (or reciprocity) as the social parallel of rationality, and as a pillar of moral development. Mutual respect and rationality are often combined in cooperation. Learning to play, work, and live cooperatively is a very general means of moral development that needs to be adapted to each age, individual and circumstance as described earlier.

CONCLUSION

It seems to me that the development of problem finding in relation to arenas of the problematic is at least as important as the development of creative thinking in relation to traditional academic subject areas. Indeed, these developments should probably be inextricably intertwined so that by the end of high school, creative thinking and critical reflection blend. Just as heroic figures in science—such as Piaget and Einstein—illustrate this blend in their own thinking, so tragic figures in science illustrate creative thinking without adequate consideration of the relation between personal practice and moral standards. The achievements of tragic figures are not cause for celebration, and they continually raise ethical or moral issues. The question, "What good am I serving?" is not one that students should ignore in the pursuit of sense-making. Indeed, a person's answer to it—elaborated into a personal philosophy from everyday problematizing—may be the best way to make sense of a life.

REFERENCES

Anderson, J. R. (1995). *Learning and memory: An integrated approach.* New York: Wiley.

Bredekamp, S. (1987). *Developmentally appropriate practice in early childhood programs serving children from birth through age 8.* Washington, DC: National Association for the Education of Young Children.

Bruner, J. (1975). The ontogenesis of speech acts. *Journal of Child Language, 2,* 1-40.

Case, R. (1993). Theories of learning and theories of development. *Educational Psychologist, 28,* 219-233.

Einstein, A., & Infeld, L. (1938). *The evolution of physics.* New York: Simon & Schuster.

Erikson, E. H. (1982). *The life cycle completed.* New York: Norton.

Freire, P. (1993). *Pedagogy of the oppressed.* New York: Continuum.
Gardner, H. (1982). *Art, mind, and brain: A cognitive approach to creativity.* New York: Basic Books.
Gardner, H. (1989). *To open minds: Chinese clues to the dilemma of contemporary education.* New York: Basic Books.
Getzels, J. W., & Csikszentmihalyi, M. (1976). *The creative vision: A longitudinal study of problem finding in art.* New York: Wiley.
Glasser, W. (1990). *The quality school.* New York: Harper & Row.
Goodman, K. S. (1986). *What's whole in whole language.* Portsmouth, NH: Heinemann.
Guilford, J. P. (1967). *The nature of human intelligence.* New York: McGraw-Hill.
Habermas, J. (1974). *Theory and practice.* Boston, MA: Beacon Press.
Hawkins, J., Pea, R. D., Glick, J., & Scribner, S. (1984). "Nerds that laugh don't like mushrooms": Evidence for deductive reasoning by preschoolers. *Developmental Psychology, 20,* 584-594.
Katz, L. G., & Chard, S.C. (1989). *Engaging children's minds: The project approach.* Norwood, NJ: Ablex.
Kuhn, D., & Ho, V. (1977). The development of schemes for recognizing additive and alternative effects in a "natural experiment" context. *Developmental Psychology, 13,* 515-516.
Leinhardt, G. (1988). Getting to know: Tracing students' mathematical knowledge from intuition to competence. *Educational Psychologist, 23,* 119-144.
Lipman, M. (1988). *Philosophy goes to school.* Philadelphia, PA: Temple University Press.
Macworth, N. H. (1965). Originality. *American Psychologist, 20,* 51-66.
Markovits, H., Schleifer, M., & Fortier, L. (1989). Development of elementary deductive reasoning in young children. *Developmental Psychology, 25,* 787-793.
Means, M. L., & Voss, J. F. (1985). Star wars: A developmental study of expert and novice knowledge structures. *Journal of Memory and Language, 24,* 746-757.
National Council of Teachers of Mathematics. (1989). *Curriculum and evaluation standards for school mathematics.* Reston, VA: Author.
O'Brien, T., & Shapiro, B. (1968). The development of logical thinking in children. *American Educational Research Journal, 5,* 531-541.
Overton, W. F., Ward, S. L., Novek, I., Black, J., & O'Brien, D. P. (1987). Form and content in the development of deductive reasoning. *Developmental Psychology, 23,* 22-30.
Piaget, J. (1948). *The moral development of the child.* Glencoe, IL: The Free Press.

Piaget, J. (1969). *Psychologie et pédagogie* [The science of education and the psychology of the child]. Paris: Denoël/Gonthier.

Piaget, J. (1977). The *Limnaea* of the lakes of Neuchatel, Bienne, Morat, and their surroundings. In H. E. Gruber & J. J. Voneche (Eds. & Trans.), *The essential Piaget: An interpretive reference and guide* (p. 8). New York: Basic Books. (Original work published 1911)

Quellmalz, E. S. (1987). Developing reasoning skills. In J. B. Baron & R. J. Sternberg (Eds.), *Teaching thinking skills: Theory and practice* (pp. 86-105). New York: Freeman.

Resnick, L. B. (1987). Constructing knowledge in school. In L. S. Liben (Ed.), *Development and learning: Conflict or congruence?* (pp. 19-50). Hillsdale, NJ: Lawrence Erlbaum Associates.

Resnick, L. B., Bill, V. L., Lesgold, S. B., & Leer, M. L. (1991). Thinking in arithmetic class. In B. Means, C. Chelemer, & M. S. Knapp (Eds.), *Teaching advanced skills to at-risk students* (pp. 27-67). San Francisco, CA: Jossey-Bass.

Roberge, J. J., & Paulus, D. H. (1971). Developmental patterns for children's class and conditional reasoning abilities. *Developmental Psychology, 4,* 191-200.

Schneider, W., Korkel, J., & Weinert, F. E. (1989). Domain-specific knowledge and memory performance: A comparison of high- and low-aptitude children. *Journal of Educational Psychology, 81,* 306-312.

Searle, D. (1984). Scaffolding: Who's building whose building? *Language Arts, 61,* 480-483.

Shulman, L. S., & Tamir, P. (1973). Research on teaching in the natural sciences. In R. M. W. Travers (Ed.), *Second handbook of research on teaching* (pp. 1098-1148). Chicago, IL: Rand McNally.

Shure, M. B. (1993). I Can Problem Solve: Interpersonal cognitive problem solving for young children. *Early Child Development and Care, 96,* 49-64.

Souriau, P. (1881). *Théorie de l'invention.* Paris: Librairie Hachette.

Thurstone, L. L. (1955). *The differential growth of mental abilities.* Chapel Hill: University of North Carolina Psychometric Laboratory.

Torrance, E. P. (1962). *Guiding creative talent.* Englewood Cliffs, NJ: Prentice-Hall.

Van Manen, M. (1977). Linking ways of knowing with ways of being practical. *Curriculum Inquiry, 6*(3), 205-228.

Vygotsky, L. S. (1978). *Mind in society.* Cambridge, MA: Harvard University Press.

Wakefield, J. F. (1992). *Creative thinking: Problem-solving skills and the arts orientation.* Norwood, NJ: Ablex.

Wakefield, J. F. (1994). Problem finding and empathy in art. In M. A. Runco (Ed.), *Problem finding, problem solving, and creativity* (pp. 99-115). Norwood, NJ: Ablex.

Wakefield, J. F. (1996). *Educational psychology: Learning to be a problem solver.* Boston, MA: Houghton Mifflin.

Ward, S. L., & Overton, W. F. (1990). Semantic familiarity, relevance, and the development of deductive reasoning. *Developmental Psychology, 26,* 488-493.

Whitehead, A. N. (1929). *The aims of education.* New York: Macmillan.

Winograd, K. (1993). Selected writing behaviors of fifth graders as they composed original mathematics story problems. *Research in the Teaching of English, 27,* 369-394.

PART II
INTERPERSONAL PROCESSES

12

TEACHING INVENTION AS CRITICAL CREATIVE PROCESSES: A COURSE ON TECHNOSCIENTIFIC CREATIVITY

Michael E. Gorman
The University of Virginia

Jonathan A. Plucker
Indiana University

In children, creativity is a universal. Among adults it is almost non-existent. The great question is: What happened to this enormous and universal human resource? This is the question and the quest of our age.
—Harold Anderson (1958, p. xii)

There are schools and courses given for practically every field of human endeavor except inventing. We have schools for engineers, doctors, lawyers, artists, musicians, and hundreds of other professions and occupations but there are no schools for the inventor. . . . Assuming that inventing also requires certain traits and native ability why have no attempts been made to teach inventing in the schools? Must we depend on pure chance for our supply of inventors? Why should it not be possible to train people to invent? These questions are extremely interesting and of great social importance.
—Joseph Rossman (1964, p. 216)

Rossman's views on the neglect of invention education are still applicable at the start of the 21st century: Three decades later, more information on invention is available (Gorman, 1990; Jewkes, Sawers, & Stillerman, 1969; Kivenson, 1977; Weber & Perkins, 1989), but few publications deal with teaching invention and design to students at the high school level and younger. In the education and creativity literature, most of the few available articles and books either provide a rationale for teaching invention to students or provide heuristics for teaching invention (Gilmore, 1959; Kuehn, 1988; McCormack, 1984; Schlesinger, 1987a, 1987b). Only a few published studies report investigations of the process of teaching invention to children (Kuehn & Krockover, 1986), rating student inventions as creative products (Treffinger, 1989; Westberg, 1991), or determining the presence of inventive characteristics in children (Colangelo, Kerr, Hallowell, Huesman, & Gaeth, 1992).

In this chapter, we describe our experiences with a course on invention and design offered to gifted secondary students in a summer enrichment program, as a springboard for an analysis of how students learn and can be taught the role of critical creative processes in invention and design. The course was developed to meet the existing need for invention education for younger students and to serve as a collaborative learning environment in which both students and teachers would explore technological creativity. The four specific objectives of the course were as follows:

1. Offer students a better understanding of the creative process in the development of technology.
2. Help students understand that invention is a process that can be improved by reflection (intrapersonal critical processes).
3. Encourage students to take advantage of different intelligences and abilities in a team effort (interpersonal critical processes).
4. Enable students to see the benefits of a multidisciplinary team approach (interpersonal critical processes).

This course was offered first at the university level, where these goals were emphasized with good results (Gorman, Richards, Scherer, & Kagiwada, 1995). Most university students have already selected majors by the time they enter this course. The potential for life change is greater at the secondary level, where an inspiring set of team activities might also entice more students to pursue careers related to technology.

In order to discuss this course and its implications for critical creative processes, we introduce concepts associated with invention and design that may not be familiar. The knowledge and skills possessed by creative technologists is in their hands as well as their minds; it is visual, kinesthetic and intellectual. Inventors and designers learn by "tinkering," altering existing devices to see what new possibilities emerge. Typically, these efforts fit within an overall "mental model," a three-dimensional conception of a technological system that can be run in the "mind's eye"; these mental models are incomplete in certain important respects, and tinkering is one of the means by which an inventor tries to complete them. (For a more complete description of this process, see Gorman, 1992).

Working Effectively in Groups: Interpersonal Critical Processes

Interdisciplinary collaboration is an important aspect of creative technological work that has not received the attention it deserves (Abra, 1994). As stated in the announcement of the Leadership Opportunity in Science and Humanities Education, sponsored by the National Science Foundation, the Fund for the Improvement of Post-Secondary Education and the National Endowment for Humanities: "Increasingly, the challenges of both scholarship and the world demand a multiplicity of perspectives. To address these challenges, individuals will need to appreciate and understand subject matter beyond the area of their formal education, communicate and work with others who have different experiences and expertise, and be flexible and responsive to change" (p. 2).

These experiences and expertises may include different disciplinary backgrounds and talents (Abra, 1994), differences in learning styles (Gregorc, 1985; Renzulli & Smith, 1978), and what Gardner (1983, 1993) called *multiple intelligences*. Another characteristic that a student brings into any group situation is the ability to present creative ideas or products and evaluate the ideas of others (Necka, 1992; Plucker, 1994; Runco & Chand, 1994; Stein, 1974, 1975). Amabile (1983) and her colleagues (Amabile, Hennessey, & Grossman, 1986) suggested that the presence of external evaluation may inhibit creative production, although this view is becoming more controversial (Plucker, 1994; Runco, McCarthy, & Svenson, 1994). Regardless of the possible effect of external evaluation on creativity, present day manufacturing and engineering requires individuals to invent and design in groups. Students who enter these fields without the ability to use and provide external evaluation effectively will be at a disadvantage. Once again, however, the literature contains little information pertaining to how students can be taught to use interpersonal evaluation effectively while creating (Plucker, 1994).

Becoming Reflective Problem Solvers: Intrapersonal Critical Processes

Combining inter- and intrapersonal evaluations requires reflective cognition (cf. Norman, 1993). Inventors and innovative designers begin with experience in one or more domains; this experience allows them to solve familiar problems rapidly, without much reflection.[1] Simon (1988) and his colleagues at Carnegie-Mellon compared the expert's knowledge to a compiled program that executes rapidly. The novice, in contrast, has to ponder over each step, going through the process slowly and self-consciously. To put it in other terms, the expert possesses tacit knowledge gained through years of experience (Sternberg & Horvath, 1999).

When inventors are stretching beyond what is known, both in terms of information and heuristics, they are a bit like novices—they are moving into areas where no one is an expert. Each inventor must transform the problem into one he or she can solve, given his or her background, expertise, and tacit knowledge. Alexander Graham Bell, for example, had expertise in speech and audition but limited expertise in the building of sophisticated electromagnetic apparatus.

> It became evident to me, that with my own rude workmanship, and with the limited time and means at my disposal, I could not hope to construct any better models. I therefore from this time (November, 1873) devoted less time to practical experiment than to the theoretical development of the details of the invention. (Bell, 1876, p. 8)

Bell built a device that showed how the bones of the middle ear translated sound into sinusoidal curves. His first patent argued that the electrical "wave" or current that transmitted speech, or musical tones, would have to have a similar shape (Gorman, Mehalik, Carlson, & Oblon, 1993).

Bell's decision to focus on theoretical developments rather than building complex circuits was reached after frustrations and failures with complex apparatus; he reflected on his strengths and weaknesses, and changed course. Inventors need to be able to do this kind of reflection, analyzing and altering their goals and strategies.

Reflection also is important for design teams moving into new domains. Such reflection can help avoid groupthink, in which a

---

[1]When Gorman discussed the role of reflection in familiar problems with Duane Bowker, one of the inventors of True Voice(sm), he disagreed, arguing that reflection is important even when personal experience guides one toward an "obvious" solution.

group reaches premature closure on an apparent solution that turns out to have negative consequences that could have been anticipated (see Janis, 1982). As Schauble, Klopfer, and Raghavan (1991) noted:

> If the eventual objective of instruction is to provide the additional capability to flexibly adapt various forms of thinking when they are appropriate, then it is important that instruction not end precisely at the point where it should begin. All science teachers can tell anecdotes in which the classroom demonstration is completed, and two weeks later children recall the "magic effect" but not the associated principle. As Dewey suggested, interest in generating effects may help engage children in the reasoning process, but sustained effort is required for progress beyond that to a model of scientific inquiry oriented toward achieving understanding. (p. 878)

The best problem solvers are those who continuously engage in the sustained effort of reflection, clarifying and sometimes transforming their goals, improving their strategies, and evaluating their processes as well as their products.

Sternberg (1990; Sternberg & Grigorenko, 1993) proposed a mental self-government theory of thinking styles. The scope of mental self-government may be either internal (i.e., involving individual tasks) or external (i.e., involving collaboration with other individuals). Sternberg argued that students who understand the different thinking styles and can use them flexibly will be better able to take advantage of their other talents and abilities. There are two ways in which this can be done:

1. Intrapersonal reflection: The problem solver adapts his or her own thinking style to fit the problem.
2. Interpersonal reflection: The group assesses the learning styles of its members and divides the task appropriately.

COURSE STRUCTURE

According to a 1991 study done by the Manufacturing Studies Board and the National Research Council, graduates of engineering schools have a difficult time transferring school-based lessons about design to work situations (*Improving Engineering Design*, 1991). One proposed solution has been the recent swell of case-based approaches to teaching design (see, e.g., Chou & Calkins, 1994). Cases permit students to apply what they are learning to situations that have a higher potential to transfer to real-world problems, including those that are ill-structured and open-ended (Spiro, Coulson, Feltovich, & Anderson, 1988).

Design exercises such as developing a portable shelter for the homeless (see the Howard University design activity described in Chou & Calkins, 1994) that require student involvement over an extended period of time are referred to as *active learning modules*, to distinguish them from brief case studies that can be done in a single class session. These active learning modules plunge students into the design process, requiring them to plan, build, and present their designs.

Typically, these modules do not include a reflection component—the students finish one activity and go onto another without describing and comparing the processes they used. One unique feature of the modules created for this course is that they included a reflection component.

As part of a 6-week, residential summer program for gifted students, two active learning modules were assigned to 31 students in Grades 9 through 11 during two 3-week sessions. Each module had its own set of subgoals related to the overall course goals and included the following assignments:

1. Create a team invention or design activity that included construction of a prototype.
2. Deep detailed notebooks to record experiments and speculate about alternate approaches.
3. Give oral and written presentations of an interim stage and of the final results of this activity.
4. Provide case studies of actual inventors working on similar problems.
5. Prepare a final notebook entry in which your group processes are compared to those of other groups and to those of the inventors.

Instructions for each module were distributed in a lengthy packet that included background readings and information. Lectures covered topics in physics that were relevant to the problems students were encountering.

Module 1: The Invention of the Telephone

The first module was based on the invention of the telephone, arguably one of the most important inventions of the 19th century. Bell's first patent for what is now called a telephone (at that time it was called a speaking telegraph) was one of the most valuable patents in history; it became the basis for the Bell corporation.

In addition to the course goals just mentioned, this module had two additional goals: First, to encourage students to experience the invention process firsthand, from idea to device to patent, and second, to permit students to compare their own invention processes with those of master inventors working on the same problem. Student packets included sections from Bell's notebooks, and lectures compared his processes to those of his rivals, Edison and Gray.[2]

Students received a packet of materials that set up the problem as follows:

> There are those who believe that the inventions we see in the world around us today were inevitable—even if Alexander Graham Bell and Thomas Edison had chosen different careers, we would still be using telephones and electric lighting systems like the ones we use today. To determine whether that is true or not, we are going to put you in the position of a 19th-century competitor with Bell and his rival telegraph inventor Elisha Gray, and see whether you can come up with an alternate communications design that could have changed history if it had been implemented at that time.
>
> In this case, you and a group of other students will attempt to design and build a system that improves on Alexander Graham Bell's famous telephone patent and a caveat submitted on the same day by Elisha Gray. (Copies of these materials appear at the end of this packet of materials.) You will be assuming the role of a 19th-century inventor like Edison who used a research team to compete with these two. Even though Bell has a patent for a system, your team can patent improvements so significant that others will be able to use them without infringing on the Bell patent, thereby leading to "fame and fortune" for you and your team. In addition, we will ask you to imagine the long-term consequences of its adoption—how would our 20th-century communications have looked different if your improvements were adopted?

Student packets included background information on the invention of the telephone, explaining the rivalry between Bell and Gray and including comparisons of transmitters created by each inventor. Students were also given descriptions of several transmitter and receiver designs that used simple, modern components to recreate 19th-century designs. Students were told that they could not simply reproduce one of these designs; they had to improve on it. They were also provided with simple materials—a variety of batteries,

---

[2]An overview of Bell's invention process, including sketches and other materials, is available on the World Wide Web under "Research Reports" (2nd series) at the following address: http://jefferson.village.virginia.edu/home.html.

types of wire, nails, bolts, cans, and multimeters and amplifiers for testing. Students were not expected to produce speech in the limited time available, but all should have been able to create changes in a multimeter reading or sounds through an amplifier.

Working in Groups. Students were asked to work in groups of three or four and were given the following advice on working in groups, based in part on the example of Duane Bowker, one of the inventors of TrueVoice (sm), a technology that greatly improves the quality of long-distance transmission. At Bell Labs, where Bowker works, every successful project eventually becomes a team effort. Bowker created the idea for TrueVoice with his best friend, Jim James. They knew each other well and had worked together for a long time, so they did not need to formally divide labor. When it came time to implement the idea, Bowker became the product champion as he sold the idea to the rest of the company and helped organized the teams that took the rough prototype and turned it into a new technology (D. Bowker, personal communication, June 1994).

Bowker and the course instructors provided the following advice to the students:

1. Divide the labor: In a bad team, nobody knows who does what. A good team divides the labor into microtasks. These tasks should be suited to the expertise and interests of individual members, as much as possible.
2. Schedule: Groups begin with a schedule imposed from the outside, but effective groups also develop an internal schedule that sets goals for the completion of microtasks. For example, while two people are building a transmitter, another two can be writing a caveat.
3. Create rules: Group members often find that they need to set up a set of rules or guidelines for participation and decision making. For example, one of the dangers of dividing labor is that an individual working on one part of the device may get out of touch with an individual working on another—and the components will not work together. One way around this is to get the group together at regular intervals and discuss progress.
4. Lead intelligently and cooperatively: Having a leader like Bowker, who serves as a product champion, can be extremely beneficial if the leader listens and makes sure the rest of the team is on board. A group can make a rule that everyone gets a chance to talk at meetings, to avoid one member becoming too dominant; groups can also pick a moderator who is not the champion to ensure that alter-

natives are considered, but the discussion does not bog down—one who has to make decisions about what to do and move ahead.

Assignments. In addition to building a prototype of their device that would illustrate its workings and potential, students were required to do the following:

1. Keep group and individual invention notebooks: Inventors use notebooks to imagine how new systems might be created, to sketch parts they are thinking about building, to plan new ventures, and to reflect on the methods they are using. A notebook can also be used in court, to establish that the invention has priority over a rival's invention. In one famous case, DeForest used a confusing notebook entry to prove that he, and not his rival Armstrong, deserved a patent for the regeneration circuit that was crucial to the development of radio (Lewis, 1991).

    In the group notebooks, students were asked to record rough sketches of devices or parts of devices, results of every experiment, and tentative conclusions. Bell made a key discovery related to his second telephone patent by carefully examining his notebook; he found a positive result he had obtained on July 11, 1876, and wondered why he had not followed up on it. In this case, good record keeping led to a patent.

    In their individual notebooks, students were asked to record their individual thoughts about the invention path their group followed, and also their reflections on their groups' processes and their role in the group. In addition, students were given questions related to specific readings or films.

2. Prepare a caveat: This is a practice that is no longer followed in the patent office, but was widely used in the 19th century to signal an intention to test and perfect a new invention. If another inventor later submitted a patent for the same idea, then the Caveator was notified and given an opportunity to submit a patent. The caveat was also used to establish priority for an invention.

    In this course, the caveat assignment forced the groups to decide on the type of system to be patented. The caveat could include several alternate designs. For example, Gray, in his caveat, raised the possibility that his system for transmitting speech might require multiple transmitters and receivers or might need only one transmitter.

Module 2: Inventing for the Environment

This module fulfills the overall course goals and the goals for the telephone module, but includes three additional goals: (a) teach the students the importance of designing for a better environment and calculating the environmental costs of any invention; (b) remind students that successful inventors create markets (this is especially important when one is trying to persuade people to use an environmentally beneficial technology); and (c) have students link library research with experimental evidence that they generate themselves.

To limit the scope of this module, we constrained the students to the area of solar energy. There are a wide range of devices, choices, and strategies one can use to harness the sun. Students could focus on a passive technology, like a solar oven or water heater, or an active technology involving photovoltaic cells, which can be used to power cars, power plants, computers, and so on. One could focus on a different source of energy (e.g., wind, biomass) in an environmental module or on conservation technologies like recycling.

The telephone module included examples of the work of several inventors, especially Bell. In this module, we used an inventor of solar heating systems, A. C. Rich, as an example; he came up with an innovative design, patented it, and tried to found a business based on it with the goal of improving the global environment while generating a profit.

In Rich's case, he used the sun to heat water—a passive solar application. In addition, students were given information on photovoltaic cells, an active solar technology. They were allowed to select their own design project but were encouraged to consider situations like a village in a remote, underdeveloped country that could use solar power to pump and heat water, refrigerate vaccines, and generally improve the quality of life without causing environmental degradation (Jintang & Weide, 1991).

Group Projects. Groups in this project tended to favor solar cars, boats, and airplanes—even a solar train—constructing clever prototypes out of simple materials. Some of these groups engaged in extensive market analysis to show that their inventions would actually save money, but none of the groups adequately considered the environmental savings that might result. One group tried to design a solar water heater that would not only provide hot water but also generate steam for electricity, resulting in the only passive solar design created in this course. Another group adopted the goal of improving life for a village in the Amazon; they hit on the idea of sending solar cells aloft on a balloon and designed a device to hold the cells and make sure they were angled properly. This was not a practical solution, but it showed imagination and ingenuity. In almost every case, students were able to demonstrate that their prototypes generated power.

RESULTS OF THE COURSE

In order to assess whether the four course objectives were met, students completed several Likert scale and open-ended surveys, were observed extensively, completed daily individual journals and group notebook entries, and participated in individual interviews.

Changes in Perceptions of the Invention Process

Students were surveyed extensively about their perceptions of invention, and they also completed numerous journal entries that revealed their attitudes toward certain aspects of the invention process. Initial entries and surveys from the beginning of the course contained surprising detail, but many students did not put enough time into the end-of-the-course surveys. As a result, drawing conclusions about student attitude change from the pre- and postcourse surveys was problematic. However, several aspects of student perceptions are covered in journal entries and surveys administered during the course, and a discussion of these areas follows.

In general, students appeared to gain a greater appreciation for the effort required in the invention process, and many became aware of the variety of influences on the invention process, such as the importance of collaboration, the role of politics, and the need for patience and persistence. The teacher noted other specific areas in which student attitudes were impacted:

> First [students] found out that just having an idea for an invention is only the beginning, not the end; instead of feeling like they know it all, they learn how little they know. The invention process pulls them into a situation that creates the *need to know*, an intrinsic motivation brought about by having them immersed in a scenario that they helped create.

> They learn that when things are first assembled, they rarely work; or if they work at first, they might not work later. They find themselves in the process of *tinkering*: trying different things, making adjustments, retrenching and starting over. True exploration toward one's goal is an experience that rarely occurs in a science setting.

through the use of group notebooks, the preparation and presentation of caveats and patents, the problem-solving aspect of the activities, and individual journals (in which students responded to guiding questions). By the end of the course, more than 70% of the students remarked on the importance of reflection in their creative and problem-solving processes. For example:

> I feel that the remembrance and understanding of knowledge and former experiences are the most vital to reflect. You can branch off of former creative ideas to create more useful ones.

> Reflection plays an important role. . . . At times, I reflect on past times in which I needed or wanted something that doesn't exist. Ideas also come from my imagination and my fields of interest, such as music and art. I think of solutions to problems in fields that I know.

> Reflection has helped me with respect to decision making. A conscious effort was made to take into account the mistakes made in the telephone project when working on the solar project. While these are very different projects in terms of objectives, many aspects of the telephone project are applicable in the solar project.

Observations of the students revealed that reflection played a more significant role at the end of the course than it had at the beginning, but the first and only reaction of most students to any problem was to tinker with the apparatus until it began to work properly. Because of this, several groups made little progress after initial stumbling blocks were encountered. Although students reported that they valued reflection as a result of the course, their actions did little to confirm this.

Evaluation of Ideas. Students were also asked about a specific type of reflection—judgment of their ideas before they presented them to other group members. First session students were evenly split between feeling that they evaluate their ideas before they mention them and feeling that they do not pre-judge their ideas. All but one second session student wrote that they evaluated their ideas before sharing them. Some representative comments from students who claimed not to have judged their ideas:

> I usually tell my team members about my idea as soon as I get one. The group and I then refine the idea together to make it better.

> In my group, we all throw out ideas and thoughts even if they are not practical or sensible. We all brainstorm and don't care what ideas we have.

> Sometimes, I think about my idea, but I'm not very aware of its sensibility. I say what thoughts are on my mind.

> When I contribute ideas to the group, I don't think about judging them beforehand. I feel that group members should feel open to each other, making a comfortable environment in which one does not feel they will be criticized for their ideas. . . . Even if an idea seems useless, another group member may hear that idea, which immediately triggers an idea in their head.

> A group is supposed to build on your ideas and support them. Therefore, I don't think I should have to judge my ideas first.

> I try to be open with my ideas about the project. Before an idea is implemented, it is discussed and debated. If the idea is not feasible, it will be thrown out or, more likely, altered in a way that makes it workable. Since many of my ideas are bizarre and unrelated to the project, it appears through reflection that this has occasionally taken the focus off the project objective. On the whole, however, I feel that this openness contributed to the project.

Representative comments from students who feel that intrapersonal evaluation is important:

> I judge my ideas to the fullest extent before I present my ideas to the group. I think about whether it would be cost efficient and environmentally safe. I also think about whether or not we could work on it as a group and if all the materials we would need would be available.

> I judge an idea before mentioning it to the group to a fairly far extent. I look at the possibilities and capabilities of building or making the idea work. I think of the potential of our group and the idea.

> You have to think about practicality, marketability, and all other factors. If I came up with an idea that would require zillions of solar cells, I wouldn't say anything because it would never pass, and there's no point to doing that.

> I think through the mechanics and the process of my idea. I try to think what may happen if we make it. If I see any flaws in it then I do not mention it.

> I consider if the idea has any potential. If my idea is ridiculous, then I won't mention it. If it has any value or could be benefitted from then I would mention it.

The importance placed on "value" of the idea is interesting. Two students mentioned a combination of both evaluation and nonevaluation:

try to accept everyone's opinion by listening carefully and then making comments.

Even the students who had major difficulties when working with the other members of their group reflected on the lessons they had learned. For example, one member of a group got sick and left the program, leaving only two students to complete the projects:

> What I think I've learned the most about is teamwork. Even when [the sick student] was gone, we accomplished a lot because we worked together and didn't goof off. If we had worked this way from the start, I think we would have had a much better project.

Students from two other groups remarked that they realized that each person required a different amount of praise. For example, Andy noticed that Rebecca became upset if her every activity was not praised enthusiastically. During an interview, Andy stated that he did not realize this at first because he needs very little praise. By giving Rebecca more positive feedback during the last week and a half of the course, he felt that he allowed the group to function more smoothly.

The following quotations are perhaps the most telling examples of the impact of the course. The first student explains her objections to the group, then discusses the positive nature of the experience, and the second student describes in detail the benefits of the course:

> Like in every project that I have encountered with a group, I have received this feeling that I have to do most of the work (in this case one other student and I felt that way, not just me) because nothing will happen if we try to evenly divide the work. I felt this because there seemed to be a lack of attention toward the project and therefore motivation. I really wanted to be able to choose our own team. . . . After we have picked "the perfect team," I would have liked to analyze the results of our decisions after choosing the team.
>
> I enjoyed this very much. [It was] challenging, which means more exciting. Thanks for doing this. It's a lot better than filing papers like they make me do when I'm finished or bored at my school.
>
> I've learned a lot of things from this experience. It not only was my first experience to make/invent something on our own, but I learned more skills and how to deal with people. That is the most important thing that I learned—how to accept one's opinions and then to make my comments. Also . . . I learned to deal

well with people and work out anything. Best of all, I learned to forgive, help, and trust people.

Pattern of the Group Experiences. Initially, students were separated into either four-person (first session) or three-person groups (second session). Group membership remained the same for both projects, and although each group had a different dynamic, the following description of the students' group experiences is typical. At first, delegation and compromise were nonexistent in almost every group. Each student either came up with an idea or deferred to those students who had ideas. After the group decided on an idea to pursue (or were told by a certain group member that his or her idea was the best one), the group proceeded. The "idea losers" generally dropped out of the group processes or became disruptive and engaged in off-task behaviors such as playing with the equipment, teasing the students who were working, or drawing other group members off-task. These negative group interactions persisted until the preparation of the caveat. This was the flashpoint for most major confrontations within the group, since many groups tried to delegate by having the least helpful group members write the caveat. Of course, these students were the least familiar with what the group was doing and could not write the caveat. They became frustrated and verbally lashed out at the other group members.

Soon after the preparation of the caveat, students participated in a group activity. During this activity, students were each asked to fill out a sheet about group dynamics. Questions included: Where's the group in solving the problem? How well is the group working together? How well are the group members helping each other? What are the problems you think the group needs to work on? How can you work on these problems? Each of these main questions was followed by a number of subquestions to which students responded. Students were then asked to fill out an additional copy of the sheet for the group after discussing their individual responses. Nearly all of the 30 students reported that this experience was constructive:

> [The activity] helped us to work out our problems and tell our other group members our thoughts without hurting any feelings. We were able to help someone recognize that he was becoming too dominate, and [the group] decided to discuss all action beforehand.
>
> The group activity helped our group very much. I feel better about the project and the way our group functions.
>
> I find the group analysis sheets to be very helpful. They help you to see what areas your group is having problems with and helps

The contrast between the two groups is revealing: The first group was highly motivated after its initial success with the photophone, yet produced a product of lesser quality on the solar project; the second group produced a poor product on the telephone, yet (perhaps partly out of embarrassment) group members managed to produce a relatively high quality solar design. The creative regression to the mean effect was not universal among the groups, but it has also been observed in the undergraduate course on which this summer opportunity was based. More intensive research is needed to determine the dynamics and universality of this effect and strategies to minimize it.

CONCLUSIONS

One of the most difficult and challenging things about this course was the interpersonal aspect of creativity. Students seemed to understand the importance of brainstorming and coming up with alternatives, but were not used to the hard negotiations involved in selling an idea and making compromises with other members of a group. Theories of creativity often imply that creativity is an individual act, best done when there is little or no external evaluation (Amabile, 1994). But creativity often requires the ability to make use of interpersonal evaluations (Runco & Chand, 1994). For example, the original idea for True Voice(sm) occurred not to one person but to two collaborators, Duane Bowker and Jim James; from the earliest stage, they interacted with others who helped them transform it into a technology appropriate for long-distance lines.

Experience with interpersonal evaluation should lead one to make better intrapersonal evaluations. Students in this course did reflect on their individual problem-solving styles and strategies, but the group element was more salient—there were more class activities directed at working effectively in groups, but these were driven, in part, by student concerns. In a 1-year follow-up evaluation, students remembered very few of the frustrations of working within groups and talked more about the benefits (Plucker & Gorman, 1999). In particular, what is needed is a better method for groups and individuals to record their processes as they are working, a method that would facilitate comparison with other groups and with the actual inventors. Such a method already exists: protocol analysis, used by psychologists to track and compare the ways in which experts and novices solve problems. However, this method has never been used by students to record and compare their own processes. Gorman (1995) developed a version of protocol analysis particularly suited to inventors, and used it to track Bell's path to the telephone. We would like to train students in this course to use this technique to record their own invention processes, and then build-in comparisons with other groups and inventors. In effect, this technique will allow groups to see similarities and differences in cognitive processes and from this comparison, learn how to visualize and change their own problem-solving strategies.

Future research should also relate these intra- and interpersonal evaluations to evaluations by persons outside the group, including teachers, patent examiners, other members of the class, or independent judges. Group interaction does not always predict group performance (Hirokawa, 1982). In this class, groups that improved their interpersonal dynamics did not always produce superior designs, although their presentations were generally smoother and more coherent. But evaluations of final designs in this class were loose and subjective, since the focus of the class was on teaching the invention process. What is needed is to take the best measures of intra- and interpersonal evaluation, see how well they predict others' ratings of the final product, and then see how well groups incorporate feedback from others in a new round of intra- and interpersonal evaluations (Hirokawa, 1988). This kind of research will offer a better sense of the types of reflection about critical creative processes that lead to better designs.

ACKNOWLEDGMENT

The modules and research reported in this chapter were supported by a grant from the Geraldine R. Dodge Foundation. We gratefully acknowledge the contributions of Michael Brittingham, the high school physics teacher who ran this course.

REFERENCES

Abra, J. (1994). Collaboration in creative work: An initiative for investigation. *Creativity Research Journal, 7,* 1-20.

Amabile, T. M. (1983). *The social psychology of creativity.* New York: Springer-Verlag.

Amabile, T. M. (1994). The "atmosphere of pure work": Creativity in research and development. In W. R. Shadish & S. Fuller (Eds.), *The social psychology of science* (pp. 316-328). New York: Guilford.

Spiro, R. J., Coulson, R. L., Feltovich, P. J., & Anderson, D. K. (1988). Cognitive flexibility theory: Advanced knowledge acquisition in ill-structured domains. In *Tenth Annual Conference of the Cognitive Science Society*. Montreal, Quebec, Canada: Cognitive Science Society and Hillsdale, NJ: Lawrence Erlbaum Associates.

Stein, J. O. (1974). *Stimulating creativity. Vol. 1. Individual procedures.* New York: Academic Press.

Stein, M. I. (1975). *Stimulating creativity. Vol. 2. Group procedures.* New York: Academic Press.

Sternberg, R. J. (1990). Thinking styles: Keys to understanding student performance. *Phi Delta Kappan, 71*, 366-371.

Sternberg, R. J., & Grigorenko, E. L. (1993). Thinking styles and the gifted. *Roeper Review, 16*, 122-130.

Sternberg, R. J., & Horvath, J. A. (1999). *Tacit knowledge in professional practice.* Hillsdale, NJ: Lawrence Erlbaum Associates.

Treffinger, D. J. (1989). *Student invention evaluation kit: Field test edition.* Sarasota, FL: Center for Creative Learning.

Weber, J. J., & Perkins, D. N. (Eds.). (1989). *Inventive minds.* New York: Oxford University Press.

Westberg, K. L. (1991). *The effects of instruction in the inventing process on student's development of inventions.* Dissertation Abstracts International, 51. (University Microfilms No. 9107625)

13

EVALUATIVE PROCESSES DURING GROUP IMPROVISATIONAL PERFORMANCE

R. Keith Sawyer
Washington University-St. Louis

Can true novelty exist? How can something be created out of nothing? In a pre-scientific era, philosophers often attributed creativity to divine inspiration. Twentieth-century social science has instead pursued empirical approaches that locate originality in psychological and social sources. Psychologists have focused on the processes whereby individuals generate creative products, whereas social theorists have explored how originality might be an emergent social fact (Sawyer, 1999). The issues stemming from this philosophical question transcend creativity theory alone. George Herbert Mead, stated that this was the key issue facing contemporary philosophy, particularly in the face of an increasingly deterministic physical science: "It is the task of the philosophy of today to bring into congruence with each other this universality of determination which is the text of modern science, and the emergence of the novel" (Mead, 1932, p. 14). Perkins (1988) noted that this problem was fundamental to creativity theory, and referred to it as the *ex nihilo* problem.

Beginning with Guilford's (1963, 1968) seminal efforts in the 1950s, creativity researchers have usually placed the source of nov-

of describing the social processes which come into play after an individual has generated a creative product. Individuals' new creative products are the "divergent" step of the process, and the social field of production (representing the discipline or field) evaluates the new product, judging whether it is "creative" or not. An apparently original or innovative idea which is not judged to be so by this field gets labeled "eccentric," "crackpot," or simply "uninteresting." The collective selection processes of the field are the social equivalent of the second psychological stage, evaluation. I explore these two issues through an examination of group improvisational performance.

Collective improvisation has interesting implications for both of these issues. With respect to the cognitive process issue, for each individual performer and for the group, the creative product and process are co-occurring. Because the creative product is generated in real time, without an opportunity for the iterative evaluation and revision common in other forms of creativity, there may not be a distinct evaluation stage. If the ideation and evaluation stages are temporally indistinguishable during improvisation, why must they be distinct temporal stages for other forms of creativity? With respect to the social process issue, when performing an improvisation with a group, no single performer dominates the performance. The performers collectively create the performance, through an ongoing symbolic interaction, whether musical or verbal. When one performer introduces a new idea, the other performers evaluate it immediately, determining whether or not the performance will shift to incorporate the proposed new idea. This social process of spontaneous evaluation has interesting parallels with the evaluation performed by a field when an individual proposes a new creative product. Likewise, it has implications for theoretical models which are based on temporally distinct stages of ideation and evaluation.

Because improvisational creativity is ephemeral and does not generate any lasting ostensible product, it has been easy to neglect. Although improvisational creativity has rarely been a subject for creativity research, it may actually represent a more common, more accessible form of creativity than privileged domains such as the arts and sciences (Sawyer, 1995a). If one recognizes that all social interactions display improvisational elements, then everyday activities such as conversation become relevant to creativity theory. Creativity in interactional domains, including teaching, parenting, and mentoring, is recognized to be important to our lives and our culture. Yet this type of creativity has been resistant to operationalization and analysis.

Improvisation has been surprisingly neglected in all fields which might be expected to claim the phenomenon, including folkloristics, ethnomusicology, musicology, and creativity studies.[4] The few treatments that exist have been ethnographic descriptions of musical and verbal performance genres. Ethnographies have described a wide range of improvisational genres, both musical and verbal. In music, in addition to the recent focus on jazz (Berliner, 1994; Monson, 1996; Sawyer, 1992), European and U.S. writers have written widely on the Indian *raga*, the Javanese *gamelan*, the Arabic and Turkish *maqam*, the Iranian *dastgah*, and group African drumming. With respect to verbal improvisation, a group of linguistic anthropologists and sociolinguists have been engaged in the ethnography of speaking (Bauman & Sherzer, 1974; Hymes, 1962). These researchers focus on public verbal performance in a variety of cultures; most of these performance genres incorporate improvisational elements. Despite the recent availability of these ethnographies, creativity studies (as well as other fields including folklore, conversation analysis, and ethnomusicology) have retained a "compositional" approach to improvised performances, often using techniques developed for the analysis of notated text artifacts. For example, musicologists who analyze improvisational performances tend to analyze transcripts of the performance, implicitly treating the performance as if it had been a composed creative product. These approaches originate in formalist or structuralist methodologies which are inadequate to the processual, interactional elements of group performance.

Improvisational performance is a type of *mediated action*. Several psychologists have suggested that mediated action is fundamental to a wide range of interactive behaviors, including cognitive development (Lave, 1992; Rogoff, 1982; Wertsch, 1985), planning (Baker-Sennett & Matusov, 1997; Baker-Sennett, Matusov, & Rogoff, 1992), education (Forman & Cazden, 1985), and the mediation of culture (Cole, 1985; Silverstein, 1985). The term *mediated action*, as defined by Wertsch (1985), is meant to emphasize that symbolic social action is subject to two influences: the socioculturally provided mediational means, a semiotic system such as a language or a culture, and the situation or context of the action. Studies of mediated action derive from the recent introduction of semiotics and sociolinguistics into psychology, associated with the writings of Vygotsky (1978, 1934/1986), cultural psychologists (Bruner, 1990; Stigler, Shweder, & Herdt, 1990; Wertsch, 1992), and those studying situated action and cognition (Baker-Sennett et al., 1992; Lave, 1992;

---

[4]This oversight may be due to the dominance of structuralist and formalist paradigms in the study of the arts, and to a lesser extent, in the social sciences. Some post-structuralists have attempted to address the improvisational nature of social interaction (Bourdieu's *habitus*, 1977, or Foucault's *discourse*, 1972), but these theorists have not turned their attention to creativity per se.

allows its communication, such as a journal article or painting.

Most of these theories of the creative process have the following aspects in common:

1. There is a period of conscious, directed thought that precedes the generation of novelty. Somehow this period prepares the unconscious mind, filling it with raw material to be used by divergent thought processes.
2. Divergent thought processes, usually placed below the level of conscious awareness, manipulate this raw material, generating ideas, concepts, or configurations. This second stage, which can last a very short time or go on for years, is the stage of *incubation*. The theorists cited here differ on just what occurs in the subconscious; Hadamard argued that active, guided processing is taking place, whereas most current researchers believe that chance combinations of thought processes below the threshold of awareness alone provide an adequate explanation (Langley & Jones, 1988; Simonton, 1988a, 1988b).
3. A *filter* or *evaluation* determines which of these many novel ideas advances into conscious awareness. This evaluative filter is also largely preconscious, and is sometimes associated with convergent thought processes.
4. The conscious mind further evaluates the insight, attempting to elaborate it into a completed creative product, whether a theory, artwork, or scientific paper. This stage is sometimes referred to as *elaboration*, but also involves evaluative processes.

From the aforementioned, one can see that the term *evaluation* means at least two things in creativity research. It refers to the preconscious, convergent processes that select which ideas move into consciousness, and it refers to the conscious process of careful, deliberative evaluation of the insight, after it has moved into consciousness. Although both of these processes are certainly evaluative, they may be qualitatively different; one preconscious and yet "directed" after a fashion; one conscious and very clearly directed. Runco (1993; Runco & Chand, 1994) is one of the few researchers who has observed that evaluation must occur on many levels, from the preconscious to the deliberate.

The notion of preconscious evaluation is perhaps the more problematic of the two. With conscious evaluation, one simply posits, like Poincaré (1913), that the conscious mind is "illuminated" by those unpredictable ideas mysteriously emerging from the unconscious, and the rational conscious mind carefully and deliberately evaluates each idea to see if it's sensible or foolish. But if the preconscious has some ability to evaluate and filter ideas, how sophisticated could it be? Would it look like the conscious mind, only automatized? Assuming that it's not as sophisticated as the conscious evaluation, wouldn't it discard some ideas which really weren't so bad? In other words, wouldn't it make mistakes? Creativity research hasn't shed much light on the nature of this preconscious evaluative process.

SOCIAL PROCESS MODELS OF CREATIVITY

Stage models, like those reviewed previously, have been widely used by psychologists as frameworks for analyzing creativity. These models have focused on *psychological* stages of the individual's creative process, without attempting to represent social influences. But even after the creative product is generated, social forces come into play, and in effect act as another level of evaluation. How does the individual integrate his or her insights with an ongoing domain of scientific or artistic activity? To what extent is the preparation stage dependent on the symbolic domain, or on the social group within which the individual works? Creative individuals rarely work in a vacuum, isolated from the social systems which constitute their domain of activity. Even psychological evaluation implies a social dimension: How can divergent thoughts be evaluated, unless the individual makes use of an internalized model of the domain (e.g., by using the formal mathematical procedures endorsed by a scientific discipline), and without an intimate familiarity with experts in the field who help select and define what is worthwhile?

In 1938, the philosopher R. G. Collingwood summarized the range and extent of social forces influencing individual creativity:

> The work of artistic creation is not a work performed in any exclusive or complete fashion in the mind of the person whom we call the artist. That idea is a delusion bred of individualistic psychology. . . . This activity is a corporate activity belonging not to any one human being but to a community. It is performed not only by the man whom we individualistically call the artist, but partly by all the other artists of whom we speak as "influencing" him, where we really mean collaborating with him. It is performed not only by this corporate body of artists, but (in the case of the arts of performance) by executants . . . and . . . there must be an audience, whose function is therefore not a merely receptive one, but collaborative too. The artist stands thus in collaborative relations with an entire community. (p. 324)

authorship, to suggest that the forces resulting in a specific art work are cultural, political, and historical. But this still leaves unanswered the philosophical question: From whence novelty?

Psychologists tend to be dismissive of such approaches to creativity. If creativity is strictly a sociohistorical phenomenon, then how can one explain individuals who labor in obscurity during their lifetime, only to be judged geniuses who were "ahead of their time" long after death? The classic counterexample to social models of creativity is Mendel's genetics; but in fact, such examples are few and far between. To many, it seems heartless and deterministic to deny that creativity could be a psychological trait; it is believed that sometimes an individual is truly creative even when all of his or her peers think the individual is a crackpot. Partly because of the emphasis on scientific creativity, researchers often hold to a positivistic model in which objective truth exists apart from any intersubjective social construction; in such a domain, the truly original creative products will eventually become obvious to everyone. Of course, this could not be the case in nonscientific creative domains like painting or literature. The reality, as acknowledged by Csikszentmihalyi's (1990) model, is likely to be some complex and messy blend of the positivist and the sociological positions.

IMPROVISATIONAL PERFORMANCE

In a series of recent papers, I proposed that the study of group improvisational performance can contribute to the broader study of creative processes (Sawyer, 1992, 1995a, 1996, 1997). I focused on three improvisational performance genres: jazz, children's pretend play, and improvisational theater. Group improvisation is particularly valuable as a way of studying how social processes are fundamental in the evaluation of creativity. For example, in musical improvisation, when a performer plays a new melody or rhythm, there is no possibility for a separate, temporally distinct evaluation by the other performers, because they are playing simultaneously. As a result, evaluation during improvisation must be a constant, ongoing aspect of the creative process.

Collective verbal improvisation has been studied by sociolinguists (Gumperz & Hymes, 1972/1986), linguistic anthropologists (Bauman & Sherzer, 1974), and folklorists (Fox, 1974; Lord, 1960/1965), and musical improvisation has been studied by ethnomusicologists (Berliner, 1994; Monson, 1996; Nettl, 1974; Powers, 1980). These researchers' descriptions of group improvisational performance display remarkable parallels to Csikszentmihalyi's (1990) systems view of how social processes affect the evaluation and selection of creative products. In improvisational performance, interaction between creating agents is immediate, durationally constrained to the moment of creation, and is mediated by signs (whether linguistic or musical). The process of creation is coincident with the moment of reception and interpretation by other performers and the audience. In product domains, interaction between creating agents occurs over time, the interaction is mediated by ostensible creative products (in the case of linguistic creativity, text artifacts such as novels or poems), and the process of creation is distinct temporally and spatially from the receipt and interpretation of the product by other individuals.[6]

Verbal improvisational genres provide opportunities for novel contributions at every utterance turn. Studies of linguistic interaction, in both linguistics and the ethnography of speaking, suggest that any given utterance is subject to a variety of interactional forces: (a) the performer (i.e., the speaker) who contributes something new to the flow of interaction through *creative entailment*; (b) the other participants in interaction; (c) the definition/constraints of the performance genre;[7] and (d) the independent regimenting force operating on the utterance that derives from the prior course of interaction.

The metaphor of interaction as improvisation is similar in many respects to Mead's (1932, 1934) concept of the *emergent*. "The emergent when it appears is always found to follow from the past, but before it appears, it does not, by definition, follow from the past" (Mead, 1932, p. 2). Mead was commenting on the *contingency* of improvisational interaction: although a retrospective examination reveals a coherent interaction, each social act provides a range of creative options, any one of which could have resulted in a radically

---

[6]In many product domains, the creative process involves social interaction such as collaboration and brainstorming. This creative process can, of course, be considered a form of interactional improvisation, just like any other conversation. The study of improvisation can increase understanding of how these social processes contribute to product creativity as well. However, the historical interaction, mediated by ostensible products, is unique to product domains, where the product is generated by, and comes temporally after, the (collaborative) process. In improvisation, the product and process are synonymous.

[7]Whether or not culturally recognized as such. In fact, more ritualized interactional genres are more likely to be noted as genres in the folk theory of the culture; more improvisational genres, including various types of "everyday conversation" such as gossip and information exchange, are often not recognized as "verbal performance genres" per se. This "taken for granted" aspect of many forms of improvisation is one factor in their neglect by creativity theory, which has instead focused on highly marked creative genres.

different performance. The emergent was the fundamental analytic category for Mead's philosophy, and the paramount issue for social science. The difficulty, Mead (1932) pointed out, is that once the emergent (read "transcripted performance") appears, the analyst attempts to "rationalize" it, showing (incorrectly) that it can be found "in the past that lay behind it" (p. 14). Mead's observations have an uncanny predictive validity when one examines the ensuing history of research in cognitive science and conversation analysis; rather than exploring the improvisational, contingent nature of interaction, most research has focused on "structuralizing" models of scripts, frames, discourse grammars, or routines. The same developments are found in creativity theory: Research has focused on creative genres that generate static, ostensible products, rather than on the contingent creative processes found in performative genres.

Using the notion of the emergent, one can characterize the process of interactional creativity during verbal improvisation as follows (see Fig. 13.2). All performers are constrained to act within the performance genre. A given performer's turn (whether speaker order is prespecified by the genre definition or whether it is collectively determined, as in ordinary conversation) is more narrowly constrained by the emergent. The nature of this constraint is unique and specific to the performance and the moment of interaction. In improvisational performance genres, the performer is expected to contribute something original to the performance in each turn, through the act of creative entailment. In the choice of creative entailment, the performer is subject to the constraints of the emergent operative at his or her turn. After the performer's turn, the other participants in the performance evaluate the turn, and the subsequent interaction determines to what extent the creative entailment resulting from the turn affects the (still evolving) emergent. A more skillful creative entailment is more likely to enter the emergent, thus operating with more force on subsequent turns. Thus, there is a continuing process: A performer, constrained by the collectively created emergent, originates an utterance with some creative entailment; the interlocutors, through their responses in subsequent utterances, collectively determine the extent to which this utterance enters the emergent; the new emergent then similarly constrains the subsequent speakers. Throughout, the "meta-regimentation" of genre definition controls many properties of this interactional process (e.g., how much creative entailment is considered acceptable, how speaker's turns are allocated, how speakers form utterances that retain coherence with the prior emergent).

Evaluation processes are constant and essential to the characterization of improvisational performance. Improvisational genres require innovations—creative entailments—from the performers; yet

```
                E(t) = the emergent active for a specific interactional time (t)
                   ( E(1) )   ( E(2) )   ( E(3) )   ( E(4) )     The emergent
   Vectors of
indexical presupposition
                                                              Portion of entailment
   Performers   P(1)       P(2)       P(3)       P(4)         entering the emergent
                                                              after evaluation by others
   Indexical
   entailments

                                                              Other performers

   interactional time
```

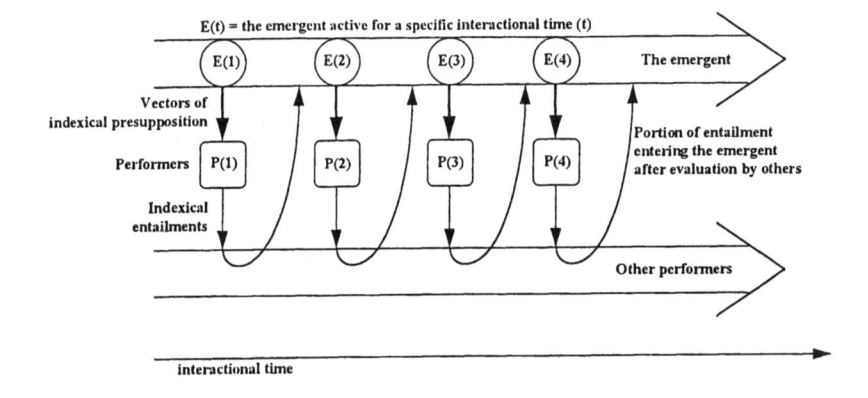

Figure 13.2. Improvisational interaction

these entailments are subject to a social process of evaluation. When a performer introduces a new creative entailment, the entire group of performers collectively determines whether that entailment will be accepted into the emergent, ongoing performance.

Because the emergent is a collective effort, an innovative entailment will not enter the emergent unless it is accepted by the coperformers. They collectively have the option of accepting the innovation (by working with it, building on it, making it "their own"), rejecting the innovation (by continuing the performance as if it had never occurred), or partially accepting the innovation (by selecting one aspect of it to build on, and ignoring the rest). This evaluative decision is a group effort, and cannot be identified clearly with any specific moment in time, nor with any single individual. The performance may evolve for some time before it becomes clear what has or hasn't been accepted. For example, in an improvised dramatic performance, a suggested plot twist may not be clearly integrated into the play until 10 or 15 minutes after its introduction. In many cases, the performers do not know what will happen either because no single individual has the authority to make these evaluative judgments. This uncertainty is inherent to improvisational performance.

The characteristics of improvisational evaluation just outlined do not fit neatly into any of the theories of creativity summarized here. In music, the evaluation occurs simultaneously with the entailment being evaluated, making it difficult to identify an "evaluation stage" (in verbal improvisation, there is a slight temporal delay between speakers). Evaluation is a collective, social process, making it difficult to associate it with individual intentionality or agency. Finally, the result of the evaluation may not be obvious until some time after the entailment.

IMPROVISATION AND PSYCHOLOGICAL MODELS OF EVALUATION

I have discussed two broad classes of improvisational performance: musical and verbal, focusing on jazz and improvisational theater. In group verbal improvisation, the performers take turns: Only one performer speaks at a time. Whether the proposed plot twist is accepted is determined subsequently, by the ensuing conversational flow. However, in musical improvisation such as jazz, the performers do not take turns: All instruments are performing simultaneously. This parallel performance is a special puzzle for the staged models of creativity. How can separation occur between the preparation, insight, and evaluation stages, when the time constraints of a performance do not allow conscious reflection and evaluation?

In Sawyer (1992), I reported on an interview study in which jazz musicians were asked about their creative processes during improvisational performance. A prominent theme of these interviews was the complex interaction of both conscious and nonconscious processes during an improvisation. Jazz musicians uniformly expressed a preference for a mental state during performance in which the "intellectual" aspect is minimized. During a performance, musicians move along a continuum between two poles: at one extreme, consciously directing the solo, and at the other, playing in a "heightened state of consciousness" in which the conscious mind seems removed from the process, and the solo seems to come from a deeper place:

> I find what I'm playing is sometimes conscious, sometimes subconscious, sometimes it just comes out and I play it; sometimes I hear it in my head before I play it, and it's like chasing after it, like chasing after a piece of paper that's being blown across the street; I hear it in my head, and grab onto it, and follow it; but sometimes it just comes out, it falls out of my mouth. . . . When you start a solo, you're still in thinking mode; it takes a while to get yourself out of thinking mode . . . and you start giving yourself a little line to follow along, and you start following along that line, and if it's a productive thought, way of expressing yourself, you keep following it, and after a while it's like getting farther and

farther into your mind, a way of burrowing in; and if you find the right thread to start with, intellectually, and keep following it, feeling it, you can turn it into something. (pp. 256-257)

Jazz musicians believed that their solos were better when they were maximally nonconscious. Simultaneously, the musicians realized that some conscious awareness was always essential: The "inner" performance state must be balanced with a simultaneous awareness of the other musicians, or of the song form:

It's all a matter of listening to the people you're playing with. . . . This is a real difficulty—you have to be able to divide your senses, but still keep it coherent so you can play, so you still have that one thought running through your head of saying something, playing something, at the same time you've got to be listening to what the drummer is doing. (p. 257)

There is a constant tension between fully conscious and fully nonconscious performance, and each musician must continuously resolve this tension to achieve a balance appropriate to the moment.

Thus, it seems that in jazz improvisation, ideation and evaluation can occur at both conscious and nonconscious levels, in some cases simultaneously: "Sometimes I catch myself playing things that I like, or ideas that came from somewhere and I can't exactly see where" (Sawyer, 1992, p. 257). When a performer's nonconscious component is active, the more conscious levels of processing may continue to evaluate ideas generated at the nonconscious level. The conscious activities of monitoring other musicians or attempting to stay aware of the song form may likewise contribute ideas to the ongoing nonconscious generation. These dual phenomena suggest that these creativity theories may need to be extended to accommodate dual stages of ideation and evaluation. In contrast to product creativity, which can be viewed as a largely conscious process with only occasional "inspiration" from a nonconscious source, in improvisational creativity the nonconscious contribution is reported to be salient, continuous, and essential.

Jazz musicians frequently discussed an internal tension between their own personally developed "patterns" or "structures" and the need to continually innovate at a personal level, to continue growing musically. Musicians practice and perform the same songs repeatedly, and can often express themselves more effectively when they have a predeveloped set of musical ideas available. However, if this process is carried too far, the spontaneous, improvisational nature of the performance is compromised. Jazz musicians are aware of the tension between the need to develop ideas in advance and the potential for a gradual evolution toward patterned rigidity: "Sometimes you get technically good with the chords, you can start to feel constrained; if you reach that point, it would be freeing, to free your ears to play a note, that normally wouldn't belong there" (Sawyer, 1992, p. 260). Musicians often characterize "mistakes" in this manner; they perform a valued function of interrupting the prearranged ideas and forcing an innovative alternative. A mistake is a note that "gets by" the preconscious evaluative stage, but then fails the conscious evaluative test.

All of these points raise a fundamental issue for staged psychological models: Is it appropriate to represent creativity as occurring in sequential stages? In improvisational performance, it is unclear whether there are distinct creative stages corresponding to divergent and convergent processes. If there is such a thing as evaluation, it must occur in part at the ideation stage; otherwise, too many ideas would be generated for the limited processing capacity available during live performance. The presumed evaluation stage would be overwhelmed, unable to properly filter the large number of musical ideas. We know that this is not what happens, because then there would be a lot of "bad" ideas getting through, and a jazz performance would have a random quality. This is true, in part, of improvisation: One never knows which nights a band will be "on" or not; and it remains the case that some bands and musicians are better than others. Clearly, some form of evaluation does occur, although perhaps less than in product creativity. It is this uncertainty that results in the tension and excitement of experiencing an improvisational performance.

CONCLUSION

The phenomenon of improvisational performance suggests two sets of implications for theories of evaluative processes. First, more sophisticated psychological models of the creative process are needed. Sequential, staged models of creativity are inadequate to explain psychological processes during improvisational performance. This discussion of improvisation clarified and emphasized the dual uses of the concept of evaluation in creativity research: Evaluation has been referred to both as a preconscious and as a conscious stage. My interviews (Sawyer, 1992) with jazz musicians suggested that both of these stages are operating in parallel during musical performance. Improvisation problematizes frameworks that suggest a sequential cognitive process for creativity.

Runco (1993) argued at length that evaluation processes must take place during divergent thought, beyond conscious awareness. Without some filtering at the ideation stage, random ideas unrelated to each other—and unrelated to the problem at hand—would overwhelm the system. Runco referenced a series of studies that showed that the ideas generated are not unrelated, but instead reflect associative patterns (Mednick, 1962; Runco & Okuda, 1991). Thus, even if it is psychologically meaningful to distinguish ideation from evaluation, to distinguish divergent and convergent thought, there is no compelling reason to insist that they cannot occur in parallel. Both types of thought may be constant, ongoing components of the creative mind.

Another question raised by improvisation is the cognitive structure of preconscious evaluation. In Csikszentmihalyi and Sawyer (1994), we proposed that evaluation processes result from an internalization of the social processes of person-domain-field. An evaluation is, in part, a judgment about whether or not the new insight will be acceptable to the field, and how it can be integrated with the domain (through an appropriately skillful elaboration). Thus, when an individual evaluates the new idea, whether during a preconscious evaluation or a conscious evaluation, knowledge of the domain and field plays an important role. Because of the long period of professional socialization required by most creative domains, there is ample time for this social process knowledge to be internalized, even "automatized," by creative individuals. We hypothesized that this social process knowledge was internalized to such an extent that it took effect at the preconscious level of evaluation. This is part of what it means to be expert in a discipline: to have this almost intuitive ability to judge what is an interesting problem, or what is a potentially valuable solution. This judgment involves an internalized representation of the social processes of the discipline.

By proposing that creative evaluation results from an internalization of social processes, I have been inspired by American pragmatism. The pragmatists, including James (1905), Dewey (1934), and Mead (1934), suggested that mental processes were a reflection of social processes. I propose that preconscious and conscious evaluative processes may be isomorphic to social processes, with the creative individual having internalized the domain of activity. If it is not simply a coincidence that social processes of evaluation display a similar processual pattern to intrapsychic processes of evaluation, then it would be interesting to explore why and how these parallels exist. Perhaps the psychology of creativity is, in fact, the social process of creativity, absorbed and internalized by those individuals called "creative."[8]

---

[8] It is much more common in recent creativity theory to reference Vygotsky as the source of the social internalization hypothesis (Runco, 1993; Smolucha, 1992); yet the American pragmatists predate Vygotsky's original Russian publications, and tend to be better elaborated versions of a social internalization theory (see also Lawrence & Valsiner, 1993; Sawyer, 1995b, 1997).

The second set of implications relates to interpersonal processes of evaluation. In Csikszentmihalyi's (1990) systems view, these processes take effect after the individual's creative process is complete. The individual's role is to generate variation, in the form of a new creative product, at the social system level. The social group then filters and selects among new products to evaluate which are appropriate to enter the domain. From the historical perspective, changes to a domain depend on both group-level evaluative processes and psychological processes. Social groups play an essential role in evaluating creative products. An individual's evaluative filter may be faulty; he or she may propose creative products that the field determines are uninteresting, repetitive, or wrong. This is the definition of crackpots, eccentrics, or perennial inventors with hundreds of patents at the patent office, and no money in the bank.

Improvisation is unlike product creativity in that one cannot identify a temporally distinct evaluation stage. The social filtering occurs in parallel with the creative process of each performer, in the same way that each performer's evaluative processes must be operating in parallel with his or her internal psychological processes of ideation. Thus, not only must intrapsychic evaluation occur in parallel with ideation; interpsychic evaluation also occurs in parallel with creative performance.

The systems model has implications at the intrapsychic level as well because I have proposed that intrapsychic processes may be internalizations of social processes. Studies of both the social and intrapsychic processes of creativity could have mutually beneficial implications. The social processes active in most creative domains are difficult to study directly. The evolution of a new scientific model may involve years of apprenticeship, lab work, and collaboration with colleagues. It is simply not feasible to study all of these social influences empirically. Creativity researchers have approached these issues indirectly through interviews (Csikszentmihalyi & Sawyer, 1994) or the examination of log books and journals (Gardner, 1993; Gruber & Davis, 1988). In contrast, the social processes active during improvisational performance are salient and readily available to empirical analysis. The study of group improvisation could thus serve as a technique for the study of social influences on the creative process.

If psychologists someday provide an answer to the *ex nihilo* problem, it will most likely be in the form of an empirically supported cognitive or neuroscientific model that describes the mental mechanisms giving rise to true originality. Today, the psychological answer to this question is buried deep in the mind, beyond those processes that have yielded to cognitive and neuroscientific methodologies. This discussion suggests that the search for novelty should be conducted at both the psychological and the social levels. Even if true novelty is to be found in divergent processes, one can learn a great deal about creativity by focusing on evaluative processes. If evaluation and ideation are not completely distinct, as I argued in this chapter, then by studying evaluation, we may end up contributing a part of the answer to the *ex nihilo* question

REFERENCES

Baker-Sennett, J., & Matusov, E. (1997). School "performance": Improvisational processes in development and education. In R. K. Sawyer (Ed.), *Creativity in performance.* Norwood, NJ: Ablex.

Baker-Sennett, J., Matusov, E., & Rogoff, B. (1992). Sociocultural processes of creative planning in children's playcrafting. In P. Light & G. Butterworth (Eds.), *Context and cognition: Ways of learning and knowing* (pp. 93-114). Hillsdale, NJ: Lawrence Erlbaum Associates.

Bauman, R., & Sherzer, J. (Eds.). (1974). *Explorations in the ethnography of speaking.* New York: Cambridge University Press.

Berliner, P. (1994). *Thinking in jazz: The infinite art of improvisation.* Chicago: University of Chicago Press.

Bourdieu, P. (1977). *Outline of a theory of practice.* New York: Press Syndicate of the University of Cambridge.

Bourdieu, P. (1993). *The field of cultural production: Essays on art and literature.* New York: Columbia University Press.

Bruner, J. (1990). *Acts of meaning.* Cambridge, MA: Harvard University Press.

Campbell, D. T. (1960). Blind variation and selective retention in scientific discovery. *Psychological Review, 67,* 380-400.

Cole, M. (1985). The zone of proximal development: Where culture and cognition create each other. In J. V. Wertsch (Ed.), *Culture, communication, and cognition: Vygotskian perspectives* (pp. 146-161). New York: Cambridge University Press.

Collingwood, R. G. (1938). *The principles of art.* New York: Oxford University Press.

Crease, R. (1993). *The play of nature: Experimentation as performance.* Bloomington: Indiana University Press.

Csikszentmihalyi, M. (1988). Society, culture, and person: A systems view of creativity. In R. J. Sternberg (Ed.), *The nature of creativity* (pp. 325-339). New York: Cambridge University Press.

Csikszentmihalyi, M. (1990). The domain of creativity. In M. A. Runco & R. S. Albert (Eds.), *Theories of creativity* (pp. 190-212). Newbury Park, CA: Sage.

Csikszentmihalyi, M., & Sawyer, R. K. (1994). Creative insight: The social dimension of a solitary moment. In R. J. Sternberg & J. E. Davidson (Eds.), *The nature of insight* (pp. 329-363). Cambridge, MA: MIT Press.

Dewey, J. (1934). *Art as experience.* New York: Perigree Books.

Epstein, R. (1990). Generativity theory and creativity. In M. A. Runco & R. S. Albert (Eds.), *Theories of creativity* (pp. 116-140). Newbury Park, CA: Sage.

Feldman, D. H. (1988). Creativity: Dreams, insights, and transformations. In R. J. Sternberg (Ed.), *The nature of creativity* (pp. 271-297). New York: Cambridge University Press.

Feyerabend, P. (1975). *Against method.* New York: Verso.

Firestien, R. L., & Treffinger, D. J. (1992). Ownership and converging: Essential ingredients of creative problem solving. In S. J. Parnes (Ed.), *Sourcebook for creative problem solving* (pp. 157-161). Buffalo, NY: Creative Education Foundation.

Forman, E. A., & Cazden, C. B. (1985). Exploring Vygotskian perspectives in education: The cognitive value of peer interaction. In J. V. Wertsch (Ed.), *Culture, communication, and cognition: Vygotskian perspectives* (pp. 323-347). New York: Cambridge University Press.

Foucault, M. (1972). *The archeology of knowledge and the discourse on language.* New York: Pantheon Books.

Fox, J. J. (1974). "Our ancestors spoke in pairs": Rotinese views of language, dialect, and code. In R. Bauman & J. Sherzer (Eds.), *Explorations in the ethnography of speaking* (pp. 65-85). New York: Cambridge University Press.

Gardner, H. (1993). *Creating minds.* New York: Basic Books.

Gruber, H. E., & Davis, S. N. (1988). Inching our way up Mount Olympus: The evolving-systems approach to creative thinking. In R. J. Sternberg (Ed.), *The nature of creativity* (pp. 243-270). New York: Cambridge University Press.

Guilford, J. P. (1963). Intellectual resources and their values as seen by scientists. In C. W. Taylor & F. Barron (Eds.), *Scientific creativity* (pp. 101-118). New York: Wiley.

Guilford, J. P. (1968). *Creativity, intelligence, and their educational implications.* San Diego, CA: EDITS/Knapp.

Gumperz, J. J., & Hymes, D. (Eds.). (1986). *Directions in sociolinguistics: The ethnography of communication.* New York: Basil Blackwell. (Original work published 1972)

Hadamard, J. (1949). *The psychology of invention in the mathematical field.* Princeton, NJ: Princeton University Press.

Heider, F. (1958). *The psychology of interpersonal relationships.* New York: Wiley.

Hymes, D. (1962). The ethnography of speaking. In T. Gladwin & W. C. Sturtevant (Eds.), *Anthropology and human behavior* (pp. 13-53). Washington, DC: Anthropological Society of Washington.
James, W. (1905). *Psychology*. New York: Henry Holt.
Jones, E. E., & Nisbett, R. E. (1971). The actor and the observer: Divergent perceptions of the causes of behavior. In E. Jones, D. Kanouse, H. Kelly, R. Nisbett, S. Valins, & B. Weiner (Eds.), *Attribution: Perceiving the causes of behavior* (pp. 79-94). New York: General Learning Press.
Langley, P., & Jones, R. (1988). A computational model of scientific insight. In R. J. Sternberg (Ed.), *The nature of creativity* (pp. 177-201). New York: Cambridge University Press.
Lave, J. (1992). Word problems: A microcosm of theories of learning. In P. Light & G. Butterworth (Eds.), *Context and cognition: Ways of learning and knowing* (pp. 74-92). Hillsdale, NJ: Lawrence Erlbaum Associates.
Lawrence, J. A., & Valsiner, J. (1993). Conceptual roots of internalization: From transmission to transformation. *Human Development, 36*, 150-167.(Harvard Studies in Comparative Literature, No. 24.
Lord, A. B. (1965). *The singer of tales*. New York: Atheneum. (Original work published 1960)
Martindale, C. (1990). *The clockwork muse: The predictability of artistic change*. New York: Basic Books.
Mead, G. H. (1932). *The philosophy of the present*. Chicago: University of Chicago Press.
Mead, G. H. (1934). *Mind, self, and society*. Chicago: University of Chicago Press.
Mednick, S. A. (1962). The associative basis of the creative process. *Psychological Review, 69*, 222-232.
Milgram, R. M. (1990). Creativity: An idea whose time has come and gone? In M. A. Runco & R. S. Albert (Eds.), *Theories of creativity* (pp. 215-233). Newbury Park, CA: Sage.
Monson, I. (1996). *Saying something: Jazz improvisation and interaction*. Chicago: University of Chicago Press.
Nettl, B. (1974). Thoughts on improvisation: A comparative approach. *The Musical Quarterly, 60*, 1-19.
Ohlsson, S. (1984). Restructuring revisited: An information processing theory of restructuring and insight. *Scandinavian Journal of Psychology, 25*, 117-129.
Perkins, D. N. (1988). The possibility of invention. In R. J. Sternberg (Ed.), *The nature of creativity* (pp. 362-385). New York: Cambridge University Press.
Poincaré, H. (1913). *The foundations of science*. New York: The Science Press.

Powers, H. S. (1980). Language models and musical analysis. *Ethnomusicology, 24,* 1-60.
Rogoff, B. (1982). Integrating context and cognitive development. In M. E. Lamb & A. L. Brown (Eds.), *Advances in developmental psychology* (pp. 125-170). Hillsdale, NJ: Lawrence Erlbaum Associates.
Rogoff, B. (1995). Observing sociocultural activity on three planes: Participatory appropriation, guided participation, apprenticeship. In J. V. Wertsch, P. del Rio, & A. Alvarez (Eds.), *Sociocultural studies of mind* (pp. 139-164). New York: Cambridge University Press.
Ross, L. (1977). The intuitive psychologist and his shortcomings: Distortions in the attribution process. In L. Berkowitz (Ed.), *Advances in experimental social psychology* (Vol. 10, pp. 173-220). New York: Academic Press.
Runco, M. A. (1990). Implicit theories and ideational creativity. In M. A. Runco & R. S. Albert (Eds.), *Theories of creativity* (pp. 234-252). Newbury Park, CA: Sage.
Runco, M. A. (1993, May). *Critical creative thought.* Wallace Symposium, University of Kansas, Lawrence, KS.
Runco, M. A., & Albert, R. S. (Eds.). (1990). *Theories of creativity.* Newbury Park, CA: Sage.
Runco, M. A., & Chand, I. (1994). Problem finding, evaluative thinking, and creativity. In M. A. Runco (Ed.), *Problem finding, problem solving, and creativity* (pp. 40-76). Norwood, NJ: Ablex.
Runco, M. A., & Okuda, S. M. (1991). The instructional enhancement of the ideational originality and flexibility scores of divergent thinking tests. *Applied Cognitive Psychology, 5,* 435-441.
Runco, M. A., & Smith, W. R. (1992). Interpersonal and intrapersonal evaluations of creative ideas. *Personality and Individual Differences, 13,* 295-302.
Sawyer, R. K. (1992). Improvisational creativity: An analysis of jazz performance. *Creativity Research Journal, 5,* 253-263.
Sawyer, R. K. (1995a). Creativity as mediated action: A comparison of improvisational performance and product creativity. *Mind, Culture, and Activity, 2,* 172-191.
Sawyer, R. K. (1995b). A developmental model of heterglossic improvisation in children's fantasy play. *Sociological Studies of Children, 7,* 127-153.
Sawyer, R. K. (1996). The semiotics of improvisation: The pragmatics of musical and verbal performance. *Semiotica, 108*(3/4), 269-306.
Sawyer, R. K. (1997). *Pretend play as improvisation: Conversation in the preschool classroom.* Norwood, NJ: Lawrence Erlbaum Associates.

Sawyer, R. K. (1999). The emergence of creativity. *Philosophical Psychology, 12*(4), 447-469.
Silverstein, M. (1985). Language and the culture of gender: At the intersection of structure, usage, and ideology. In E. Mertz & R. J. Parmentier (Eds.), *Semiotic mediation: Sociocultural and psychological perspectives* (pp. 219-259). Orlando, FL: Academic Press.
Simon, H. A. (1977). *Boston studies in the philosophy of science: Vol. 54. Models of discovery.* Boston: Reidel.
Simonton, D. K. (1988a). Creativity, leadership, and chance. In R. J. Sternberg (Ed.), *The nature of creativity* (pp. 386-426). New York: Cambridge University Press.
Simonton, D. K. (1988b). *Scientific genius: A psychology of science.* New York: Cambridge University Press.
Smolucha, F. C. (1992). The relevance of Vygotsky's theory of creative imagination for contemporary research on play. *Creativity Research Journal, 5,* 69-76.
Sternberg, R. J. (Ed.). (1988). *The nature of creativity.* New York: Cambridge University Press.
Stigler, J. W., Shweder, R. A., & Herdt, G. (Eds.). (1990). *Cultural psychology: Essays on comparative human development.* New York: Cambridge University Press.
Vygotsky, L. S. (1978). *Mind in society* (A. Kozulin, Trans.). Cambridge, MA: Harvard University Press.
Vygotsky, L. S. (1986). *Thought and language* (E. Hanfmann & G. Vakar, Trans.). Cambridge: MIT Press. (Original work published 1934)
Wallas, G. (1926). *The art of thought.* New York: Harcourt, Brace, & World.
Wertsch, J. V. (1985). The semiotic mediation of mental life: L. S. Vygotsky and M. M. Bakhtin. In E. Mertz & R. J. Parmentier (Eds.), *Semiotic mediation: Sociocultural and psychological perspectives* (pp. 49-71). Orlando, FL: Academic Press.
Wertsch, J. V. (1992). Keys to cultural psychology. *Culture, Medicine, and Psychiatry, 16,* 273-280.

14

MOTIVES FOR CRITICISM: SOME THEORETICAL SPECULATIONS AND INTROSPECTIVE DATA

Jock Abra
University of Calgary

Evaluation is an inescapable aspect of creative work. *Creativity* usually carries positive connotations (Stein, 1974), thus it must achieve products that possess not only novelty and originality but value, quality, merit, or the like. These attributes are unavoidably matters of opinion (Pirsig, 1974), so what most distinguishes art and science from problem solving (Abra, 1988a) is that the appropriateness of any solution is decided by subjective rather than generally agreed on criteria. As a result, disagreements will be common. Given this state of affairs, those persons known as critics who render such judgments must play seminal roles. Indeed, whether a product attains renown or oblivion may depend as much on their attitudes, motives, and moods as on its own intrinsic qualities. As one example, most lists of history's great achievers contain far more men than women. A host of explanations is possible (Abra & Valentine-French, 1991), but one would have it that most influential critics of the past have been male, causing their judgements to reflect the biases of their sex: "This is an important book, the critic assumes, because it deals with war. This is an insignificant book because it deals with the feelings of women in a drawing room" (Woolf, 1977, p. 51).

But despite critics' importance there has been, apart from a few informal anecdotes and interviews (Hickenlooker, 1991; Rosner & Abt, 1976), little discussion about their psychological characteristics, a considerable void in the creativity literature. My main purpose here, therefore, is to make a start at reversing this situation by advancing some hypotheses and flying some kites, one way tried and true to attract scholarly attention to deserving but overlooked topics (Abra, 1994, 1997). However, I also report some data to allow these speculations to be empirically evaluated.

Primary interest is on the motives that impel the critic. Eminent creators display remarkable persistence and dedication (Simonton, 1984) and understanding the origins of these qualities may go far toward explaining their success (Abra, 1997). There is no apparent reason why the same would hold for critics, but their motives are equally puzzling and thus exert the same fascination, because neither activity, when examined with the detached eye of rationality, makes a great deal of sense. Both fly in the face of every known behavioral law (Skinner, 1971), causing one to wonder why anyone of sound mind would engage in them. Creative work, especially the artistic type, holds out many negative reinforcers—frustration, traumatic and ego-destroying failure, and insufficient material reward, to name only a few—that seem to far outweigh any euphoria or public adulation and the same is true in spades for critics. Of the incentives that Freud (1963) famously held out for the creator—honor, power, wealth, fame, and the love of women—critics may realistically hope only for the second and fourth (in its adjective form prefixed by "in") coupled with a plethora of sticks such as hatred and ridicule. The following comments typify the reactions they may expect:

> There is no scorn more profound, or on the whole more justifiable, than that of the men who make for the men who explain. Exposition, criticism . . . is work for second-rate minds. (Hardy, 1983, p. 386)

> Critics are like fleas; they love clean linen and adore any form of lace. . . . Eternal mediocrity living off genius by denigrating and exploiting it! Race of cockchafers slashing the finest pages of art to shreds. . . . How rare it is to see a critic who knows what he's talking about. (Flaubert, cited in Barnes, 1985, pp. 173-174)

> Critics are like eunuchs in a harem: they know how it's done, they've seen it done every day, but they're unable to do it themselves. (Behan, cited in Winokur, 1992, p. 72)

> Drooling, driveling, doleful, depressing, dropsical drips. (Beecham, cited in Winokur, 1992, p. 73)

Nor are such attitudes a recent development. Genesis has it that one result of original sin was the ability "to know good from evil," and the New Testament warns:

> Judge not, that ye be not judged. For with what judgment ye judge, ye shall be judged: and with what measure ye mete, it shall be measured to you again. (*Mathew* VII: 1-2)

Still, the Old Testament does devote two entire books to Judges, who are highly esteemed as epitomies of wisdom and virtue: "Nevertheless, the Lord raised up judges, which delivered [The Israelites] out of the hand of those that spoiled them" (*Judges* II: 16). Furthermore God, having completed His/Her/Its work as Creator Par Excellence, has reportedly taken up criticism as a secondary career, to decide for each of us whether we deserve Eternal Bliss or Damnation. Few mortal critics, however powerful, can dish out accolades or stones that remotely compare to these (although Carpenter, 1991, pointed out one exception that hopefully will not be fulfilled— the Ayatollah's death sentence on Salman Rushdie)!

In summary, in The Bible as elsewhere criticism provokes many of the same mixed, ambivalent reactions as does creativity (Arieti, 1976). Nonetheless, there are those who continue to practice it, suggesting that critics even more than creators must include among their attributes a goodly helping of masochism. Or as theatre prophet Gordon Craig said to Kenneth Tynan, "You have the right face for a critic . . . the look of a blooming martyr" (cited in Kenneth Tynan, 1961, p. 142).

The Critic's Task

That the critic's task is so colossally misunderstood is one reason for the abuse critics suffer. Their main purpose, it is widely believed, is to be destructive, to discourage innovation, and to severely punish those who dare risk it. Perhaps because the first requirement for survival is to avoid potential dangers, the human psyche takes far more note of negative than positive phenomena; professors invariably remember one student's harsh comment over a veritable chorus of approval ("That One Negative Comment," 1990). This being the case, even the odd act of censure by a generally encouraging critic will ensure a reputation as a sadistic assassin. Actually, eliminating critics would have catastrophic results. Even if it were possible, which I doubt (see later), quality work would soon disappear beneath a mass of mediocrity.

Arguably, therefore, their most crucial task is to recognize excellence, especially when genuinely innovative, and bring it to attention. The general public does usually prefer the familiar, so helpful interpretative commentary can enhance its appreciation. In this way John Martin of *The New York Times* served the fledgling modern dance movement as it struggled against the tide of the European import, classical ballet. By the same token, Popper (1972) saw criticism as among humanity's most admirable inventions. According to his doctrine of *falsifiability*, because scientific ideas can only be proven false, never true, science progresses by the disproof of erroneous ideas—in other words, through criticism. Thus, Popper disputed the prevalent belief that a totalitarian society, because decision making is more centralized, functions more efficiently than do open ones. By discouraging criticism it is less able to discover errors or adjust to change. Recent events in eastern Europe add credibility to this opinion.

Another source of misunderstanding is that laypeople would have critics evaluate each work on its own merits without intrusion of personal biases, and be "objective." Moreover, one school of criticism (Kisselgoff, 1976) agrees that it should aim not to judge but merely describe, allowing audiences to decide for themselves. Such approaches I find unappealing. First, critics become mere reporters and writing that is devoid of opinion is sterile, as Russell (1969) intimated when he claimed that books are held together by their point of view. More to the point, to ask for objectivity, let alone to follow such dreamy romantics as Rogers (1970) and Kohn (1986) and advocate avoiding judgment entirely and viewing every product as equivalent, is to ask the impossible. The tendency to judge is deeply rooted in the human psyche, well nigh a knee-jerk reflex. For example, after viewing a film, among the first questions one asks of his or her companions will assuredly be, "Well, what did you think of it?" One *assumes* that they will have an opinion. As Pirsig (1974) so persuasively (and stylishly) argued, value-free perception is not in humans repertoires; people cannot experience anything, be it films, hamburgers, or displays of home furnishings without evaluating them. So I would again second Russell (1969), that persons without bias do not exist. As is truly said: Everyone is a critic.

Criticism, in short, will not go away. It follows that it should be performed, certainly when success and careers are at stake, by the most capable and knowledgeable, who can compare new work to what has gone before and to the genre's possibilities. Not every opinion should carry equal weight, for as commercial television demonstrates, when majority rules, a catering to the lowest common denominator and a deluge of schlock will surely follow. As Hamlet advised the players:

> This overdone, or come tardy off, though it make the unskillful laugh, cannot but make the judicious grieve; the censure of the which one must in your allowance o'erweigh a whole theatre of others. (Act III: 2)

This is not to say that the enlightened are never wrong. Consider these morsels from Rigg's (1983) entertaining collection of "the worst ever theatrical reviews" (The Reverend Joseph McCulloch's comment that critics leave *No Turn Unstoned* provided her wonderful title):

- By Samuel Pepys, in his *Diary*, "*Romeo and Juliet* . . . is a play, of itself, the worst that ever I heard in my life" (p. 125), and again, ". . . saw *Twelfth Night* acted well, though it be but a silly play" (p. 136).
- By James Agate: "(Fred) Astaire is neither a stage-shaking dancer nor a world-shaking dancer" (p. 150).
- By Harold Hobson: "*Guys and Dolls* is . . . an interminable, an overwhelming and in the end intolerable bore" (p. 151).
- By George Bernard Shaw: "*Othello* . . . is pure melodrama; There is not a touch of characterization that goes below the skin" (p. 232).
- By Lord Byron: "Shakespeare's name . . . stands absurdly too high and will go down" (p. 277).

But despite gaffes such as these, such enlightened opinion must carry the day. If that ultimate critic, time, were in the pizza business it would soon go bankrupt, so leisurely is the pace at which it delivers its verdicts. In the meantime, that those legions who know nothing about art but know what they like should decide yay or nay is even less palatable.

The Relationship to Creativity

Another common misconception sees critics as failed artists, forced to fall back on this inferior career so that jealousy distorts their every perception. This belief will not stand scrutiny either. Some of the finest critics—Coleridge, Johnson, T. S. Eliot, and Mathew Arnold; Schumann, Berlioz, and Shaw; Truffaut and Goddard of the filmic French New Wave—need not apologize for their artistic credentials, and many a creator has like Dylan Thomas (Ferris, 1978) made a dreadful critic because as egocentric and stubborn in outlook as any successful creator must be, they have proved unable to brook any alternatives to their own approaches.

As well, effective criticism like creativity of any kind (Abra, 1988b) requires special talents. Appropriate instruction and environments are necessary to refine them (Kauffmann, 1976), but these experiences will only prove effective where some potential exists. Thus, critics of talent are as rare and arguably as valuable as are creators of other kinds. Absolutely requisite are the abilities to sense quality, especially in radically innovative work, to work out and explain to befuddled others why a given work does or does not possess it (reportedly, at first very few individuals could grasp Einstein's relativity proposals), and to interpret its various meanings and connotations, because these even its author may only dimly comprehend. Another necessity is a boundless enthusiasm for one's genre. Each new work, to get a fair hearing, must be approached with a fresh rather than jaded outlook, yet every critic must endure a numbing parade of mediocrity or worse. That the capacity to rebound diminishes is one likely reason why many eventually burn out (Simon, 1976).

Media critics at least must also be able to write well. Most in their own estimation (Rosner & Abt, 1976) took up their calling not because they failed at creating but because they wanted to write about a field that appealed to them so they have become successful writers, albeit of a special kind. As Cardus (cited in Daniels, 1976, p. 167), the respected music critic of *The Manchester Guardian* said, "A critic's job . . . is to produce literature." Thus great critics and creators both are distinguished less by their opinions or beliefs than by their reasons for holding them and by the style with which they defend them. As someone said, Shaw is more interesting when dead wrong than most critics are when they are right! In short, superior criticism like all great work will stand the test of time and reveal to the future "what it was like to be there on that night."

Most creators, among other things, try to express in external form an inner personal experience, whether of external or internal origin (Langer, 1951, 1953). The same may be said of critics, who part company only in that this experience arises from creative products contrived by others. Here is Oscar Wilde:

> The critic is he who can translate into another manner of a new material his impression of beautiful things. The highest, as the lowest, form of criticism is a mode of autobiography. (cited in Redman, 1959, p. 174)

Indeed, Camus (1956) intimated that every artist performs this critical function. The definitive metaphysical rebels, artists by implication criticize God's greatest concoctions by suggesting alternatives and improvements to them. In any event, that critics must rely on the work of others to do theirs explains still another routine, derogatory accusation, that they are parasites. Yet because criticism feeds on both life experience and creation, whereas the arts use only the first, Wilde, that master of paradox, saw it as superior (Kauffmann, 1976).

As a final rejoinder, criticism is an integral part of any creative act. According to most analyses (Hutchinson, 1949; Stein, 1974; Wallas, 1970), a major component of the process is *verification*, wherein an initially vague vision or idea is polished to achieve a product able to communicate that vision to others. The Mozarts who purportedly realize excellence in a single draft, even if not apocryphal (Perkins, 1981), are far fewer than the Beethovens and Brahms who constantly revise while sweating blood over every note. Indeed it is ability for such self-criticism that may most distinguish winners from also rans.

By the same token, in many opinions creators have much in common with both children (Gardner, 1982; Kris, 1952) and the psychologically disturbed (Becker, 1973; Rank, 1932), but are set apart precisely by this capacity for detached criticism and viewing their work through others' eyes. Psychotic artists on the other hand may achieve sometimes astonishing originality but they will never, on no account revise what they have done (Rothenberg, 1990). Once again, Oscar Wilde:

> That fine spirit of choice and delicate instinct of selection by which the artist realizes life for us, and gives to it a momentary perfection . . . that spirit of choice, that subtle tact [sic] of omission, is really the critical faculty in one of its most characteristic moods, and no one who does not possess this critical faculty can create anything at all in art. (cited in Redman, 1959, p. 175)

In short, critics and creators of other kinds are siblings. But not identical twins. There must be something different about those who would rather consume, judge, and interpret than produce creative work; as Ebert (1991, p. 365) said, "the function of the critic is to be an ideal member of the audience." Although critics should have at least learned the techniques and tried to practice that on which they comment, to appreciate the difficulties and hazards involved (Bookspan, 1976; Kisselgoff, 1976). Schrader, a film critic turned screenwriter (of such landmarks as *Taxi Driver* and *Raging Bull*) summarized the differences as follows:

> Criticism is essentially a cadaverous business: you perform an autopsy on something and try to determine how and why it lived. Screenwriting and film-making are much more embryonic—something is growing and you have to nourish it and not pass judgement on it until it is born. (Jackson, 1990, p. 134)

Now one could retort that criticism also focuses on a living entity (i.e., personal experiences engendered by creative ones), but Schrader intimated one likely distinction. To use Ornstein's (1972) language, criticism mainly demands intellectual/linear/left hemisphere activity, creation also the intuitive/nonlinear/right hemisphere kind. Thus, to borrow Getzels and Jackson's (1970) distinction between high IQ-high creatives and high IQ-low creatives, many critics may represent the second category. They "know the way but can't drive the car" (Kenneth Tynan, 1967, p. 171). Nevertheless, it is my premise that criticism has enough in common with creating that it can be tackled using similar approaches. These are described next.

METHODS OF STUDY

The Eclectic Approach

Both Guilford (1973) and Gardner (1988) advocate attacking creativity from several perspectives, and I too, after surveying various theoretical outlooks (Abra, 1988a), concluded that each has something helpful to offer. Therefore, for a given topic of concern, be it creativity's decline with age (Abra, 1989), gender difference (Abra & Valentine-French, 1991), or motivation (Abra, 1997), my eclectic approach adopts by turn each perspective's outlook, whether of a psychoanalytic, existential, behavioristic, or some other kind, to determine its account of that topic, so a variety of such accounts are realized. The same tactic is adopted here because its benefits are several. If as one is informed, nothing is so practical as a good theory, then a multiplicity should prove still more effective, especially when the aim is to stimulate discussion. Then too, Darwin asserted that generating more possibilities than can ultimately survive provides more alternatives among which selection can then choose. Likewise, the more kites one flies the better are the chances that a few will remain aloft.

Eclecticism need not follow Nature to the bitter end and select only the most viable possibilities while condemning the remainder to extinction. Rather, it can view them all as pieces in a complex puzzle, as not adversaries but complements, with each applying to some of the people some of the time. Moreover this seems a better premise to adopt here because criticism like creativity (Abra, 1997) is probably *multimotivated*, with not only different people but the same person at different times having differing aims. Eclecticism does invite intellectual inconsistency, but this is a minor danger to those who see "schizophrenic" as a less pejorative label than "narrow specialist."

The Introspective Method

In contrast to my previous applications of eclecticism, however, I also report some data gathered from people who actually do the work—in this case, critics—to evaluate the various speculations. Some such data concern hypotheses previously advanced (Abra, 1988a) about their likely personality characteristics, but of special interest will be their reactions to various motive possibilities. One obvious difference between psychology and the natural sciences is that the target of study, human beings, can and will evaluate every aspect of the body of knowledge, be it a theoretical idea, fact, or whatever, against their own experience. If it does not ring true on an introspective level and increase their understanding of that experience then it will be given little credibility, regardless of its other merits, and be thereby called into question. Thus, few people would claim to be expert about, say, physics or geology, but about matters psychological everyone thinks themselves qualified to comment and in a real sense they are. This is not to say that they know everything there is to know about psychology. Much of that knowledge is dormant, so an investigator's task is to bring it to light so that the personal relevance of a hypothesis can be evaluated against it. Hence, the questions put to critics about their motives.

Still and all, Nisbett and Wilson's (1977) several valid criticisms of introspection as a method must be answered (also see Howe, 1991). At base, they reduce to one undeniable fact: Most people are not very good at it, and this becomes still more likely when motives are the target, if Freud's notion is at all sound that many influential ones are hidden in an unconscious that by definition lies beyond ordinary awareness. Which may explain why creators, when asked about their motives, provide such uninformative answers as "Because I enjoy it!"

Nonetheless, one reason for introspection's failings, notably when used by the Wundt-Titchener consortium (Watson, 1963), may be that training subjects is not enough. Being an extremely difficult task, it may be that like creating (Abra, 1988b) only the talented few can carry it off, but if so, then creative persons represent promising possibilities. Several notions, notably Freud's (1963) of *flexibility of repression*, surmise that such persons must have unusual access to the unconscious. It supposedly provides the content for their work whose very essence, therefore, is to find some publicly available means to express and communicate private experiences, and given that this represents the essence of introspection as well, skill at it seems integral to creative success (Wallace, 1989). Moreover, if critics, when all is said and done, muse in verbal form about the experiences that a creative work induces, and if their genuine creativity is allowed, then they too should be adept.

As a second rejoinder, introspection's difficulties may be offset by judicious questioning. Asking only "Why do you do it?" is likely to yield equally vague answers, but inquiring whether more specific possibilities (i.e., the motives proposed by various theoretical perspectives) sound right intuitively may encourage affirmative responses. Focusing the introspective search in this way, so subjects know what they are looking for, should heighten accuracy, as does recognition compared to recall for memory searches (Hintzman, 1978). Admittedly, proposing specific possibilities may heighten suggestibility and cause subjects to observe what they expect, but in an exploratory investigation such as this, such risks are worth taking.

As for the objection that motives resist introspection because they are locked in the unconscious, this is troublesome when unflattering ones are involved, notably that critics might seek power or notoriety. However, I would contend that this should not be problematic for less threatening possibilities and also that even for these others, an answer's tone can be as suggestive as its content. A casual "No, I don't think so!" gives a different impression than vehement, angry denials that suggest someone who doth protest too much! And if nothing else, it will be useful to learn what critics rightly or wrongly *believe* their motives to be.

The Subject Population: The Varieties of Criticism

Critics come in many guises, practicing their craft under diverse conditions and in various fields. Oscar Wilde for one deplored such specialization:

> For a man to be a dramatic critic is as foolish and inartistic as it would be for a man to be a critic of epics or a pastoral critic or a critic of lyrics. All modes of art are one, and the modes of the art that employs words as its medium are quite indivisible. The result of the vulgar specialization of criticism is an . . . entire incapacity . . . to receive any artistic impression at all. (cited in Redman, 1959, p. 176)

Nevertheless, such specialties are as much a fact of critical life as of most others nowadays, so representatives from several are sampled. Therefore, these variations should be described because it is likely that for criticism as for creativity, ability in a given field such as music depends on both some general, widely applicable factors and on others specific to it (Spearman, 1927).

The arts and humanities, as against the sciences, present one obvious difference. Influential critics in most artistic fields apart from literature tend to be full-time professionals, whereas scientists, whether reviewing for journals or granting agencies, usually also do other creative work themselves; indeed, their reputation here more than for critical acumen is usually the cardinal reason for their employment. Several considerations follow. Because the latter may also face judgment from those they judge, a mutual scratching of backs may color the results, as will the presumably greater appreciation of the pain that negative assessments produce, however constructive and kindly worded (some arts critics, judging by the sarcasm of their pronouncements, have little clue on this score). On the other hand, judges directly involved may be less open to approaches that contradict their own, a troubling consideration because given modern science's realities, they have virtual life and death power over creators. Without grants and frequent publication, the latter literally cannot do their work, whereas although negative commentaries about painters and composers can certainly harm their careers, in the last analysis, if they can compromise on such luxuries as nutrition and domicile they can still practice their crafts, albeit in probable obscurity. After all, a writer needs only a typewriter, a large pile of paper, and an even larger wastebasket.

Another difference is the intended audience. The most visible arts critics, those in the media, aim at nonspecialist laypersons, scientists at more knowledgeable groups such as those who edit or read journals. Then too, the work that the latter evaluate is invariably new, whereas in some artistic fields, notably music and ballet, a great deal of it concerns the latest renditions of familiar warhorses, be it a Tchaikovsky symphony or yet another *Nutcracker*. Still, this does not hold for, say, visual art or literary criticism, revealing that the various arts also differ among themselves. In some such as those mentioned critics can contemplate works in solitude, but in others such as film and theater they are members of audiences whose collective reactions must affect their own. As well, some critics, notably of theatre, must function under time deadlines of the most stringent kind. It is obscene that due to a higher-up's obsession with topicality a critic should have 1 hour to consider and express his or her reactions to a work to which its producer has devoted several years of obsessive labor (Kauffmann, 1976).

Furthermore, the lay audience to which arts critics address themselves can vary, and so influence their role. In provincial centers, a critic with any sense of responsibility must attach high priority to encouragement and fostering growth. Certainly minimal standards must be set and gradually raised, but never at the expense of killing plants still implanting roots; presumably it is better to have inferior art than none at all! Such critics may also have to become politically involved by advocating and lobbying for adequate funding and recognition for the arts, as *Southam Newspaper*'s Jamie Portman has so tirelessly done in Canada. In cosmopolitan centers where such traditions are well established, critics can when necessary afford to be more negative.

Data Gathering: The Questionnaire

This questionnaire was submitted to 60 Canadian media, mainly newspaper critics of various arts. It had been planned to do likewise for scientists involved in grant and journal reviewing, but conclusions from preliminary, informal discussions with this group were unanimous so that this was not deemed worthwhile. Without exception, their involvement reflected a sense of duty to the profession, with the sole satisfaction being the periodic opportunity to experience and encourage promising new work. Each item on the questionnaire, other than those relating to personal information, posed a possibility that has been advanced and requested either a rating on a 7-point scale as to its seeming personal relevance, or an agree or disagree decision.

Preliminary Findings

The number of returns (27 or 45%) was gratifying for a mail-in survey, indicating substantial interest in the findings (feedback was offered if desired) or an unusually conscientious population. Regardless, it does add to the data's credibility. The respondents represented a variety of genres, and some of them covered several. Six different Canadian provinces were represented (although British Columbia, Alberta, and Ontario were disproportionately represented). However, the opinions they expressed did not vary systematically with these considerations so the data will be presented only for the population as a whole. Seventeen respondents were male, 10 female, with the number representing various age groups being 20 to 30 (n = 4), 31 to 40 (n = 9), 41 to 50 (n = 10), and 51+ (n = 4), and the number of years spent as a professional critic: less than 5 (n = 1), 5 to 10 (n = 12), 11 to 15 (n = 5), 16 to 20 (n = 2), 21+ (n = 7).

The reactions to each theoretical speculation are provided as that speculation is described in the section to follow, but those pertinent to the opinions already expressed in the introduction are presented now. First, when asked whether they wonder about their motives, 30.8% answered *frequently,* 53.8% *on occasion,* and only 15.4% *never,* so evidently the puzzlement earlier expressed is shared by most to some extent at least. As well, the supposition that criticism is multimotivated seems to be borne out. A possibility given a rating of 5 or higher presumably represents a fairly potent motive, and of the 23 statements, the mean number so rated was 8.9.

Table 14.1 contains reactions to some other opinions:

Table 14.1. Reactions to Opinions.

	Percentage Agreeing
Criticism is a creative activity	96.2
Critics are failed artists, like eunuchs in a harem	0.0
You have the right face for a critic, of a martyr	0.0
A critic knows the way, but can't drive the car	7.7
Criticism should be constructive	53.8
Criticism should never be cruel or sarcastic	34.6
Criticism should be objective	23.1
Criticism requires special abilities	57.7
The highest criticism is a mode of autobiography	34.6
Criticism is as inevitable as breathing	73.1
A critic is three things: a writer, a teacher and a thinker—and also a philosopher of sorts	76.9
You must have tried creating to do criticism	26.9
I look for whether they succeed on their own terms; I don't review a Disney film the way I review Truffaut	84.6
Saying yay or nay is the least interesting part; I only do it because that's what others want	53.8

THEORETICAL SPECULATIONS

Before these bases for introspection are introduced, a disclaimer is in order. A good number represent extensions of theories about creativity, yet rarely have their authors directly confronted the critical enterprise, so the analyses to follow are very much my interpretations. It is possible that those authors would find the words put in their mouths unpalatable. Moreover, the critics' reactions are expressed as percentage agreeing if the decision merely required this. However, for those involving a 7-point rating, the means and standard deviations of these ratings, along with the rank order of the means in the 23 statements so assessed, are presented.

Evolutionary Mechanisms

If among human beings the tendency to judge is truly reflexive, if as T. S. Eliot (1951, p. 714) asserted, "criticism is as inevitable as breathing," then a possibility exists of an advantage to survival over value-free reactions. In primitive environments, it is critical that stimuli be judged quickly and accurately as to their potential for benefit or harm, so a tendency to routinely notice such features would be adaptive. Thus, critics may in the last analysis merely refine and intensify this tendency, and base it on other criteria besides sheer survival value.

Adaptive mechanisms could have other effects as well. First, an important aspect of criticism, certainly in the arts and letters, is to relate a given work to others, to give it a context and discern general movements such as Romanticism or Impressionism. This practice first of all points to another similarity to creative work. In many opinions (Mednick, 1962; Poincaré, 1952), it too involves what Koestler (1970) called *bisociation*, drawing similarities between previously unconnected events, be it an artist discerning an effective metaphor or Darwin tying evolution to natural selection.

But more to the point, the practice also reflects a tendency to group various phenomena into the same category that offers substantial adaptive benefits and everyone does routinely. Were every stimulus to be treated as unique, past experience could not be put to effective use, nor the wildly heterogeneous external world responded to in any consistent or efficient fashion. Grouping stimuli together, be they shoes, lions, or VCRs, which although not identical are similar enough for practical purposes, makes the world seem more comprehensible. By the same token, placing innovative products in a lineage of traditions and trends can reduce the befuddlement they might otherwise invoke, and also unmask overpraised new entries that are little more than variations on previously voiced themes. Now many creators find this search for parallels objectionable because by implication it downplays the uniqueness of their work, but it can be valuable for consumers.

Finally, that critic *nonpareil*, Dr. Sam Johnson (1951), defended reliance on those ultimate judges, time and history, by taking a page from Darwin's book before it was written. While verifying Shakespeare's rights to immortality, he asserted:

> To works . . . of which the excellence is not absolute and definite, but gradual and comparative, to works not raised upon principles demonstrative and scientifick, but appealing wholly to observation and experience (i.e., creative works), no other test can be applied than length of duration and continuance of esteem. What mankind have long possessed they have often examined and compared, and if they persist to value the possession, it is because frequent comparisons have confirmed opinion in its favor. . . . The reverence due to writings that have long subsisted arises therefore not from any credulous confidence in the superi-

or wisdom of past ages, or gloomy persuasion of the degeneracy of mankind, but is the consequence of acknowledged and undubitable positions, that what has been longest known has been most considered, and what is most considered is best understood. (p. 444)

Selection mechanisms, whether exercised by humans or nature, operate slowly, but ultimately the cream rises to the surface.

Moreover, this tardiness can be beneficial because evaluation, like many other adaptive tendencies (including creativity itself), can be a mixed blessing, especially if exercised too soon. It can lead to half-baked, seemingly off-the-wall possibilities being rejected that given further development might prove fruitful. The primary goal of one pioneering technique to assist creative thinking, Osborn's (1963) *brainstorming*, was to minimize premature judgment especially of the derogatory variety. Unfortunately, this technique tends to work better in theory than in practice (Stein, 1974) because the judgmental tendency is so reflexive, so that obtaining an atmosphere where anything truly does go becomes a challenging business. Easier said than done!

Reinforcement Mechanisms

According to Skinner (1971), all behaviors are governed by their consequences; those that result in positives will persist, those in negatives or nothing will extinguish. On the face of it, then, both creative and critical behaviors are embarrassing because they apparently produce so few dividends and so many downers, yet both behaviors are extraordinarily persistent. Advocates can fall back on several defenses. First, partial reinforcement conditions increase resistance to extinction, so it may be these very mixed blessings that make these activities so durable. As well, the concept of reinforcement, if used with sufficient ingenuity, can be wonderfully circular and invulnerable to disproof, because for The True Believer a behavior's repetition provides evidence enough that reinforcement of some kind, however subtle, must be present; a behavior continues because it is reinforced and it must have been reinforced or it wouldn't continue. Furthermore, for Skinner at least, reinforcers must be delivered by an external source because if individuals could reinforce themselves (Amabile, 1983; Bandura, 1977) it would imply, unthinkably for such an arch-determinist, control over their own behaviors.

At any rate, reinforcement principles can encompass many creative phenomena, although difficulties do arise (Abra, 1988a). Certainly, many of the motives considered here could be interpreted in these terms, and at least one eminent critic, Dr. Johnson, was a strong advocate, asserting "No one but a blockhead ever wrote except for money . . . which is the only motive to writing that I know of" (cited in Bate, 1979, pp. 334, 331). Only 19.2% of the present sample agreed with this statement, but in any event could lucre, whether filthy or laundered, be the root of not only all evil but all virtue, at least of the literary kind?

The Search for Meaning

This possibility, like the previous ones, implies a motive shared by all humanity, but parts company in that it presumably occurs in no other animal. It has been most notably propounded by existentialists. Existence, as supposedly experienced, defies understanding. It suggests a myriad of interpretations that all seem equally valid, so truth and knowledge become personal and subjective rather than reliable. Yet this freedom to make of existence whatever one chooses engenders not euphoria but anxiety; it is certainty that provides security (Fromm, 1960), whereas "Opinion is the source of all suffering" (*Man Alive*, 1991). As Osborne's (1961) Martin Luther exclaimed, "I am a man struggling for certainty, struggling insanely like a man in a fit, an animal trapped to the bone with doubt" (p. 73).

Camus (1956, 1969) especially stressed existence's inherent absurdity. Although it makes no sense, people have an unquenchable need to try to understand it and this search for personally satisfying explanations, a search one realizes in advance is futile, gives existence its sole meaning. Thus, the legendary Sisyphus gained a perverse happiness from the futile and hopeless labor to which the gods had condemned him: pushing a rock up a mountain for all eternity. For Frankl (1984), too, having a sense of meaning to life is crucial or neurosis and depression will surely follow. Creative activities can provide that sense. Apart from the passionate commitment they invoke, they perhaps more than any other try to wrestle with and impose a personal meaning on an unformed medium. A blank canvass or slab of marble presents the same opportunities for many subjective interpretations as does existence itself, and once again none is objectively speaking more valid than another. Criticism could reflect the same mechanism, except that here it is an initially baffling creative work that instills the propelling insecurity. In a word, critics may be attempting to work out what it means to themselves, and why. Kael responded, when asked what she thought about a film, "I don't know, I haven't written my review yet" (cited by Simon, 1976, p. 176), and 50% of the present sample agreed with her answer.

Yet, it may be that both creativity and criticism attempt not so much to wrestle with and defeat as to escape from absurdity; Greene (1981) indicatively titled his autobiography *Ways of Escape*.

Both activities involve artificial worlds that offer the prospect of understanding and comprehension. Most novels and plays, for example, offer attributes real life seems to lack—comprehensible characters; plots with beginnings, middles, and ends; and above all control; we become masters rather than slaves of events. As Einstein asserted,

> One of the strongest motives that lead persons to art and science is flight from everyday life, with its painful harshness and wretched dreariness, and from the fetters of one's shifting desires. (cited in John-Steiner, 1985, p. 180)

Persons who immerse themselves in such worlds, whether to concoct or evaluate them, live in unreality. Is this one of the attractions?

Individuation and the Sense of Self

It is widely held (e.g., Rank, 1932) that *individuation*, setting oneself apart from others to gain a sense of uniqueness, represents another powerful human motive. Thus, for Sartre (1969), human anxiety also arises because humans have complete psychological freedom to choose their own actions, unencumbered by antecedent determinants of either nature or nurture. Every new act defines a momentary self, or being, which is therefore constantly under construction, changing unpredictably with each such act, so questions about "Who am I?" resist consistent answer quite as much as do those about the meaning of life. Nonetheless, one's fundamental project in existence, futile though it may be, is to seek permanent being, to unite the subjective and dynamic with the objective and unchanging. Every act one chooses supposedly serves this purpose, but creative ones would seem especially promising candidates, resulting as they do in products that are both a reflection of oneself and yet that once finished have the longed for constancy. Alas, any such satisfaction can only be momentary. We will continue to change while the product remains fixed as it was, no longer to reflect who we are.

To deny that people possess any permanent being or *essence* whatsoever surely goes too far. The humanists' notion of a semiconsistent potential or "real self" seems more plausible; although individuals may lack essence in the sense of a universal human nature shared by all (Stern, 1967), each person does have an essence that is individual and particular. Which in turn means that those arbitrary decisions do not so much define as *reveal* oneself to oneself. As Storr (1976) said, creative acts are *quests for identity*.

But whichever variation is preferred, criticism may also serve it. A value judgment I render about a phenomenon clarifies my sense of self. A fact is impersonal, something on which by definition everyone agrees. But the various impressions and associations that ambiguities such as Rorshach ink blots engender in me, my subjective reactions to puzzling things with which others may disagree, heighten my sense of how I as against others interpret the world. By striving to decide what I think about a creative product, and why, I learn that I am the person who holds this opinion and prefers such and such. The present group found these possibilities moderately appealing, with a statement describing them gaining a mean rating of 4.43 (SD = 1.81), ranking seventh.

And Sartre's (1969) contention that in these endeavors people are trying to make the subjective (opinion, value) objective, is persuasive. As individuals pass a judgment, do they not experience it in part as "true" and beyond dispute, even though they know rationally that it is not? If it expresses who the individual is that point in time, he or she will strongly resist attempts to change it, because that is tantamount to *denying* who that individual is. Similarly, any disagreement with it, the individual may *take personally*—because this questions who he or she is as a person. There is a lot of ego tied up in one's opinions. Arguments about value judgments can be enjoyable and fruitful, but not because people change their minds. On matters about which they feel strongly, how often do they? Rather, by attempting to convince others to change theirs, they form and discover their own.

The Need to Express

This need also sees creative activity as aiming more to satisfy oneself than others. It has been most persuasively voiced by Langer (1951, 1953). People are periodically afflicted with feelings that are too vague to be expressed precisely in words but that induce tension and demand release, so they try to give them tangible expression in external form, usually in symbols. For these, being equally ambiguous (Kreitler & Kreitler, 1972) and lending themselves to quite as many valid interpretations, are peculiarly fitted to capture feelings having these qualities. Thus, creative work's primary aim is not to communicate to others, which is all well and good if it happens but is at best a by-product of the process, but to *express for oneself*. Similarly, Arieti (1976) proposed that creators have vague but haunting images or *endocepts* in their mind's eyes, an ultimate entity that they are trying to express, as a rule not successfully because more often than not it remains tantalizingly just beyond reach.

Might the critic seek a similar purpose, differing only in that it is other creative works that initiate vague feelings and endocepts? The present sample found the possibility moderately appealing. The relevant statement achieved a mean rating of 3.14 (SD = 2.13), giving it a rank of 13, and 57.7% agreed with a corollary of Langer's views, that if marooned alone on a desert island with no chance that one's review would be read by others, one would still be motivated to write it. Still, in cases where this motive does operate, a problem arises. Langer was adamant that any attempt to interpret expressions in words is "vicious," a contradiction in terms. After all, they come about in the first place to capture a feeling that could not be put into words—if it could have been, it would have been—so any attempted interpretation must inevitably misrepresent them. Yet, just such attempts represent one essential aspect of criticism. This does not mean that Langerian mechanisms do not give rise to the activity, but that it would presumably have earned her disfavor.

The Search for Perfection

Freud's (1958b) contention, that only dissatisfied people create, is difficult to gainsay. Great creators in other respects may differ substantially, but far more often than not they are driven if not obsessed people (Simonton, 1984; Storr, 1976). One likely reason is their propensity for perfectionism. Even results that others admire, they find unsatisfactory, which in turn suggests that their work may represent a search for that elusive perfection. Given that creativity has long been seen as God's/the gods' bailiwick, every human creator may be seeking to realize Its/their by definition unblemished status. The desired perfection may come during the process, in those peak experiences (Maslow, 1970) that provide glimpses of existence at its best. It may come in the finished product, in that one episode in the novel or moment of critical insight that provides that rarity, a perfect realization of an endocept. Whatever: that Great Experimenter In The Sky, inflicting a partial reinforcement schedule of unrivaled cruelty, seems to dole out just enough such food pellets to encourage the persistent coming-back-for-more that such schedules always induce (Ferster & Skinner, 1957).

In any event, those who achieve great things conform to Browning, "Ah but a man's reach should exceed his grasp/ Or what's a heaven for," because two necessities are thereby ensured: eternal dissatisfaction and lofty aims. Those content to reach the summit of a foothill are not likely to conquer Everest. Granted, perfectionism can have unattractive aspects, notably that affliction that is so rampant among writers: procrastination (Pacht, 1984). How many who enjoy having written something will seize any excuse—sharpening pencils, making pots of coffee, phoning relatives—to avoid the doing? And critics are as susceptible to procrastination as any—Dr. Johnson (Bate, 1979) was one victim—because if one's standards are impossible to reach and an undertaking's only possible outcome is failure at least in one's own eyes, one will be understandably reluctant to begin. Therefore, those deadlines that so many critics deplore may be blessings in disguise.

Given perfectionism's importance, its emphasis by otherwise diverse theoretical accounts, albeit in various forms, is not surprising. For Sartre (1969), when creators try to unite the subjective with the objective they are also trying to emulate God, the only being actually able to carry off this project. Likewise Rank (1932) contended that *productive* (i.e., creative) personalities are most distinguished from the normal by their dissatisfaction, first and foremost with their mortality. This instills an intense desire to achieve godlike eternal life by perpetuating themselves in products in which their names can symbolically live on. And more than one critic, especially of ephemeral events such as dance, has admitted a desire to leave for the future a permanent record of the occasion. For the present sample, however, the notion that criticism tries to defeat mortality held few allures, achieving a mean rating of 2.04 ($SD = 1.60$) for a rank of 20th overall.

Gestalt accounts (Henle, 1974; Wertheimer, 1959) provide another perspective. Creative work begins with a gap, a sense of incompleteness or inconsistency in a situation because things do not quite add up. The preferred feelings of integrated unity that a genuine Gestalt provides are missing, generating desires to eliminate gaps. So an Einstein (Wertheimer, 1959) perceives them in situations that to a lesser light seem harmonious, and will settle for nothing less than solutions that completely restore the simple perfection of closure. In turn, another of criticism's attractions (M. Morris, personal communication, October 1993) may be that it allows one to contemplate the components of complex creative works with the detachment needed to perceive otherwise overlooked gaps, as well as possible ways to alleviate them. Whereas those actively involved in concocting such works, because of their intimate proximity to the individual trees, may miss the forests lurking beneath.

For Adler on the other hand, perfectionism related more to wishes for the future (Ansbacher & Ansbacher, 1956). In children, feelings of inferiority are supposedly inevitable, but one way to compensate is to construct an ideal self, the person that one wishes to become, and such *fictional goals* profoundly influence the prevailing approach to living or *style of life*. Similarly, for humanists (Maslow, 1962; Rogers, 1970), creativity is the definitive means to self actualization, to achieving one's maximum potential as a person, that real self.

Unfortunately, according to Adler ideal selves are buried in the unconscious mind, so time may be needed before a person realizes their calling; certainly this seems to be the case for many writers. Few child prodigies are found in this field (Feldman, 1980), and Shaw (1965) claimed that for some little time he no more thought of himself as a writer than a fish thinks of itself as a swimmer! Furthermore, criticism in particular seems to be a career to which most come relatively late in life. Very few youngsters grow up with dreams of becoming critics, an impression substantiated by the group here. None considered it seriously for the first time before age 21, and for other age ranges the percentages doing so were 21 to 25 (22.2%), 26 to 30 (25.9%), or 31+ (51.2%). Likewise, according to Maslow (1976), most people fail to self-actualize because of fear of the hard work and sacrifice required, of the arrogance and seeming hubris that it can suggest (see later), of the responsibility that follows from realizing one's destiny. Any or all of these might dissuade someone from a critical career, given its onerous, egocentric, and unsavory aspects.

But Bandura (1977, 1978) provided an unusually compelling perspective on perfectionism. In a certain situation, each person establishes an *internal standard* of the performance he or she expects of him or herself. Each person then evaluates his or her actual deeds therein against it, with perceived success depending more on that comparison than on performance per se. So, comparable achievement, such as a course grade may indicate success to one person, yielding pride and self-satisfaction, and failure to another, resulting in dissatisfaction or shame. Moreover, the same person may set different standards in different activities, being a perfectionist in one while elsewhere content to wallow in happy mediocrity.

How do high standards come about? A Skinner (1968) would emphasize shaping toward them; for behaviors of great difficulty (including the creative kind), one gradually demands ever more of oneself as reinforcement waits upon increasingly close approximations. Thus, Greer (1979) blamed the historic mediocrity of female painters in part on *poisonous praise* from others, the patronizing kind too easily won. Why strive to improve if lesser performance will gain the same rewards? Bandura, however, as usual stressed *vicarious conditioning*, imitating influential role models. Indicatively, most high achievers have had parents who were themselves perfectionists, who not only preached but themselves practiced such creeds as "anything worth doing is worth doing well" (Bloom, 1985).

The notion of internal standards has several implications for criticism. First, although some (Fulford, 1988) would not agree, to many critics (e.g., Daniels, 1976) one duty is to maintain standards of excellence and resist their deterioration, even when the less demanding public chastises them for this. Certainly, this seems to be a prevalent view among the present group, for the relevant statement achieved a rating of 5.46 (*SD* = 1.43), ranking third overall. So impossible to satisfy critics should not be, difficult to satisfy they must be because greater experience has presumably brought home to them the ultimate possibilities of their medium. Incidentally, those critics who are impossible to please may also reflect parental reactions, in this case insufficient love, which according to Pacht (1984) instills an excessive perfectionism that fosters not achievement but neurosis. The child may conclude that nothing less than flawless performance will earn that love and later impose these standards on others.

Regardless, the best critics, I suspect, are not jaded cynics but enthusiasts and eternal optimists. Each occasion provides another possibility for that greatest of privileges: witnessing firsthand the birth of a fresh new talent or certified masterpiece. Furthermore, this suspicion is strengthened by two questionnaire items. First, that which directly expressed this possibility had a mean rating of 4.39 (SD = 1.79) placing it eighth, but of even greater moment, the statement "I love the genre in which I do criticism, and I want to do what I can to assist and improve it" attained the highest rating of all, a mean of 5.93 (SD = 1.18).

That hope springs eternal in the critical breast may explain another intriguing aspect of its psyche, the sometimes venomous reactions to perceived incompetence. Disappointment is understandable, but why outrage as if one had been personally insulted? Wasted time and money, which may explain such reactions from other audience members, will not suffice here; attendance is the critic's job and admission is free. The *frustration-aggression hypothesis* (Kimble, 1961) is more helpful. Frustration supposedly results when anticipated goals are blocked (Amsel, 1958), as when one has hoped for miracles but encountered dross, and a predominant response to frustration is aggression, typically against the perceived source. Thus Shaw, wearing his critic's hat:

> The artist . . . who accounts for my disparagement by alleging personal animosity on my part is quite right. When people do less than their best, I hate them, loathe them, detest them, long to tear them limb from limb and strew them in goblets about the stage or platform. . . . The true critic is the man who becomes your personal enemy on the sole provocation of a bad performance and will only be appeased by good performances. (cited in Nathan, 1969, p. 11)

Of the present group, 23.1% agreed with these sentiments, and an identical percentage with a similar statement from Nathan (1969):

> Any normal critic must periodically be guilty of vulgarity and bad manners or he is a weak and ineffective critic. If a (creator) hits

me in the face with a contemptible cheese pie, I must hit him in the face in turn with an even larger and juicier critical equivalent. (p. 19)

Yet it may console the targets of such wrath that so many of them behave still more aggressively toward their own work when it falls short of the exacting standards set by their own internal critics, (known to Freudians as superegos). Not even the most sadistic critic would slash a canvass to ribbons, burn an entire manuscript representing several years labor, let alone resort to the ultimate self chastisement to which van Gogh, Mark Rothko, and Hemingway fell tragic victim: ending the creator's very life.

Still, the most perfectionistic creators cannot constantly maintain lofty standards. At times, even such a dauntless personification of unadulterated will power as Martha Graham (de Mille, 1992) will be tempted to sigh, "Aw, that's good enough," and now an external force—for Graham, accompanist/father-confessor/lover Louis Horst—is needed to demand improvements. And critics too, if as respected as was John Martin can also, by chastising more in sorrow than in anger, foster the discontent that the lapsed superego usually provides. Because whether called guilt or *cognitive dissonance* (Festinger, 1957), it is indeed a great motivator! But the feelings of the talented toward critics who perform this service must vacillate between love and hate. Be they coaches, teachers, or whomever, those who take on the responsibility of dragging talented people, kicking and screaming, to their maximum potential and accepting nothing less are doomed at times to be fiercely resented. If they are not, they are probably not doing their job. So, if as is seen here, many critics are motivated by desires to teach, then they must also be willing to take up this cross.

Erotic Needs

No discussion of motivation would be complete without psychology's most notorious contributions to this topic, those emanating from Freud (1958a). Creativity grows mainly from the defense mechanism of *sublimation*, the expression of socially unacceptable desires (primarily, needless to say, sexual/erotic ones) in socially acceptable ways. Thus, a work of art, like a dream, subtly expresses its creator's unconscious material in symbols, which the usual Freudian catalogue can decode to reveal the underlying pornography. But because creators rely on this material for their work, they must have that flexibility of repression that provides fuller access to it than others have. They must also have more of the child about them (Freud, 1958b); they indulge more freely in thinly veiled versions of play and other forms of childlike mentation to exploit the unconscious mind's outrageous, unrealistic possibilities (a possibility Kris [1952]), pursued with his notion of *regression in the service of the ego*).

How might all this clarify critics' activities? Not much, according to the present sample. The statement summarizing these possibilities obtained the lowest rating of all, a mean of 1.32 (SD = .77). Orthodox Freudians, of course, so ingenious at rescuing doctrine in the face of any and every finding, would take this to indicate that the defense mechanism of denial is at work. I prefer to deny denial! In any event, Freud's theory of developmental stages suggests other possibilities. First, if the typical creator leans toward childlike or id tendencies, the id's sworn antagonist, the superego, may in critics carry the day:

> you worthy critics . . . in the constraint which your intellect imposes on your imagination . . . are ashamed of the momentary and passing madness which is found in all creators. . . . You reject too soon and discriminate too severely. (Schiller, cited in Brill, 1938, p. 193)

Although not one of the present sample agreed with these assertions, if critics do not only suppress their own id-based possibilities but chastise any work wherein they suspect they lurk, then this does suggest a dominant superego. As does a fondness for judgment.

Still, at least one first-rate critic, Kenneth Tynan, could author among the most ribald theatrical productions ever, *Oh Calcutta*, outspokenly advocate untrammeled sexuality, and blatantly practice what he preached (Kathleen Tynan, 1987). While flying over Newfoundland he once began—in most un-English fashion, before they had even been properly introduced—to grope the comely female in the next seat. She immediately headed for the washroom, causing him to fear (needlessly as things turned out because she, as willing as any Barkis, wanted only to facilitate proceedings by removing her girdle) she had taken umbrage. He envisioned public humiliation in screaming headlines: CRITIC CHARGED: WOMAN GOOSED OVER GANDER! (p. 201).

Another difficulty. The superego is thought to first appear as a result of resolving the Oedipus complex, so excess of superego presumably reflects fixation in this, a relatively late stage of development. Whereas judgmental tendencies come about during the earlier, anal stage, so fixation here would seem a more likely beginning for prospective critics, particularly in this stage's later part that results in an *anal-retentive character*. This type supposedly displays such traits as orderliness and perfectionism (Hergenhahn, 1984) that also seem to typify critics (see later). Certainly more than one creative person believes that critics are overly anal retentive.

Ambition

This motive resembles the perfectionistic one. According to Hardy (1983), a talented young person's first duty is to be ambitious, as all great work has grown from this root. Similarly for Freud (1963). Although most wishes underlying the sublimation mechanism were unmistakably kinky, he also indicted those of ambition, notably in his claim that creators seek honor, power, wealth, fame, and the love of women—and not necessarily in that order. But anyone who aims high, whatever it be for, must not lack for self-confidence. Creative people do not (Barron, 1965; May, 1975) and several critics (Rosner & Abt, 1976) observed that it also takes arrogance to foist your judgments on others because this clearly assumes that those judgments are worthwhile. Furthermore, 53.8% of the present group agreed that it takes a lot of confidence and ego to do criticism. To complicate the picture, however, another statement to this effect achieved only a moderate rating, of 2.86 (SD = 1.80), placing it 14th overall, and the reverse possibility, that criticism does not result from but is a means to increase confidence and self-esteem, was even less enthusiastically received, its mean rating being 2.29 (SD = 1.38) for a rank of 17.

Be that as it may, one certified possessor of the necessary *chutzpa, The Toronto Star*'s late Nathan Cohen, routinely claimed that he was not just the best drama critic in Canada but the only one (Fulford, 1988) and in most opinions including his own, "devoted his life to creating one star—Nathan Cohen" (p. 124). (Adlerians, incidentally, might cite Cohen, a poor shopkeeper's son from the cultural backwater of Cape Breton, as a textbook example of overcompensation for inferiority.)

If ambition also impels critics then what, we might ask, are they ambitious for. The influential 18th century music critic, Dr. Burney, wanted acceptance by the wealthy and influential (Grant, 1983), and commenting on the art to which they attached considerable importance was a means to this end. Other likely incentives, although some would deny it (Kerr, 1970), are those that also reign among scientists (Merton, 1973; Roe, 1965): recognition and fame. It must be no mean ego trip to know that one's opinions carry great weight and to see them, even if lifted hilariously out of context, emblazoned on four-story high billboards. Thus criticism can be a high profile career, especially nowadays with the unprecedented coming of media superstars such as Siskel and Ebert. However in Schickel's (1991) opinion, the superstar phenomenon has harmed the profession, and for the present group these considerations held few attractions, garnering a mean rating of 2.68 (SD = 1.59), which placed it in a tie for 15th place. At any rate, other targets for ambition are best dealt with under other possibilities to follow.

Competence and Efficacy

According to both Bandura (1989) and Feldman (1980), people want to feel competent at something. There are few roads more conducive to unhappiness than being trapped in a career at which one knows one is not very good! As well, Guilford (1967) and Gardner (1983) argued convincingly that talent is field-specific, so potentially creative persons are at promise for not any and all endeavors but *for something*, such as mathematics, music, or athletics. The rejection of any wide-ranging component for creativity is debatable (Abra, 1993), but that specific talents must tell at least part of the story seems too sensible to be entirely off base. Who is not far better at some things than others? But if this much is accepted, then the aim of ambition could be to discover the niche where one's talents lie, as this would represent a crucial first step towards feeling competent—to realize, in the words of a song from *A Chorus Line*, "I Can Do That!". Indeed, Feldman held that a primary goal of education should be to assist this process of discovery, because minimizing the number of round pegs in square holes is in the best interests of both society and its individual members.

These considerations should influence prospective critics as much as anyone, especially if Jung's (1923) notion of personality types is valid. While famously distinguishing between introverts and extraverts, he also claimed that most creative people occupy the first category (and my informal impression is that very few critics are hail-fellows-well-met either). But of particular note, Jung also specified within each category four types of preferred psychological functioning (thinking, feeling, sensation, and perception). Thus came about *The Myers-Briggs Type Indicator* (Myers, 1962), which assesses four bipolar dimensions, with each extreme on one dimension representing one of the eight types. One such dimension ranges between judging and perceiving, so whereas MacKinnon (1978) found that prospective creators tend to fall toward the latter, scoring at the other extreme might help critics in the making identify their calling. Furthermore, the present sample tended to view such considerations as relevant. The motive of doing something, in this case evaluation and writing, at which they feel competent received a rating of 4.61 ($SD = 1.71$) and ranked sixth.

An influential role model might be another means to discovering one's niche. Even if talent is nonspecific, the desire to imitate such a one can determine the field in which it is manifest (Greenacre, 1971). But Walters and Gardner's (1986) suggestion is more appealing. *Crystallizing experiences* with seminal contributions to a field can set those at promise in it on their life's course, whereas those not so inclined are unaffected by that same experience.

Exposure to Wagner's music purportedly aroused Debussy from his dogmatic slumbers, and in Neville Cardus' case (Daniels, 1976), it was his predecessor at the *Manchester Guardian*, Earnest Newman who set him on his critical career. Some members of the present sample reported similar influences (Shaw, Tynan, and Robert Brustein were mentioned by several drama critics, and Edwin Denby by critics of dance) and overall they found the desire to imitate an admired role model to be a moderately relevant motive; it gained a mean rating of 3.64 (SD = 1.93) and ranked 12th.

Power, Competition, and Cooperation

According to accounts so far discussed, criticism is done mainly for oneself. Yet, because human beings attach great importance to interpersonal relations (Ansbacher & Ansbacher, 1956; Fromm, 1962), there is reason to suspect that these too might provide powerful propellents, and *communication of results* (Stein, 1974) might represent as necessary a stage in the critical as creative process. Because here again it would otherwise make little sense to risk the negative reactions that public display risks. Why not simply write the review, then file it away? Relations with others offer two possibilities: cooperation and competition.

Adler (Ansbacher & Ansbacher, 1956) presumed that the critical factor for later developments is the manner in which children compensate for those inevitable feelings of inferiority. They may choose *social interest* and emphasize togetherness with others, or *competition* and seek power and domination. In my view (Abra, 1988a), Adler's position about the choice typical of creators is unclear, but in any event, representative views advocating each possibility are considered here.

Sartre (1969) provided one compelling account of the power motive. In the neverending process of creating being via those constant choices that existence demands, interactions with other people, summarized in the moment called *the gaze* of eye to eye contact, are seminal events. Egalitarian interactions are impossible. Power struggles inevitably ensue as each adversary tries to retain the freedom to create itself as it will while imposing on The Other any Being it should choose for them. The victorious *sadist* will decide it for both parties, while the submissive *masochist* has it imposed by that Other. In several studies of creative persons, including of himself (Sartre, 1981), Sartre showed why they may voluntarily choose masochism. In essence, because sadists need masochists the latter can, through their very submission, gain power over these antagonistic partners.

This raises another likely target for a critic's purported ambition. Several prominent ones, including Walter Kerr and John

Simon, began as teachers, and many others (Rosner & Abt, 1976, although see Daniels, 1976), have viewed teaching and educating the public as an important part of the job. (So did many in the present sample; the statement to this effect garnered a mean rating of 5.14, $SD = 1.33$, placing it fourth in rank). In Dr. Johnson's (1951, p. 452) words, "it is always a writer's duty to make the world better" (a statement with which 23.1% of the present sample agreed). This implies a desire to influence and hence have power over others (although reactions to this possibility were even less enthusiastic, achieving a mean rating of 2.07, $SD = 1.15$ and ranking 19th). So does another truth about the critic's calling, albeit one that usually goes unspoken but may be attractive for some: One's opinions can literally make or break careers. Still, this is not so in every field, with pop and mass culture being one notable exception. What film or music critics have to say about *Jurassic Park* or Madonna will not influence the box office in the slightest.

In addition, Sartre's (1971) fascinating account of writer/criminal/passive homosexual queen Jean Genet's unorthodox psyche is germane to understanding a certain type of critic, so it too deserves scrutiny. Because Genet played the masochistic role and received his selfhood from others, the particular labels they fixed on him ruled his destiny; he then had to live up to these labels or suffer guilt. In his case, he was from childhood branded a thief, a social outcast, because orthodox society needs such scapegoats. His sole remaining choice was to perfect the role assigned to him anyway. "I was a thief, I will be the thief," he decided (p. 50) so "He remains in his place conspicuously when nobody has requested him to leave it" (p. 55). By such machinations did he gain the perverse, subtle power of the masochist and provide the *lietmotif* of Sartre's evocative analysis: "This is a game in which the loser wins" (p. 68).

Similarly, are there not critics who, judging by the constant cruelty of their invective, take a warped delight in being hated, who contradict the definition of criticism in *Webster's New Collegiate Dictionary*: "the art of evaluating and analyzing with knowledge *and propriety*" (italics added)? One such assassin, *The Chicago Tribune*'s notorious Claudia Cassidy, denied an entire city the pleasures of several noted performers who were unwilling to risk her wrath, and *New York* magazine's John Simon can be so cruelly sadistic as to singlehandedly give the lie to those who defend the arts on grounds that they foster civilized behavior. Consider these remarks:

> Liza Minelli: That turnipy nose overhanging a forward-gaping mouth and hastily retreating chin, that bulbous cranium with eyes as big (and as inexpressive) as saucers.

Shelly Duval: is the worst and homeliest thing to hit the movies since Liza Minelli.

Carol Kane: You have to have a stomach for ugliness to endure Carol Kane. (cited in Winokur, 1992, pp. 48, 49)

Any responsible critic must on occasion render negative judgments about someone's abilities. But in my view, even here cruelty and sarcasm are never justified, and personal ridicule such as Simon's is as unacceptable as are disparaging remarks about mental or physical handicaps. About half of the present sample agreed and the others condoned such practices only under certain circumstances, notably for someone such as Madonna who is cynically exploiting or misleading the public.

Why would a John Simon then, of apparently sound if not superior mind choose to become a social pariah? Simon (1976) himself excused his outbursts of invective on grounds that they exorcise the anger that inadequacies induce, to cleanse him for experiencing the next candidate afresh. Then too, critics who never like anything build an audience, especially among sneering sophisticates for whom "enthusiasm" is a four-letter word (Kauffmann, 1976) and so long as you sell papers or keep up your ratings, what else matters? But another possibility suggests itself. Because adolescents are notoriously prone to forming cliques, perhaps some of those later drawn to media work, and criticism therein, were for whatever reason condemned early on by the prevailing culture and the all-powerful peer group to this outcast role. Therefore, for a Simon as for Genet the only choice left is to play that role better than anyone could have hoped, to garner the masochist's perverse satisfactions by becoming another loser who wins. If so, then masochism, it seems, can paradoxically give rise to matchlessly sadistic behavior.

Still, desires for cooperation and togetherness provide another venue for understanding critics. Sartre (1965) himself portrayed the relationship between writer and reader (and by implication critic) as an egalitarian exception to the usual dominance struggles. Every writer needs a reader to perceive their books as those writers cannot, because these are products of themselves (can anyone read their own writing as they do someone else's?) so readers are invited to be partners, to freely interpret those books however they choose. Thus, reading becomes both a truly creative act and an *exercise of generosity*, because writers need readers' gifts of their entire persons in order to complete their work. This collaborative view of the creator-critic relationship the present group found moderately compelling, being given a rating of 4.04 ($SD = 1.77$), for a rank of ninth.

But the most promising possibilities vis-à-vis cooperation involve the human desire, whether called *encounter* (May, 1975), *relatedness* (Fromm, 1962), or *intimacy* (Abra, 1988a), to seek not only physical but psychological connection with others. However, on one important point there is disagreement. For May, creative work adequately consummates this need but for Fromm it does not, because unlike genuine acts of love it does not provide direct contact with another person.

Fromm's position seems the more convincing (Abra, 1993). Apart from rare exceptions such as Tolstoy (Green, 1983) and Jane Austen (Cecil, 1980), few great lives have manifested abundant amounts of intimacy, especially in childhood. Therefore their work may represent a compensatory attempt to contact or offer a gift (Greenacre, 1971) to others, one that in some respects may seem preferable to genuine intimacy. For intimacy carries, as both May and Fromm pointed out, substantial appreciable risks such as rejection, or loss of self and independence. First and foremost, creating offers a sense of control over the direction taken by and the ultimate nature of the Significant Other, the product, whereas human inamorata are far less malleable. Furthermore, such possibilities I find equally valid for the stereotypic critic who, my informal observation suggests, is as much the introverted loner as are most creators (MacKinnon, 1978). Clearly the present group did not agree with these notions, however, because a statement of Fromm's views achieved a mean rating of only 2.18 ($SD = 1.66$), and ranked 18th.

For all that, I have argued elsewhere (Abra, 1993) that the routine portrait (Kohn, 1986) of competition and cooperation as mutually exclusive phenomena misrepresents reality. Veritable Siamese twins, in practical situations both are invariably present and nowhere more so than in the critic-creator relationship. Which may well explain why the two participants so often perceive it in contradictory terms. For the firstnamed, donning their rose-colored glasses, it is a cooperative partnership in which each works towards the same end: improvement. Thus, it exemplifies Skinner's (1971) notion of *reciprocity of reinforcement* wherein participants in any interaction both deliver and receive reinforcement in equal measure, a mutual scratching of backs that gives each equal control. This being the case, many critics profess befuddlement when their partners take negative judgments personally (Rosner & Abt, 1976). "Why are they so upset?" they ask, "I was only trying to help!" But to many creators, the relationship must be adversarial. In their view, critics are parasites who exploit the fruits of their labor for their own selfish purposes, at best a necessary evil, if not The Enemy. Furthermore, some critics do understand the creators' outlook; 50% here agreed with the statement that "A creative work is a tremendous investment of ego, so if authors hate me for negative things I've written, I never resent it. Why shouldn't they?"

Duty

Feeling obligated to indulge in behaviors that to oneself seem undesirable or even worse can have results that are tragic (how many young men has it induced to go like lambs to war's slaughters?), hilarious (Frederick, in *The Pirates of Penzance*, is victimized by an excessive sense of duty), but also admirable. As mentioned, it is the main reason cited by scientists for serving as journal editors, reviewers for granting agencies and the like, activities that to all appearances benefit the profession and others far more than themselves. Unlike writers of reviews they are usually unpaid and have little to gain in the way of personal expression or heightened self understanding either, let alone any thanks.

Such behaviors, then, resemble the altruistic kind, and on these several perspectives already discussed can be brought to bear. From Skinner's standpoint altruism is a contradiction in terms because all behavior requires reinforcement in some form and so is inherently "selfish." No doubt the reciprocity of reinforcement principle would once more be invoked; critics indulge so that others will in their turn perform similar services to benefit them. A more appealing variation, however, on which several subthemes suggest themselves (see Davis, 1994), comes from a less rigidly behavioristic angle. Here, the selfish purpose is to alleviate some negative internal state. For example, a Bandurian or cognitive dissonance standpoint might stress the guilt that arises respectively from not living up to internal standards of professional conduct, or to self-concepts. The present sample clearly did not agree, however. This possibility achieved a mean rating of only 1.50 (SD = .79), and ranked next to last.

Still, my informal impression is that the duty motive, so prevalent among scientific/scholarly evaluators, is less so among others, a suspicion given credibility by the present sample of arts critics. They gave it a mean rating of only 2.68 (SD = 2.07), which placed it in a tie for 15th place. Why this discrepancy? Feelings of empathy facilitate altruism (Eisenberg & Miller, 1987) and because as a rule science critics are themselves active contributors they should empathize more readily with other workers and realize the negative effects on them if these distasteful but necessary tasks were left undone. By the same token, tendencies to assist increase with helper-helpee similarity, and this too is greater here than in the arts (literature excepted). Although such presumed empathy does not prevent a few science critics, especially when hidden behind the veil of an anonymous review, from indulging in sarcastic ridicule that their artistic alter-egos would be hard pressed to equal.

Experiences While Creating

The creative process is routinely seen as a means to an end, which is a product. However many a creator reports that various peak experiences (Maslow, 1970) or "highs" that occur while completely engrossed in the activity represent another inducement and if such is the case it reverses the situation. Now concocting products becomes the means to achieving the process and its kindred experiences. As a climber acquaintance put it, sometimes its more important to climb the mountain than to reach the top. In any event, certainly many creators, when asked, explain their involvement on grounds of enjoyment, "Because it's 'fun'!"

It is not surprising then that products having higher judged creativity should result from intrinsic motivation conditions that emphasize creating for sheer enjoyment, than from the extrinsic kind in which the activity is portrayed as a means to another end, such as material reward or impressing others (Amabile, 1983). But more to the point, although such answers raise problems in that "fun" as used is a woefully circular term (I do something because it's fun, and it must be fun or I wouldn't be doing it), given their ubiquity they cannot be ignored simply because they are messy, and they could well hold for critics also. Several competent critics stated (Rosner & Abt, 1976) that they like to write, which suggests first that they are not failed artists but successful journalists, and second that writing criticism may also offer those periodic highs. A fair number of the present sample agreed; a statement expressing this possibility received a mean rating of 3.96 (SD = 1.90), and ranked 10th.

What is meant by "fun"? The opposite of "boring" represents one possibility among others (Abra, 1993). The brain's reticular formation keeps other areas aroused and alert (French, 1957) for if this were not accomplished, responding to incoming information would be inefficient. But the reticular formation itself needs novel and varying stimulation or it becomes unresponsive, resulting in underarousal, lethargy and, well, boredom. Thus, various pursuits including creative ones that may seem biologically useless in fact are nothing of the kind (Hebb, 1955). They provide this stimulation and are therefore "fun" precisely because they counteract a not only repellent but maladaptive state.

Might criticism offer the same benefits? Although some events are boring—William Archer (Rigg, 1983) claimed that the first requisite for the prospective critic is the ability to sleep while sitting bolt upright—it offers more prospects than do most careers for regular exposure to experiences that, whatever their quality, feature novelty and variety. And even periodic exposure to boring ones might be advantageous, because too much arousal can be as deleterious as too little (Hebb, 1955; Yerkes & Dodson, 1908). But might not the ordinary audience member gain the same benefits without the detriments of the critic's calling? Yet introspection suggests that attending as a critic, knowing that later on one will have to work out in writing what one thought and why, intensifies one's involvement in and reactions to the event. Thus, arousal and in turn enjoyment is heightened, to be enhanced still further by the actual writing. Many of the present sample felt as much; the relevant statement's mean rating was 5.00 (SD = 1.91), and ranked fifth.

Miscellaneous

The questionnaire also assessed a few other motive possibilities suggested informally rather than by theories. These data too should be presented, particularly because one was highly rated. The statement "a critic's aims should be to increase the public's awareness of and enthusiasm for work in their field" attained a mean rating of 5.50 (SD = 1.69) and ranked second, which again suggests the pull of missionary-educational considerations. On the other hand, a statement more suggestive of those of power and influence, "Critics want to influence the direction and form that creative activity takes in the future," in keeping with other possibilities in this vein held fewer attractions; its mean rating was 3.75 (SD = 1.92), for a rank of 11th. Likewise, one that seemed to tap into ego-confidence factors, that "I did creative work myself, and was so disgusted by the incompetence of the critics that I decided to become one myself" was rated on average at only 1.89 (SD = 1.60), and ranked 21st.

The critics themselves suggested other possibilities. Practical considerations of career and livelihood was one, as in "because it's my job," although only in some genres is it possible to eke out a living entirely through criticism—and even for these, several cited poor remuneration as another reason for critic burn out. Other frequently cited motives were to reach an audience—to entertain—and also assist them in deciding whether they should spend time and money on this event.

Finally, one item asked about early environmental factors that in retrospect might have fostered the career choice and revealed several consistencies. Not surprisingly, one was a fondness as a child for reading, but among other things for works of criticism and commentary—not, I submit, items high on most youngsters' reading lists. As well, homes tended to have books and magazines abundantly available, reading was common, and the arts and humanities respected and frequently discussed. Perhaps most indicative, several mentioned being encouraged to express their own opinions and think for themselves rather than toe parental lines. Children taught to be seen and not heard, it seems, are not likely to become critics!

FURTHER CONSIDERATIONS AND CONCLUSIONS

The questionnaire also gathered personal data and two items warrant discussion. With increasing age, creative work may decline both in quantity and quality (Lehman, 1953) or at least change in its attributes (Simonton, 1983). A plethora of explanations can be offered (Abra, 1989), but there is evidence (Saltuklaroglu, 1994) that changes in prevailing motives may be part of the story. Do critics show similar alteration? Although 76% of the present sample felt that their motives had not changed since they began professional work, there are indications that this belief may not be entirely accurate. Specifically, several critics who did respond in the affirmative suggested that they had become more fatalistic and pragmatic, less driven by ego and desires to change the world, and these possibilities a discriminant analysis (Diekhoff, 1992) of the four age categories did somewhat bear out. Discriminant Function 1 was significant, χ^2 (66) = 100.34, $p < .005$, and when all three discriminant functions were taken into account, classified members to groups with 100% accuracy. Inspection of group centroids indicated that this effect was primarily due to differences between the 20 to 30 and 31 to 40 age groups, with the statement concerning the role of confidence and ego being the main contributor; the two groups gave it a mean rating of 4.8 and 2.7, respectively. Given that the younger group had only four subjects, this finding should be viewed cautiously, and this is even more the case for other possibilities that also contributed somewhat to the effect in that the absolute sizes of the differences were moderate at best. For what it is worth, desires for encounter/relatedness increased slightly ($n = 1.5$ and 2.4, respectively), while the belief that egalitarian partnership with creators is possible decreased, from 4.8 to 3.8, and the latter could suggest that in the face of reality, initial idealistic beliefs that this partnership is possible may suffer.

The second noteworthy attribute is gender. It is beyond contention that in the past at least most of the achievements called "great" have come from men, and of the many viable explanations that can be offered (Abra & Valentine-French, 1991), some suggest motivation differences. Might these too operate in the critical sphere? On the face of it the answer is affirmative. Discriminant analysis of the sex variable resulted in χ^2 (23) = 37.10, $p < .05$, with 100% accuracy in classifying subjects to groups. In descending order of magnitude, the statements that most contributed to this effect, along with the mean ratings for males and females respectively for each, had to do with (a) ego and confidence (3.7 and 1.5), (b) expression and self-discovery à la Langer (5.3 and 3.3), (c) recognition and fame (3.2 and 1.8), (d) the influence of role models (4.3 and 2.7), and (e) increasing the aesthetic experience through writing about it (5.6 and 4.2).

Moreover, after the fact most of these effects suggest plausible explanations. For example, women of the past may have been less driven to creative work of any kind (Ferris, personal communication, 1980) because cultural conditioning provided a clearer sense of self (wife and mother) and the meaning of life (to marry and reproduce), and today's female critics did have few role models in the profession to imitate. However two considerations complicate interpretation. First, one persistent problem here is that ratings may indicate a motive's actual power or simply the respondent's *belief* in its power, and this difficulty becomes especially troublesome in the present context. Are women genuinely less driven by ego and desires for fame, or for whatever reason are they merely less willing to admit it? Second, for every possibility alluded to above, the male ratings were higher. Do the differences therefore indicate a difference on these specific factors or on a more general willingness to assign high ratings? The second alternative cannot be dismissed. The difference in ratings given to all items, while small in absolute terms ($n = 3.7$ and 3.1 for males and females, respectively) after a correction for heterogeneity of variance was significant, $t(13.76) = 2.16$, $p < .05$. Why women were more reluctant to use the scales' higher echelons is unknown, but it does muddy the waters.

In conclusion, what can be said about the motives that impel critics? As with any population of creative people, rugged individualists all, generalization can be foolhardy. That said, what is most striking is the emphasis this sample placed on serving the audience and readership—through teaching, education, maintaining standards, increasing appreciation and enthusiasm for the genre, and so on. This represents a significant departure from creative people of other kinds, for whom these candidates have rarely been mentioned as plausible possibilities (Abra, 1994). By the same token, most motives that purportedly predominate among creators held for these critics few allures. Yet another puzzle that creative work presents is the choice of field. Given sufficient portions of the talent and drive that is required, what factors draw one person to music, another to dance, and a third to problems posed by nature? The present study suggests an explanation at least for critics: different motivational priorities.

ACKNOWLEDGMENTS

I thank Morley Hollenberg for surveying science critics and for several stimulating discussions, those critics who took the time and effort to fill out and return the questionnaires, Theresa Kline for suggesting the data analysis, and Gord Abra and Linda Plotkins who assisted in carrying it out.

APPENDIX: CRITICS QUESTIONNAIRE

Name _____
(leave blank if you prefer to remain anonymous):
Field(s) (Theater, Film, Dance, etc.): _____

Part I

<u>Personal Information</u> (Circle the option for each that best describes you.)

1. Age: 20-30   31-40   41-50   51+
2. Gender: Male   Female
3. Place of Residence: BC   AB   SK   MB   ON   PQ   Maritimes
4. Age at which you first though seriously about becoming a critic:
   Before 15   16-20   21-25   26-30   31+
5. Number of years you have been doing criticism:
   less than 5   5-10   11-15   16-20   21+
6. Do you know of any previously published discussions about critics' motives, and/or other topics that might be relevant to my interests?
                    YES   NO
   If Yes, please list references_____
   _____
   _____

7. Have you wondered about your motives for doing criticism and why you do it?
              Frequently   On occasion   Never

Part II

The following items each suggest a possible motive for criticism that has been advanced. For each, show on the rating scale provided how relevant it seems for you.

1. Creative works induce in the consumers a variety of vague feelings and emotional reactions that produce discomfort unless expressed in words or some other form. Thus, such feelings are like itches and writing criticism provides relief, a sort of psychological scratching.

no relevance	an intermittent, secondary motive	a dominant motive
1 2	3 4 5	6 7

2. Critics want recognition, fame, and renown.

no relevance	an intermittent, secondary motive	a dominant motive
1 2	3 4 5	6 7

3. Criticism is the expression of socially, unacceptable, uncivilized tendencies, be they erotic, aggressive, hostile, or whatever, in socially acceptable ways.

no relevance	an intermittent, secondary motive	a dominant motive
1 2	3 4 5	6 7

4. I love the genre in which I do criticism, and I want to do what I can to assist and improve it.

no relevance	an intermittent, secondary motive	a dominant motive
1 2	3 4 5	6 7

5. Criticism is a voyage of self-discovery. Because reactions to a creative work are complex and difficult to express in words (being in good part intuitive, "gut reactions"), one is not sure what one thinks of it or why, so one tries to discover this, and by extension more about oneself, by writing about it.

no relevance	an intermittent, secondary motive	a dominant motive
1 2	3 4 5	6 7

6. A critic's aims should be to increase the public's awareness of and enthusiasm for work in his or her field.

no relevance	an intermittent, secondary motive	a dominant motive
1 2	3 4 5	6 7

7. Creating attempts to defeat mortality via works that, should they survive one's death and be perceived by future generations, symbolically keep oneself alive. Criticism, by permanently recording one's reaction to a work, serves the same purpose.

no relevance	an intermittent, secondary motive	a dominant motive
1 2	3 4 5	6 7

8. It takes a lot of confidence to believe that your opinions are worth inflicting on the public, so criticism aims to express one's ego.

no relevance	an intermittent, secondary motive	a dominant motive
1 2	3 4 5	6 7

9. The reverse of #8: Rather than confidence fostering criticism, criticism is a means to increase confidence. Specifically, the act of sharing one's opinions with others in a public forum increased the sense of self-esteem.

no relevance	an intermittent, secondary motive	a dominant motive
1 2	3 4 5	6 7

10. Writing about a work intensifies the aesthetic experience. For example, one's reactions to that work, whether positive or negative, are deepened by contemplating more fully and at leisure how its various components fit together like pieces in a puzzle.

no relevance	an intermittent, secondary motive	a dominant motive
1 2	3 4 5	6 7

11. Critics want power and influence over others.

no relevance		an intermittent, secondary motive			a dominant motive	
1	2	3	4	5	6	7

12. High standards of creative work must be maintained, otherwise quality work will be lost beneath masses of mediocrity. Criticism aims to establish and maintain those standards, even in the face of majority opinion that is willing to settle for less.

no relevance		an intermittent, secondary motive			a dominant motive	
1	2	3	4	5	6	7

13. Critics are eternal optimists in whose breasts hope springs eternal. Their incentive is that each new work represents another possible chance to discover a masterpiece and/or a new talent.

no relevance		an intermittent, secondary motive			a dominant motive	
1	2	3	4	5	6	7

14. I did creative work myself in my field, and I was so disgusted by the incompetence of the critics that I decided to become a critic myself to try and improve the situation.

no relevance		an intermittent, secondary motive			a dominant motive	
1	2	3	4	5	6	7

15. Feelings of guilt, perhaps stemming from realizations that one has special abilities or responsibilities, would prove overwhelming if one did not practice criticism, so it attempts to forestall these feelings.

no relevance		an intermittent, secondary motive			a dominant motive	
1	2	3	4	5	6	7

16. Critics, by expressing their preferences, want to influence the direction and form that creative activity takes in the future.

no relevance	an intermittent, secondary motive	a dominant motive
1 2	3 4 5	6 7

17. People like to feel competent, but they are good at different things, so personal satisfaction comes from discovering one's niche(s). Critics have found theirs to be evaluation and writing.

no relevance	an intermittent, secondary motive	a dominant motive
1 2	3 4 5	6 7

18. The critic wants to teach, to educate the public.

no relevance	an intermittent, secondary motive	a dominant motive
1 2	3 4 5	6 7

19. Critics, like many other people, have been inspired by influential role models they admire and in whose footsteps they want to follow. (Note: mention particular persons, if you wish)

no relevance	an intermittent, secondary motive	a dominant motive
1 2	3 4 5	6 7

20. Creators can no more evaluate their own work as if it was done by someone else than can parents be detached about their children. Critics try to provide the necessary detached contemplation and interpretation, so creator and critic collaborate in a partnership in which each serves a different, but complementary role.

no relevance	an intermittent, secondary motive	a dominant motive
1 2	3 4 5	6 7

21. Most critics, like creative people generally, are introverts or loners. Therefore, the review represents a means for reaching out to other people, the readership, for the contact they need.

no relevance	an intermittent, secondary motive	a dominant motive
1 2	3 4 5	6 7

22. Critics are motivated by various intense experiences, or "highs," that sometimes occur during the process of writing itself.

no relevance	an intermittent, secondary motive	a dominant motive
1 2	3 4 5	6 7

23. A sense of duty and obligation, to do something that may be personally unrewarding or even worse but that needs to be done, is what drives the critic.

no relevance	an intermittent, secondary motive	a dominant motive
1 2	3 4 5	6 7

Part III

Please provide any answers you can to the following (use reverse side if necessary):

1. Describe any other possible motives for doing criticism that occur to you but were not presented above.

2. With the benefit of hindsight, do you see anything in the way you spent your childhood, particularly in your interests and preferred activities, to indicate that here might be a budding critic? If so, what were they?

3. Do you see anything in your family background (e.g., influences from parents or relatives) that might have predisposed you to a critical career, and to your genre?

4. How do you deal with variations in moods, fatigue, domestic worries, and other factors that might influence your judgments?

5. Many critics seem to burn out. Why do you think this might be, and how do you counteract it?

6. Do you think vindictive or personally cutting reviews are sometimes justified? If so, why?

7. As Letters To The Editor sections reveal, not just creators but other people frequently get angry at critics with whom they disagree. Why do you think this is? Does it bother you, and if so, how do you deal with it?

8. Have your motives for doing criticism changed in the time since you began? If so, explain how.

Part IV

Here are some statements made (not by myself I hasten to add but by critics and others). For each circle YES if you agree, leave blank if you do not (Elaborate on your answers if you wish).

Motive for Criticism

1. Criticism is a creative activity.	YES
2. Most critics are failed artists. They are like eunuchs in a harem: they know how it's done, they've seen it done every day, but they can't do it themselves.	YES
3. You have the right face for a critic—the look of a blooming martyr.	YES
4. A critic is someone who knows the way, but can't drive the car.	YES
5. Criticism should be constructive.	YES
6. Criticism would never be cruel or sarcastic.	YES
7. Criticism should be objective.	YES
8. Effective criticism requires special abilities. If YES, what do you think they are?	YES

_____

_____

If YES, can they be taught? _____

9. The highest form of criticism is a mode of autobiography.	YES
10. Criticism is as inevitable as breathing.	YES
11. No one but a blockhead ever wrote except for money, which is the only motive for writing that I know of.	YES
12. The artist who alleges personal animosity on my part is quite right. When people do less than their best, I hate them, loathe them, detest them.	YES
13. You worthy critics are ashamed of the momentary and passing madness that is found in all creators.	YES
14. It is always a writer's duty to make the world better.	YES
15. Any normal critic must periodically be guilty of vulgarity and bad manners or he or she is a weak and ineffective critic. If a (creator) hits me in the face with a contemptible cheese pie, I must hit him in the face in turn with an even larger and juicier critical equivalent.	YES
16. A creative work is a tremendous investment of ego, so if authors hate me for negative things I've written, I never resent it. Why shouldn't they?	YES
17. It takes a lot of ego and confidence to do criticism.	YES

18. A critic is three things: a writer, teacher, and thinker— YES
and also a philosopher of sorts.

19. You need to have tried to do creative work in a field, YES
successfully or not, in order to evaluate other work.

20. What I look for is do they succeed on their own terms; YES
I don't review a Disney film the way I review Truffaut.

21. Saying yay or nay is the least interesting part of the YES
job; I only do it because that's what others want.

22. (Q) What did you think of it? YES
(A) I don't know, I haven't written my review yet.

23. Criticism is a dialogue with an imaginary audience, YES
present and future.

24. If I was marooned alone on a desert island, and YES
encountered a work of art with no chance that my
review would be read by someone else, I would still be
motivated to write it.

REFERENCES

Abra, J. C. (1988a). *Assaulting Parnassus: Theoretical views of creativity.* Lanham, MD: University Press of America.
Abra, J. C. (1988b). Is creative ability widespread? *Canadian Review of Art Education, 15,* 69-89.
Abra, J. C. (1989). Changes in creativity with age: Data, explanations and further predictions. *International Journal of Aging and Human Development, 28,* 105-126.
Abra, J. C. (1993). Competition: Creativity's vilified motive. *Genetic, Social and General Psychology Monographs, 119,* 291-342.
Abra, J. C. (1994) Collaboration in creative work: An initiative for investigation. *Creativity Research Journal, 7,* 1-20.
Abra, J. C. (1997). *The motives for creative work: An inquiry.* Cresskill, NJ: Hampton Press.
Abra, J. C., & Valentine-French, S. (1991). Gender differences in creative achievement: A survey of explanations. *Genetic, Social and General Psychology Monographs, 117,* 233-284.
Amabile, T. M. (1983). *The social psychology of creativity.* New York: Springer-Verlag.
Amsel, A. (1958). The role of frustrative nonreward in noncontinuous reward situations. *Psychological Bulletin, 55,* 102-119.
Ansbacher, H. L., & Ansbacher, R. R. (Eds.). (1956). *The individual psychology of Alfred Adler.* New York: Basic Books.
Arieti, S. (1976). *Creativity: The magic synthesis.* New York: Basic Books.
Bandura, A. (1977). *Social learning theory.* Englewood Cliffs, NJ: Prentice-Hall.
Bandura, A. (1978). The self system in reciprocal determinism. *American Psychologist, 33,* 344-358.
Bandura, A. (1989). Perceived self-efficacy in the exercise of personal agency. *The Psychologist: Bulletin of the British Psychological Society, 10,* 411-424.
Barnes, J. (1985). *Flaubert's parrot.* London: Pan Books.
Barron, F. (1965). The psychology of creativity. In *New directions in psychology* (Vol. 2, pp. 1-134). New York: Holt, Rinehart & Winston.
Bate, W. J. (1979). *Samuel Johnson.* New York: Harcourt, Brace, Jovanovich.
Becker, E. (1973). *The denial of death.* New York: The Free Press.
Bloom, B. S. (Ed.). (1985). *Developing talent in young people.* New York: Ballentine Books.
Bookspan, M. (1976). Interview. In S. Rosner & L. E. Abt (Eds.), *The creative expression* (pp. 221-234). Croton-on-Hudson, NY: North River Press.

Brill, A. A. (Ed.). (1938). *The basic writings of Sigmund Freud*. New York: Random House.
Camus, A. (1956). *The rebel*. New York: Vintage Books.
Camus, A. (1969). *The myth of Sisyphus and other essays*. New York: Knopf.
Carpenter, J. (1991). Interview. In G. Hickenlooper (Ed.), *Rebel conversations* (pp. 329-343). New York: Citadel Press.
Cecil, D. (1980). *A portrait of Jane Austen*. Harmondsworth, Middlesex: Penguin Books.
Daniels, R. (1976). *Conversations with Cardus*. London: Victor Gollancz Ltd.
Davis, M. H. (1994). *Empathy: A social psychological approach*. Madison, WI: Brown & Benchmark.
de Mille, A. (1992). *Martha: The life and work of Martha Graham*. New York: Vintage Books.
Diekhoff, G. (1992). *Statistics for the social and behavioral sciences*. Dubuque, IA: Wm. C. Brown.
Ebert, R. (1991). Interview. In G. Hickenlooper (Ed.), *Rebel conversations* (pp. 357-372). New York: Citadel Press.
Eisenberg, N., & Miller, P. A. (1987). Empathy and prosocial behavior. *Psychological Bulletin, 101*, 91-119.
Eliot, T. S. (1951). Tradition and the individual talent. In J. H. Smith & E. W. Parks (Eds.), *The great critics: An anthology of literary criticism* (3rd ed., pp. 713-721). New York: Norton.
Feldman, D. H. (1980). *Beyond universals in cognitive development*. Norwood, NJ: Ablex.
Ferris, P. (1978). *Dylan Thomas*. Markham, Ontario: Penguin Books.
Ferster, C. B., & Skinner, B. F. (1957). *Schedules of reinforcement*. New York: Appleton-Century-Crofts.
Festinger, L. (1957). *A theory of cognitive dissonance*. Palo Alto, CA: Stanford University Press.
Frankl, V. (1984). *Man's search for meaning*. New York: Washington Square Press.
French, J. (1957). *The reticular formation* (Scientific American offprint No. 66). San Francisco: Freeman.
Freud, S. (1958a). The most prevalent form of degradation in erotic life. In B. Nelson (Ed.), *On creativity and the unconscious* (pp. 173-186). New York: Harper & Row.
Freud, S. (1958b). The relation of the poet to daydreaming. In B. Nelson (Ed.), *On creativity and the unconscious* (pp. 44-54). New York: Harper & Row.
Freud, S. (1963). Introductory lectures on psychoanalysis (Part III). In J. Strachey (Ed.), *The complete psychological works of Sigmund Freud* (Vol. 16). London: Hogarth Press.
Fromm, E. (1960). *Fear of freedom*. London: Routledge & Kegan Paul.

Fromm, E. (1962). *The art of loving: An inquiry into the nature of love.* New York: Harper & Row.
Fulford, R. (1988). *Best seat in the house.* Toronto: Collins.
Gardner, H. (1982). *Art, mind and brain: A cognitive approach to creativity.* New York: Basic Books.
Gardner, H. (1983). *Frames of mind: The theory of multiple intelligences.* New York: Basic Books.
Gardner, H. (1988). Creative lives and creative works: A synthetic scientific approach. In R. Sternberg (Ed.), *The nature of creativity* (pp. 298-324). New York: Cambridge University Press.
Getzels, J. W., & Jackson, P. W. (1970). The highly intelligent and the highly creative adolescent. In P. E. Vernon (Ed.), *Creativity* (pp. 189-202). New York: Penguin Books.
Grant, K. S. (1983). *Dr. Birney as critic and historian of music.* Ann Arbor: University of Michigan Press.
Green, M. (1983). *Tolstoy and Gandhi: Men of peace.* New York: Basic Books.
Greenacre, P. (1971). The childhood of the artist: Libidinal phase development and giftedness. In P. Greenacre (Ed.), *Emotional growth* (Vol. 2, pp. 479-504). New York: International Universities Press.
Greene, G. (1981). *Ways of escape.* New York: Penguin Books.
Greer, G. (1979). *The obstacle race.* London: Secker & Warburg.
Guilford, J. P. (1967). *The nature of human intelligence.* New York: McGraw-Hill.
Guilford, J. P. (1973). A psychometric approach to creativity. In M. Bloomberg (Ed.), *Creativity: Theory and research* (pp. 229-246). New Haven, CT: College and University Press.
Hardy, G. H. (1983). A mathematician's apology. In R. S. Albert (Ed.), *Genius and eminence* (pp. 386-391). New York: Pergamon Press.
Hebb, D. O. (1955). Drives and the C. N. S. (conceptual nervous system). *Psychological Review, 62,* 243-254.
Henle, M. (1974). The cognitive approach: The snail beneath the shell. In S. Rosner & L. E. Abt (Eds.), *Essays in creativity* (pp. 23-44). Croton-on-Hudson, NY: North River Press.
Hergenhahn, B. R. (1984). *An introduction to theories of personality* (2nd ed.). Englewood Cliffs, NJ: Prentice-Hall.
Hickenlooker, G. (1991). *Rebel conversations.* New York: Citadel Press.
Hintzman, D. L. (1978). *The psychology of learning and memory.* San Francisco: Freeman.
Howe, R. B. K. (1991). Introspection: A reassessment. *New Ideas in Psychology, 9,* 25-44.
Hutchinson, E. D. (1949). *How to think creatively.* New York: Abingdon Press.

Jackson, K. (Ed.). (1990). *Schrader on Schrader*. London: Faber & Faber.
Johnson, S. (1951). Preface to Shakespeare. In J. H. Smith & E. W. Parks (Eds.), *The great critics: An anthology of literary criticism* (3rd ed., pp. 443-460). New York: Norton.
John-Steiner, V. (1985). *Notebooks of the mind*. Albuquerque: University of New Mexico Press.
Jung, C. G. (1923). *Psychology of types*. London: Routledge & Kegan Paul.
Kauffmann, S. (1976). Literary criticism. In S. Rosner & L. E. Abt (Eds.), *The creative expression* (pp. 201-220). Croton-on-Hudson, NY: North River Press.
Kerr, W. (1970). *Thirty plays hath September*. New York: Simon & Schuster.
Kimble, G. (1961). *Hilgard and Marquis' conditioning and learning* (2nd ed.). New York: Appleton-Century-Crofts.
Kisselgoff, A. (1976). Interview. In S. Rosner & L. E. Abt (Eds.), *The creative expression* (pp. 153-167). Croton-on-Hudson, NY: North River Press.
Koestler, A. (1970). *The act of creation*. London: Pan Books.
Kohn, A. (1986). *No contest: The case against competition*. Boston: Houghton Mifflin.
Kreitler, H., & Kreitler, S. (1972). *Psychology of the arts*. Durham, NC: Duke University Press.
Kris, E. (1952). *Psychoanalytic explorations in art*. New York: International Universities Press.
Langer, S. K. (1951). *Philosophy in a new key*. New York: Mentor Books.
Langer, S. K. (1953). *Feeling and form*. New York: Charles Scribner's Sons.
Lehman, H. C. (1953). *Age and achievement*. Princeton, NJ: Princeton University Press.
MacKinnon, D. W. (1978). *In search of human effectiveness*. Buffalo, NY: Creative Education Foundation.
Man Alive. (1991). CBC-TV, March 29.
Maslow, A. H. (1962). *Toward a psychology of being*. Toronto: D. van Nostrand (Canada) Ltd.
Maslow, A. H. (1970). *Religions, values and peak-experiences*. New York: Viking Press.
Maslow, A. H. (1976). *The farther reaches of human nature*. Markham, Ontario: Penguin Books.
May, R. (1975). *The courage to create*. New York: Norton.
Mednick, S. A. (1962). The associative basis of the creative process. *Psychological Review, 69*, 220-227.
Merton, R. K. (1973). *The sociology of science*. Chicago: University of Chicago Press.

Myers, I. B. (1962). *Myers-Briggs type indicator manual.* Princeton, NJ: Educational Testing Service.

Nathan, G. (1969). *Passing judgements.* New York: Greenwood Press.

Nisbett, R. E., & Wilson, T. B. (1977). Telling more than we can know: Verbal reports on mental processes. *Psychological Review, 84,* 231-259.

That one negative comment. (1990, April). *The Teaching Professor,* p. 5.

Ornstein, R. (1972). *The psychology of consciousness.* San Francisco: Freeman.

Osborn, A. F. (1963). *Applied imagination.* New York: Scribner's.

Osborne, J. (1961). *Luther.* London: Faber & Faber.

Pacht, A. R. (1984). Reflections on perfection. *American Psychologist, 39,* 386-390.

Perkins, D. N. (1981). *The mind's best work.* Cambridge, MA: Cambridge University Press.

Pirsig, R. M. (1974). *Zen and the art of motorcycle maintenance.* New York: Bantam Books.

Poincaré, H. (1952). Mathematical creation. In B. Ghiselin (Ed.), *The creative process* (pp. 33-42). New York: New American Library.

Popper, K. (1972). *The logic of scientific discovery.* London: Hutchinson.

Rank, O. (1932). *Art and artist.* New York: Alfred A. Knopf.

Redman, A. (1959). *The wit and humor of Oscar Wilde.* New York: Dover.

Rigg, D. (1983). *No turn unstoned: The worst ever theatrical reviews.* London: Arrow Books.

Roe, A. (1965). Changes in scientific activities with age. *Science, 150,* 313-318.

Rogers, C. R. (1970). Towards a theory of creativity. In P. E. Vernon (Ed.), *Creativity* (pp. 137-151). New York: Penguin Books.

Rosner, S., & Abt, L. E. (Eds.). (1976). *The creative expression.* Croton-on-Hudson, NY: North River Press.

Rothenberg, A. (1990). *Creativity and madness.* Baltimore, MD: Johns Hopkins University Press.

Russell, B. (1969). *The autobiography of Bertrand Russell. The middle years: 1914-1944.* New York: Bantam Books.

Saltuklaroglu, J. (1994). *Motivation for creativity from a developmental perspective.* Unpublished honors thesis, University of Calgary.

Sartre, J. P. (1965). *What is literature?* New York: Harper Row.

Sartre, J. P. (1969). *Being and nothingness.* New York: The Citadel Press.

Sartre, J. P. (1971). *Saint Genet: Actor and martyr.* New York: New American Library.

Sartre, J. P. (1981). *The words.* New York: Vintage Books.

Schickel, R. (1991). Interview. In G. Hickenlooper (Ed.), *Rebel conversations* (pp. 198-214). New York: Citadel Press.
Shaw, G. B. (1965). *The complete prefaces of Bernard Shaw.* London: Paul Hamlyn.
Simon, J. (1976). Interview. In S. Rosner & L. E. Abt (Eds.), *The creative expression* (pp. 168-183). Croton-on-Hudson NY: North River Press.
Simonton, D. K. (1983). Dramatic greatness and content: A quantitative study of eighty-one Athenian and Shakespearian plays. *Empirical Studies of the Arts, 1,* 109-123.
Simonton, D. K. (1984). *Genius, creativity and leadership.* Cambridge, MA: Harvard University Press.
Skinner, B. F. (1968). *The technology of teaching.* New York: Appleton-Century-Crofts.
Skinner, B. F. (1971). *Beyond freedom and dignity.* New York: Knopf.
Spearman, C. (1927). *The abilities of man.* New York: MacMillan.
Stein, M. I. (1974). *Stimulating creativity: Vol. I. Individual procedures.* New York: Academic Press.
Stern, A. (1967). *Sartre: His philosophy and existential psychoanalysis.* New York: Dell.
Storr, A. (1976). *The dynamics of creation.* Harmondsworth, England: Penguin Books.
Tynan, Kathleen (1987). *The life of Kenneth Tynan.* New York: William Morrow.
Tynan, Kenneth. (1961). *Curtains.* London: Longmans.
Tynan, Kenneth. (1967). *Tynan right and left.* London: Longmans.
Wallace, D. B. (1989). Stream of consciousness and reconstruction of self in Dorothy Richardson's *Pilgramage.* In D. Wallace & H. Gruber (Eds.), *Creative people at work* (pp. 147-169). New York: Oxford University Press.
Wallas, G. (1970). The art of thought. In P. E. Vernon (Ed.), *Creativity* (pp. 91-97). New York: Penguin Books.
Walters, J., & Gardner, H. (1986). The crystallizing experience: Discovering an intellectual gift. In R. J. Sternberg & J. E. Davidson (Eds.), *Conceptions of giftedness* (pp. 306-333). New York: Cambridge University Press.
Watson, R. I. (1963). *The great psychologists.* Philadelphia: J. B. Lippincott.
Wertheimer, M. (1959). *Productive thinking.* New York: Harper.
Winokur, J. (Ed.). (1992). *The portable curmudgeon.* New York: Plume.
Woolf, V. (1977). *A room of one's own.* New York: Granada.
Yerkes, R. M., & Dodson, J. D. (1908). The relation of strength of stimulus to rapidity of habit formation. *Journal of Comparative Neurology, 18,* 459-482.

15

INTERMEDIARIES IN THE CREATIVE PROCESS: SERVING THE INDIVIDUAL AND SOCIETY

Morris I. Stein
New York University

No person is an island unto themselves. Generally true: assuredly true of creativity. The myth of the hero springing from Jupiter's head, leading a solitary life conquering dragons all along the way is just that—a *myth.*

Difficult although it be, it must be admitted that "Even the Muses Had Parents" (Stein, 1984a). From start to finish, creativity occurs in a social context (Stein, 1974, 1975).

Contemporary efforts to understand creativity focus on both its intra- and interindividual components. The former consist of psychological factors that facilitate or block the creative process. The latter range from studies of the zeitgeist to those that spell out organizational effects on creativity. Relatively little attention, however, is paid to the intermediaries in the creative process—those who stand between the creative individual at one end and the public or audience at the other. This is a serious oversight because intermediaries are critical to the social context in which the creative process occurs.

WHO ARE THE INTERMEDIARIES?

Intermediaries are many and varied. They are one's immediate family: parents and siblings. They may also be one's extended family: grandparents, uncles, aunts, and cousins; family of procreation: spouses and offspring; neighbors; friends and lovers; teachers at all grade and educational levels: kindergarten, grade school, high school, college, university, and professional school; peers and colleagues at work and in one's profession (Stein, 1993). They can be government bureaucrats, foundation heads, university administrators, investment bankers (Stein, 1981), publishers, gallery owners, reviewers, critics, and many others, including international creativity trainers.

To add some spice to the stew, intermediaries may be dead or alive, real or imagined, in one's awareness or in one's unconscious but always in one's life space (Lewin, 1935). They may constitute formal or informal groups. Wherever they are or whomever they are, they are powerful individuals. At one time, a reviewer of Broadway plays for *The New York Times* could "make" or "break" a play in a review written right after opening night. Without intermediaries' support and protection the "hero's" work may never see the light of day. Without intermediaries' "stamp of approval" and guidance, society may be at a loss as to how to react to and evaluate works in science and technology, the arts and the humanities.

There are many ways of classifying intermediaries. The criterion proposed for purposes here is "focus of allegiance." Those who nurture and foster the individual's work are *developers*. Those who serve as gatekeepers (Lewin, 1958) for society are *regulators*. Developers' and regulators' roles and functions overlap. In each of them, supportive, nurturing, and evaluative factors can be found. In some, the balance is tipped in favor of complete acceptance and support and a minimum of evaluation. In others, the balance shifts to the weight placed on evaluative factors, but here to one may still find some evidence for acceptance and support. Developers' and regulators' roles are separated here for heuristic purposes only.

Developers

Developers nurture talents, gifts, and creative potential. They shape, direct, discipline, and "prune." Some of the following ways that they do this are discussed here.

Support.

Emotional Support. The psychosocial development of all individuals requires the emotional support of others. In this respect the creative person is no different than other people. It is the *gestalt* of the creative person's needs and his or her intensity that makes the creative individual unique. The creative individual is on the cutting edge of things. At times, the creative individual expresses him or herself with such ease that bystanders do not perceive how well problems have been solved. On other occasions, a creative individual can become very frustrated and aggravated by the very tasks that have been imposed and the very goal that has been selected. The creative individual may not know how to express what he or she desires to communicate. Solutions are not easy. Risks are high. The creative individual may be out on a limb and it is very lonely out there. Emotional highs and lows may be the order of the day.

Some intermediaries take the creative individual's needs in stride and find satisfaction in fulfilling them. They are happy being part of a special relationship and process. Others find it too demanding, narcissistic, and emotionally draining—all precursors to the end of the relationship.

Early in a creative person's developmental history, a very strong bond may be formed with another that is based on unconditional love and acceptance. All of which is crucial for future self-esteem and self-confidence that will stand the creative individual in good stead while exploring new vistas. In other relationships, an intermediary's emotional support is conditional. The creative individual is no longer independent and autonomous but a tool, an instrument through which the intermediary intends to make his or her mark in life. Such relationships may produce ill effects, not immediately, but at some later date when the creative individual suffers self-doubt, and can no longer produce or enjoy the fruits of his or her labor and falls into a depression. No longer does the creative person satisfy the needs of the internalized insatiable tyrant.

In these support systems, one is the giver and the other is the receiver. Another set of fascinating relationships are the *collaborative* ones. Two persons collaborate on one or more pieces of work. Or, two persons, of the same or opposite gender, each recognized for their own creativity, are involved in a caring, loving, and sexual relationship with each other (Chadwick & de Courtivron, 1993).

Financial Support. Emotional support is only one type of support that might occur. Another is *financial.* In hereditary and affluent societies creativity was generally an indulgence of the wealthy either for themselves or for whom they patronized. On the contemporary scene, even in more democratic settings, it is next to impossible to get the education one requires and the tools one needs without funds.

When funds are provided without any strings attached, the situation is ideal. But if funding leads to debt or excessively long working hours then creative work may be carried out with pressure and only when one has enough energy left over from one's labor. Inadequate funds may lead some people to change the course of their careers moving from "pure" to "applied" areas because that is where the money is. Motivation may shift from intrinsic to extrinsic. Creativity then becomes a commodity deteriorating as it is traded for the coin of the realm.

Stimulation.

The postnatal world provides the neonate with stimulation it needs to grow and develop. Emotional stimulation, previously discussed, is crucial to the infant's development. Physical and cognitive stimulation are equally important. Deprivation in one or both of these types of stimulation can lead to marasmus and defective neuronal development (Gazzaniga, 1988; Jerison, 1973). Stimulation overload can be a problem but effective intermediaries intuit or learn how to provide an optimal amount.

It is impossible to discuss all of the important sequelae to stimulation but it should be kept in mind that in each area—emotional, physical, and cognitive—stimulation has as its important psychological sequelae—security and trust, self-esteem, power, and self-confidence, all of which lead to curiosity, questioning, exploration, experimentation, and effective communication with oneself and others.

Appropriate cognitive stimulation may be dependent on having appropriate resources and a rich environment. When these are lacking, they might be compensated for by reading good books and other means of developing a fantasied environment.

Stimulation is often associated with environmental riches, however, deficits and losses can also bring out the best in some people. Roe (1952) reported on the loss of the father early in the lives of a sample of Nobel Prize winners. Building on her work, Stein (1983) suggested that the cognitive complexity brought on by such losses and other crises in life, together with a source of emotional security may actually prove to be the winning combination.

Stimulation is crucial to a person's early development but it is no less important as all the other stages throughout the life cycle.

Recognition.

Through rewards, intermediaries provide the creative individual with valuable feedback for works produced. And, it is here that one sees most clearly how intermediaries' evaluations produce their effects. Rewards help shape and direct individual's individual's efforts. They also highlight for others who are yet to manifest their creativity, the persons to be emulated, the processes to be employed, and the products to be produced.

The downside of the reward system is that it siphons off energy from creativity to competition. All the persons who had a hand in the creative work usually go unrewarded because the reward is to be given to only one person. Other conditions limit recognition only to living persons or to works produced during a specific segment of time (e.g., a calendar year). And, the fact that a work is recognized with a reward does not mean that it is completely without fault or error (Gleitman, 1981, 1984; Stein, 1984b, 1985).

Mentoring.

There are groups of intermediaries who facilitate an individual's work with guidance and advice. They are called *mentors*. Mentors have a long history and go way back in time. In Greek mythology, Odysseus appointed Mentor to watch over his son, Telemachus. Mentors, according to Torrance (Frey & Noller, 1992), appear in many cultures under different names. In Europe there is the *patron*, in India the *guru*, and in Japan, the *sensei*.

The mentoring relationship may be formal or informal. The success of the mentoring relationship depends on the mentor's ability to recognize and evaluate talent or ability, sensitivity in personal relationships, ability to be giving and supportive, ability to manifest courage, ability to show warmth, and the like, as well as the mentor's competence, skills, and know-how. The mentor's protege must have drive and ambition, ability, trust in the mentor, and the capacity to accept the mentor's acceptance, support, guidance, and evaluation.

On the negative side, it is important to guard against jealousy, tension, and resentment. Consequently, it is important that the nature of the mentoring relationship be reviewed as the protege develops creatively.

On the contemporary scene, as women are getting more and more opportunity (although not as great as they or others would like for them) to rise to important positions in management and administration of companies, the role of the mentor may well play a crucial role in their future administrative mobility and success.

Modeling.

The modeling function of intermediaries is similar to the mentoring function. Mentoring involves a much more conscious effort to advise, direct, and facilitate a protege's efforts. In modeling, for purposes here, there is also more of the master-apprentice relationship in which the apprentice learns a great deal incidentally and unconsciously while working with the master.

A conference of prominent scientists and philosophers of science (Maugh, 1974) assumed that the capacity to generate ideas might be innate and could not be changed. They agreed, however, that the master-apprentice relationship helps the apprentice develop a "critical faculty"—the ability to ask the "right kind" and "worthwhile questions" and the capacity for self-criticism—all of which lead to "finding problems that can be solved."

Championing.

Intermediaries champion and publicize creative individuals' works. This added push is necessary at time to get others' attention. It may also be necessary to goad the creative person into completing a work in progress, and presenting it to peers or the public for their reactions and evaluations. Darwin was a good case in point (Gruber, 1981). He published his data and theory only after Wallace had already sent him a paper in which his work carried out independently was similar to what Darwin had in mind.

Family and friends, peers, and colleagues usually are in a position to serve as excellent champions. In some fields, the role of champion is formalized in that of the *publicist* who gets publicity for the individual and at the same time protects the individual from overexposure to others.

Not only celebrities have publicists. Publicists also play roles in academia, in the sciences, and the arts where they may or may not function discretely behind the scenes. Thomas Huxley does not always get the credit he deserves for championing Darwin's theory of evolution even though he was known at a crucial point in time as "Darwin's bulldog" (Peel, 1984).

Protection.

The roles and functions of intermediaries discussed thus far may or may not be formalized and institutionalized. In most instances they are not. They are fulfilled in some informal manner by nonprofessionals and professionals who need not necessarily be paid for their time and effort. Whatever they do, they do for their profession and even for themselves but certainly for the creative individual.

In turning to "protection," we are at a transition point. This function, especially in terms of the example discussed here, is performed by an institutionalized group, actually a governmental agency (e.g., the U.S. Patent Office) that serves both the individual and the society. It gives the individual rights to the sole use of the patent as well as protection from patent infringement (and hence possible loss of income). The community is protected because the work has been reviewed, evaluated, and considered "workable."

Patents are guaranteed by the Bill of Rights and when assigned give patentees the sole right to exploit their works commercially for a period of 17 years. Why are works of art, for example, not given similar protection? For what it is worth, it has been suggested that the protection given to inventors might be related to the fact that some of the founding fathers of the United States who had a hand in writing the Bill of Rights were themselves inventors.

Artists, painters, and sculptors were not accorded the same protection as inventors. Artists have argued that they should receive royalties for their works. As works of art are sold and resold from one collector to another or from one dealer to another, prices may go up and up and artists responsible for the work never share in the profit. Art collectors and those who invest in art do not necessarily agree that artists should share in the profits. They argue that once the artist is paid for art work he or she loses all right to it as would be the case with anyone who sells a commodity. Artists counter with the argument that their art works are not commodities.

Developments in computer software have recently attracted a great deal of attention. These are patented works and a great deal of creativity, time, effort, and money are usually invested in them. However, knowing or unknowingly, intentionally or unintentionally, the patents of these works are infringed on by students, hackers, and others.

A case (Lewis, 1994) involved a 20-year-old student at the Massachusetts Institute of Technology who was accused by a federal grand jury of illegally distributing pirated software that cost such a vast amount of money. Another case was cited at Brown University. Currently, the law states "it is illegal to distribute or make unauthorized copies of copyrighted programs regardless of whether a profit motive is involved or not" (Lewis, 1994, p. 4). These cases are seen as "one of the major tests of how new copyright laws, as well as old First Amendment protections, could function in a society that increasingly communicates over electronic networks" (Lewis, 1994, p. 1).

In this whole arena, still another important case has recently come to the fore (Bulkeley, 1994a, 1994b). A computer consultant developed a means of sending messages via computer that is "uncrackable, or as close to it as a secret code has ever been" (Bulkeley, 1994a). This may have been sent worldwide over Internet (which is illegal) "making it easy for foreign governments and terrorists to use it and render their computer traffic impervious to U.S. spying" (Bulkeley, 1994b). A federal grand jury is still studying this matter.

Regulators

Having considered intermediaries whose role it is primarily to serve the individual, I come now to a large group of intermediaries whose primary role it is to serve society. These persons generally fulfill some formal professional or governmental function and, hence are here called *regulators*. Basically, their overriding function to serve society as gatekeepers (Lewin, 1958) determining that which will or will not get through to the public.

Like developers, regulators also vary in training and number. Like developers, regulators can be very powerful individuals insofar as the creative process is concerned. Unlike developers, regulators' decisions more often than not have the power of law behind them. And, when it is not the power of the law, it is the power of a professional group or association. Some of the roles and functions fulfilled by regulators are discussed here.

Review.

Government agencies require review and evaluation of projects and proposals even before they are financed and set in motion so that money and time are not wasted. Careful, objective, and incisive reviews by in-house or external experts are mandatory.

The experts may have achieved their status because they are senior people with a broad knowledge and a history of creative contributions to the field, or because they are specialists in the field under discussion, or because for one reason or another they are considered "peers" of those who submitted a proposal or plan for review.

Judging from the history of progress in the arts and sciences this system of review, generally referred to as *peer review* has served society rather well. The status and high regard in which such review is held is reflected in the fact that in some academic situations research personnel whose work has passed peer review receive greater rewards—large salary increases, promotions, and the like.

As in other situations, so here there is also a negative side. Insiders can be quite hostile and refuse to acknowledge outsiders' contributions with what is referred to as an "NIH" attitude—if a work has "not been invented here,"[1] it is no good. The competitive attitude of peers toward each other has been highlighted by psychologist David Rappaport, who is reported to have defined a peer as follows: "A peer is someone who gets on behind you in a revolving door and comes in front of you." Such competitiveness can even result in the refusal to acknowledge in print that a peer has been proven correct when earlier one was quick to say he was wrong (Dewsbury, 1993).

Review committees, whether they are charged with considering salary or proposals, are composed of people. Consequently, they are subject to all the foibles that one can expect of people. When it comes to salary decisions the buddy system may operate, where "x" rewards "y" and then "y" returns the favor by increasing "x's" salary.

Backscratching can also block adequate peer review of scientific studies. Friendship, the expectation of a returned favor, an attitude of *noblesse oblige* can all interfere with proper standards.

Criticism.

Criticism is implicit or explicit in most of the roles and functions fulfilled by intermediaries. They are most explicit and most obvious in the behavior of those persons who are actually designated as "critics." These persons earn their livelihoods by writing critical evaluations of books, movies, exhibitions, and the like. They are expected to be objective, in the sense that they will not play favorites. It is clear that they are evaluating and stating opinions that are highly regarded by their employers and their large number of followers. In their reviews they can "make" or "break" works and reputations.

This is a very serious matter because vast sums of money are invested in plays, in publishing books, and the like. What should not be overlooked is the stress, strain, and investment of time and money by the person who created a work that is reviewed.

For example, the publication of a book-length murder mystery may have a long and involved history. (Mack, 1994) said that "Most mystery writers write four complete books before they sell one. . . ." After the work is completed, an agent is to be hired because publishers will not necessarily look at unsolicited manuscripts—they want others to do the screening for them. Then, if the work is accepted and it is the author's first work, the author would have to be happy with an advance of only $3,000 to $5,000.

A very positive review will be quoted and can help sales. There is little that can be done if the review is negative. Some journals and magazines will accept letters from the author disputing the review. In some instances, this opportunity will come with certain

---
[1] This is also a pun on the National Institutes of Health.

restrictions—the author may discuss only facts but not opinions, there may be limitations on space allocated to the author; and, because the author's defense is not published with the negative review, the author may or may not reach the same audience that read the earlier negative review.

All this might change pending a case that is currently in litigation (Barrett, 1994). Moldea received a very negative review for his book, *Interference: How Organized Crime Influences Professional Football* in *The New York Times*. It was said to be full of "'unfounded insinuations'" and "'sloppy journalism.'" Although the reviewer did say that the book contained "'hot stuff'" he also said "'there is too much sloppy journalism to trust the bulk of this book's 512 pages.'" Misspelled names and "'bungled anecdotes'" were cited in support of this assertion.

The author admitted that three names were misspelled and admitted the review contained errors. He wanted *The New York Times* to publish a letter from him which corrected the errors. *The Times* refused. And, so the author sued in August 1990. At least one other paper that had published a negative review did publish a letter from the author and was not sued). In his suit, the author also cited economic losses that he suffered as a result of the negative review—television appearances were cancelled and he lost income from other media as well. Media people agreed that the *The New York Times Book Review* wielded a great deal of influence.

Moldea's suit, when it was first presented before a federal judge, was thrown out of court. "But in February [1994] a U.S. appeals court panel reinstated the suit, saying criticism—literary or otherwise—isn't insulated from libel actions" (Barrett, 1994, p. B1).

According to Barrett, some journalists and First Amendment buffs regard the author as a traitor. Publishers do not want to see reviews harmed in any way because reviews "even scathing ones, are a prime means of promotion, especially for authors who aren't already famous" (Barrett, 1994, p. B1).

Finally, as Barrett reported, "The media are up in arms over the panel's decision, pointing to a dissenting judge's assertion that it could 'open up the entire arena of artistic criticism to mass defamation suits.'" Until recently, courts made a sharp distinction between assertions of fact and opinion, and opinion as completely shielded from libel suits. But in 1990, the Supreme court rejected the dichotomy, saying that statements of opinion can be libelous if they imply false facts. The appeals court's Moldea ruling is built on the 1990 precedent. Should the decision go in the author's favor one can expect important changes in the behavior of intermediaries involved in publishing critiques of books, plays, and the like.

Watchdog.

Governmental agencies, professional organizations, community groups, and others are intermediaries who fulfill watchdog functions in the creative process. In so doing, they are involved in a variety of different areas of which the following are a sample.

Technological Innovation. The federal government serves a watchdog function in the area of technological innovation. As such, it functions in part as developer and in part as regulator. As a developer the federal government puts up the money to stimulate technological development as the information highway and in flat-panel television screens. Its behavior, however, has been described as "schizophrenic" because, although it promotes the efforts of many companies, it also seems to go out of its way to pick fights with these same companies.

> Signs of the internal conflict are almost everywhere. The President and Vice President Al Gore have made several high-profile trips to Silicon Valley and have courted its executives as advisers. At the same time, however, the Justice Department is pursuing an intense antitrust investigation of the Microsoft Corporation the biggest software company. (Andrews, 1994, p. D1)

Fraud. To detect fraud on government-supported works, the U.S. government has come to rely partly on whistleblowers who are rewarded 15% of what the government collects after a legal suit. Contractors object to whistleblowers who report alleged frauds to government before going to management and giving management the opportunity to rectify the alleged wrongdoing. In 1986, the U.S. government increased the amount awarded to overcome fraud. Thus far, $750 million has been collected and it is anticipated that the figure will likely "surpass $1 billion" (Sims, 1994).

Ethics. Ethics, is another watchdog function of government. Governmental agencies as well as professional organizations have published codes of ethics to guide and regulate the behavior of scientists and other professionals with regard to each other and especially with regard to patients and clients whom they might use as subjects in their research. Stein (1993) reported on the efforts of *The New England Journal of Medicine* (Angell, 1990) and organizations of ethnobotanists (Boom, 1990).

Surely, existing codes work well but there are occasions where weaknesses in the system come to the fore. A case in point was recently reported in which "some experts say, probably caused the most deaths of all the known Government-sponsored radiation experiments since World War II" (Schneider, 1994, p. D9).

Public Health. The publics' health has to be watched over carefully. One frequent area of concern is radiation experiments and another involves biotechnology and bioengineering. With regard to these two latter areas, some of the problem may involve the public's ignorance and some of the problem may involve conflict with some existing economic interests.

Consider, for example, the use of hormone injections to increase milk production. Many people were antagonistic to this procedure fearing that the hormones would find their way into the persons who drank the milk and cause some unknown problems or illnesses. This, despite the fact that "in the natural state," some cows produce milk because of the characteristics of their hormones. Another negative side effect was the possibility of infection at the site where the hormone was injected into the cow. But, this is a quite different matter than the problem of the hormone.

One objection to the use of the hormone that did not necessarily receive the attention it deserved was that it worked too well. Cows receiving the hormone produced more milk than cows who did not. With increased milk production, the price of milk would fall and profits might well drop or small farmers might have difficulty competing with dairy farmers who have large herds of cows.

In other words, it is conceivable that the objection to the use of hormones to increase milk production stemmed not only from injecting cows with hormones but also from powerful economic interests as well.

One of the important side effects of the Food and Drug Administration's (FDA) experience with hormones and milk was increased caution with biogenetically engineered vegetables—specifically the tomato.

A U.S. company sought approval for the first genetically engineered food—a firmer tomato that can ripen longer on the vine before being picked for shipment (Hilts, 1994). In fact, the company did not need approval from the FDA but it sought it nevertheless simply to avoid confusion and turmoil in the marketplace when the tomatoes would come to market with lots of fanfare about being a good-tasting product with longer shelf life than tomatoes that are not biogenetically engineered.

Developments in bioengineering are moving at such a pace that the public might find it worthwhile to become better informed about the development of new food products. For example, it is age-old practice for farmers, while harvesting corn, to separate those ears of corn that they will send to market from those they regard as specially outstanding and worthy of serving as *seed corn* to be used in the production of future crops. Urban populations who have enjoyed the fruits of this procedure probably never realized the important role played by the farmer in the development of types of corn. Little did they realize that the end effect of what is produced by the farmer is no different from what is produced by researchers who systematically alter a vegetable's genetic structure to produce some desirable or valued characteristic.

I hasten to add that I do not mean to suggest that the study of innovations' effects on health should be done away with or bypassed. On the contrary, it should be maintained as a check. But this should be independent of educating the public about the processes involved in new development.

Albeit incomplete, let this survey of two major groups of intermediaries—developers and regulators—suffice for purposes here and let us turn to the future.

THE FUTURE

Effort should be devoted to the systematic study of the variety of roles and functions fulfilled by intermediaries in the creative process. Case studies and anecdotal material can add to the picture. In all instances, one needs to know how intermediaries become intermediaries, what their life histories are, what is the course of their careers, why they became intermediaries instead of creatives (if they had a choice), how they obtained and exercise the power they wield, and how they go about developing and regulating others in the creative process.

Ideally, the same psychological techniques administered to more and less creative persons in any domain should also be administered to intermediaries to increase understanding of their psychodynamics. Just as one studies organizational effects on creativity, so one should study organizational effects on intermediaries.

Such knowledge would go a long way to increasing the understanding of the total creative process as it occurs in a social context. If nothing else, it would highlight the fact that the total creative process is not without evaluation (Runco, 1993). It would explain the characteristics of this evaluation and how it effects creativity.

Knowledge so obtained should be fed back to participants in creativity training programs. At the present time, training programs focus almost all of their energy on the individual or the organization, but intermediaries and their effects are overlooked. Traineers should be prepared for what to expect so that they can cope more effectively with and communicate more effectively with developers, regulators, and other intermediaries.

Those who teach courses on creativity might find it worthwhile to devote some teaching time to intermediaries. Students in my creativity course interviewed gallery owners in their neighborhoods and curators in the museums they attended. Of special interest to many of them were the interviews they had with cafe and disco owners to learn how they as intermediaries went out hiring new bands and stand-up comics. Not only did these students learn about the psychosocial factors effecting creativity but they also learned about "creativity in action," something that interested them most.

Some students of creativity are too close or too immersed in their work to take notice of intermediaries. To counteract this tendency, I suggest attending a workshop in an area other than one's own. I attended a screenplay writing workshop in Hollywood and even though I shall never write a screenplay, I found the experience an eye opener. I became more aware than I had ever been with the collaborative art form movie making is. Short of attending a screenplay workshop I would recommend as a substitute step in the right direction reading the March 21, 1994 issue of *The New Yorker* which is completely devoted to the movies.

Studies of intermediaries and systematic case studies, anecdotal or otherwise, can also be of value to society at large and especially that group within it that believes that it is overregulated. This attitude is well expressed in the following quotation from a paper by a retired director of Lockheed's Advanced Development Projects Group who wrote:

> We are lucky the airplane was invented back in 1903 and developed over the following years. We would probably be stopped in developing the airplane in today's climate. The environmentalists would object to the noise, the consumers would want to have them all recalled before they got out the factory door, the pacifists would complain that they could be used to carry troops, preservationists would be afraid they could fly into city hall, and ten government study groups could prove that they definitely could cause cancer.

In the light of this discussion, it is understandable for some persons to wonder how creative works come to light at all. Hopefully, when more complete knowledge of intermediaries' roles and functions is added to knowledge of the psychosocial dynamics of the creative individual in the social context one will be able to facilitate further the course of the creative process. It will be possible to optimize the fulfillment of creative efforts so that fewer creative works will die on the vine and the quality of life of the whole society will be advanced.

REFERENCES

Andrews, B. I. (1994, April 11). Clinton and technology: Some policies clash. *The New York Times*, pp. D1, D2.

Angell, M. (1990). The Nazi hypothermia experiments and unethical research today. *New England Journal of Medicine, 322*, 1435-1440.

Boom, B. M. (1990). Giving native people a share of the profits. *Garden, 14*, 28-31.

Barrett, P. M. (1994, April 7). Author sued over scornful review is now scorned by the publishing world. *The Wall Street Journal*, p. B1.

Bulkeley, W. M. (1994a, April 28). Cipher probe: Popularity overseas of encryption code has the world worried. *The Wall Street Journal*, pp. 1, B13.

Bulkeley, W. M. (1994b, April 11). Two face computer-fraud allegations over software piracy on the Internet. *The Wall Street Journal*, pp. B6, B22.

Chadwick, W., & de Courtivron, I. (Eds.). (1993). *Significant others: Creativity & intimate partnerships*. New York: Thames & Hudson.

Decision from FDA on Calgene tomato expected in 90 days. (1994, April 11). *Wall Street Journal*, p. B6.

Dewsbury, D. A. (1993). On publishing controversy: Norman R. F. Maier and the genesis of seizures. *American Psychologist, 48*, 869-877.

Frey, B. R., & Noller, R. B. (1992). Mentoring: A legacy of success. In S. J. Parnes (Ed.), *Source book for creative problem solving* (pp. 446-449). Buffalo, NY: Creative Education Foundation.

Gazzaniga, M. S. (1988). *Mind matters: How the mind & brain interact to create our conscious lives*. New York: Houghton Mifflin.

Gleitman, H. (1981). *Psychology*. New York: Norton.

Gleitman, H. (1984). Some comments on Dr. Stein's critique of my account of Asch's social-pressure studies. *Perceptual and Motor Skills, 59*, 1003-1006.

Gruber, H. (1981). *Darwin on man: A psychological study of scientific creativity*. Chicago: University of Chicago Press.

Hilts, P. J. (1994, April 9). Genetically altered tomato moves toward U. S. approval. *The New York Times*, p. 17.

Jerison, H. J. (1973). *Evolution of the brain and intelligence*. New York: Academic Press.

Lewin, K. (1935) *A dynamic theory of personality*. New York: McGraw-Hill.

Lewin, K. (1958). Group decision and social change. In F. E. Maccoby, T. M. Newcomb, & E. L. Hartley (Eds.), *Readings in social psychology* (3rd ed., pp. 197-211). New York: The Free Press.

Lewis, P. H. (1994, April 9). Student accused of running network for pirated software. *The New York Times*, pp. 1, 9.

Mack, T. (1994, April 25). Novel advice. *Forbes*, pp. 174-175.

Maugh, T. H., II. (1974, June). Creativity: Can it be dissected? Can it be taught? *Science*, p. 1273.

Peel, J. D. (Ed.). (1984). *Herbert Spencer and social evolution.* Chicago: University of Chicago Press.

Roe, A. (1952). *The making of a scientist.* New York: Dodd, Mead.

Runco, M. (1993, May). *Giftedness as critical and creative thought.* Paper presented at the Wallace Symposium on Giftedness and Talent, Iowa City, IA.

Schneider, K. (1994, April 11). Cold war radiation test on humans to undergo a congressional review. *The New York Times*, p. D9.

Sims, C. (1994, April 11). Trying to mute the whistle-blowers. *The New York Times*, p. D1.

Stein, M. I. (1974). *Stimulating creativity: Vol 1 Individual procedures.* Amagansett, NY: The Mews Press.

Stein, M. I. (1975). *Stimulating creativity: Vol 2 Group procedures.* Amagansett, NY: The Mews Press.

Stein, M. I. (1981). The investment analyst: An intermediary in the process. *Wall Street Transcript, 61,* 61, 315-317.

Stein, M. I. (1983). The creative process and the synthesis and dissemination of information. In S. A. Ward & L. J. Reed (Eds.), *Knowledge structure and use: Implications for synthesis and interpretation* (pp. 364-396). Philadelphia, PA: Temple University Press.

Stein, M. I. (1984a). Even the muses had parents. *Journal of Creative Behavior, 18,* 185-186.

Stein, M. I. (1984b). A minority of one, a crackpot (?), in an introductory psychology textbook. *Perceptual and Motor Skills, 39,* 370.

Stein, M. I. (1985). A reply to Gleitman. *Perceptual and Motor Skills, 60,* 10.

Stein, M. I. (1993). Moral issues facing intermediaries between creators and the public. *Creativity Research Journal, 6,* 197-200.

AUTHOR INDEX

A

Abelson, R. P., 219, *224*
Abra, J. C., 19, *63*, 277, 279, *299*, 329, 330, 336, 337, 343, 354, 355, 358, 360, 362, 363, *373*
Abramson, L. Y., 215, *223*
Abt, L. E., 334, 353, 356, 358, 360, *377*
Ackerman, C. M., 61, *63*
Adams, J. L., 120, *126*
Adams, M. J., 202, 203, *206*
Adhikarya, R., 21, *66*
Albert, R. S., 21, *67*, 79, *93*, 305, *326*
Alexander, D. A., 62, *63*
Alisa, I., 26, 36, 38, *63*
Amabile, T. M., 20, 32, *63*, *64*, 116, *126*, 139, 143, 147, *148*, 211, 216, 219, *222*, *223*, 232, 235, 242, *248*, 277, 298, *299*, *300*, 343, 360, *373*
Amsel, A., 350, *373*
Anderson, D. K., 280, *302*
Anderson, H. H., 275, *300*
Anderson, J. R., 22, 58, *63*, 255, *269*
Andrews, B. I., 389, *393*
Andrews, P., 285, *301*
Angell, M., 389, *393*
Angelo, T. A., 191, *206*
Ansbacher, H. L., 348, 355, *373*
Ansbacher, R. R., 348, 355, *373*
Arieti, S., 20, *63*, 331, 346, *373*
Atkinson, J., 212, *228*

B

Bachelor, P., 226, *249*
Baer, J., 21, 32, 57, *63*, 131, 139, 141, 142, 143, 144, 145, 147, *148*, *149*, 203, *206*
Bagnall, J., 119, 120, *126*
Baker-Sennett, J., 307, *323*
Bandura, A., 349, 354, *373*
Barnes, J., 330, *373*
Barrett, P. M., 388, *393*
Barrett, P. T., 103, *113*
Barron, F., 110, 111, *112*, 176, 181, *186*, 229, *248*, 353, *373*
Basadur, M., 61, *63*, 85, 87, 88, 91, *92*, *93*, 138, *149*
Bate, W. J., 344, 347, *373*
Baughman, W. A., 23, 24, 32, 42, 56, 58, 60, 62, *63*, 65
Bauman, R., 307, 314, *323*
Beck, A. T., 216, *222*
Becker, E., 335, *373*
Bell, A. G., 278, *300*
Bell, E. T., 101, 104, *112*

Berger, D. E., 26, 66
Berliner, D. C., 140, 149
Berliner, P., 307, 314, 343
Bernstein, M., 14, 17
Beveridge, W. I. B., 5, 16
Bill, V. L., 258, 271
Birney, R. C., 212, 222
Black, J., 263, 270
Block, D., 78, 92
Block, J., 78, 92
Bloom, B. S., 349, 373
Bookspan, M., 335, 373
Boom, B. M., 389, 393
Bourdieu, P., 307(n4), 313, 323
Bousfield, W., 105, 112
Bradshaw, G. F., 8, 17
Bradshaw, G. L., 8, 17, 21, 63
Bransford, J. D., 143, 145, 151
Bredekamp, S., 260, 264, 269
Brill, A. A., 352, 374
Brock, W. H., 96, 112
Brown, J. D., 210, 222
Brown, R. T., 181, 186
Bruner, J., 262, 269, 307, 323
Bulkeley, W. M., 385, 386, 393
Burdick, H., 212, 222
Burns, M. S., 143, 145, 151
Byrnes, J. P., 36, 62, 68

C

Cacciari, C., 244, 249
Calkins, D. E., 279, 280, 300
Cameron, N., 106, 112
Campbell, D. T., 4, 5, 9, 16, 101, 102, 112, 132, 134, 135, 137, 138, 149, 309, 323
Camus, A., 334, 344, 374
Carey, S., 143, 149
Carlson, W. B., 22, 63, 278, 300
Carpenter, J., 331, 374
Carroll, J. B., 97, 112
Case, R., 256, 269
Cazden, C. B., 307, 324
Cecil, D., 358, 374
Chadwick, W., 381, 393
Chaffee, J., 20, 64
Chand, I., 27, 67, 69, 71, 80, 81, 82, 83, 90, 91, 93, 115, 125, 126, 127, 277, 298, 301, 310, 326
Chard, S. C., 262, 270

Charles, R., 78, 79, 80, 94
Chi, M. T. H., 22, 64
Chou, D. L., 279, 280, 300
Clancy, M., 108, 113
Claridge, G., 108, 114
Clark, H., 228, 229, 231, 248
Clark, R., 212, 223
Clinkenbeard, P. R., 170, 171, 187
Colangelo, N., 276, 300
Cole, M., 307, 323
Collingwood, R. G., 311, 323
Connelly, M. S., 22, 62, 65
Costanza, D. P., 23, 32, 56, 58, 62, 65
Cotropia, K. K., 61, 63
Coulson, R. L., 280, 302
Crease, R., 305(n2), 323
Cross, K. P., 191, 206
Crutcher, R. J., 210, 222
Csikszentmihalyi, M., 26, 51, 59, 64, 116, 117, 126, 139, 149, 177, 186, 196, 207, 213, 214, 222, 238, 244, 248, 253, 270, 304, 305(n12), 312, 314, 322, 323, 324

D

Daniels, R., 334, 349, 355, 356, 374
Darwin, C., 134, 149
Davidson, J. E., 26, 36, 38, 45, 64, 165, 167, 173, 186, 187
Davis, G., 233, 249
Davis, M. H., 359, 374
Davis, S. N., 322, 324
de Courtivron, I., 381, 393
de Mille, A., 351, 374
de Sanchez, M., 189, 207
Declos, V. R., 143, 145, 151
DeCock, C., 90, 92
Dewey, J., 321, 324
Dewsbury, D. A., 387, 393
Diekhoff, G., 362, 374
Dillon, J. T., 22, 64
Doares, L., 21, 23, 24, 27, 42, 56, 57, 60, 65, 65, 66
Dodson, J. D., 361, 373
Domino, G., 21, 64, 233, 237, 248
Dow, G., 91, 94
Drevet, A., 122, 126
Dryden, W., 216, 222
Duncker, K., 118, 126
Dykes, M., 108, 112

Author Index

Dykman, B. M., 215, *223*

E

Easton, S. M., 8, *17*
Ebert, R., 335, *374*
Einstein, A., 259, *269*
Eisenberg, N., 359, *374*
Eliot, T. S., 341, *374*
Elkind, D., 72, *92*
Ellis, A., 216, *223*
Epstein, R., 309, *324*
Erikson, E. H., 260, *269*
Eysenck, H. J., 4, *16*, 97, 101, 103, 104, 105, 106, 107, *111*, *112*, *113*
Eysenck, S. B. G., 106, *113*

F

Facione, P., 191, *206*
Fausto-Sterling, A., 139, *149*
Feldhusen, J. F., 26, *64*
Feldman, D. H., 309, *324*, 349, *354*
Feldon, J., 109, *113*
Feltovich, P. J., 280, *302*
Ferrari, M., 171, *187*
Ferris, P., 333, *374*
Ferster, C. B., 347, *374*
Festinger, L., 351, *374*
Feyerabend, P., 313, *324*
Fillenbaum, S., 234, *248*
Fine, G., 238, *248*
Finke, R. A., 21, 22, 23, 42, 44, 56, 60, *64*
Firestien, R. L., 309, *324*
Fleishman, E. A., 27, *66*
Fodor, J. A., 142, *149*
Forman, E. A., 307, *324*
Fortier, L., 263, *270*
Foucault, M., 307(n4), *324*
Fox, J. J., 314, *324*
Francis, W., 71, *93*, 225, *250*
Frankl, V., 344, *374*
Frearson, W., 103, 104, *113*
Frederiksen, R., 22, 58, *64*
Freire, P., 266, *270*
French, J., 360, *374*
Freud, S., 330, 337, 347, 351, 353, *374*
Frey, B. R., 383, *393*
Fromm, E., 344, 355, 358, *375*
Fulford, R., 349, 353, *375*
Fuller, R. G., 193, *206*
Furneaux, W. D., 102, *113*

Fustier, M., 122, *126*

G

Gaeth, J., 276, *300*
Gage, N. L., 140, *149*
Galanter, E., 117, *126*
Galton, F., 226, *248*
Gangley, P. W., 21, *63*
Gardner, H., 76, *92*, 139, 141, 142, 143, *149*, 260, 263, *270*, 277, *300*, 312, 322, *324*, 335, 336, 354, *375*
Garnier, H., 14, *17*
Garvey, W. D., 14, *16*
Gazzaniga, M. S., 142, *149*, 382, *393*
George, E. I., 106, 107, *114*
Gerrig, R., 231, *248*
Getzels, J., 26, 51, 59, *64*, 83(n1), *92*, 117, *126*, 177, *186*, 253, *270*, 336, *375*
Ghiselin, B., 20, *64*, 227, 242, *251*
Giacommelli, L., 234, 237, *249*
Gibbs, R., 244, *249*
Gick, M. L., 27, *64*
Gilmore, F. E., 276, *300*
Givon, T., 229, *249*
Glaser, E. M., 90, *94*
Glaser, R., 22, *64*
Glasser, W., 268, *270*
Gleitman, H., 383, *394*
Glick, J., 261, *270*
Glover, J. A., 96, *113*
Goetz, K. O., 106, *113*
Gollob, H., 240, *250*
Goodman, N., 154, *186*, 262, *270*
Gordon, W. J. J., 199, *206*
Gorman, M. E., 22, *63*, 276, 277, 278, 298, *300*, *301*
Gough, H., 229, 233, 236, 242, 243, *249*
Graen, G. B., 61, *63*
Grant, K. S., 353, *375*
Gray, J., 109, *113*
Gray, N., 109, *113*
Green, M., 358, *375*
Greenacre, P., 354, 358, *375*
Greene, G., 344, *375*
Greeno, J. G., 45, 58, *64*
Greer, G., 349, *375*
Gregorc, A., 277, *300*
Grice, H., 228, *249*

Grigorenko, E. L., 171, *187*, 279, *302*
Grossman, B. S., 277, *300*
Gruber, H., 14, *16*, 20, *64*, 322, *324*, 384, *393*
Guilford, J. P., 21, *64*, 71, *92*, 122, *126*, 139, 140, 141, *150*, 261, 270, 303, *324*, 336, 354, *375*
Gumperz, J. J., 314, *324*
Gustafson, S. B., 20, 22, 57, *65*

H

Habermas, J., 266, *270*
Hadamard, J., 308, *324*
Haensly, P. A., 177, *186*
Hall, C. S., 20, 61, *65*
Hallowell, K., 276, *300*
Halpern, D. F., 191, 194, 196, 198(n19), *206*
Hampton, J., 242, *249*
Harding, F. D., 27, *66*
Harding, S., 139, *150*
Hardy, G. H., 99, *113*, 330, *375*
Harrington, D., 78, 81, 91, *92*, 110, 111, *112*, 178, 181, *186*, 213, *223*, 229, 233, *248*, *249*
Hawkins, J., 261, *270*
Hayes, J. R., 169, 177, *186*
Hebb, D. O., 360, 361, *374*
Heider, F., 313, *324*
Heinzen, T. E., 211, 215, 220, *223*
Helson, R., 247, *249*
Hemsley, D. R., 109, *113*
Henle, M., 348, *375*
Hennessey, B. A., 32, *64*, 148, *150*, 216, *223*, 277, *300*
Herdt, G., 307, *327*
Hergenhahn, B. R., 352, *375*
Herrnstein, R. J., 189, *207*
Hickenlooker, G., 330, *375*
Hilts, P. J., 390, *393*
Hintzman, D. L., 388, *375*
Hirokawa, R. Y., 299, *300*
Ho, V., 263, *270*
Hocevar, D., 81, 91, *92*, 226, *249*
Hoepfner, R., 139, 140, 141, *150*
Hogarth, R. M., 36, *64*
Holyoak, K. J., 27, 58, *64*
Hoover, S. M., 26, *64*
Horvath, J. A., 278, *302*
Houtz, J. C., 193, *207*

Howe, R. B. K., 337, *375*
Huesman, R., 276, *300*
Huff, D., 195, *207*
Hull, D. L., 12, *16*
Hutchinson, E. D., 335, *375*
Hymes, D., 307, 314, *324*, *325*

I

Infeld, L., 259, *269*
Ironson, G., 233, *249*
Isaksen, S. G., 61, *65*

J

Jackson, K., 335, *376*
Jackson, P., 83(n1), *92*, 335, 336, *376*
James, W., 321, *325*
Janis, I. L., 279, *300*
Jausovec, N., 55, *65*
Jennings, J., 245, *249*
Jerison, H. J., 382, *393*
Jewkes, J., 276, *300*
Jintang, L., 286, *301*
John-Steiner, V., 345, *376*
Johnson, D., 245, *249*, *251*
Johnson, M., 194, *207*, 244, *250*
Johnson, S., 342, 356, *376*
Johnson-Laird, P. N., 135, 137, 138, 139, 140, 143, *150*
Jones, E. E., 210, 221, *223*, 313, *325*
Jones, R., 309, 310, *325*
Jung, C. G., 354, *376*

K

Kac, M., 100, *113*
Kagiwada, J. K., 276, *300*
Kanigel, R., 97, *113*
Kantorovich, A., 4, *16*
Karmiloff-Smith, A., 142, 143, 145, *150*
Kasof, J., 9, *16*, 21, *65*
Katz, A., 229, 232, 233, 234, 236, 237, 239, 240, 241, 243, 244, *249*, *250*, *251*
Katz, L. G., 262, *275*
Kauffmann, S., 334, 335, 339, 357, *376*
Kaufmann, A., 122, *126*
Kay, S., 26, 59, *65*
Kerr, B., 276, *300*
Kerr, W., 353, *376*
Ketton, T. L., 61, *63*
Kimble, G., 350, *376*
Kirton, M., 242, *250*

Kisselgoff, A., 332, 335, *376*
Kivenson, G., 276, *301*
Klopfer, L. E., 279, *301*
Knight, D., 96, *113*
Koberg, D., 119, 120, *126*
Kocowski, T., 120, *126*
Koestler, A., 5, 13, *16*, 22, *65*, 342, *376*
Kogan, N., 83(n1), *94*
Kohlberg, L., 76, *93*
Kohn, A., 331, 358, *376*
Korkel, J., 25, *271*
Kotovsky, K., 169, *186*
Kreitler, H., 346, *376*
Kreitler, S., 346, *376*
Kreuz, R., 229, *250*
Kris, E., 335, 352, *376*
Krockover, G. H., 276, *301*
Kucera, H., 71, *93*, 225, *250*
Kuehn, C., 276, *301*
Kuhn, D., 6, 12, *17*, 203, *270*
Kuhn, T. S., 22, 26, 36, 38, *65*, 95, *113*
Kulkarni, D., 22, 26, *65*

L

Lakoff, G., 194, *207*, 244, *250*
Lamb, D., 8, *17*
Langer, E. J., 199, *207*
Langer, S. K., 334, *376*
Langley, P., 8, *17*, 309, 310, *325*
Lave, J., 307, *325*
Lawrence, J. A., 321(n8), *325*
LeBoeuf, M., 185, *186*
Ledoux, J., 142, *149*
Leer, M. L., 258, *271*
Lehman, D. R., 202, *207*
Lehman, H. C., 362, *376*
Leinhardt, G., 259, *270*
Lesgold, S. B., 258, *271*
Lewin, K., 380, 386, *393*
Lewis, P. H., 385, *394*
Lewis, T., 283, *301*
Lin, H. T., 61, *66*
Linzdey, G., 20, 61, *65*
Lipman, M., 268, *270*
Littman, M., 231, *248*
Liu, H. C., 61, *63*
Lohman, D. R., 36, *67*
Lord, A. B., 314, *325*
Lowell, E., 212, *223*
Lowenfeld, V., 190, *207*

Lubart, F. I., 153, *187*
Lubart, T. I., 21, *67*, 116, *127*, 176, *186*
Lubow, R. E., 108, 108, *113*

M

Mack, R. W., 190, *206*
Mack, T., 190, *207*
MacKinnon, D., 213, *223*, 226, *250*, 354, 358, *376*
Mackworth, N. A., 117, *126*
Macworth, N. H., 253, *270*
Maher, M. A., 23, 56, *65*, 143, *150*
Manes, S., 285, *301*
Margaret, A., 106, *112*
Markman, E. M., 182, *186*
Markovits, H., 263, *270*
Marshall, C., 228, 229, 231, *248*
Martinage, M., 216, *223*
Martindale, C., 4, 6, *17*, 309, *325*
Martinsen, O., 21, *65*
Maslow, A. H., 347, 348, 349, 360, *376*
Masterman, M., 95, *113*
Matusek, P., 106, 107, *114*
Matusov, E., 307, *323*
Maugh, T. H., II, 384, *394*
Maultsby, M. C., Jr., 216, *223*
May, R., 357, *356*
Mayer, R. E., 145, *150*
McCarthy, K. A., 277, *301*
McClelland, D. C., 212, *223*
McCloskey, M., 143, *150*
McConaghy, W., 108, *113*
McCormack, A. J., 276, *301*
McCormack, M. H., 185, *186*
McGhie, A., 108, *112*
McGucken, W., 96, *113*
Mead, G. H., 303, 315, 316, 321, *325*
Means, M. L., 255, *270*
Mednick, M. T., 20, *65*, 321, *325*
Mednick, S., 20, *65*, 104, *114*, 227, *250*, 342, *376*
Meeker, M., 83, 90, *93*
Mehalik, M. M., 278, *300*
Merton, R. K., 8, *17*, 353, *376*
Milgram, R., 241, *250*, 309, *325*
Miller, D. T., 210, *223*
Miller, G. A., 104, *114*, 117, *126*
Miller, P. A., 359, *374*
Milton, R., 96, *114*
Mitgang, H., 183, *186*

Mobley, M. I., 21, 23, 24, 27, 42, 56, 57, 60, 65, 66
Monson, I., 307, 314, 325
Moore, B. N., 191, 207
Mordell, L. J., 98, 114
Mraz, W., 70, 79, 93, 94
Mumford, M. D., 20, 21, 22, 23, 24, 26, 27, 30, 32, 42, 45, 49, 51, 56, 57, 58, 60, 62, 63, 65, 66
Myers, I. B., 354, 377

N

Nathan, G., 350, 377
National Council of Teachers of Mathematics, 258, 270
National Education Goals Panel, 190, 207
Necka, E., 116, 123, 127, 277, 301
Nelson, L. H., 139, 150
Nettl, B., 314, 325
Newell, A., 103, 104, 114
Nicholls, J., 20, 66, 227, 250
Nickerson, R., 189, 191, 207
Nisbett, R. E., 121, 127, 202, 203, 207, 210, 223, 313, 325, 337, 377
Noller, R. B., 383, 393
Norman, D., 228, 229, 250, 278, 301
Novek, I., 263, 270
Novick, L. R., 27, 66

O

O'Brien, D. P., 263, 270
O'Brien, T., 261, 270
O'Hara, L., 153, 187
Oblon, M., 278, 300
Ohlsson, S., 309, 325
Okuda, S., 26, 66, 78, 94, 233 250, 321, 326
Ornstein, R., 336, 377
Osborn, A. F., 61, 66, 123, 127
Osborne, J., 343, 344, 377
Overton, W. F., 36, 62, 68, 263, 270, 272
Owens, W. A., 23, 66

P

Pacht, A. R., 347, 350, 377
Parker, R., 191, 207
Parnes, S. J., 61, 65, 136, 150
Parrott, G., 245, 249, 251
Parsons, J. L., 62, 63

Patrick, C., 119, 127
Paulus, D. H., 263, 271
Payne, J. W., 210, 223
Payne, R. W., 106, 107, 114
Pea, R. D., 261, 270
Peel, J. D., 384, 394
Perkins, D. N., 26, 39, 45, 66, 116, 127, 193, 207, 276, 302, 303, 309, 325, 335, 377
Piaget, J., 124, 127, 253, 254, 259, 260, 267, 269, 271
Pickering, A., 109, 113
Pirsig, R. M., 329, 331, 377
Plucker, J., 277, 298, 301
Poag, J., 233, 250
Poincaré, H., 4, 14, 17, 102, 114, 182, 186, 308, 310, 325, 342, 377
Popper, K., 332, 377
Powers, H. S., 314, 326
Prentky, R. A., 106, 114
Pribram, K. H., 117, 126
Pylyshyn, Z., 142, 150

Q

Quellmalz, E. S., 267, 271

R

Raghavan, K., 279, 301
Rank, O., 335, 345, 348, 377
Rapoport, A., 234, 248
Rathunde, K., 196, 207
Rawlings, J. P., 109, 113
Redman, A., 335, 338, 377
Redmond, M. R., 26, 27, 30, 32, 45, 49, 51, 57, 66, 334, 377
Reiter-Palmon, R., 21, 24 27, 32, 56 57, 66
Renzulli, J. S., 176, 186, 277, 301
Resnick, L. B., 258, 259, 271
Reynolds, C. R., 96, 113, 177, 186
Richards, L. G., 276, 300
Richards, R. L., 106, 114
Rickards, T., 90, 92
Rigg, D., 333, 360, 377
Roberge, J. J., 263, 271
Rodgers, E. M., 21, 66, 331, 377
Roe, A., 382, 394
Rogers, C. R., 348, 377
Rogers, R. J., 210, 222
Rogoff, B., 307, 308, 323, 326
Ronning, R. R., 96, 113

Root-Bernstein, R. S., 14, *17*
Rose, L. H., 61, *66*
Rosenblatt, E., 76, *93*
Rosner, S., 334, 353, 356, 358, 360, *377*
Ross, L., 219, 221, *223*, 313, *326*
Ross, M., 210, *223*
Rossman, B., 240, *250*
Rossman, J., 275, *301*
Rostan, S. M., 45, *66*
Rothenberg, A., 6, *17*, 22, 23, *66, 67*, 335, *377*
Rubenson, D. L., 21, *67*
Rumelhart, D., 228, 229, *250*
Runco, M. A., 21, 26, 27, 59, *66, 67*, 69, 70, 71, 72, 75, 76, 77, 78, 79, 80, 81, 82, 83, 84, 85, 87, 89, 90, 91, *93, 94*, 115, 125, *126, 127*, 130, 132, 139, 141, 143, 145, 147, 148, *150*, 213, *223*, 232, 233, 236, 242, 243, 245, *250, 251*, 277, 298, *301*, 305, 305(n12), 309(n5), 310, 312, 313, 320, 321, 321(n8), *326*, 391, *394*
Russell, B., 331, *377*

S

Saltuklaroglu, J., 362, *377*
Sanders, G. S., 214, *223*
Sanders, R. E., 215, *224*
Sartre, J. P., 345, 346, 348, 355, 356, 357, *377*
Sawers, D., 276, *300*
Sawyer, R. K., 276, *300*, 304, 305(n2), 306, 307, 312, 314, 318, 319, 320, 321, 321(n8), 322, *323, 324, 326*
Schaffer, S., 96, *114*
Schank, R. C., 219, *224*
Schauble, L., 279, *301*
Scherer, W. T., 276, *300*
Schickel, R., 353, *378*
Schleifer, M., 263, *270*
Schlesinger, B. E., Jr., 276, *301*
Schneider, K., 389, *394*
Schneider, W., 255, *271*
Scribner, S., 261, *270*
Searle, D., 262, *271*
Sedgwick, C., 105, *112*
Shahn, B., 182, *186*

Shapiro, B., 261, *270*
Shaw, G. B., 349, *378*
Shaw, J. C., 103, 104, *114*
Sherzer, J., 307, 314, *323*
Shorris, E. A., 39, *67*
Shrager, J., 8, *17*
Shulman, L. S., 263, *270*
Shure, M. B., 268, *271*
Shweder, R. A., 307, *327*
Siegler, R. S., 142, 145, *151*
Silverstein, M., 307, *327*
Simon, H. A., 8, *17*, 21, 22, 26, 45, *63, 64, 65*, 103, 104, *114*, 169, *186*, 278, *301*, 309, *327*
Simon, J., 334, 344, 357, *378*
Simon, R. J., 14, *17*
Simonton, D. K., 4, 5, 8, 9, 10, 15, *17, 18*, 22, *67*, 102, *114*, 116, *127*, 134, 135, 137, 138, 139, *151*, 199, *207*, 226, *251*, 309, 310, *327*, 347, 362, *378*
Sims, C., 389, *394*
Skinner, B. F., 330, 343, 347, 349, 358, *374, 378*
Smith, A. D., 109, *113*
Smith, L. H., 277, *301*
Smith, S. M., 21, 22, 23, 42, 44, 56, 60, *64*
Smith, W. R., 83, 84, 89, 90, *94*, 145, 147, *150*, 312, 313, *326*
Smith, W., 227, 242, 245, *251*
Smolucha, F. C., 321(n8), *327*
Snow, R. E., 36, 45, *67*
Sobel, R. S., 23, 66, *67*
Sorokin, P. A., 10, *18*
Souriau, P., 254, *271*
Spearman, C., 101, *114*, 338, *378*
Spearman, L., 101, *114*
Speedie, S., 193, *207*
Sperber, D., 228, *251*
Spiro, R. J., 280, *302*
Startha, W. E., 21, *68*
Stein, J. O., 277, *302*
Stein, M. I., 329, 335, 343, 355, *378*, 379, 380, 382, 383, 389, *394*
Steinmetz, J. L., 219, *223*
Stern, A., 345, *348*
Sternberg, R. J., 21, 26, 36, 38, 45, *64, 67*, 116, *127*, 138, 141, *151*, 153, 154, 156, 157, 165, 167,

170, 171, 173, 178, 180, *186*, *187*, 225, 232, 236, 237, 239, 242, 243, *251*, 278, 279, *302*, 305, *326*
Stigler, J. W., 307, *327*
Stillerman, R., 276, *300*
Storr, A., 345, 347, *378*
Stratton, R., 245, 249, *251*
Suler, J. R., 20, *67*
Supinski, E. P., 23, 32, 56 58, *65*
Svenson, E., 277, *301*
Swanson, H. L., 62, *67*
Swanson, J., 45, *67*
Swets, J. A., 189, *207*

T

Tamir, P., 263, *270*
Tauscher, H., 9, *16*
Taylor, C., 227, 242, *251*
Teach, R. J., 26, 30, 32, 45, 49, 51, *66*
Teevan, R. C., 212, *222*
Tetewsky, S. J., 154, *187*
Thompson, M., 232, 236, 240, 241, 243, *250*
Thompson, R. F., 20, 61, *65*
Threlfall, K. V., 32, 58, *65*
Thurston, B. J., 78, *94*
Thurstone, L. L., 141, *151*, 261, *271*
Tomita, K., 14, *16*
Torrance, E. P., 70, 71, 78, *94*, 178, 181, *187*, 263, *271*
Torrance, P., 227, *251*
Treffinger, D. J., 276, *302*, 309, *324*
Treffinger, D. T., 193, *207*
Trick, L., 244, *251*
Turner, M., 244, *249*
Tynan, Kathleen, 331, 352, *378*
Tynan, Kenneth, 336, *378*

U

Uhlman, C. E., 21, 24, 27, 56, 57, 62, 65, *66*
Urban, K. K., 116, *127*

V

Valentine-French, S., 329, 336, 362, *373*
Valsiner, J., 321(n8), *325*
Van Manen, M., 266, *271*
Vega, L., 72, 75, 76, 77, 89, *94*
Voss, J. F., 255, *270*

Vye, N. J., 143, 145, *151*
Vygotsky, L. S., 262, *271*, 307, *327*

W

Wakabayashi, M., 61, *63*
Wakefield, J. F., 254, 258, *271*, *272*
Walberg, H. J., 21, *68*
Wallace, D. B., 308, *327*, 337, *378*
Wallach, M. A., 83(n1), *94*
Wallas, G., 119, *127*, 335, *378*
Walters, J., 354, *378*
Ward, S. L., 36, 62, *68*, 263, *270*, *272*
Ward, T. B., 21, 22, 23, 42, 44, 56, 60, *64*
Ward, W. C., 78, *94*
Watson, G., 90, *94*
Watson, R. I., 337, *378*
Weber, J. J., 276, *302*
Weide, L., 286, *301*
Weinert, F. E., 255, *271*
Weisberg, R. W., 191, 193, *207*
Welsh, G., 227, *251*
Wertheimer, M., 348, *378*
Wertsch, J. V., 307, 308, *327*
Westberg, K. L., 276, *302*
Wexley, K. N., 215, *224*
White, S. H., 62, *63*
Whitehead, A. N., 259, *272*
Williams, W. M., 175, *187*
Wilson, D., 228, *251*
Wilson, T. B., 337, *377*
Wilson, T. D., 121, *127*, 210, *224*
Winner, E., 76, *93*, 143, *145*
Winograd, K., 258, *272*
Winokur, J., 330, 357, *378*
Woodward, D., 243, *249*
Woody, E., 108, *114*
Woolf, V., 329, *378*
Woolfolk, A. E., 143, 145, *151*

C

Yerkes, R. M., 361, *378*
Yukl, G. A., 215, *224*

Z

Zaccaro, S. J., 27, *66*
Zajonc, R. B., 213, *224*
Zbikowski, S. M., 148, *150*
Zythow, J. M., 8, *17*

SUBJECT INDEX

A

Abnormality, 105
Absurdity, 344
Academy of Science, 243
Acceptance of Ideas, 135
Acclaim, 218
Accommodation, 124, 257
Achievement, 20, 21
Active Learning, 280
Adaptability (see Adaption)
Adaptation, 12, 341, 343
Adaptation-Innovation Inventory, 88
Adolescence, 257
Aesthetics, 7, 12, 75
Age and Judgment, 78
Age, 78, 155, 336 (see also Adolescence, Children, Development)
Allusive Thinking, 108
Ambiguity, 35
Ambition, 353
American Pragmatism, 321
Analogies, 55, 158
Analytical Genius, 100
Animals, 3
Appropriateness, 77, 79, 229
Argument Analysis, 194
Art, 4, 26, 76, 143, 178, 238, 240, 244, 253, 311, 338
Art History, 313
Artists, 10, 213
Assimilation, 124, 256
Association of ideas, 5, 15, 20
Associative History of Ideas, 82
Associative Theory, 101
Associative Gradient, 105
Assumptions, 158
At-Risk Students, 258
Athletes, 218
Attention, 221
Attitude, 87, 196, 236, 288, 292
Attributions, 10, 83, 209
Audience, 6, 213, 232, 237, 242, 246, 339 (see also Attributions)
Audiences, 234
Authorship, 314
Autism, 142
Autobiography, 341, 344

B

BACON (computer program), 8
Balance, 16
Barron Welsh Art Scale, 106
Beethoven, 335
Behaviorism, 230
Bell, Alexander Graham, 278
Bell Labs, 282
Bias, 20, 82, 210, 332

403

Bible, The, 331
Bill of Rights, 385
Biology, 254
Bisociation, 111, 341
Blind Variation, 4, 132
Brain Damage, 142
Brain Hemispheres, 175
Brain Structure, 102
Brainstorming, 90, 132, 343
Business, 169

C

Cambridge, 99
Case Study, 392
Categories of Thought, 23, 27
Category Combination, 42
Category Selection, 39
Causes of Creativity, 106
Cervantes, Miguel, 11
Chance, 102, 134, 137, 309
Chance Configuration Theory, 4, 101
Change, 102
Chaos, 3, 8
Childhood, 9, 97 (see also Children)
Children, 70, 108, 236, 335, 349
Children's Ideas, 72
Children's Judgments, 75, 89
Citizenship, 190
Classical Conditioning, 109
Clinical Psychology, 111
Clues for Thinking, 27
Cluster Analysis, 234
Cognition, 5, 21, 70, 106, 121, 191, 237
Cognitive Development, 307
Cognitive Structures, 22, 124, 209
Cognitive Components, 71, 155
Cognitive Aliens, 72
Cognitive Style, 243
Cognitive Dissonance, 351
Cognitive Operations, 144, 147
Collaboration, 381
Colleagues, 380 (see also Collaboration)
College, 98
Communication, 135, 226, 228, 241, 309, 363
Compatator, 102
Competency, 354
Competition, 289, 355

Complementarity, 254
Composition, 315
Compromise, 296
Computational Models, 4
Computational Metaphor, 305
Computer Programs, 8 (see also Bacon)
Concept Formation, 39, 108
Conceptual Projection Problems, 154
Conceptual Boundaries, 106
Consciousness, 13, 121, 219, 308, 310, 321
Consensus Seeking, 199
Constraints, 13, 81, 137
Context, 96, 226, 230, 238
Context of Justification, 96
Context of Discovery, 96
Contingencies, 315
Conventional Domains, 241
Conventionality, 75, 158, 230
Convergence, 309
Convergent Thinking, 40, 69, 105, 110, 131
Convergent Validity, 73
Cooperation, 228, 233, 282, 355
Copernicus, 3, 101
Creation of Rules, 282
Creative Problem Solving Institute, 132
Creativity Quotient, 304
Criteria of Creativity, 4, 229
Critical Thinking, 20, 85, 123, 140, 189, 191, 267
Criticism, 116, 230, 387
Critics' Questionnaire, 363
Crystallizing Experiences, 354
Culture, 5, 6, 232, 267, 307, 313, 363
Curators, 392
Curriculum, 167, 259, 266
Cycles in the Problem-Solving Process, 26

D

Darwin, Charles, 3, 8, 9, 105, 132, 137, 341
Deadlines, 339
Deductive Reasoning, 263
Defense Mechanisms, 351
Definitions of Creativity, 20
Depression, 215

Subject Index

Determinants of Performance, 27
Determinism, 314
Developmental History, 381
Developmental Trajectories, 145
Dialectical Process, 95
Difficulty, 105
Disabled Students, 265
Disciplinary Matrix, 95
Discovered Problems, 80
Discovery, 110, 257
Discriminant Validity, 83, 89
Disposition, 106
Divergent Thinking, 21, 35, 69, 80, 87, 95-97, 105, 131, 145, 181, 233, 304-305, 309
Divergent Thinking Tests, Critics of, 70
Divergent Perspectives Hypothesis, 83
Division of Labor, 282
Domains of Performance, 21, 30, 62, 142, 203, 312, 320
Dopamine, 109

E

Eclecticism, 336
Economic Theories, 11, 153
Edison, Thomas, 285
Education, 15, 70, 96-97, 189, 254, 262
Effort, 122, 279
Ego, 6, 230
Einstein, Albert, 96, 110, 259, 334
Elaboration, 310
Electricity, 286
Elementary School, 262
Embarrassment, 297
Emergence, 315-316
Eminence, 230
Emotional Support, 381
Emotions, 15, 121, 215
Encoding, 30, 39, 49
Encouragement, 213
Endocepts, 346
Enhancement, 70, 202
Enrichment, 276
Environmental Influences, 78, 261
Epistemology, 4
Equilibrium, 15
Essays, 164

Essential Tension, 6
Ethics, 389
Ethnography, 307
Evaluation, 276
Evaluations by Managers, 85
Evaluative Thinking, 141, 147
Evaluative Accuracy, 75
Everyday Creativity, 243, 253, 258
Evolution, 3, 132, 341
Expectations, 75
Experience, 8, 76, 337
Experimentation, 96, 285
Expert Ratings, 143, 237, 386
Expertise, 21, 227, 242, 253, 255, 278
Explicit Instructions, 81, 91

F

Facilitating Creativity, 212
Factual Information, 38
Falsifiability, 332
Fame, 230
Family, 380
Fear of Failure, 212
Feedback, 118, 213
Fictional Goals, 348
Filters, 108, 310, 320
Financial Support, 381
Fit of Ideas, 7, 102
Flexibility, 15, 55, 71, 142, 199, 235, 241, 289, 337
Fluency, 79, 105, 263
Forgeries, 238 (see also Fraud)
Fourth Grade Slump, 75, 77
Fraud, 389 (see also Forgeries)
Freudian Theory, 304, 337
Frustration, 230, 350
Fundamental Attribution Error, 221, 313
Funding, 382
Future Research, 91, 299

G

Galileo, 96
Games, 78
Garden Variety Creativity, 132
Gate Keepers, 312
Gender Differences, 336
Generosity, 357
Genetics, 3, 13, 142, 314
Genius, 4, 97, 100, 106, 219
Geometry, 10

Gestalt, 348
Gifted Students, 174, 265
Goals, 4, 40, 117, 120, 255
God, 3, 331, 334
Government, 385
Grade Point Average, 84, 89, 147
Group Projects, 286
Groups, 282, 293, 303
Groupthink, 278
Guttenburg, 13

H

Habit, 118
Hamlet, 332
Heuristics, 278
Hindsight, 96
History, 96, 229, 280
Hitler, 204
Hopelessness, 215
Humanities, The, 338
Hypothesis Testing, 195

I

Idea, 5, 54, 154, 290
Idea Evaluation, 5
Ideal Creative Person, 240
Ideation, 4, 20, 69
Ideational Pools, 79
Identity, 345
Ideology, 11
Imagery, 23
Imagination, 13, 16, 130, 287
Improvisation, 135, 303, 305, 314
Incentives, 230
Incubation, 308, 310
India, 97
Individual Differences, 264
Individuation, 345
Inference, 90
Information, 24, 71, 237, 240, 278
Information Integration, 78
Information Coding, 36
Information Processing, 155, 158
Ingenuity, 287
Inhibition, 108, 212
Ink Blots, 346
Innovation, 62, 101, 216, 268, 306
Insight, 164, 166, 254, 308, 310
Instruction, 105, 145, 202, 259, 303
    (see also teaching, education)
Instructions to be Creative, 233

Intelligence, 70, 138, 141, 153, 154, 225, 240
Interactionist Model of Creativity, 116
Intermediaries, 379
Internal Standards, 349
Interpersonal Evaluations, 82, 213, 226, 245, 276, 293, 313
Interrater Reliability, 143 (see Judges, Experts)
Interview Study of Creative Individuals, 312
Interviews of Musicians, 218
Intrapersonal Evaluation, 77, 226, 245, 278, 289, 313, 322
Intrinsic Motivation, 149, 214
Introspection, 229, 341, 337
Intuition, 98, 100, 122, 213, 336
Intuitive Genius, 100
Invention, 276
Invention of the Telephone, 280
Inventors, 298
IPAR, 229
IQ, 76, 83, 89, 140, 170, 173, 176, 336

J

Japanese Business, 180
Jazz, 314, 318
Judgement, 7, 115, 306
Judges, 70

K

Knowledge, 22, 29, 102, 111, 121, 143, 204, 219, 229, 231, 268, 276, 285, 337, 391

L

Language, 78, 244
Latent Inhibition, 108
Lateral Thinking, 69
Law of Planetary Motion, 8
Leadership, 282, 293
Learned Helplessness, 215
Learning, 108
Learning Curves, 261
Line Meanings, 72
Linearity, 119
Literacy, 260
Literature, 184
Logic, 8, 122, 168, 261
Longitudinal Follow up, 298

Subject Index

M
Madness, 106
Malthus, 105
Masochism, 331
Mass Media, 334
Mathematical, 14, 97, 160, 173, 254, 258,
Maturation, 76
Mediated Action, 307
Memory, 204, 255, 338
Mendel, Gregor, 241
Mental Elements, 309
Mental Illness, 6
Mental Models, 231, 233, 240, 241, 276
Mentors, 15, 383
Metacognition, 115, 125, 145
Metaphor, 139, 341
Microdomains, 142
Middle Ages, 11
Military Advantage, 11
Mindfulness, 199
Modeling, 384
Models of Evaluation, 318
Modules, 280
Money, 239
Monitoring Problem Solving, 182
Monk Problem, 179
Morality, 10, 267
Motivation, 21, 71, 196, 236, 238, 329, 336, 360 382 (see also Intrinsic motivation)
Mozart, 335
Multidimensional Scaling, 236
Multiple Intelligences, 276
Multiple Discovery, 8
Multiple Choice Tests, 164
Muses, The, 379
Museums, 238, 392
Music, 6, 184, 217, 307, 315, 355
Myers-Briggs Type Indicator, 354

N
National Educational Goals Panel, 190
Natural Logarithms, 105
Natural Selection, 3
Naturalism, 19
Need for Expression, 346
Need for Achievement, 212
Networks of Enterprise, 14
Neural Architecture, 142
Neurology, 102 (see also Brain)
New York Times, 332
Nobel Prize, 382
Nonentrenchment, 236
Normal Science, 95, 96, 110
Novel Numerical Operations Problem, 160
Novel Number Matrix Problem, 160
Novelty, 27, 102, 115, 119, 164, 191, 242, 303
Novices, 278

O
Object Sorting Test, 108
Objectivity, 226
Observers, 313
Odyssey of the Mind, 130
Open Mindedness, 199
Open-ended problems, 22
Opera, 12
Opportunity, 139, 145, 219
The Origin of Species, 134
Originality, 6, 32, 70, 79, 253, 306, 313
Overinclusion, 106, 108
Osborn-Parnes Creative Problem Solving Theory, 85

P
Paradigm, 95, 135, 312
Parents, 70, 236, 242, 380
Patience, 288, 385
Patents, 284, 290
Pathology, 215
Pavlovian Conditioning, 109
Peer Review, 221
Penicillin, 165
Perceptions, 102
Perceptions of Invention, 287
Perfection, 347
Perfectionism, 353
Performance, 306, 316
Personality, 4, 9, 21, 106, 111, 218, 229, 230, 233, 237, 241, 296, 337, 346, 348
Philosophy, 19, 268
Physics, 143
Piagetian Theory, 124
Planning, 196

Play, 260, 314
Poetry, 6, 143
Poisonous Praise, 349
Politics, 11, 312
Pond, Ezra, 6
Popularity, 72, 84
Pornography, 225
Posterity, 9, 12
Potential, 70, 334
Power, 355
Practice, 75, 90, 256
Pragmatics, 13
Preconsciousness, 309
Preference for Closure, 85
Preferences, 30, 78
Premature Closure, 279
Preschool, 260
Private Schools, 99
Problem Spaces, 241
Problem Definition, 121
Problem Construction, 26, 30
Problem Quality, 33
Problem Solving, 4, 21, 290
Problem Identification, 15, 22
Problem Finding, 71, 253
Problem Redefinition, 154
Problematizing, 266
Problems, 13
Product Creativity, 143, 305, 360
Proof, Mathematical, 98
Protection, 384
Proteges, 142, 349
Prototypes, 55, 239
Psychopathology, 106
Psycholinguistics, 225
Psychologists, 314
Psychology, 96
Psychosis, 335
Psychoticism, 106, 107
Public Policy, 30
Public Health, 390
Public Awareness, 361
Publishers, 380
Purposeful Behavior, 108, 117

Q

Qualitative Findings, 291
Quality of Information, 26
Quality, 29

R

Rationality, 221, 269, 311
Rationalization, 216
Real-World Problems, 26, 48, 70, 279
Realistic Tasks, 80
Reality, 313
Reception, 154
Recognition, 383
Recognition of Assumptions, 90
Reductionism, 308
Reflection, 268
Reframing Strategy, 48
Regression to the Mean, 296
Regression in the Service of the Ego, 352
Reinforcement, 108, 230, 343, 358
Relativity, 95, 334
Reliability, 32, 42, 73, 84
Religion, 10, 11, 97 (see also Bible, The)
Rembrandt, 213, 241
Remote Associations Test, 20
Representation, Cognitive, 27, 145
Repression, 337, 351
Resistance, 96
Restrictions on Thought, 27, 33
Retention, 102
Revolutionary Science, 95
Risk, 15, 122
Romantic View, 62
Romantic Tradition, 19
Romeo and Juliet, 333
Rote Learning, 98

S

Satisficing, 29, 48
Scaffolding, 262, 265
Schema, 22
Schizophrenia, 6, 106, 108, 111
Scholarship, 359
School, 158, 241, 264, 268 (see also Education, Teachers)
Science, 184, 304, 332
Scientific Revolutions, 95
Scientific Methodology, 96
Scientific Revolutions, 96 (see also Paradigms)
Scientific Laws, 96
Scientists, 243
Search and Mapping, 23

Search for Meaning, 344
Secondary Education, 276
Selection Mechanisms, 343
Selection of Ideas, 102
Selective Encoding, 164
Selective Search, 39
Selective Retention, 132
Self, 345
Self-Concept, 233
Self-Criticism, 335
Self-Esteem, 221
Self-Evaluation, 149, 209
Self-Expression, 71
Self-Serving Bias, 210, 211
Self-Talk, 209 (see Verbalization)
Sentence Completion Test, 106
Shakespeare, 11, 341
Shifting Creativity, 135
Siblings, 380
Situated Cognition, 307
Skill, 143, 255, 260
Skills Taxonomy, 193
Slumps in Creativity, 263
Social Cultural Selection, 10
Social Darwinism, 4
Social Evolution, 4
Social Facilitation, 214
Social Milieu, 122
Social Processes, 306, 311
Social Psychology, 209, 222
Social Recognition, 230
Social Validation, 232
Sociology, 313
Solar Energy, 286
Soviet Union, 160
Spiritualism, 9
Sport, 244
Stability of Ideas, 102
Stage Models of Creativity, 136, 308, 311
Stages of Development, 254
Stages of Divergence, 304
Stages of Ideation, 20
Stained Glass, 166
Stamina, 15
Standards, 313, 348
Strategies, 7, 29, 45, 180
Structure of Intellect, 83, 139, 147
Student Ratings, 276
Style, 85

Style of Life, 348
Subject of Judgment, 72
Subjectivity, 96, 121, 227, 229, 289, 312, 332, 351
Supervisors, 23, 242
Supervisory Assessment of Creativity, 23
Systems Theory, 312, 315, 322

T

Task Specificity, 132, 141
Task Differences, 245
Tacit Knowledge, 278
Tacit Rules, 228
Tchaikovsky, 339
Teachers, 70, 75, 242, 265, 380
Teaching, 201, 211, 275, 276
Technological Creativity, 276
Technological Innovation, 289
Technoscientific Creativity, 275
Telephone, 23
Tension, 319
Tentative Structures, 119
Test of Critical and Analytical Thinking, 83
Testing, 78, 227
Testing Environment, 78
Tests, 158
Theater, 314
Theorems, 99
Therapy, 209, 215, 222
Time, 36, 38, 122, 158
Tinkering, 276
TOTE, 117
Tradition, 3, 16
Trail and Error, 7
Training, 48, 86, 88, 146, 209, 245
Traits of Creativity, 230
Transfer, 145
Triarchic Abilities, 171
Twins, 335
Two Tiered Model of Creative Thinking, 71

U

Uncertainty, 195
Unconscious, 20, 100, 338
Uniqueness, 81
University Education, 276

V

Validity, 70, 71, 115, 125
Value, 119, 291
Value Judgments, 341, 345
Variation, 3, 102, 309,
Variation, Cognitive, 102
Verbal Skill, 158, 225, 314
Verbal Reasoning, 194
Verbal Reports, 210
Verbalization, 121, 255

Verification, 335
Vygotsky, 106, 321

W

Wasteland, The, 6
Weltanschauung, 96
Wisdom, 225

Z

Zeitgeist, 10, 279